"Dry water? Cold fire? Short eternity? All contradictions in terms. But what about Free Church catholicity? Equally oxymoronic? Not so, says C. Ryan Fields in his engaging and substantive new study, *Local and Universal: A Free Church Account of Ecclesial Catholicity*. Who would have thought the Free Church tradition would have something to say—much less contribute—to the doctrine of the church's catholicity? Fields shows us the way, engaging both Scripture and the Free Church tradition with scholarly acumen and pastoral verve. He offers fresh theological resources for thinking about the church's claim to universality to those not only within the Free Church tradition but of any ecclesial tradition. Highly recommended!"

Todd Wilson, president and cofounder of the Center for Pastor Theologians and author of *Real Christian: Bearing the Marks of Authentic Faith*

"Catholicity is both a contested and neglected aspect of ecclesiology. It is contested in that there are several definitions for it, and it is neglected in that there are not many recent studies on its biblical and historical foundations, particularly from the Free Church traditions. C. Ryan Fields successfully speaks into this gap in ways that are both imaginative and rooted, generative and definitive. This book should be a standard for studies of catholicity for any tradition, and especially for Free Church traditions."

Matthew Y. Emerson, dean of theology, arts, and humanities at Oklahoma Baptist University and author of *"He Descended to the Dead"*

"The importance of the Free Church tradition, broadly construed, on the world stage can hardly be overestimated. Indeed, at a time where other Christian traditions often seem to be losing their way or giving in to religious liberalism (or both), Free Church communities are regularly found to be growing. While as a (Roman) Catholic I cannot agree with everything Fields says, I am deeply struck by the constructive rigor, ecumenical erudition, and biblical and theological depth found in this book on the very sensitive theme of catholicity."

Matthew Levering, James N. Jr. and Mary D. Perry Chair of Theology at Mundelein Seminary

"An astute, irenic, and worthy contribution to a two-thousand-year-old conversation about the church's catholicity. Not many books accomplish that. My own thoughts on the topic were educated, pushed, and edified, and any future conversations on the doctrine of catholicity will need to interact with Fields's careful and compelling work. I am sincerely grateful for the opportunity to recommend it."

Jonathan Leeman, editorial director at 9Marks and author of *Political Church*

"Historically, the Free Church tradition has had a weak ecclesiology. Fields's excellent work is a breath of fresh ecclesial air. Fields biblically grounds and theologically guides our thinking about the church—each local church manifests the fullness of the gospel, meaning it lacks nothing, and it also evidences a gospel-compelled catholicity, as it reveals part of the now of the kingdom, a partial embodiment of Jesus' high priestly prayer, an outpost of heaven. This is an exceptional work, one I heartily recommend, written by an outstanding pastor-theologian who lives out this truth as a pastor in a local church. We all, especially those in the Free Church tradition, are in his debt."

Gregory Strand, executive director of theology and credentialing for the Evangelical Free Church of America and adjunct professor of pastoral theology at Trinity Evangelical Divinity School

"C. Ryan Fields delivers a biblically grounded, historically informed manifesto for the catholicity of the local assembly within the Free Church traditions. Through extensive research and engagement with Scripture he examines bottom-up (Free Church) and top-down (Episcopal) patterns of ecclesial authority, finding their expressions of unified diversity as complementary. *Local and Universal* provides an important contribution to the doctrine of catholicity."

Ingrid Faro, Northern Seminary, coordinator of the MA in Old Testament—Jerusalem University College program

"In an age with pervasive calls for both diversity and unity, Christian catholicity calls for renewed and wise consideration by Protestants. When it is discussed, Free Churches are too often overlooked, from both within and without. In *Local and Universal*, C. Ryan Fields makes a unique and important contribution to ecclesiological catholicity. He has not merely worked at the intersection of catholicity and the Free Church tradition but also provides an insightful, catholic-minded, and constructive design for that intersection. This is a well-researched, contributive, and important book."

W. David Buschart, professor of theology and historical studies at Denver Seminary

"The time is long past for Free Church believers both to reclaim the word *catholic* and to live out the meaning of true catholicity—and to do so precisely as part of our own rich ecclesial tradition. This book advances that argument with rigor and nuance and thus contributes to what I believe is the Spirit's moving in our midst."

Timothy George, distinguished professor of divinity at Beeson Divinity School, Samford University

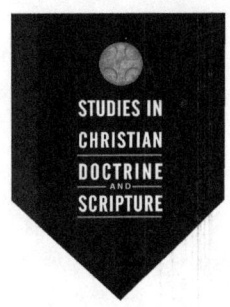

LOCAL and UNIVERSAL

A Free Church Account of Ecclesial Catholicity

◆◆◆◆◆◆◆◆◆◆◆◆◆◆◆◆◆◆◆◆◆

C. Ryan Fields

Foreword by
Kevin Vanhoozer

An imprint of InterVarsity Press
Downers Grove, Illinois

InterVarsity Press
P.O. Box 1400 | Downers Grove, IL 60515-1426
ivpress.com | email@ivpress.com

©2024 by Christopher Ryan Fields

All rights reserved. No part of this book may be reproduced in any form without written permission from InterVarsity Press.

InterVarsity Press® is the publishing division of InterVarsity Christian Fellowship/USA®. For more information, visit intervarsity.org.

All Scripture quotations, unless otherwise indicated, are taken from The Holy Bible, New International Version®, NIV®. Copyright © 1973, 1978, 1984, 2011 by Biblica, Inc.™ Used by permission of Zondervan. All rights reserved worldwide. www.zondervan.com. The "NIV" and "New International Version" are trademarks registered in the United States Patent and Trademark Office by Biblica, Inc.™

The publisher cannot verify the accuracy or functionality of website URLs used in this book beyond the date of publication.

Cover design: David Fassett
Interior design: Jeanna Wiggins
Cover images: Steven Moore / EyeEm via Getty Images

ISBN 978-1-5140-0671-9 (print) | ISBN 978-1-5140-0672-6 (digital)

Printed in the United States of America ∞

Library of Congress Cataloging-in-Publication Data
Names: Fields, C. Ryan, 1984- author.
Title: Local and universal : a free church account of ecclesial Catholicity / C. Ryan Fields.
Description: Downers Grove, IL : IVP Academic, [2024] | Series: Studies in Christian doctrine and scripture | Includes bibliographical references and index.
Identifiers: LCCN 2023033637 (print) | LCCN 2023033638 (ebook) | ISBN 9781514006719 (print) | ISBN 9781514006726 (digital)
Subjects: LCSH: Catholic Church–Doctrines. | Church–Catholicity–History of doctrines. | Church. | Mission of the church.
Classification: LCC BX1751.3 .F54 2024 (print) | LCC BX1751.3 (ebook) | DDC 230/.2–dc23/eng/20230921
LC record available at https://lccn.loc.gov/2023033637
LC ebook record available at https://lccn.loc.gov/2023033638

This work is dedicated to my parents, Ernie and Pat,
whose continual support has enabled me to come this far;

to my daughters, Penelope, Amelie, and Madeline,
whose vibrant life fills me with joy each day;

to my wife, Emily, whose matchless love
has made this dream come true;

and to my God, Father, Son, and Holy Spirit,
whose grace has made it possible for me to offer this
sacrifice of praise unto Him; Soli Deo Gloria.

Contents

Foreword by Kevin Vanhoozer	ix
Acknowledgments	xiii
Series Introduction	xv
Introduction: Free Church Catholicity?	1
1 Biblical Warrant for the Doctrine of Catholicity	21
2 Catholicity: The Development of a Doctrine	61
3 Engaging Anglican Accounts of Catholicity	98
4 Free Church Catholicity Explored: Examining Reformational Manifestations	131
5 Free Church Catholicity Expounded: Assessing Contemporary Proposals	162
6 Free Church Catholicity Embodied: Locating Catholicity	193
Conclusion: Local Catholicity and Catholic Locality	249
Bibliography	257
General Index	279
Scripture Index	281

Foreword

Kevin Vanhoozer

THERE IS NO USE MINCING WORDS. This book is about the *catholicity* of the Christian church. It is a controversial and often misunderstood term. Ryan had entitled an earlier version of this book (his doctoral dissertation, which it was my privilege to supervise) "Locating Catholicity." Why is a Protestant pastor who belongs to the Evangelical Free Church of America writing a book on catholicity? Doesn't that term belong to another tradition (viz., Roman Catholic)? Well, some Protestants may want to ask, as Luther did when he wondered why the devil should have all the good (bar) tunes, why one church should have exclusive rights to all the good descriptors.

In fact, a good case can be made (and Ryan makes it) for seeing the church's catholicity as an aspect of the gospel message itself: "For he himself is our peace, who has made us both one and has broken down in his flesh the dividing wall of hostility" (Eph 2:14 ESV). In Christ, there is a new humanity, in which old divisions, such as Jew and Greek, or master and slave, are no more. Catholicity is a characteristic of this new humanity, this new people of God that the apostle Peter calls a "holy nation" (1 Pet 2:9). Ethnic and social distinctions that divide have passed away, yet differences that enrich remain.

Local and Universal helps us better understand how the church—the people of God, body of Christ, and fellowship of the Holy Spirit—is a result of the gospel by delving deeper into the meaning of catholicity, and explaining why no one denomination can monopolize it. All Christians confess the oneness of the church, but catholicity involves more than unity. As Ryan helpfully points out, *universality* means something different from *uniformity*. We must ascribe both unity and diversity to the church if we are to do justice to the biblical teaching that it includes those "from every tribe and language and people and nation" (Rev 5:9). One way of thinking about the book you are about to read, then, is to see it as a fresh reflection on the ancient problem of "the one and the many," insofar as the latter relates to the question of the unity and diversity that make up the church.

The popular "church growth" movement of the 1970s encouraged evangelists and missionaries to direct their energies to "homogeneous people groups," communities that shared common cultural and ethnic characteristics. It was a pragmatic strategy that often proved successful: like attracts like. However, as a description of the church, homogeneity connotes *sameness*, not difference, and falls short of the picture of the church that we see in the New Testament, which is not merely provincial but worldwide.

Before diversity became a requirement of the academy—a mandate to reflect the various people groups and perspectives of students and faculty—it was an imperative of the gospel. The *one* body of Christ is made up of *many* members. *Local and Universal* is a biblically grounded, historically informed, and pastorally sensitive theological reflection on the kind of diversity that should characterize the body of Christ. The one church may be invisible in some respects, but Christians are called to make visible their unity-in-diversity—not the dull monochrome of homogeneity, but the multichromatic glory of catholicity.

Ryan's book calls for and clarifies catholicity, then goes on to specify what it means in his Free Church tradition. In so doing, he practices what he preaches, for the way in which he relates the universality of the church to its many localities contributes not only to his own Free Church tradition but, fittingly enough, to the church as a whole.

For me, Ryan's first reader, there were three main takeaways. I learned, first, that there is historical precedent in the Free Church tradition for confessing catholicity. Second, though I already knew that catholicity refers to God's people in all times and places, I appreciated the way Ryan highlighted the importance of *place*, indeed, multiple places. He even made me wonder if *locality* should count as a fifth mark of the church, in addition to "one, holy, catholic, and apostolic." Third, I was struck by Ryan's argument that, precisely because Free Church ecclesiology emphasizes the completeness of local congregations (rather than locating unity and authority in bishops, as churches in Episcopal traditions tend to do), Free Churches are in a better position to provide a theologically robust account of the church's catholicity.

Saint Ignatius of Antioch famously said millennia ago that the presence of a bishop is a unifying factor for the church. However, bishops alone do not make for diversity. Ryan's book thus raises an important question: Where is the one catholic church, the unity-in-diversity of the people of God, to be found? Can there be catholicity where only two or three are gathered in Christ's name?

In a post-pandemic age in which various cultural forces foster increasing polarization, threatening to split the church into diverse homogeneous people groups rather than exhibiting a peaceful unity-in-diversity, this reflection on the church's multifarious wholeness may be just the tonic Christians need.

Acknowledgments

I WISH TO ACKNOWLEDGE THE CONTRIBUTIONS of so many who have helped this research project come to completion. I owe an enormous debt to the students and faculty of Trinity Evangelical Divinity School, with whom I have had the joy of growing in greater love and knowledge of God as those entrusted with the gospel. In particular, I would like to thank Douglas Sweeney, Graham Cole, Richard Averbeck, David Dockery, James Arcadi, and Eric Tully for their helpful feedback and consistent encouragement throughout my doctoral studies.

I also wish to express thanks to the many folks who have cultivated within me a love of the church and a desire to serve her as a pastor-theologian. The congregations of Creekside Community Church, Evanston Bible Fellowship, and Faith Evangelical Free Church have played a critical role in this cultivation. In particular, I would like to thank Steve Gregg, Richard Horner, Jason Lancaster, and Leo Sandgren for the ways they have helped me see that theology is for the church, that doctrine is for disciples, and that helping God's people grow in greater love and knowledge of God through his Word is one of the great privileges of pastoral ministry.

Last, I wish to express a special word of gratitude to Kevin Vanhoozer, who has been generous to me and so many others with the time and talent the Lord has entrusted to him. I am thankful he has impressed on me the high calling of shepherding the flock of God from the depths of the Word of God, for showing me why evangelicals, particularly Free Church evangelicals, need both canon sense and catholic sensibility, and for his consistent teaching that *evangelical* and *catholic* aren't the enemies they have been made out to be, but are actually good friends indeed.

Series Introduction
Studies in Christian Doctrine and Scripture (SCDS)

DANIEL J. TREIER AND KEVIN VANHOOZER

THE STUDIES IN CHRISTIAN DOCTRINE and Scripture (SCDS) series attempts to reconcile two disciplines that should never have been divided: the study of Christian Scripture and the study of Christian doctrine. Old walls of disciplinary hostility are beginning to come down, a development that we hope will better serve the church. To that end, books in this series affirm the supreme authority of Scripture, seeking to read it faithfully and creatively as they develop fresh articulations of Christian doctrine. This agenda can be spelled out further in five claims.

1. We aim to publish constructive **contributions to systematic theology** rather than merely descriptive rehearsals of biblical theology, historical retrievals of classic or contemporary theologians, or hermeneutical reflections on theological method—volumes that are plentifully and expertly published elsewhere.

The initial impetus for the SCDS series came from supervising evangelical graduate students and seeking to encourage their pursuit of constructive theological projects shaped by the supremacy of Scripture. Existing publication venues demonstrate how rarely biblical scholars and systematic theologians trespass into each other's fields. Synthetic treatments of biblical theology garner publication in monograph series for biblical studies or evangelical biblical theology. A notable example is a companion series from IVP Academic, New Studies in Biblical Theology. Many of its volumes have theological significance, yet most are written by biblical scholars. Meanwhile, historical retrievals of theological figures garner publication in monograph series for historical and systematic theology. For instance, there have been entire series devoted to figures such as Karl Barth or the patristic era, and even series named for systematic theology tend to contain figure-oriented monographs.

The reason for providing an alternative publication venue is not to denigrate these valuable enterprises. Instead, the rationale for encouraging constructively evangelical projects is twofold and practical: The church needs such projects, and they form the theologians undertaking them. The church needs such projects, both addressing new challenges for her life in the world (such as contemporary political theology) and retrieving neglected concepts (such as the classic doctrine of God) in fresh ways. The church also needs her theologians not merely to develop detailed intellectual skills but also ultimately to wrestle with the whole counsel of God in the Scriptures.

2. We aim to promote **evangelical** contributions, neither retreating from broader dialogue into a narrow version of this identity on the one hand, nor running away from the biblical preoccupation of our heritage on the other hand.

In our initial volume, *Theology and the Mirror of Scripture*, we articulate this pursuit of evangelical renewal. We take up the well-known metaphor of mere Christianity as a hallway, with particular church traditions as the rooms in a house. Many people believe that the evangelical hallway is crumbling, an impression that current events only exacerbate. Our inspection highlights a few fragmenting factors such as more robust academic engagement, increased awareness of the Great Christian Tradition and the variety of evangelical subtraditions, interest in global Christianity, and interfaces with emergent Christianity and culture. Looking more deeply, we find historical-theological debates about the very definition of *evangelical* and whether it reflects—still, or ever—a shared gospel, a shared doctrine of God, and a theological method that can operationalize our shared commitment to Scripture's authority.

In response, prompted by James 1:22-25, our proposal develops the metaphor of a mirror for clarifying evangelical theology's relation to

Scripture. The reality behind the mirror is the gospel of God and the God of the gospel: what is revealed in Christ. In disputes about whether to focus on a center or boundaries, it may seem as if evangelicalism has no doctrinal core. But we propose treating what is revealed in Christ—the triune God and the cross of Christ, viewed in the mirror of Scripture—as an evangelical anchor, a center with a certain range of motion. Still, it may seem as if evangelicalism has no hermeneutical coherence, as if interpretive anarchy nullifies biblical authority. But we propose treating Scripture as *canonical testimony*, a God-given mirror of truth that enables the church to reflect the wisdom that is in Christ. The holistic and contextual character of such wisdom gives theology a dialogic character, which requires an evangelical account of the church's catholicity. We need the wisdom to know the difference between church-destroying heresy, church-dividing disagreements that still permit evangelical fellowship, and intrachurch differences that require mutual admonition as well as forbearance.

Volumes in the SCDS series will not necessarily reflect the views of any particular editor, advisory board member, or the publisher—not even concerning "evangelical" boundaries. Volumes may approach perceived boundaries if their excellent engagement with Scripture deserves a hearing. But we are not seeking reform for reform's sake; we are more likely to publish volumes containing new explorations or presentations of traditional positions than radically revisionist proposals. Valuing the historic evangelical commitment to a deeply scriptural theology, we often find that perceived boundaries are appropriate—reflecting positions' biblical plausibility or lack thereof.

3. We seek fresh understanding of Christian doctrine **through creatively faithful engagement with Scripture**. To some fellow evangelicals and interested others today, we commend the classic evangelical commitment of *engaging Scripture*. To other fellow evangelicals today, we commend a contemporary aim to engage Scripture with *creative fidelity*. The church is to be always reforming—but always reforming according to the Word of God.

It is possible to acknowledge *sola Scriptura* in principle—Scripture as the final authority, the norming norm—without treating Scripture as theology's primary source. It is also possible to approach Scripture as theology's primary source in practice without doing that well.

The classic evangelical aspiration has been to mirror the form, not just the content, of Scripture as closely as possible in our theology. That aspiration has potential drawbacks: It can foster naive prooftexting, flatten biblical diversity, and stifle creative cultural engagement with a biblicist idiom. But we should not overreact to these drawbacks, falling prey to the temptation of paying mere lip service to *sola Scriptura* and replacing the Bible's primacy with the secondary idiom of the theologians' guild.

Thus in *Theology and the Mirror of Scripture* we propose a rubric for applying biblical theology to doctrinal judgments in a way that preserves evangelical freedom yet promotes the primacy of Scripture. At the ends of the spectrum, biblical theology can (1) rule out theological proposals that contradict scriptural judgments or cohere poorly with other concepts, and it can (5) require proposals that appeal to what is clear and central in Scripture. In between, it can (2) permit proposals that do not contradict Scripture, (3) support proposals that appeal creatively although indirectly or implicitly to Scripture, and (4) relate theological teaching to church life by using familiar scriptural language as much as possible. This spectrum offers considerable freedom for evangelical theology to mirror the biblical wisdom found in Christ with contextual creativity. Yet it simultaneously encourages evangelical theologians to reflect biblical wisdom not just in their judgments but also in the very idioms of their teaching.

4. We seek **fresh understanding of Christian doctrine**. We do not promote a singular method; we welcome proposals appealing to biblical theology, the history of interpretation, theological interpretation of Scripture, or still other approaches. We welcome projects that engage in detailed exegesis as well as those that appropriate broader biblical themes and patterns. Ultimately, we hope to promote relating Scripture to doctrinal understanding in material, not just formal, ways.

As noted above, the fresh understanding we seek may not involve altogether novel claims—which might well land in heresy! Again, in *Theology and the Mirror of Scripture* we offer an illustrative, nonexhaustive rubric for encouraging various forms of evangelical theological scholarship:

projects shaped primarily by (1) hermeneutics, (2) integrative biblical theology, (3) stewardship of the Great Tradition, (4) church dogmatics, (5) intellectual history, (6) analytic theism, (7) living witness, and (8) healing resistance. While some of these scholarly shapes probably fit the present series better than others, all of them reflect practices that can help evangelical theologians to make more faithfully biblical judgments and to generate more creatively constructive scholarship.

The volumes in the SCDS series will therefore reflect quite varied approaches. They will be similar in engaging one or more biblical texts as a key aspect of their contributions while going beyond exegetical recital or descriptive biblical theology, yet those biblical contributions themselves will be manifold.

5. We promote scriptural engagement **in dialogue with catholic tradition(s)**. A periodic evangelical weakness is relative lack of interest in the church's shared creedal heritage, in churches' particular confessions, and more generally in the history of dogmatic reflection. Beyond existing efforts to enhance understanding of themes and corpora in biblical theology, then, we hope to foster engagement with Scripture that bears on and learns from loci, themes, or crucial questions in classic dogmatics and contemporary systematic theology.

Series authors and editors will reflect several church affiliations and doctrinal backgrounds. Our goal is that such commitments would play a productive but not decisive hermeneutical role. Series volumes may focus on more generically evangelical approaches, or they may operate from within a particular tradition while engaging internal challenges or external objections.

We hope that both the diversity of our contributor list and the catholic engagement of our projects will continually expand. As important as those contextual factors are, though, these are most fundamentally studies in Christian *doctrine* and *Scripture*. Our goal is to promote and to publish constructive evangelical projects that study Scripture with creative fidelity and thereby offer fresh understanding of Christian doctrine. Various contexts and perspectives can help us to study Scripture in that lively way, but they must remain secondary to theology's primary source and soul.

We do not study the mirror of Scripture for its own sake. Finding all the treasures of wisdom in Christ to be reflected there with the help of Christian doctrine, we come to know God and ourselves more truly. Thus encountering God's perfect instruction, we find the true freedom that is ours in the gospel, and we joyfully commend it to others through our own ministry of Scripture's teaching.

Introduction

Free Church Catholicity?

THIS BOOK SEEKS TO REMEDY the issue Miroslav Volf identified when he said that when it comes to reflecting on the catholicity of the local church from a Free Church perspective: "Free church theologians have barely studied this problem."[1] And though we can say that there has been *more* reflection on the church's catholicity from a Free Church vantage point since Volf's writing, his observation remains largely and lamentably true. Curtis Freeman, a Free Church theologian from the Baptist tradition, can cite as the impetus for his study of "contesting catholicity" the fact that "it is fair to note that 'catholic' is not a term with which Baptists readily identify."[2] Volf goes further, noting that it is easily (though mistakenly, in his view) concluded that "a catholic Free Church is a contradiction in terms—it understands itself as free precisely with regard to those relationships that would tie it to the whole and thus make it catholic in the first place."[3] Herman Bavinck observed that "the free churches undoubtedly have the promise of the future," but held that this would only be true if "they preserve the catholicity of the Christian faith and the Christian church."[4] Many believe that

---

[1] Miroslav Volf, "Catholicity of 'Two or Three': Free Church Reflections on the Catholicity of the Local Church," *The Jurist* 52, no. 1 (1992): 528.
[2] Curtis W. Freeman, *Contesting Catholicity: Theology for Other Baptists* (Waco, TX: Baylor University Press, 2014), 15.
[3] Miroslav Volf, *After Our Likeness: The Church as the Image of the Trinity* (Grand Rapids, MI: Eerdmans, 1998), 260.
[4] Herman Bavinck, "The Catholicity of Christianity and the Church," trans. John Bolt, *Calvin Theological Journal* 27, no. 2 (November 1992): 250.

global Christianity has substantiated Bavinck's prediction and thus raised the stakes of his proviso even higher.[5] Indeed, the critical question for the burgeoning Free Church tradition is this: Can it not only account for the church's catholicity, but also preserve and enact the doctrine of ecclesial catholicity, even contributing to its fullness? In other words, can the Free Church tradition truly hold that the church is both local and universal?

So we must ask the critical question, Is the notion of a catholic Free Church a contradiction in terms? Does the fact that Free Church folk don't readily identify as catholic preclude the possibility of *ever* doing so (or ever *having* done so)? Is the underdeveloped sense of catholicity in the tradition due more to its defining characteristics undercutting catholicity (e.g., "the autonomy of the local church" demonstrating inevitably anticatholic "DNA") or to the reality Volf observed that Free Church theologians have not given sufficient attention to this particular creedal attribute from their distinctive ecclesiological vantage point? If the latter, what sort of retrieval and appropriation of catholicity is possible within the Free Church tradition if theologians were to give due attention to this lacuna? And what distinctive (and currently untapped) contribution would the Free Church tradition make to the doctrine of catholicity such that not only the Free Church but also the universal church would stand to benefit?

It is to this set of interconnected questions that we turn in this book, arguing ultimately that the biblical basis for the church's catholicity, the parameters of the doctrine's development through church history, the oversights and unresolved issues within Episcopal accounts of catholicity, and certain manifestations of a "catholic sensibility" within Free Church history prompt us to articulate a distinctively Free Church account of the church's catholicity. This book also seeks to demonstrate the vital contribution such an account can make to a fuller-orbed doctrine of ecclesial catholicity, one that is informed by the insights of the Free Church tradition, which have remained largely underleveraged. Indeed, such a contribution is important not only for the health of the Free Church tradition but also for the vitality

---

[5]Volf, *After Our Likeness*, 260. We could also cite John Howard Yoder's claim in 1978 that "the Church of Tomorrow cannot but be a Believers' Church," quoted in Teun van der Leer, "Which Future Church (Form)? A Plea for a 'Believers' Church' Ecclesiology," *Journal of European Baptist Studies* 9, no. 3 (May 2009): 43.

of the universal church, especially given the claim that the Free Church might be "the church of the future," globally speaking.

It is important to clarify at this point my usage of a few key terms. For this project, *catholic* (lower-case *c*) will indicate association with the creedal attribute, while *Catholic* (upper-case *C*) will indicate identification with the Roman Catholic tradition. Though the Free Church tradition has been characterized at times as being both "anticatholic" and "anti-Catholic," it is the former that I seek to address in this work. By *Episcopal* here I mean the larger ecclesial tradition that sees the constitution of the church as bound up with the oversight of bishops participating in apostolic succession. This includes Eastern Orthodox, Roman Catholic, Anglican, and certain Lutheran communions. Volf is right to recognize that the vast majority of theological reflection that has been done on the doctrine of catholicity to date has been done from within this larger Episcopal tradition.

I will be arguing that though catholicity has indeed been oft-neglected in the Free Church tradition, this is not because the two are mutually exclusive. On the contrary, I will make the case that certain streams of the larger Free Church tradition have articulated a vision for the church's catholicity consistent with church tradition and grounded in the witness of Scripture. Thus we can say that the Free Church tradition not only has the theological resources to account for the church's catholicity, but actually stands to make a substantial contribution to the catholic church's understanding of the nature of the catholicity that we confess. In other words, I believe that the Free Church tradition can, and indeed must, contribute to positive doctrinal development by bringing its distinctive yet neglected theological resources to bear in constructing a richer doctrine of ecclesial catholicity.

My thesis is that the Free Church tradition provides the most consistent account of the local dimension of the church and the corresponding pattern of ecclesial authority that finds its proper locus in a gathered church; such an account is necessary for any confession of the church's catholicity to be sufficiently robust and faithful to the biblical vision of the church's nature as one of unified diversity manifesting through the multifarious whole. This Free Church account brings a necessary complement to the insights of the Episcopal tradition by insisting that because the church's catholicity involves the church of all times, peoples, *and places*, the catholicity of the church is best understood as a *local* catholicity. By locating catholicity where even just two or three gather ecclesially in Christ's name (see Mt 18:20), the church's catholic nature is guarded, spotlighted, and maximized because the one church is properly understood as manifesting amid an ever-increasing, *localized* diversity. In short, we adhere to this doctrinal rule: *no fulsome catholicity without sufficient locality and no fulsome locality without sufficient catholicity.*

OUTLINE OF CHAPTERS

My work seeks to clarify the nature of our creedal confession that the church is catholic by assessing its biblical warrant, its doctrinal development, its content as understood by various ecclesial traditions, and its precedent and possibility within the Free Church tradition. To do this will require an appeal to multiple theological authorities, but always with Scripture as preeminent. Thus in chapter one, "Biblical Warrant for the Doctrine of Catholicity," I seek to demonstrate the biblical basis for our confession of the church's catholicity. This chapter is all-important in seeking to provide an evangelical account of catholicity under the Protestant principle of *sola Scriptura*, especially because the term *catholic* is never applied to the church in the biblical witness and is often viewed suspiciously by many Free Church folk (particularly because of its historical association with the Roman *Catholic* Church). In asking how the doctrine of the church's catholicity might be founded in the witness of Scripture, I propose that biblical warrant for the doctrine can be found by exploring how the *scope* of God's covenant people develops over the course of redemptive history, and particularly by seeing how this scope expands to include *all times, peoples, and places*, enabling God's people to be increasingly marked by a *unified diversity*. It will be concluded that the witness of Scripture provides us both sufficient warrant and orienting content for the doctrine of ecclesial catholicity.

In chapter two, "Catholicity: The Development of a Doctrine," I survey the major contours of the doctrine of catholicity as it develops from the apostolic era to the contemporary period, seeking to consolidate a taxonomy of catholicity and offer concluding evaluations of the various conceptions that emerge over the course of church history. Important stages in the doctrine's development we will examine include the following: (1) the early fathers, (2) the creeds and later fathers, (3) medieval "consensus," (4) Reformational developments, and (5) modern contributions. Special attention will be given to notions of catholicity that emerge with the Reformation, which served as the first real test of catholicity (at least in the West) and became the fountainhead for diverging Free Church versus Episcopal notions of the church's catholicity.

In chapter three, "Engaging Anglican Accounts of Catholicity," I enter into dialogue with Episcopal accounts of catholicity by interacting with one representative tradition: Anglicanism. Anglicanism offers us a via media between Rome and Geneva, one that largely maintains the Episcopal conception of catholicity from above (that is, via a bishop in apostolic succession) and has a long track record of interaction with the Free Church tradition. Historic and contemporary Anglican voices will be probed to elucidate the nature of the church's catholicity according to this tradition. I will consolidate the best of what Anglicanism has to offer in developing a full-orbed doctrine of catholicity while simultaneously noting oversights and unresolved issues that lead me to conclude that its contribution is ultimately insufficient. This comparative vantage point is vital as I move to the second half of the book and seek to articulate what is distinctive and necessary in the Free Church understanding of catholicity.

In chapter four, "Free Church Catholicity Explored: Examining Reformational Manifestations," I seek to answer a critical question regarding Free Church catholicity: Have there been manifestations of the Free Church tradition that have affirmed and offered a robust understanding of the church's catholicity? In answering this question I will argue that certain sixteenth-century Anabaptists and seventeeth-century English Baptists and Congregationalists exhibit a substantial doctrine of catholicity and a catholicity of doctrine and practice. This bolsters the claims that the Free Church isn't inherently anticatholic (and thus that the neglect of catholicity downstream is historically contingent) and that the tradition has significant theological resources to contribute toward a fuller-orbed doctrine of ecclesial catholicity.

In chapter five, "Free Church Catholicity Expounded: Assessing Contemporary Proposals," I examine current proposals of Free Church catholicity and consolidate the insights of the Free Church tradition regarding catholicity to date. I engage both "broad" and "Baptist" Free Church theologians, identifying their strengths but also noting where their proposals are insufficient for setting forth either a robust enough vision of Free Church *catholicity* or a faithful enough picture of a distinctly *Free Church* catholicity (one that is fully consistent with Free Church ecclesial distinctives). I then distill insights from the trajectory explored in chapters four and five into a proposal of *Free Church catholicity as local catholicity*, one that builds on biblical emphases, is in continuity with church tradition, and offers a robust understanding of catholicity while being faithful to both the biblical witness and Free Church ecclesial convictions.

In chapter six, "Free Church Catholicity Embodied: Locating Catholicity," I set out to consolidate all that has come before by answering this question: What contribution to a fuller-orbed doctrine of catholicity could be made from a distinctly Free Church ecclesial vantage point, one that complements the insights of the Episcopal tradition? The answer, in sum, is that because the Free Church tradition provides the most consistent account of the *local* dimension of the church and its corresponding pattern of ecclesial authority that finds its proper locus in a gathered church, it stands to provide a more theologically robust account of the church's catholicity than the Episcopal tradition *alone* can provide by insisting that this catholicity is always a "local catholicity." Indeed, the work of "locating catholicity" asks the question, *Where is the catholic church we confess to be found*? The answer, to the Free Church mind, is that it is to be found in local churches of even just two or three manifesting at all times, among all peoples, and in all places. This emphasis on the gathered church as the proper locus of catholicity allows us to maintain the tension inherent in confessing the church's unity alongside its catholicity by holding that the church is best understood as having a unified-yet-diverse nature that manifests through the *multifarious* whole of all times, peoples, and places; in other words, its unity is in tandem with an ever-increasing, *localized* diversity. Indeed, in light of the witness of Scripture, we hold that there is no fulsome catholicity without sufficient locality, for catholicity comes into its fullness only amid a diverse whole made up of many parts, and local churches, as the smallest catholic "units," maximize that diverse wholeness.

After this chapter, I provide a brief conclusion reflecting on some implications of my research for the Free Church tradition, especially reflecting on the corollary that there is no fulsome locality without sufficient catholicity, meaning that one cannot represent Christ locally without connection to the rest of his body, manifest in innumerable other local churches. I close with a call for Free Church folk to see their freedom as a freedom to embrace catholicity and a call for those in every ecclesial tradition to continue to work out the implications of our confession that the church is catholic.

Defining Catholicity

But before we can proceed, we must provisionally define our terms, especially what is meant by *catholicity* and the *Free Church tradition*. Beginning with the former, we start by recognizing that the term is extremely significant in church tradition as one of four ecclesial attributes confessed in the ecumenical creeds. Churches across the globe and through the centuries have taken up the language of the Apostles' Creed in confessing their belief in "the holy, *catholic* church" (alongside belief in "the communion of saints"). This twofold confession of the church's nature becomes fourfold in the Nicene Creed: we believe in "one, holy, *catholic* and apostolic church." Considering the abundance of ecclesial images provided in the New Testament, the four creedal attributes nicely summarize what we believe about the church *based ultimately on the testimony of Scripture*.[6] We insist that the creeds are best understood as providing ancient, ecumenical summaries of the biblical narrative (providing a rule of faith outlining redemptive history) and biblical doctrine (providing the groundwork for church dogmatics), summaries that serve the church by distinguishing orthodox from heterodox interpretations of the gospel.[7]

Among the many things we could say about this creedal content, one of the most important is that each of these attributes is interdependent with, yet distinct from, the others. We can thus begin delineating our understanding

---

[6]Paul Minear identified at least ninety-five ecclesial images in his classic work. Paul S. Minear, *Images of the Church in the New Testament* (Philadelphia: Westminster Press, 1960).
[7]On the nature of creeds being rightly understood as *norma normata* that help us synthesize biblical teaching (our *norma normans*), see Carl R. Trueman, *The Creedal Imperative* (Wheaton, IL: Crossway, 2012), 17.

of catholicity by exploring its interrelationship with, and distinction from, the other creedal attributes.

We begin with the church's oneness. The unity of the church is emphasized in many places in the New Testament, but perhaps is nowhere more clearly expressed than in Ephesians 4:3-6. There the oneness of the church derives from the oneness of our common Spirit, Lord, and God (thus exhibiting a trinitarian basis) as well as our common faith and baptism (thus exhibiting a twofold emphasis on orthodoxy and orthopraxy; Paul also sees a similar oneness expressed in the Eucharist in 1 Cor 10). In John 17 Jesus' prayer demonstrates a distinct theme of ecclesial unity, one that mirrors the unity that exists between Father and Son. This New Testament emphasis on the church's oneness is important to see because often unity and catholicity are conflated rather than properly distinguished (even as we recognize that they are closely related). Minimally this means that in confessing the church's catholicity we are confessing something *other* than its oneness; we are confessing an attribute that, while interconnected with unity, is not equivalent to it.

The next attribute is holiness. That the church is "set apart" or "sanctified" for a particular purpose is perhaps the most frequent creedal attribute attested in Scripture. Jesus prays for this very thing in John 17:17-19, and Paul mentions it multiple times in Ephesians 1 as he describes the blessedness of the church. Peter can both exhort the church *to be* holy (1 Pet 1) and remind them, based on their identification with Israel and promises made in Exodus 19, that they *are* holy (1 Pet 2). But perhaps most dramatically, the infamous Corinthians vividly portray the fact that a church that exhibits disunity, litigation, sexual scandal, abuse of the Lord's Supper, and wrong doctrine can still be said to be "sanctified in Christ Jesus and called to be his holy people" (1 Cor 1:2) and identified as a temple of the Holy Spirit (1 Cor 3:17).[8] Here we simply note that catholicity involves something distinct from but related to this holiness.

Next is apostolicity. This attribute draws attention to the connection between the church and the apostles along with their witness; the church is both derived from, and is called to be faithful to, the apostolic message, the gospel. Again we see this attribute emerge in John 17, where we hear Jesus

---

[8]All Scripture quotations in this project, unless otherwise noted, are taken from the New International Version.

praying for "those who will believe [the apostles'] message" (Jn 17:20). We recall the significant image of the church Paul provides in Ephesians 2:20 where he identifies it as "built on the foundation of the apostles and prophets." Indeed, the earliest church community in Jerusalem was characterized by, among other things, a dedication to the apostles' teaching (Acts 2:42). Paul sees the apostles and their witness to the resurrection as part of the gospel message that Christ died for our sins according to the Scriptures (1 Cor 15:1-5). Thus we recognize that catholicity is distinct from apostolicity; whatever we confess when we say the church is catholic, it is something different from yet interconnected with its apostolic foundation and calling.

In light of these other three attributes, we can now offer a preliminary orientation to what we mean by the church's catholicity. Significantly, the term itself is never applied to the church in the New Testament; it is first used in this way by Ignatius in the early second century.[9] But before this identification of the church as catholic, the term simply meant something to the effect of "wide-ranging" or "general" or "universal in scope"; in this sense it can be directly contrasted with "provincial" or "bounded."

This initial starting point opens up avenues for glimpsing the biblical basis for the church's catholicity as well as its interrelationship with the other creedal attributes. For instance, we see the catholicity of the church affirmed in Jesus' prayer that the disciples would be sent out "into the world" (Jn 17:18), connecting with *apostolicity* by marking out the universal scope of the church's mission. We see the catholicity of the church manifest in the fact that God's new covenant people, in stark contrast to the old covenant centering on ethnic Israel, is composed of "persons from every tribe and language and people and nation" (Rev 5:9), connecting with *holiness* by identifying that it is this multifarious people who have been set apart "to be a kingdom and priests to serve our God" (Rev 5:10). And we see the catholicity of the church testified to in the stunning reality that the one body of Christ is made up of many parts with distinctive functions that cannot be conflated or minimized (Rom 12:3-8).[10] Catholicity thus connects most

---

[9]See Angelo Di Berardino, ed., *We Believe in One Holy Catholic and Apostolic Church* (Downers Grove, IL: IVP Academic, 2010), 72.

[10]Those distinct parts include, but are not limited to, vocational capacity (1 Pet 4:10-11), spiritual gifting (1 Cor 12:4), ministerial calling (1 Cor 12:5), spiritual background (1 Cor 12:13), social standing (1 Cor 12:13), class ranking (1 Cor 1:26), economic means (Jas 2:1), religious

centrally to the church's *unity*, with Ephesians 4 providing compelling evidence on this score. There we see that the church is defined by a deep unity as one body, indwelled by one Spirit, unto one hope, under one Lord, professing one faith, undergoing one baptism, looking to one Father (Eph 4:4-6). And yet this *unity* is matched with a corresponding *diversity* as Christ apportioned it (Eph 4:7-16), such that the unity is perfected only through the work of every distinct office and member, a work of "build[ing] [the church] up in love, as each part does its work" (Eph 4:16). Here Douglas Koskela's observation is apt: Catholicity "reflects, in many ways, a theologically robust account of diversity."[11]

Now, we must acknowledge that the nature of ecclesial catholicity is, along with every creedal attribute, highly contested. In fact, just here we find an initial difficulty: to begin the work we must define catholicity, and yet in defining catholicity in a certain way we have revealed a confessional bias. But if we fail to recognize the complexities involved in confessing that the church is catholic, we ignore the obvious: incredibly varied interpretations of this attribute have been offered across the ecclesial spectrum, and stunningly diverse notions of catholicity have emerged over the course of church history and are still on offer today.

The challenge of ecclesial disagreement exists across the various loci of systematic theology but is particularly acute in ecclesiology and especially pointed when dealing with catholicity. This is because, as Volf has noted, "the content of the concept of catholicity always depends on the respective understanding of the church. The dispute concerning catholicity . . . is always a struggle to come to a correct understanding of the church."[12] This observation helps explain not only *why* there exists a multiplicity of

---

accomplishments (Gal 3:28), biological sex (Gal 3:28), marital status (1 Cor 7:7), ethnic identity (Col 3:11), generational association (Titus 2:2-4), strength of conscience (Rom 14:1-2), and ecclesial office (Eph 4:11-16).

[11]Douglas M. Koskela, "Holiness and Catholicity: A Fruitful Tension for the Wesleyan Tradition," *Wesleyan Theological Journal* 49, no. 1 (Spring 2014): 73.

[12]Volf, *After Our Likeness*, 261. He continues, "The conditions of catholicity largely coincide with those of ecclesiality . . . [because any] recognition of the ecclesiality of a community simultaneously implies recognition of its catholicity." Volf, *After Our Likeness*, 269. This interrelationship is why Nikos Nissiotis can not only say that the problem of catholicity is "the primary question of ecclesiology" but he can also draw out the implications by noting that catholicity acts as "the primary problem in dialogue between Christians estranged from one another." Quoted in Volf, *After Our Likeness*, 269.

conceptions of catholicity across ecclesial traditions (and even within the same), but also *what is at stake* in the debates over catholicity: a determination regarding the content of catholicity implies a certain understanding of the church's nature, determines a proper pattern of ecclesial authority, and ultimately makes evaluative judgments regarding what groups are (and are not) a part of the catholic "whole." To say that the ecclesiological stakes of how catholicity is conceived are quite high is no overstatement.

Thus, we must proceed with a definition that is as confessionally neutral as possible, moving slowly but surely toward greater conceptual clarification by returning to the biblical and church-historical sources while continually seeking theological synthesis. In offering a provisional definition of catholicity, then, we do well to remain close to the etymology of the word: to be "catholic" (from the Greek *katholikos*, *kata* "with respect to" + *holos* "whole") is to be in keeping with the whole, to be universal in orientation. One can thus speak of individuals, churches, and even church traditions demonstrating a "catholic spirit," by which we mean an irenic mood that seeks to be in constructive dialogue with the whole, that is, with other parts of the universal church that is one in Christ by faith.

But to speak of the *church* as catholic is specifically to signify "the church as the whole people of God, spread out over space, across cultures, and through time."[13] Thus to believe that the church is catholic is to "recognize the Spirit's work in the church's reception of the gospel over the centuries and across cultures."[14] Appropriately this insight connects catholicity with the Holy Spirit (the ecclesial attributes come in the third article of the creed) and with the church's belief of the gospel and ongoing effort to live in light of it (for the creed summarizes biblical narrative and doctrine that makes the gospel understandable). We thus hold that the catholic church manifests wherever, whenever, and among whomever the gospel is received by faith as enabled by the Spirit and verified by the apostolic witness of Scripture, for the gospel is set forth in Scripture, and only a church that brings its message

---

[13]Kevin J. Vanhoozer, *The Drama of Doctrine: A Canonical-Linguistic Approach to Christian Theology* (Louisville, KY: Westminster John Knox, 2005), 27.

[14]Kevin J. Vanhoozer, "Imprisoned or Free: Text, Status, and Theological Interpretation in the Master/Slave Discourse of Philemon" in *Reading Scripture with the Church: Toward a Hermeneutic for Theological Interpretation*, by A. K. M. Adam, Stephen E. Fowl, Kevin J. Vanhoozer, and Francis Watson (Grand Rapids, MI: Baker Academic, 2006), 77.

(apostolicity) and life (holiness) into conformity to Christ by the Spirit as revealed in the Scriptures is part of the unified (one), universal (catholic) church of God.[15]

Another important issue is the extent to which we should understand catholicity as not just quantitative (marking out the *scope* of the church), but also qualitative (marking out a substantial *characteristic* of the church). With Avery Dulles, whose *The Catholicity of the Church* provides one of the most significant contributions to the contemporary doctrine of ecclesial catholicity, I hold that catholicity is a complex attribute that can only be understood multidimensionally and must be assessed in terms of *both* quantitative *and* qualitative categories.[16] The previously discussed distinction-yet-interconnectedness between the church's unity (oneness) and its universality (catholicity) is particularly important to register here. Kevin Vanhoozer rightly insists that "the evangelical unity of the church is compatible with a catholic diversity."[17] But here we seek to build on that insight by arguing that *quantitative* catholicity speaks to the church's unity being increasingly diversified as the missional scope of redemptive history expands all the way to glory, while *qualitative* catholicity speaks to the church's diversity being properly unified in Christ by faith according to the gospel.

Quantitative catholicity increases as redemptive history marches on; qualitative catholicity belongs to the church in equal measure from Pentecost to parousia. Quantitative catholicity *increases* as the church inhabits a greater plurality of contexts and cultures; qualitative catholicity is *more fully displayed* as the unity of Christ's body is exhibited amid greater and greater degrees of diversity. Both are necessary for a full-orbed confession of the church's catholicity, and both are integrally connected to the creedal

---

[15]Vanhoozer has deftly observed that "catholic and evangelical belong together. To be precise: 'catholic' qualifies 'evangelical.' The gospel designated a determinate word; catholicity the scope of its reception." Vanhoozer, *The Drama of Doctrine*, 27. Webster agrees, noting that to be "catholic" is to "seek reflectively to trace the universal scope of the truth of the gospel." John Webster, "The Self-Organizing Power of the Gospel of Christ: Episcopacy and Community Formation," *International Journal of Systematic Theology* 3, no. 1 (March 2001): 70. For more see Kevin J. Vanhoozer, "Improvising Theology According to the Scriptures," in *Building on the Foundations of Evangelical Theology*, ed. Gregg R. Allison and Stephen J. Wellum (Wheaton, IL: Crossway, 2015), 45-50.

[16]Avery Dulles, *The Catholicity of the Church* (Oxford: Oxford University Press, 1985).

[17]Vanhoozer, *The Drama of Doctrine*, 27.

attribute of unity. I thus follow Volf in understanding catholicity as involving "the fundamental question of the relationship between *unity and multiplicity*"[18] and Vanhoozer in understanding catholicity as the church's participation in "a differentiated unity, a fulsome wholeness."[19] For this work, then, I demarcate catholicity as a *unified diversity through the whole of all times, peoples, and places*, which particularly distinguishes the concept from uniformity (for what is unified is a *diversity*), pluralism (for the diversity is *unified*) and sectarianism, exclusionism, and provincialism (for it is *through the whole of all times, peoples, and places*). In short, ecclesial catholicity indicates the unified-yet-diverse nature of the church as it manifests universally.

Defining the Free Church Tradition

In defining what we mean by the Free Church tradition for this project, we must recognize that this, too, is a much-contested notion (perhaps even more so). Kevin Bidwell rightly observes that when it comes to the Free Church, "the defining boundaries have historically been somewhat fluid . . . therefore, a measure of caution should be exercised in any strict usage of this expression."[20] Indeed, the difficulty of defining this ecclesial tradition is heightened by the fact that the Free Church banner attempts to group churches that often exhibit a deep commitment to the autonomy of the local church and a degree of skepticism regarding the existence of any earthly ecclesial entity beyond the local congregation. Those who have attempted to delineate the contours of the Free Church have often offered starkly different pictures of the tradition, with some asking whether we can characterize it as a cohesive tradition at all. For his part, Donald Durnbaugh seeks to bring clarity by identifying the Free Church through five marks: (1) an adherence to congregational polity, (2) an implementation of "low" liturgy (often through the nomenclature of "nonliturgical"), (3) an eschewing of

---

[18] Volf, *After Our Likeness*, 261-62.
[19] Kevin J. Vanhoozer, "A Mere Protestant Response," in *Was the Reformation a Mistake? Why Catholic Doctrine Is Not Unbiblical*, by Matthew Levering (Grand Rapids, MI: Zondervan, 2017), 229. This is also to follow Yves Congar when he defined catholicity as "the quality of the Church through which its actual multiplicity enters into harmony with its actual unity." Quoted in Josef Neuner, "The Idea of Catholicity—Concept and History," in *The Church: Readings in Theology*, ed. Gustave Wegel (New York: P. J. Kenedy & Sons, 1963), 67.
[20] Kevin J. Bidwell, *"The Church as the Image of the Trinity": A Critical Evaluation of Miroslav Volf's Ecclesial Model* (Eugene, OR: Wipf & Stock, 2011), 58.

formal adherence to creeds (often through the nomenclature of "non-creedal"), (4) a high value on individual conscience and religious liberty, and (5) an insistence on the separation of church and state.[21] Volf believes he can get the list down to two primary characteristics: "[The Free Church] designates first those churches with a congregationalist church constitution, and second those churches affirming a consistent separation of church and state."[22] Meanwhile, Yoder is content, at least in one place, to simply mark out the tradition as encompassing any churches shaped by evangelical nonconformity to the Constantinian model of the church.[23] Of the making of lists of Free Church defining marks there is, it seems, no end. Nonetheless, this project will require our own articulation of the tradition's most central characteristics in due course.

But beyond a list of marks, how might we arrive at a proper definition of the Free Church tradition? Yoder assists us here by pointing out two false paths for this task. The first attempts to mark out the tradition *too broadly* by following the designation that emerges largely out of the twentieth-century British context, where "free churches" designate everything but the national church (thus including Presbyterian and Methodist churches in the Free Church fold, full stop). Such a "formal and non-evaluative" definition is clearly insufficient, as exhibited by the fact that by this definition every church in America (Anglican, Orthodox, and Roman Catholic included) could technically be designated a "free church."[24] But Yoder insists there is also an opposite error of drawing the Free Church lines much *too narrowly* by defining the term according to a purity of "vision that even the 'radical reformation' groups . . . do not fully live up to"; this indicates a sectarian, rather than an ecclesial, spirit.[25] A proper definition of the tradition, according to Yoder, would combine a formal description (such as voluntary membership and institutional independence from civil authorities) with a

---

[21]Donald F. Durnbaugh, *The Believers' Church: The History and Character of Radical Protestantism* (Scottdale, PA: Herald Press, 1985), 5-8. Durnbaugh understands "Free Church" and "Believers' Church" as largely interchangeable terms.
[22]Volf, *After Our Likeness*, 9.
[23]See Michael G. Cartwright, "Radical Reform, Radical Catholicity: John Howard Yoder's Vision of the Faithful Church," in *The Royal Priesthood: Essays Ecclesiastical and Ecumenical*, by John Howard Yoder, ed. Michael G. Cartwright (Scottdale, PA: Herald Press, 1998), 29-30.
[24]Yoder, *The Royal Priesthood*, 264.
[25]Yoder, *The Royal Priesthood*, 264.

normative claim that "those differentiae . . . are also important, *biblically warranted* testimonies."[26] This desideratum is duly noted.

Franklin Littell, for his part, agrees that the first of Yoder's false paths ("too broad") is indeed of very little help, and yet is the one quite often taken. To define the Free Church tradition simply in terms of nonestablishment and separation from state interference, Littell insists, is to mark out the tradition *negatively* rather than establish what it is *positively*. Taking the positive route would require a theological account of "the disciplined community witness[ing] to the work of the Holy Spirit."[27] In another place he elaborates that "to begin the discussion of the Free Church at the wrong point, *e.g.,* with the question of relations with the state, will prejudice every issue in the wrong way. . . . The place to begin *is with the view of the church and her mission*."[28] Similarly Yoder has observed that "'Freedom' [for this tradition] is not only a descriptive trait but also a theological value. Behind those formal ways in which it has been tested or stated in the past lie deeper concerns regarding the faithfulness of the individual and the Body, their mission and their renewal."[29] In light of Littell's and Yoder's guidance, we believe that a proper identification of the Free Church tradition must go beyond a *formal* description to an articulation of what *normative* ecclesiological claims are made by its churches; this means that the tradition should be defined in a *fully theological*, rather than in a *narrowly political*, manner.

Another avenue for properly marking out the "Free Church" tradition comes by comparing it with its *conceptual alternatives*. One oft-touted possibility is the label of the "Believers' Church" tradition, first used by Max Weber in more narrowly describing the Anabaptist and Quaker ecclesial impulses.[30] Since then the concept has been broadened out, perhaps most famously at the "Concept of the Believers' Church Conference" held at the Southern Baptist Theological Seminary in 1968. At that time around

---

[26] Yoder, *The Royal Priesthood*, 264, emphasis added.
[27] Franklin H. Littell, *The Free Church* (Boston: Starr King Press, 1957), 149-50.
[28] Franklin H. Littell, "The Historical Free Church Defined," *Brethren Life and Thought* 50, nos. 3–4 (Summer–Fall 2005): 53, emphasis added.
[29] Yoder, *The Royal Priesthood*, 264. Littell can similarly observe that "classical Free Churchmanship involved religious liberty in a secondary sense, whereas the primary emphasis was upon a new concept of a [free] community of discipleship." Littell, *The Free Church*, 1.
[30] See Max Weber, *The Protestant Ethic and the Spirit of Capitalism* (New York: Charles Scribner's Sons, 1958), 145-46.

150 participants from communions as diverse as the Assemblies of God, the Brethren Church, the Churches of Christ, the Presbyterian Church of Japan, the Mennonite Church, the Southern Baptist Convention, the United Church of Christ, and the United Methodist Church came together to discuss one central question: "What [is] the meaning and the contemporary significance of the Believers' Church?"[31] In his introduction to the conference proceedings, James Leo Garrett offered an apologetic of sorts for this label over alternatives like "free church," "gathered church," "pilgrim church," "pure church," or "antipaedobaptist church" because, to his mind, "believers' church" more properly "fashion[s] an instrument of identification, however imperfect, for that segment of the Protestant Christian heritage which is distinct from Classical Protestant and from Catholic—Roman, Eastern, Anglican, *et al*—understandings of the church by its insistence on the indispensability of voluntary churchmanship with its many implications."[32] Garrett rightly understands the tradition as within the broader Protestant family, one that he labels "Radical Protestantism" as distinguished from classical (i.e., magisterial) Protestantism.[33]

But even more to the point, we agree with Yoder's insistence, registered amid the Louisville conference, that the labels *Free Church* and *Believers' Church*, while largely signifying the same terrain, should not ultimately be understood as interchangeable because the former is *more comprehensive* than the latter.[34] This observation is borne out by reflection on the trajectory of subsequent Believers' Church conferences, which have been convened intermittently since the inaugural 1968 conference.[35] As the particular participants and topics of these conferences made clearer as they progressed, the Believers' Church label seems to always entail the practice of credobaptism and often connotes a more direct association with the stream of

---

[31]See James Leo Garrett Jr., "Preface," in *The Concept of the Believers' Church: Addresses from the 1968 Louisville Conference*, ed. James Leo Garrett Jr. (Scottdale, PA: Herald Press, 1969), 5-7.
[32]Garrett, "Preface," 5.
[33]Garrett, "Preface," 15. This resonates with the work of Littell in identifying this tradition as a "'third force' in Western Christianity, a force just as original as Roman Catholicism or 'magisterial Protestantism.'" See Littell, "The Historical Free Church Defined," 51.
[34]See Garrett's introductory comments to Franklin H. Littell, "The Concept of the Believers' Church," in Garrett, *Concept of the Believers' Church*, 16.
[35]For a full listing of these conferences (eighteen to date) up until the latest conference in 2017, see www.believerschurchconferences.com/previous-conferences.html.

"peace churches" than the broader Free Church label does. The insistence on believer's baptism unnecessarily excludes Congregational, Wesleyan, and Evangelical Free/Covenant traditions despite their "family resemblance" with the other churches in view.[36] It seems best, then, to follow Yoder's lead in insisting that if we want to speak of "Radical Protestantism" in the broadest sense (which is the aspiration of this work), the label *Free Church*, while not without its drawbacks, is the best option currently available.

Thus to mark out the Free Church in its broadest conception means, as Michael Cartwright has observed, grouping continental Anabaptists of the sixteenth century with separatist Puritans of the seventeenth century with certain Lutheran Pietists and Wesleyan Revivalists of the eighteenth century with Disciples of Christ of the nineteenth century with the German Confessing Church of the twentieth century with global Pentecostals of the twenty-first century.[37] Of course there is much that distinguishes these various groups and their churches. But to speak of them under the Free Church label is to discern that they can be understood as ecclesial streams within a common tradition. These streams would include what we might label "Peace churches" (Mennonite, Brethren), "Holiness churches" (Pentecostal, Wesleyan), "Radical/Separatist Puritan churches" (Congregational, Baptist), "Restorationist churches" (Churches of Christ, Disciples of Christ), and "Pietist churches" (Evangelical Free Church, Evangelical Covenant), among others.

The similarities of these streams in terms of a Free Church family resemblance come into particular focus when questions of the church's constitution and the nature of its authority are raised. This is because the Free Church tradition is best understood, and its distinctive ecclesiological convictions and theological contributions best glimpsed, when it is placed alongside its *ecclesiological opposite*: the broader "Episcopal tradition" with

---

[36]We follow Littell in recognizing the "radical puritans" of seventeenth-century Congregationalism (which were paedobaptist) as the "other wing" of the emerging Free Church tradition, alongside the wing that insisted on credobaptism as the proper outworking of Free Church ecclesiology (Mennonites, Baptists, etc.). Congregationalists justify infant baptism without appealing to the *corpus Christianum*, demonstrating that while credobaptism has been the majority position within the larger Free Church tradition, there is no reason to see paedobaptism as incompatible with the tradition as it is understood here. See Franklin H. Littell, "The Claims of the Free Churches," *The Christian Century* 78, no. 14 (April 5, 1961): 417-18.

[37]Cartwright, "Radical Reform, Radical Catholicity," 25.

its particular ecclesial streams: Eastern Orthodoxy, Roman Catholicism, Anglicanism, and, to a lesser extent, Lutheranism.[38] Volf particularly makes this clear by highlighting two ecclesial convictions of the Episcopal tradition that directly contrast with the Free Church conception of the church: (1) the church's constitution is via a bishop in apostolic succession (vs. being congregationally constituted), and (2) the church's ministry is objectively effective regardless of subjective conditions such as faith or holiness (vs. understanding the church's ministry effectiveness as to some extent dependent on certain subjective conditions, such as the presence of saving faith).[39] In many ways these convictions stem from understanding ordained ministers, particularly bishops, as belonging to the *esse* of the church. The Free Church rejection of these convictions reveals a deep fault line that runs between the two traditions, especially in their differentiation of a "bottom up" versus "top down" pattern of ecclesial authority and in their attendant conceptions of catholicity as "from below" versus "from above."[40]

It is important to observe that the issues I have in mind here in defining the Free Church tradition in relationship to the Episcopal tradition are not limited to questions of congregational or Episcopal polity *alone*; rather, I am seeking to offer what might be summarized as a *theological* account of the Free Church tradition and the pattern of ecclesial authority it entails. The Free Church tradition has often been identified simply in terms of an expressed polity, specifically that of congregationalism: the church is governed under the authority of Christ by the collective congregational membership of regenerate persons (who appoint leaders, vote on propositions, etc.). But I believe to do so ultimately confuses *a form of polity*

---

[38]This is to follow Volf and the authors of *The Catholicity of Protestantism* in discerning the scope of these two traditions quite broadly and in contrast with each other. See R. Newton Flew and Rupert E. Davies, eds., *The Catholicity of Protestantism: Being a Report Presented to His Grace the Archbishop of Canterbury by a Group of Free Churchmen* (London: Lutterworth Press, 1950).

[39]Volf, *After Our Likeness*, 133-35. Volf offers another contrast in saying that from an Episcopal vantage point the church's being depends on Christ's mediated presence in the sacraments (vs. depending on the local gathering of God's covenantally assembled people). But this is a false dichotomy, for Free Church ecclesiology in the broadest sense is compatible with many understandings of the sacraments as they relate to Christ's presence.

[40]Bidwell also sees these two traditions in contrast with each other, noting that the Free Church is "an umbrella term today that houses a somewhat fluid and loosely defined worldwide movement that encompasses a host of *non-Episcopal church streams*." Bidwell, *"Church as the Image of the Trinity,"* 84, emphasis added.

(congregationalism) with *an ecclesial tradition* that enacts a form of polity to organize its affairs (the Free Church tradition). Paul Harrison rightly notes that an ecclesial tradition derives from a distinctive doctrine of the church ("the beliefs Christians hold about the nature of the church, its relation to God, and its purpose in the world") and only enacts a polity ("the administration and government of the church") to work out its ecclesial convictions by organizing and regulating church life in a particular way.[41] Ecclesial tradition (focused on the church's nature) and ecclesial polity (focused on the church's order) are interrelated but not to be conflated, following John Owen's insistence that "the church is considered either as it is essential[ly], with respect unto its nature and being, or as it is organical[ly], with respect unto its order."[42] Here we focus primarily on the former while tracing out potential implications for the latter, holding that the Free Church tradition is concerned fundamentally with ecclesiality (what makes the church the church, what are the conditions of being a church, etc.) and only secondarily with working out the implications of its ecclesial convictions in terms of the church's mission and polity.[43]

We must now draw the strands together. Beginning with a delineation of defining criteria, I hold that the churches of the Free Church tradition exhibit three interrelated marks. (1) Free Churches are *congregationally constituted*; that is, they hold that their ecclesiality is established "from below" in the Spirit-enabled, voluntary gathering around Christ of God's faith-filled, priestly people rather than "from above" in the acts of a bishop or monarch. (2) Free Churches are *conscientiously nonconformist*; that is, they emphasize the necessary holiness and "otherness" of the church and reject Constantinian arrangements out of a conviction that the church's distinctiveness is best preserved when it is nonestablished, kept from state interference, and identified with the *corpus Christi* (the body of Christ) rather than the *corpus Christianum* (the body of Christendom). (3) Free Churches are *corporately*

---

[41]Paul H. Harrison, *Authority and Power in the Free Church Tradition* (Carbondale, IL: Southern Illinois University Press, 1959), 4.

[42]John Owen, *The True Nature of a Gospel Church and Its Government*, ed. John Huxtable (London: James Clarke, 1947), 51.

[43]This follows Webster's axiom that "an adequate doctrine of the church will maximize [theology] . . . and relativize (but not minimize or abolish) ecclesial action and its ordered forms." John Webster, "The Self-Organizing Power of the Gospel of Christ," 74.

local; that is, they insist on the primacy of the local, gathered church (vs. the church as a translocal institution or an invisible aggregate of the elect) as the proper manifestation of the catholic church, convening under the authority of Christ by the power of the Spirit for covenanted fellowship marked by word, sacrament, and oversight while seeking conformity to the pattern of Scripture and God's greater glory.

In sum, we understand the Free Church tradition as an *ecclesial* tradition, one that views the church in a particular way, namely as congregationally constituted (dealing with the *establishment* of the church in the world), conscientiously nonconformist (dealing with the *way* of the church in the world), and corporately local (dealing with the *locus* of the church in the world). Stated theologically, we might say that the Free Church ecclesial tradition holds that the church has its life from first to last fully and completely in and by the triune God, gathered together around the Son by the Spirit unto the Father as the new covenant people of God called to offer a distinctive witness to the world everywhere it assembles. Such life in God rightly expresses itself in a congregational pattern of ecclesial authority, one that recognizes the freedom that has been won for and ought to be exercised by all of God's gospel-liberated people to act as priest-kings who believe, guard, and live out the gospel in gathered assemblies of even just two or three. So understood, we recognize that there is broad ecclesial expression within the Free Church tradition: churches from Brethren to Baptist to Congregational to Disciples to Evangelical Covenant to Evangelical Free to Mennonite to Pentecostal, along with the broad spectrum of nondenominational and independent churches, can be placed under this banner, even as they represent distinctive streams within it.[44]

---

[44]This represents a similar Free Church scope to that found in D. H. Williams, *Retrieving the Tradition and Renewing Evangelicalism: A Primer for Suspicious Protestants* (Grand Rapids, MI: Eerdmans, 1999), 2.

Biblical Warrant for the Doctrine of Catholicity

HERE WE TAKE UP the foundational enterprise of determining whether there is biblical warrant for the creedal confession of the church's catholicity. To show that the church's catholicity is grounded not only in tradition but ultimately in Scripture is not only *proper* according to the Protestant principle of *sola Scriptura*; it is also *wise* given the contested nature of the doctrinal content down church-historical stream. This chapter thus seeks to heed, first and foremost, God's very own words in Scripture as the *norma normans* of theology. To do so is nothing less than an attempt to do theology "according to the Scriptures" (1 Cor 15:3).

THE NEED FOR BIBLICAL WARRANT

Though every exercise in systematic theology ought to begin (and end) with the Word of God, it is all the more critical when it comes to the doctrine of the church's catholicity and the parameters of this book. This is for three primary reasons. The first, as we have already mentioned, is the contested nature of the doctrine. Catholicity could represent the quintessential case study of ecclesial division and doctrinal disagreement, quite ironic given the fact that catholicity concerns the whole church and justifies an understanding of the church as having a diversified nature. Due to conflicting claims regarding the content of catholicity, each ecclesial tradition is obligated to account for its understanding of the doctrine, be open to the insights of other traditions, and be willing to have its account evaluated in light of Scripture.

The second reason is that, simply put, the biblical basis for this creedal attribute is vastly understudied. That studies of the church's catholicity abound, especially post–Vatican II and amid the rise of the ecumenical movement, is clear. But a closer examination of these studies reveals one key oversight: biblical warrant is rarely a primary concern. In fact, very little work has been done developing a *biblical* notion of the church's catholicity.[1] Clowney can say "the burning issues of church unity or division, apostolicity or apostasy, holiness or worldliness, universality or sectarianism—*all hinge on an understanding of the biblical doctrine of the church.* . . . Only as the church stands under the Word of God can it discover its own nature and calling."[2] We thus need to better articulate the biblical warrant for, and content of, catholicity.

Third, establishing biblical support for the doctrine is especially important for the Free Church tradition. Indeed, if large swaths of this tradition are to retrieve catholicity and even contribute toward a fuller-orbed expression of the doctrine, we must make clear that such a doctrine has biblical support.[3] This is particularly true of the tradition's more evangelical manifestations, which have been characterized (not without basis) as often being apathetic, suspicious, or even outright hostile regarding any notion of the church's catholicity. Indeed, Timothy George's observation regarding evangelicals at large is perhaps even truer of Free Church evangelicals. He notes that "most evangelicals are happy to confess that the church is one, holy, and apostolic. These are, after all, not only biblical concepts but also New Testament terms. But . . . many contemporary evangelical churches have long abandoned the word 'Catholic,' and would even consider it an insult to be called such."[4] If we are seeking to spur those in the Free Church

---

[1] For example, there is no monograph-length biblical theology of catholicity to date; such a lacuna is not only astonishing but also speaks to the relative lack of emphasis on *biblical* (vs. creedal) foundations for rightly understanding the church's catholicity.

[2] Edmund P. Clowney, *The Doctrine of the Church* (Philadelphia: Presbyterian and Reformed, 1974), 2, emphasis added.

[3] The Free Church tradition has earned the reputation of positing a central question in evaluating doctrinal proposals: "Where stands it written?" For example, see the way the Evangelical Free Church of America understands this question as stemming from a right understanding of the Scripture's authority in matters of faith and practice in *Evangelical Convictions: A Theological Exposition of the Statement of Faith of the Evangelical Free Church of America* (Minneapolis: Free Church Publications, 2011).

[4] Timothy George, "Toward an Evangelical Ecclesiology," *Evangelical Review of Theology* 41, no. 2 (April 2017): 112.

tradition on in retrieving the doctrine of the church's catholicity and contributing to its fullness, we must demonstrate Clowney's affirmation to be true: catholicity "flow[s] from the more fundamental teaching of the Bible regarding the nature of the church."[5]

THE PROCESS OF ESTABLISHING BIBLICAL WARRANT

But we also must ask, *How* do we go about establishing this all-important biblical warrant? It is one thing to want to "be biblical" in establishing a doctrine of the church's catholicity; it is quite another to actually *demonstrate* that biblical basis, especially given the fact that there is no passage we can turn to for a face-value exposition of the church's catholicity. Graham Cole helps us face this challenge by reminding us that proper interpretation of Scripture requires moving from micro to macro, examining specific texts within their immediate contexts within their distinctive literary units within their particular books within the larger canon and in light of the entire flow of redemptive history from Genesis to Revelation.[6] We thus approach the biblical text less as a storehouse to be mined for propositional content (in this case, propositions affirming the church as catholic) and more as a unified narrative of God's redemptive-historical ways with and for his people, looking for distinctive themes and motifs that emerge across the entire canon. In this case we'll explore the biblical warrant for catholicity by examining how the *nature* of God's people as a *unified diversity* and the *scope* of that people *through the whole of all times, peoples, and places* develop over the course of the whole redemptive narrative.

But before we proceed, we must also deal with one other concern: Should we *really* use the term *catholic* to describe the church if the Bible never does so? Two comments can be made here. First, we must recognize that terms such as *catholic* or *catholicity* are not required to speak about the church's universal scope and nature; other nouns such as *fullness* and *wholeness* and other adjectives such as *all* and *whole* function in much the same way. But second, we must remember that *catholicity* is

---

[5]Edmund P. Clowney, "The Biblical Theology of the Church," in *The Church in the Bible and the World*, ed. D. A. Carson (Grand Rapids, MI: Baker, 1987), 16.
[6]Graham A. Cole, *He Who Gives Life: The Doctrine of the Holy Spirit* (Wheaton, IL: Crossway, 2007), 28.

not alone in this regard. Many of the great terms of the Christian tradition, including *Trinity* and *homoousios* ("of the same substance," used to defend the claim that Christ was equally divine with the Father), are not found in Scripture. It is important, as David Yeago has claimed, to distinguish between judgments and the conceptual terms in which those judgments are rendered. In his "The New Testament and the Nicene Dogma," Yeago argues convincingly that Nicaea's judgment that the Son was *homoousios* says "the same thing" as Paul's judgment that Jesus had "equality with God" in Philippians 2:6.[7]

Here we follow a similar line of argumentation regarding the creedal confession that the church is catholic, namely that the creeds synthesize and express the same judgment as Scripture, but in slightly different terms. Specifically we will follow and adjust Yeago's argumentation to insist that the term *catholic* "is neither imposed *on* the New Testament texts, nor distantly deduced *from* the texts, but rather describes a pattern of judgements present *in* the texts, in the texture of scriptural discourse."[8] The present chapter is thus an attempt to discern the pattern of judgments in the text of Scripture that warrants and orients our confession that the church is catholic. It is an attempt to show, in the words of Jason Hallig, that "the story of the catholic church is a *biblical* story.... It is a story of God's redemptive history—rescuing men and women from sin... [and intending] to create a people for himself—a community not only of one nation but of many nations, who would serve as the kingdom people... [and as] a catholic community."[9] The warrant for the doctrine is thus derived from one of the most central themes of Scripture: God's covenantal intention to call a people to himself.[10] An inquiry regarding the biblical basis for the doctrine of the church's catholicity is thus an inquiry into a particular characteristic of this people, especially as it manifests in God's *new covenant* people, the church.

---

[7]David Yeago, "The New Testament and the Nicene Dogma: A Contribution to the Recovery of Theological Exegesis," *Pro Ecclesia* 3, no. 2 (Spring 1994), 160.
[8]Yeago, "New Testament and the Nicene Dogma," 153.
[9]Jason Valeriano Hallig, *We Are Catholic: Catholic, Catholicity, and Catholicization* (Eugene, OR: Wipf & Stock, 2016), 56, emphasis added.
[10]See Gen 17:7; Ex 6:7; Lev 26:12; Deut 7:6; Jer 31:33; Ezek 36:28; Zech 8:8; Rom 9:26; 2 Cor 6:16; Rev 21:3.

Redemptive-Historical Context: Genesis 1–11

In inquiring about the catholicity of God's people, we might ask why we should begin by examining Genesis 1–11, long before the covenant made with Abram and ages before the New Testament speaks of the *ecclesia*? We might answer that this is because, as Cornelius Plantinga has argued, these foundational chapters on creation and the story of humanity prior to Abraham are vital to properly understanding the redemptive-historical narrative that follows them. Particularly, it is important to grasp God's design and intention for creation and for humanity set forth in Genesis 1–11 in order for the remainder of the biblical narrative to make sense.[11] Properly understanding the biblical story that flows from creation to new creation also requires understanding why our world is now "not the way it's supposed to be" due to sin's devastating effects and the creational context for God's solution to this problem: calling a covenant people to himself ultimately by the work of a promised redeemer (Gen 3:15).

Here we seek to apply Karl Barth's insight that "creation is the external basis of the covenant" while "covenant is the internal basis of the creation."[12] Specifically we should see that there is no covenantal content (in this case, the catholicity of God's people) without creational context (in this case, the unified diversity of the created order). Because catholicity relates more directly to God's *covenantal* purposes, we look to Genesis 1–11 to establish the creational context that will give covenantal catholicity meaning. That is to say, because catholicity is properly an *ecclesiological* category, one that describes the nature of God's redeemed people, it belongs to the realm of *soteriology* rather than *protology*. But soteriology presupposes protology; we can't speak of humanity redeemed without first speaking of humanity created (and fallen). Here we seek to isolate the part of the creational context most relevant to the covenantal content of catholicity, namely that the created order exhibits an inherent unity-in-diversity and has the capacity to demonstrate increasing amounts of unified diversity as time

---

[11]Plantinga summarizes this design under "shalom" defined as "the webbing together of God, humans, and all creation in justice, fulfillment, and delight . . . universal flourishing, wholeness . . . the way things ought to be." Cornelius Plantinga, *Not the Way It's Supposed to Be: A Breviary of Sin* (Grand Rapids, MI: Eerdmans, 1995), 10.

[12]Karl Barth, *Church Dogmatics* III/1, trans. G. W. Bromiley, ed. T. F. Torrance (Edinburgh: T&T Clark, 1975), 51.

goes on.¹³ Recognizing this allows us to see how God's creational design of unified diversity sets the stage for the covenantal catholicity of God's people displayed in redemptive history; particularly we see Genesis 1–11 set forth creational "raw material" that develops into the catholicity of God's people according to God's wisdom and grace in his administration of the gospel (Eph 3:1-11).¹⁴

Genesis 1–3. We can only offer here the briefest of surveys of this creational context. In this survey we must not neglect the fact that it is God's own life that is the fount for this creational unified diversity. There is a unity, a oneness, that characterizes God's being.¹⁵ In Genesis 1 this is seen in the way God implements a well-ordered creation with no hint of challenge or inner division. What God wills comes to pass with nothing to hinder his plan: God creates the heavens and the earth (Gen 1:1); God sees that his creation is good (Gen 1:4, 10, 12, 18, 21, 25, 31); God orders his creation (Gen 1:4, 7); God names portions of his creation (Gen 1:5, 8, 10); God commissions elements of his creation (Gen 1:6, 14-18, 26, 28); and God delights in his completed creation (Gen 1:31–2:2).

And yet even within the first chapter of the Bible there are hints that this unity of God's being is of a diversified type. The Christian tradition (based on NT witness) will come to identify this using the language of *triunity* or *Trinity*, and here it manifests most clearly in a delineation of roles in the act of creating. So while in Genesis 1:1 we are told that "in the beginning God created the heavens and the earth," in only the next verse we hear that "the Spirit of God was hovering over the waters." And then in Genesis 1:3 we are introduced to the means of God's creating: his word, which will eventually be identified as the Word of God (who is also the Son of God, Jn 1:1-14; Col 1:16), distinct from and yet one with both God (the Father) and the

---

[13]This is not because of some determinative element in the order of creation itself, but because of God's good pleasure in enacting the covenant of grace to make it so. At most, then, we can say that there is a creaturely *analogy* to the church's catholicity, namely the unified diversity of all creation: every element of creation is united in its creatureliness and yet every element is diverse in the particulars of its creaturely identity and role.

[14]For a different framing of the same concept, see Avery Dulles, *The Catholicity of the Church* (Oxford: Oxford University Press, 1985), 48-67. Dulles has labeled these creational foundations the "depth dimension of catholicity" or "catholicity from below."

[15]This will be driven home again and again throughout God's covenantal dealings with his people. See Deut 6:4; Mk 12:29; 1 Cor 8:6; Gal 3:20; Eph 4:6; 1 Tim 2:5; Rev 11:17.

(Holy) Spirit of God. The significance of this trinitarian fount from which all unified diversity in the created order flows should not be overlooked.[16] God's trinitarian life, marked by a unified diversity, is the source of all; that unity-in-diversity shows up in every aspect of creation and in the very nature of the church in God's redemptive program should be no surprise.

Indeed, Genesis 1 goes on to showcase a unified diversity in the created order itself: all the things God creates are united in their creatureliness and God-glorifying capacity, and yet there is manifold diversity in what is created. Each day of creation unfurls new and varied forms of being, each of which contains the seed for seemingly infinite variety. Again and again we are told that God created "according to their kinds": seed-bearing plants (Gen 1:12), fruit-bearing trees (Gen 1:12), sea-dwelling creatures (Gen 1:21), flying animals (Gen 1:21), beasts of the earth (Gen 1:25), livestock (Gen 1:25), and even "creeping things" (Gen 1:25). We are told that when God surveyed *all* of what he had made, the heavens and the earth "in all their *vast array*," (Gen 2:1) he concluded that it was all very good (Gen 1:31).[17] God rejoices in creational diversity unified under his creative provision and care. David Smith thus doesn't exaggerate when he proclaims, "At the very outset of the biblical narrative we are presented with a God who revels in diversity, in rich creativity."[18]

But there is a particular segment of God's creation where we see unified diversity particularly manifest, and that is in human beings, who alone are made in the image of the triune God (Gen 1:26-27). There are many dimensions of unified diversity found in humans. The earliest mentioned, and the one given the most emphasis in Genesis 1–2, is the fact that we image God in distinct yet complementary ways as male and female. Genesis 2 fleshes this out by drawing attention to the fact that uniformity

---

[16]On this, Allison says "[The] trinitarian nature of God is not uniformity, but unity in diversity.... They are diverse persons enjoying different eternal relationships and being principally responsible for different kinds of trinitarian works in which they inseparably share. Yet they are not diverse in terms of being three different gods; rather, they are three diverse persons of the one eternal Godhead. Theirs is unity in diversity." Gregg Allison, *Sojourners and Strangers: The Doctrine of the Church* (Wheaton, IL: Crossway, 2012), 169.

[17]Emphasis added. Any italics in biblical quotations in the remainder of this work are my addition. Any italics added to nonbiblical quotations will be indicated.

[18]David Smith, "What Hope After Babel? Diversity and Community in Gen 11:1-9; Exod 1:1-14; Zeph 3:1-13 and Acts 2:1-3," *Horizons in Biblical Theology* 18, no. 2 (December 1996): 169-70.

of the male form was incomplete, the first "not good" arising in the created order (Gen 2:18). God then moves to remedy the insufficiency by creating the woman out of the man, demonstrating their unified status as equally imaging the divine (Gen 2:22). Adam's poetic celebration of God's goodness in creating the woman recognizes both her similarity to, and distinctness from, him (Gen 2:23).

Other forms of unified diversity within human beings are visible here, one of which surrounds geographical expansion: human beings will always dwell on the earth (unity, established in Gen 1:26) and yet will inhabit a myriad of places and climates within it (diversity, hinted at in Gen 2:10-14). Again Smith is helpful here, noting that in the commission to be fruitful and increase in number, filling the earth and subduing it (Gen 1:28), "the command to subdue is preceded by a command to fill. The move out of the garden which follows the fall is already implicit in the dynamic initiated by this command. The garden is a place *from* which ... people are to spread, bringing blessing.... Spreading, like diversity, is rooted in creation prior to the fall."[19] In short, we see a multifaceted unity-in-diversity at the beginning, in seed form; unified diversity, particularly in God's image bearers, is being prepared to go through the whole (earth).

But the creational unity-in-diversity that marks the shalom of God's good creation is shattered in the account of humanity's fall and its aftermath set forth in Genesis 3 and following. Indeed, the rebellion of human beings manifests in their alienation from God, one another, and the created order (seen in God's rebuke and curse of Gen 3:14-19). The unified diversity that once defined the created order in terms of manifold expressions of God-glorifying creatureliness is now broken. The unity of the human race has now splintered into blame shifting and resentment (Gen 3:12-13); the diversity once so beautiful is now a primary source of division, marginalization, and abuse (Gen 3:16).[20] Mysteriously God promises to address the tragedy by initiating a plan of redemption (hinted at in Gen 3:15, 21). Even

---

[19]Smith, "What Hope After Babel?," 170.
[20]But Udo Middelmann is correct to note that "Adam and Eve's original mandate to subdue the earth and to have dominion was to continue after the fall in pursuit of a more varied, creative, and righteous life. Both creation before the Fall ... and after the Fall ... were never to be embraced as final, repetitive, unquestioned, and without change." Udo W. Middelmann, *The Innocence of God* (Colorado Springs, CO: Paternoster, 2007), 201-2.

as Adam and Eve are banished "east of Eden," the creational pattern of unified diversity remains, with humans still united in dependence on God while continuing to demonstrate greater degrees of diversity.

Genesis 10–11. But the portion of Genesis 1–11 that does the most to highlight how God's creational design of unified diversity lays the foundations for the glories of covenantal catholicity in redemptive history is undoubtedly Genesis 10–11; indeed, it is the material known as the "Table of Nations" (Gen 10) and the "Tower of Babel" (Gen 11:1-9) that most directly sets the context for the catholic nature of God's covenant people. This is seen when we recognize that Genesis 10–11 has been designed with a "deliberate dischronologization," which Smith explains by saying, "[The] linguistic uniformity in Genesis 11:1 is [not] in conflict with the references to the [prior] linguistic diversity in Gen 10:5, 18 and perhaps 25. . . . [And thus] it is quite clear that Gen 10–11 are not arranged chronologically. Genesis 10 presents three successive historical sweeps with vague timescales before returning in summary to the time of Noah in verse 32 (and again in 11:10!)."[21] In other words, it makes sense to understand Genesis 11 as *preceding* Genesis 10 chronologically (providing an explanation for the cultural/linguistic diversity on display in the previous chapter) even as it *follows* Genesis 10 in the narrative. This raises an important question: What motivated this chronological reversal? Answering this question will go a long way in helping us see the unified diversity of God's creational order affirmed within.

We begin with the Tower of Babel narrative. While there are multiple interpretations of the account,[22] here we will briefly engage the interpretation offered by Theodore Hiebert.[23] On his reading the primary issue that Yahweh responds to is not a swelling hubris but rather a commitment to homogeneity and permanence of locale as a source of safety in the postdiluvian world. Hiebert says, "The story of Babel . . . [describes] the human

---

[21]Smith, "What Hope After Babel?," 172.
[22]By far the most pervasive is the traditional interpretation, what Theodore Hiebert has labeled the "pride-and-punishment" interpretation. On this reading the builders of the tower are motivated by pride, and Yahweh's response is primarily to punish them for their ambition in order to prevent a repeat of Genesis 6.
[23]See Theodore Hiebert, "Cultural Diversity: Punishment or Plan? Two Interpretations of the Story of the Tower of Babel," in *Toppling the Tower: Essays on Babel and Diversity*, ed. Theodore Hiebert (Chicago: McCormick Theological Seminary, 2004), 2.

longing for homogeneity in conflict with the divine plan for cultural diversity. The human problem is not pride but the fear of spreading out into a multicultural world. And God's response . . . [enacts] a divine plan that the world after the flood be filled with diverse languages and peoples and cultures."[24] On this reading Babel marks the auspicious advance of human diversity, especially in language and geographical distribution, despite human effort to the contrary.

Hiebert's reading helps us further grasp the creational context for the church's catholicity down redemptive-historical stream when we return to our question: Why did the author of Genesis 1–11 reverse the chronological order of the Tower of Babel (Gen 11) and Table of Nations (Gen 10)? Clines's answer has tremendous payoff:

> If the material of chap. 10 had followed the Babel story, the whole Table of Nations would have to be read under the sign of judgment; where it stands it functions as the fulfillment of the divine command of 9:1 "Be fruitful and multiply, and fill the earth," which looks back in its turn to 1:28. All this means that the final author of the primeval history understands that the dispersal of the nations may be evaluated both positively (as in chap. 10) and negatively (as in chap. 11).[25]

That is, according to Clines the author decided to reverse the order so that continuity with what preceded in Genesis is evident: God's creational intention for and blessing on increasing degrees of diversity precede its corruption by human sin and remain despite that corruption.

Indeed, when we look back at Genesis 10 from this perspective we recognize that the Table of Nations is framed not as *consequence* of human sin but rather as an *outworking* of God's good creational design for increasing degrees of diversity among human beings united in their common image bearing. This is the first place we get a large-scale picture of humanity as exhibiting a unified diversity through the whole (earth).

---

[24]Theodore Hiebert, "Babel: Babble or Blueprint? Calvin, Cultural Diversity, and the Interpretation of Genesis 11:1-9," in *Reformed Theology: Identity and Ecumenicity II: Biblical Interpretation in the Reformed Tradition*, ed. Wallace M. Alston Jr. and Michael Welker (Grand Rapids, MI: Eerdmans, 2007), 139.

[25]D. J. A. Clines, "Theme in Genesis 1–11," in *I Studied Inscriptions from Before the Flood: Ancient Near Eastern, Literary, and Linguistic Approaches to Genesis 1–11*, ed. Richard S. Hess and David Toshio Tsumura (Winona Lake, IN: Eisenbrauns, 1994), 296.

While the Table of Nations is difficult to interpret,[26] we know that the chapter provides us with an account of how seventy "nations" relate to Noah's three sons after the flood. Daniel Hays helpfully orients us to four significant terms in the chapter, noting that "Genesis 10 described the division of the world according to the family/tribe/clan, language, land/country/territory, and nation (Gen 10:5, 20, 31)."[27] B. Oded points to these same verses and concludes that the table is thus a conglomerate of "ethnopolitical (after their families, nations), linguistic (after their tongues) and geographic (in their countries)" divisions.[28] The layers of *diversity* on display in light of this recognition are staggering. But Elizabeth Sung helpfully observes that the table does just as much to emphasize *unity*, reminding us that "Genesis 10 begins by reaffirming that humankind in the postdiluvian era fundamentally comprises a single extended family that stems from Noah and his household (v. 1; cf. 9:18-19)."[29] It thus portrays humanity as a unified diversity through the whole. The fact that this is on display *prior* to Babel enables us to see, in Bill Arnold's words, that "the Table of Nations in its current location fulfills the divine command to 'be fruitful and multiply, and fill the earth' (9:1, reflecting also 1:28), and is therefore predominantly a positive appraisal of human dispersion. . . . Had it been placed after 11.1-9, the Table of Nations in Gen 10 would of necessity be transformed into a sign of God's judgment."[30] As it stands, it is a sign of God's blessing on the cultural, linguistic, political, geographic, and familial diversity that is nevertheless united by a common lineage and a common calling to bear God's image and to live in conformity to his creational intentions. The Babel narrative drives home that things have gone awry and that a much deeper remedy than even a worldwide flood will be required. But for now we see that the foundational chapters of Genesis 1–11, far from being irrelevant to developing a biblical theology of catholicity, are actually quite significant in setting the covenantal

---

[26]For a helpful orientation see B. Oded, "The Table of Nations (Genesis 10): A Socio-Cultural Approach," *Zeitschrift Für Die Alttestamentliche Wissenschaft* 98, no. 1 (1986): 14-31.
[27]J. Daniel Hays, *From Every People and Nation: A Biblical Theology of Race* (Downers Grove, IL: InterVarsity Press, 2003), 61-62.
[28]Oded, "Table of Nations," 14.
[29]Elizabeth Yao-Hwa Sung, "'Race' and Ethnicity Discourse and the Christian Doctrine of Humanity: A Systematic Sociological and Theological Appraisal," PhD diss., Trinity Evangelical Divinity School, 2011, 263.
[30]Bill T. Arnold, *Genesis* (Cambridge: Cambridge University Press, 2009), 119.

scene by portraying (1) God's design that humans exhibit a God-glorifying unified diversity through the whole of creation and (2) how such a design was corrupted (but not eradicated) by human sin.

Redemptive-Historical Commencement: Genesis 12–Malachi 4

While in Genesis 1–11 we saw the *creational context* for catholicity, with Genesis 12 we move to the *covenantal content* of catholicity: by God's grace he calls a people to himself marked by increasing degrees of unified diversity over the course of redemptive history as the scope of this people continuously works through the whole of all times, peoples, and places. The catholicity of God's people is thus a covenantal glory on greater and greater display as we move from Genesis 12 to Revelation 22.[31] God's covenantal intention to call a people has a particular focus: calling a *diverse* people to be his *unified*, special possession. The catholicity of this people is anticipated in the old covenant, climaxes with the new covenant, and comes to consummate expression only at the end of redemptive history as *all* of God's people from *all* times, peoples, and places finally dwell together in Christ by the Spirit for all eternity.

Genesis 12. It is this larger redemptive-historical perspective that allows Yoder to proclaim that catholicity "is a reality . . . flowing down through human history, ever since Pentecost, or if you will ever since Abraham."[32] Why make *Abraham* a distinctive focus when speaking of the church's catholicity? Because the calling of Abraham and the promise given to him in Genesis 12:1-3 (especially that "all peoples on earth will be blessed through [him]") is the answer to the cosmic problem as it has been portrayed in Genesis 3–11, even as this covenantal promise to graciously provide a redeemer comes only after the scope has significantly narrowed from Genesis 10–11. Indeed, we move from Babel and a broad concern with how Noah's sons became the ancestors of the "seventy nations" of the world to a particular concern with Shem's line (Gen 11:10) and then to a narrow branch of his family tree: Terah and his three sons (Gen 11:27).

---

[31]God's creational design of unified diversity also continues to develop through the whole of human history. Here see David Bruce Hegeman, *Plowing in Hope: Toward a Biblical Theology of Culture*, 2nd ed. (Moscow, ID: Canon Press, 2007).

[32]John Howard Yoder, *The Royal Priesthood: Essays Ecclesiastical and Ecumenical*, ed. Michael G. Cartwright (Scottdale, PA: Herald Press, 1998), 302.

It is only when we are told of God's call of *one* of those sons to go from "Ur of the Chaldeans" (the land of the Babelites) to the land of Canaan (the land given to God's people) that we see the redemptive promise emerge: God's original intention to dwell with his image bearers, disturbed by the fall, will be restored through the calling of one man who will become the father of one nation and also the father of many peoples. The fact that the language of "peoples" and "nations" is so pervasive in the promises to Abram is no coincidence; it establishes a definitive link back to Genesis 10–11. Hays nicely summarizes this:

> Genesis 10 described the division of the world according to the family/tribe/clan, language, land/country/territory, and nation (Gen 10:5, 20, 31). The call of Abraham picks up on these terms. . . . The term "families" in 12:3 provides a tight connection . . . for this term occurs not only in the summary statements (10:5, 20, 31) but also in 10:18 and 10:32. . . . In Genesis 18:18 . . . God restates the promise with a slight change. He promises that all the *nations* of the earth will be blessed through Abraham, referring back to the *fourth* element in the fourfold list of Genesis 10. The two promises, taken together, imply that the totality of the fourfold list is to find blessing through Abraham.[33]

In short, a proper reading of the promises given to Abraham recognizes the intentional connections to the Table of Nations, connections that help us understand that Abraham's covenantal call is God's answer to the corruption of his creational intentions seen at Babel.

Indeed, on a canonical reading of Genesis 12 it is impossible not to see the promise that "all peoples on earth will be blessed through [Abram]" as anticipating the *catholic* nature of God's people as their scope comes to include all peoples in all times and all places. The reality that Israel ultimately existed for the sake of the nations is only hinted at in the OT, with the missional calling of God's people on behalf of the nations being more veiled and centripetal in the old covenant and becoming more explicit and centrifugal in the new.[34] But this ultimate missional trajectory is evident amid

---

[33] Hays, *From Every People and Nation*, 61–62.
[34] So Wright can observe that "beginning with the call of Abraham in Genesis 12 . . . Israel came into existence as a people with a mission entrusted to them from God *for the sake of God's wider purpose of blessing the nations*. . . . Arguably God's covenant with Abraham is the single most important biblical tradition within a biblical theology of mission. . . . It generates a vast, arching, trajectory that carries us from Genesis 12 to Revelation 22." Christopher J. H. Wright, *The*

indications that the nations will be blessed by their proximity to, and even their inclusion within, the people of God traditionally restricted to Israel. This is made clear by Jesus himself in Luke 24:44-47, where he says, "Everything must be fulfilled that is written about me in the Law of Moses, the Prophets and the Psalms. . . . [And] this is what is written: The Messiah will suffer and rise from the dead on the third day, and repentance for the forgiveness of sins will be preached in his name *to all nations*, beginning at Jerusalem." The fact that Jesus says that the missional scope including all nations was *already attested* in the OT gives us permission to investigate where this "proto-catholic vision" is attested there. Though each segment of the OT bears this out, space constraints prevent us from examining the Law[35] or the Writings.[36] Here we focus on how the Prophets testify to this redemptive-historical development and thus to the increasingly catholic identity of God's covenant people.

Prophets. It is with the Prophets that we see hints of missional inclusion of the nations accelerate and the redemptive-historical development toward a more catholic scope for God's people become increasingly evident. The Minor Prophets offer a concentrated expression of this. For one example, Zephaniah is told (in Zeph 3:9) that one day God "will purify the lips of *the peoples*, that *all of them* may call on the name of the LORD and serve him shoulder to shoulder," thus hinting that a linguistic/cultural diversity would one day mark God's covenant people even as they were united in common worship of him. This striking vision of unified worship in diverse expression is also signaled in Zechariah 8:23 where we hear that in the last days "ten people *from all languages and nations* will take firm hold of one Jew by the hem of his robe and say, 'Let us go with you, because we have heard that God

---

Mission of God: Unlocking the Bible's Grand Narrative (Downers Grove, IL: IVP Academic, 2006), 65, 187, emphasis added.

[35]Particularly noteworthy is how Deuteronomy, though it recognizes that Israel's relationship to the nations is complicated and at times full of animosity (see Deut 7:1, 15:6, 33:17), presents Israel's vocation as ultimately to be a light unto the nations, who would observe their wisdom and way of life as an attractive force and source of blessing (Deut 4:6).

[36]The reference in Luke to the "Psalms" is likely to the Writings as a whole, with the book of Psalms standing as its representative head. The Psalms make for an enlightening case study since the book offers several "hints" of multiethnic inclusion in the covenant people of God. Examples include Ps 47:8-9; 50:1; 65:2; 72:17; 87:4-6; 148:14; and 150:6 along with the entirety of Ps 62. We could say that it is the *hope* of the Psalms that the nations will ultimately join with Israel in giving praise to Yahweh and experiencing the blessing of being part of his covenant people.

is with you.'" In contrast to an ethnocentric vision of God's people, Zechariah sees a day when "*many peoples and powerful nations* will come to Jerusalem to seek the LORD Almighty and to entreat him" (Zech 8:22). The animosity that once existed between the nations and Israel will be no more (Zech 14:16). These passages indicate the Lord's intention to one day expand the scope of his covenantal people to include all nations.[37]

But the fullest expression of this proto-catholic vision no doubt comes from the book of Isaiah; nowhere else in the OT do the hints of multinational inclusion become more frequent and explicit. For instance, Isaiah 2:2-4 envisions "all nations" streaming into Zion that "many peoples" might be taught God's ways, walk in his paths, and turn their swords to plowshares. In Isaiah 11:10-12 we encounter the promise that the Root of Jesse will stand "as a banner for the peoples" and a rallying point for "the nations"; so inclusive is this vision that it includes a remnant from the despised Egypt, Assyria, and Babylon and even representatives from "the islands" (Is 11:10-12). The vision in Isaiah 19:19-25 of a future where there is "an altar to the LORD in the heart of Egypt" and where "the LORD will make himself known" to Israel's long-standing foes leads Clowney to say, "So unthinkably great will be God's sanctifying blessing . . . that Israel's position as the covenant people will be shared by Egypt and Assyria, the former enemies!"[38] Isaiah 25:6-8 demonstrates a staggering scope of redemption in the image of a feast prepared by Yahweh himself "for all peoples," saying that God

> will destroy
>   the shroud that enfolds *all peoples*,
> the sheet that covers *all nations*;
>   he will swallow up death forever.
> The Sovereign LORD will wipe away the tears
>   from *all faces*;
> he will remove his people's disgrace
>   from *all the earth*.

---

[37]Amos 9 and Obadiah 1 also provide examples worthy of consideration. A study of the book of Micah, especially through the lens of a remnant brought out from both Israel and the nations, would also be illuminating in developing a biblical theology of catholicity from the Minor Prophets. Thanks to Eric Tully for this observation.

[38]Clowney, *Doctrine of the Church*, 26.

In many ways the proto-catholic vision crescendos in Isaiah 40–66 as the focus of the book turns from pre-exilic concerns (Is 1–39) to the trajectory of God's people in an exilic (Is 40–55) and post-exilic (Is 56–66) context. Perhaps the greatest expression of Gentile inclusion in God's covenant purposes comes in Isaiah 49:6, where the Lord says,

> It is too small a thing for you to be my servant
>   to restore the tribes of Jacob
>   and bring back those of Israel I have kept.
> I will also make you a light for the Gentiles,
>   that my salvation may reach *to the ends of the earth.*

Indeed, this serves as a wonderful summary of what God has been doing with Israel throughout the old covenant stage of redemptive history: preparing a people (and a Person) to be a light to the nations. Isaiah 56:6-8, a text that becomes quite significant in light of Jesus' appropriation of it at the cleansing of the temple (cf. Mk 11:17), goes on to promise that

> foreigners who bind themselves to the Lord
>   to minister to him,
> to love the name of the LORD,
>   and to be his servants . . .
> these I will bring to my holy mountain
>   and give them joy in my house of prayer.
> Their burnt offerings and sacrifices
>   will be accepted on my altar;
> for my house will be called
>   a house of prayer for *all nations.*

The text then affirms that the Lord who gathers the exiles of Israel "will gather still others to them besides those already gathered," a sentiment picked up in John 10:16 where Jesus says there are "other sheep . . . not of this sheep pen. I must bring them also. They too will listen to my voice, and there shall be one flock and one shepherd."

The book ends with the stunning promise of Isaiah 66:18-23. Most astonishingly perhaps is the fact that God himself declares in Isaiah 66:18 that there will be a day when he will "gather the people *of all nations and languages,* and they will come and see my glory." Isaiah 66:19 is as good a

Biblical Warrant for the Doctrine of Catholicity 37

candidate as any for Jesus' claim in Luke 24 that the Old Testament proclaimed ahead of time that repentance for the forgiveness of sins will be preached to all nations, for in this verse we are told that God will direct his people "to the nations—to Tarshish, to the Libyans and Lydians . . . to Tubal and Greece, and to the distant islands that have not heard of my fame or seen my glory" and thus that his people will "proclaim [his] glory among the nations." James Scott comments that Isaiah 66:18-19 "stands out among OT texts [by] containing a positive eschatological expectation for the nations. . . . By alluding to [the Table of Nations tradition], the partial list of nations in v. 19 . . . provides concrete examples of God's intention to gather 'all nations' in v. 18."[39] This intention is reinforced in the following verses, for while the promise is made that Israelites will return from "all the nations" (Is 66:20), that promise is now set within the much larger frame of Isaiah 66:23: "'From one New Moon to another and from one Sabbath to another, *all mankind* will come and bow down before me,' says the LORD." That Isaiah particularly, and the Prophets collectively, testify that the scope of God's people will ultimately come to include representatives from all times, all peoples, and all places is quite clear.

As we complete our survey of these redemptive-historical developments in the OT, we are left with an unresolved tension when it comes to the scope of God's people and their nature as one marked by unified diversity. On the one hand, there is a clear animosity toward the nations, particularly heard in the call for Israel to be separate from them and the consistent drumbeat that the nations will be judged. And yet there are also hints that point in the direction of an ever-increasing catholic scope. Throughout Israel's history, in a way that echoes the promise to Abraham, representatives from the nations are blessed in their encounter with Abraham's descendants. We could cite Rahab (Josh 2), Ruth, the widow of Zarephath (1 Kings 17), Naaman (2 Kings 5), and the Ninevites (Jonah) as examples. These encounters prove to be proleptic, especially with the proclamation of a new covenant (cf. Jer 31 and Ezek 36). This new covenant promise, though it centers on a renewed Israel, ultimately makes clear that this renewal is for the sake of gathering in the

---

[39]James M. Scott, *Paul and the Nations: The Old Testament and Jewish Background of Paul's Mission to the Nations with Special Reference to the Destination of Galatians* (Tübingen: Mohr Siebeck, 1995), 14.

Gentiles. Indeed, the trajectory of the new covenant promise brings the catholic scope of God's people more clearly into view. Not only is the covenant itself described as an "everlasting covenant" (all times, Ezek 37:26), but in light of other OT passages we can conclude that it is inclusive of "all the nations" (all peoples, Is 56:7), proclaimed in "all languages" (all tongues, Is 66:18), and understood as spreading "to the ends of the earth" (all places, Is 49:6). At the end of the Old Testament it is clear that "in the future all nations will be blessed by Abraham's seed. Torah, history, and prophecy . . . point to this glorious future. The day is coming when . . . the light of Israel will shine upon the nations, and the Lord's salvation will reach to the ends of the earth."[40] The question that remained: *How* was this going to happen?

REDEMPTIVE-HISTORICAL CLIMAX: THE GOSPELS AND ACTS

The answer to that question becomes clear only when we arrive at the New Testament and see the veiled previews give way to a full-orbed vision of God's covenant people as a unified diversity through the whole of all times, peoples, and places. The catalyst for this movement is the Christ event: the coming of the long-awaited Messiah who fulfills God's intention to call a people to himself. This is the climax of redemptive history, and with it comes the replacement of Israel's ethnocentric, centripetal orientation with the church's multiethnic, centrifugal one.[41] The catholic scope of the church is established definitively with the risen Christ's commission to make disciples of all nations (Mt 28:19) and giving of the Spirit for that mission (Acts 2).

But prior to this crescendo in redemptive history, we see in Jesus' ministry an initial continuity with Israel's anticipatory role. Jesus explicitly limits the scope of his ministry ("I was sent only to the lost sheep of Israel," Mt 15:24) and the ministry of his disciples ("Do not go among the Gentiles or enter any town of the Samaritans. Go rather to the lost sheep of Israel," Mt 10:5-6) to the people of Israel. But amid these restrictions, Christ's ministry is sprinkled with Gentile encounters that are revelatory of the catholic

---

[40]Herman Bavinck, "The Catholicity of Christianity and the Church," trans. John Bolt, *Calvin Theological Journal* 27, no. 2 (November 1992): 223.

[41]Indeed, Hagner sees "a clear distinction between the time of Jesus' earthly ministry and the time following the resurrection . . . [as] a movement from particularism to universalism." Quoted in Andreas J. Köstenberger and Peter T. O'Brien, *Salvation to the Ends of the Earth: A Biblical Theology of Mission* (Downers Grove, IL: InterVarsity Press, 2001), 93.

scope which will emerge as a result of his ministry. For instance, in examining Jesus' interaction with the woman at the well (Jn 4), the demoniac (Mk 5), the centurion (Mt 8), the Syrophoenician woman (Mt 15), and the Samaritan leper (Lk 17), not only do we learn much more about the nature of Jesus' ministry (particularly that it is *not* ultimately restricted to the nation of Israel), but we also see that these exchanges are *anticipatory* in nature, "unusual events that were harbingers of the things to come."[42] Thus we can speak of the "catholicity of the gospel" already on display in the four Gospel accounts. It is worth examining how John and the Synoptics bear this out.

John. John's presentation joins the Synoptics in presenting Jesus and his work as having massive implications for the scope of God's covenant people, but the nature of this presentation is distinctive. For one, John focuses much less on the "nations" and much more on the "world." This leads Hallig to describe John's unique presentation of Jesus as "the Word for the world,"[43] noting that "the evangelist's presentation of the life and ministry of Jesus is more theological than historical. . . . [As such] it is more explicit than implicit . . . that the gospel of Jesus Christ is not exclusively for the Jews but also for the Gentiles. It is a gospel for the world."[44] As evidence we could cite the inclusiveness of the vision found in John 1:9 ("the true light that gives light to *everyone* was coming into the world"), John 1:12 ("yet to *all* who did receive him, to those who believed in his name, he gave the right to become children of God"), John 1:29 ("Look, the Lamb of God, who takes away the sin *of the world*"), John 3:16 ("For God so loved *the world* that he gave his one and only Son, that *whoever* believes in him shall not perish but have eternal life") and John 8:12 ("I am the light *of the world. Whoever* follows me will never walk in darkness, but will have the light of life."). John presents Jesus as teaching that the mission (commencing at Pentecost) involves "other sheep that are not of this fold" (i.e., the Gentiles) and promising that "I must bring them also. They too will listen to my voice" (Jn 10:16). In fact, heading to the cross, Jesus anticipates that his cross work will bring about salvation

---

[42] Allison, *Sojourners and Strangers*, 438.
[43] We recognize that the term *world* in Johannine literature does not just have positive connotations and indeed can be used to describe forces in opposition to Christ (for example, Jn 17:9). Here we are simply isolating those particular contexts where *world* has positive value based on God's redemptive love.
[44] Hallig, *We Are Catholic*, 52.

on a global scale: "And I, when I am lifted up from the earth, will draw *all people* to myself" (Jn 12:32).

But perhaps the greatest contribution of John's Gospel to a biblical theology of the church's catholicity comes in its vision of God's people as exhibiting unified diversity. In many ways John focuses more on the mission of Jesus than the mission of his people, but, significantly, in John's version of the disciples' commissioning (Jn 20:21-23) these two are intrinsically linked.[45] Indeed, Jesus says, "As the Father has sent me, I am sending you." And just as Jesus' mission had a universal scope ultimately in view, so there is a universal scope inherent in the church's mission: "If you forgive *anyone's* sins, their sins are forgiven; if you do not forgive them, they are not forgiven." But Köstenberger and O'Brien bring out the most distinctive Johannine contribution when they say: "The evangelist maintains an overlap between Jesus' shepherding and witnessing functions and that of his chosen representatives . . . [an overlap that] accentuates the believers' need to be knit together in love, unity and mutual service, *modeled closely after Jesus' relationship with the Father.*"[46] Indeed, for John the catholic scope of the mission is wrapped up in the way God's people imitate God, particularly the unity-in-diversity that marks his life (especially as seen in the relationship of the Father and the Son).

The greatest manifestation of this is found in Jesus' "high priestly prayer" of John 17.[47] There Jesus prays in a way that both rehearses the universal scope of his mission ("For you granted [the Son] authority over *all people* that he might give eternal life *to all those* you have given him," Jn 17:2) and grounds the universal mission of the disciples in his mission ("As you sent me into the world, I have sent them into the world," Jn 17:18). Jesus goes on to pray for *all those* who would believe the message proclaimed by the disciples, that "all of them may be one, Father, *just as you are in me and I am in you*. May they also be in us so that the world may believe that you have sent me. I have given them the glory that you gave me, *that they may be one as we are one*—I in them and you in me—so that

---

[45]Köstenberger and O'Brien, *Salvation to the Ends of the Earth*, 203.
[46]Köstenberger and O'Brien, *Salvation to the Ends of the Earth*, 204, emphasis added.
[47]For an attempt to show how the offices of Christ align with the creedal attributes of the church, see Tom Greggs, *Dogmatic Ecclesiology: The Priestly Catholicity of the Church* (Grand Rapids, MI: Baker Academic, 2019).

they may be *brought to complete unity*" (Jn 17:21-23). Here Jesus prays that this flock of ever-increasing diversity will be unified in a way that is patterned after the unity-in-diversity of the Father and the Son, all with vast missional implications.[48] In other words, the unity and catholicity of the church go together because it is the triune God who has constituted them as a people. Since John's Gospel was written that *whoever* reads it "may believe that Jesus is the Messiah, the Son of God, and that by believing . . . have life in his name" (Jn 20:31), we see that the type of unity God's people will exhibit (modeled on the relationship of the Father and the Son) is one of unified *diversity*.

Synoptics. Each of the Synoptics emphasizes the *continuity* between the promises of the old covenant and their fulfillment in Jesus. Beginning with Matthew, it is thus not insignificant that the very first words of the book make explicit connection back to Genesis 12 with its messianic promise for all nations. Indeed Matthew 1:1 presents us with "the genealogy of Jesus the Messiah, the son of David, *the son of Abraham*." Here we see redemptive history climaxing with the coming of the Messiah, the seed that was promised from those earliest chapters of Genesis (Gen 3:15; 9:9; 12:7). Matthew's unique presentation of the "magi from the east" (Mt 2:1) shows us early on the scope of redemption that Christ will usher in. But Jesus' interaction with the centurion in Matthew 8 is perhaps the most revelatory of his Gentile encounters in Matthew. After all, Jesus' commendation of the soldier ("I have not found anyone in Israel with such great faith," Mt 8:10) comes with a promise expanding the scope of God's people far beyond Israel: "many will come from the east and the west, and will take their places at the feast with Abraham, Isaac and Jacob in the kingdom of heaven" (Mt 8:11). Though the promise is framed in centripetal versus centrifugal terms, it spotlights the inclusion of the nations in a manner reminiscent of OT promises. We also see a proto-catholic scope inherent in Jesus' promise that "I will build my church" (Mt 16:18) and the promise given to this

---

[48] Allison notes here that church unity "is grounded most fundamentally in the perichoretic harmony enjoyed by the triune God. . . . [For] this mutual indwelling of the three distinct persons in one another portrays and prompts a church unity that is not uniformity, nor union, but unity in diversity." Gregg Allison, "Holy God and Holy People: Pneumatology and Ecclesiology in Intersection," in *Building on the Foundations of Evangelical Theology*, ed. Gregg R. Allison and Stephen J. Wellum (Wheaton, IL: Crossway, 2015), 253.

ecclesia that "Where two or three gather in my name, there am I with them" (Mt 18:20).[49]

It is only at the end of Matthew's Gospel that the church's centrifugal mission is made explicit and the scope of God's people is portrayed as encompassing all times, peoples and places. Köstenberger summarizes how this is all in fulfillment of OT promises: "Jesus, the 'son of Abraham,' fulfills the Abrahamic promise—that God would bless all nations through his descendent—by sending out the representatives of this new messianic community to take the gospel of salvation in Jesus Christ to the ends of the earth."[50] In short, the Great Commission is the christological means by which the Abrahamic commission will finally be fulfilled.[51]

Many similar things could be said regarding Mark's Gospel.[52] Indeed, though it is clear in Mark that Jesus' work is still constrained to Israel *during* his ministry, it is also clear that Mark is the Gospel most interested in stressing the implications of Jesus' work for the scope of God's people *after* his ministry. As Köstenberger and O'Brien have claimed, Mark specifically emphasizes the inclusion of all nations where other Gospels neglect it.[53] For instance, during the cleansing of the temple episode of Mark 11:17, Mark includes the reference that the temple would be a house of prayer "for all nations" in the quotation of Isaiah 56:7, where both Matthew and Luke exclude that portion of the reference. And when we recall that Mark powerfully places the greatest confession of the whole book in the mouth of a Gentile centurion standing at the foot of the cross (Mk 15:39, "Surely this man was the Son of God!"), we conclude that Mark believes the gospel has vast implications for who can be included in God's covenant people.

---

[49]For a compelling discussion of the interrelated foundational ecclesial promises of Matthew 16 and 18 from a Free Church vantage point, see Jonathan Leeman, *Political Church: The Local Assembly as Embassy of Christ's Rule* (Downers Grove, IL: IVP Academic, 2016).

[50]Andreas Köstenberger, "The Church According to the Gospels," in *The Community of Jesus: A Theology of the Church*, ed. Kendell H. Easley and Christopher W. Morgan (Nashville: B&H Academic, 2013), 38.

[51]Yoder discerns multiple catholic elements in this text, including the ascending Lord's claim of all authority *in heaven and on earth* (all places), the fact that the eleven were to make disciples *of all nations* (all peoples), and the promise that Christ would be with them *always* (all times). See Yoder, *Royal Priesthood*, 309.

[52]This is especially true in light of shared material with Matthew, such as the stories of the demoniac (Mt 8 and Mk 5) and the Syrophoenician woman (Mt 15 and Mk 7).

[53]Köstenberger and O'Brien, *Salvation to the Ends of the Earth*, 84.

In the Gospel of Luke we have what Hallig argues is "the most catholic of the Gospels" because it is integrally connected with a second volume (Acts) that collectively shows us an expanded scope for God's people anticipated (volume 1) and portrayed (volume 2).[54] If Hagner is right to argue that the greatest pivot between the proto-catholic possibility for God's people and the actualized catholic vision for the church is Jesus' resurrection, then Luke is the only Gospel writer who shows us what the outworking of this catholic vision looks like.[55] But before Acts, Luke's Gospel anticipates a more universal scope for God's people in unique ways. For instance, Köstenberger notes the particular significance of Luke tracing Jesus' genealogy all the way back to Adam rather than stopping with Abraham: this emphasizes the universal scope of Jesus' mission as the Savior for "all the people" (Lk 2:10).[56] Luke's widely recognized concern for the poor and marginalized also contributes to this unique vision: social and economic barriers to inclusion among God's people are shown to be incompatible with the gospel. But most significantly, Luke places continued emphasis on the inclusion of the Gentiles among God's people. Simeon's song rejoices that the coming of the Messiah brings about a salvation "prepared in the sight of all nations: a light for revelation to the Gentiles" (Lk 2:31-32); Luke is the only Gospel writer to connect Jesus' proclamation that "no prophet is accepted in his hometown" with evidence derived from Old Testament Gentile encounters (Lk 4:24-27); Luke is unique in providing us the story of the Samaritan leper, showcasing a "foreigner" who alone returns to praise God (Lk 17:11-19); and Luke is the only Gospel writer who tells of Jesus' claim that part of what was written in the Law, Prophets, and Writings about him was that "repentance for the forgiveness of sins will be preached in his name *to all nations*, beginning at Jerusalem" (Lk 24:47).

Acts. But Acts is where Luke's vision for the universal scope of God's people is vividly displayed. Indeed, Luke structures his second volume around the motif of geographical expansion: "you will be my witnesses in Jerusalem, and in all Judea and Samaria, and to the ends of the earth" (Acts 1:8). The fact that we begin the book in Jerusalem (and particularly

---

[54] Hallig, *We Are Catholic*, 49.
[55] Quoted in Köstenberger and O'Brien, *Salvation to the Ends of the Earth*, 93.
[56] Köstenberger, "The Church According to the Gospels," 54.

centered on the temple) and end in Rome (the center of the known world) is a sign that a universal scope has been enacted and will remain ever-expanding to the ends of the earth and the end of the age.

That witness is inaugurated by *the* constitutive event that makes the church a catholic entity: the giving of the Spirit at Pentecost recounted in Acts 2. Pentecost has long been recognized as integrally connected to the claim that the church is catholic.[57] Volf has called Pentecost the "primal catholic event," one that shows itself to be more than simply the reversal of Babel because "communication comes about through the speaking of *different* languages . . . [demonstrating] a catholicity in which the unity of all is coupled with the affirmation of . . . uniqueness."[58] Stephen Wellum can even describe the inauguration of the new covenant portrayed here as a "universalization," pointing to Peter's citation of Joel 2 to explain the phenomenon of Pentecost as a guarantee that the scope of the new covenant "promises to be universal . . . [for] he empowers and gifts every member . . . for ministry and mediating the knowledge of God to [all] unbelieving nations."[59] Indeed, Peter emphasizes that the promise in Joel was that God would "pour out [his] Spirit on *all people*" (Acts 2:17), that all generations and classes would receive this gift (Acts 2:17-18), that the scope of signs demonstrating the coming of "the great and glorious day of the Lord" would indeed be worldwide (Acts 2:19-20), and that "*everyone* who calls on the name of the Lord will be saved" (Acts 2:21). The universal implications of Pentecost are driven home at the end of the sermon, where Peter assures his hearers: the promise that forgiveness of sins is available in Jesus' name and that the Spirit can be received personally "is for you and your children and *for all who are far off*—for *all* whom the Lord our God will call" (Acts 2:38-39). The temporal (indicated by generational language), ethnic

---

[57] For instance, Dulles observes that "thanks to the gift of Pentecost, the early Christian community burst out of its Jewish shell and became . . . catholic in scope." Dulles, *The Catholicity of the Church*, 46. Similarly, Henri de Lubac noted that the church was already catholic "on the morning of Pentecost, when a small room was big enough for all its members." Quoted in Miroslav Volf, *After Our Likeness: The Church as the Image of the Trinity* (Grand Rapids, MI: Eerdmans, 1998), 265.

[58] Volf, *After Our Likeness*, 268.

[59] Stephen J. Wellum and Kirk Wellum, "The Biblical and Theological Case for Congregationalism," in *Baptist Foundations: Church Government for an Anti-Institutional Age*, eds. Mark Dever and Jonathan Leeman (Nashville: B&H Academic, 2015), 54.

(implied by those who were far off, including Gentiles), and geographical (indicated by a near to far trajectory) dimensions of the church's catholic scope are emphasized.

But there is more. It is likely that Luke draws on the Table of Nations and the Tower of Babel narratives in his portrayal of Pentecost.[60] We can thus understand the event as both a "renewal" of the Table of Nations *and* a "reversal" of the Tower of Babel.[61] Smith even argues that the Babel story provides the model for Luke's account of Pentecost, noting not only verbal similarities between Acts 2:1-13 and the LXX version of Genesis 11:1-9 but also the way that echoes of Babel enumerate: both narratives have a call to spread into all the earth as their background (Gen 9:1, Acts 1:8); both narratives describe people gathering together and God coming down in response; both narratives involve confusion with the end result being dispersion (noting the significance of Acts 8:1 for the latter).[62] But even in the narratives' differences there seems to be an intentional inversion: the Babelites chafe against God's purposes, while the disciples embody dependent submission to the divine plan; God's descent at Babel communicates condemnation and judgment, while at Pentecost the descent of the Spirit conveys commendation and blessing; Babel produced a failure to communicate and further alienation, while Pentecost is characterized by a renewed ability to understand and be united in a common, God-honoring purpose.[63]

Other passages in Acts demonstrate God's intention for the church to manifest as a unified diversity through the whole of all times, peoples, and places, especially those dealing with the mission to the Gentiles. Indeed, from the time we are told that "all except the apostles were scattered throughout Judea and Samaria" (Acts 8:1), attention increasingly turns to the emerging catholic scope of the church and the accompanying difficulties

---

[60]For instance, Luke's structural map found in Acts 1:8 both conforms to the progression of Christian mission after Pentecost and alludes back to the groupings of the nations in Gen 10. This progression moves from Jewish Shemites (Jerusalem, Acts 1–7) to Shemites more broadly (Judea and Samaria, Acts 8–12) and ultimately to the Japhethites (the ends of the earth, Acts 13–28). But at the central pivot point (Acts 8) we see Philip encountering an Ethiopian eunuch, a representative of the Hamites. For detailed and persuasive argumentation in this regard, see Scott, *Paul and the Nations*.

[61]An influential framework set forth by John G. Davies, "Pentecost and Glossolalia," *The Journal of Theological Studies* 3, no. 2 (October 1952): 228-31.

[62]Smith, "What Hope After Babel?," 184.

[63]Smith, "What Hope After Babel?," 184.

the church had to wrestle through. While Phillip's engagement with the Samaritans (Acts 8:4-25) and his evangelization of the Ethiopian eunuch (Acts 8:26-40) are the first breaks in the dam, Peter's meeting with Cornelius is the pivotal turn. With Peter's recognition that "God gave [the Gentiles] the same gift he gave us [Jews]," the resulting conclusion that "even to Gentiles God has granted repentance that leads to life" (Acts 11:17-18), and the subsequent description of the church in Antioch as having many "Greeks ... [who] believed and turned to the Lord" (Acts 11:20-21), the Gentile mission becomes the focus of Acts 13–28 and showcases the church's increasingly universal scope.[64]

One particularly compelling example is the "Jerusalem Council" of Acts 15. The chapter is honest about the Jewish Jerusalem church grappling with the implications of God raising up a new covenant people increasingly marked by a diversity that included Gentiles. The question before the council was essentially one of *how much diversity* was acceptable as the Gentiles came into the fold. Particularly this question remained: Did Gentiles need to become Jews by taking on their boundary markers, especially that of circumcision? This was ultimately a question about whether the church was going to be catholic or provincial in its pursuit of unity. The remainder of the book serves as evidence that the former won out over the latter. Indeed, at the very end of the book it is significant that Luke speaks even of Paul's limited house-arrest ministry as still having a universal focus. Alexander points out that "the open-ended conclusion to the book is emblematic: it shows Paul ... preaching the kingdom to all comers ... [reinforcing that] the mission to the Gentiles is one of the major themes of Acts."[65] Gentile inclusion led to an exponential increase in ecclesiological diversity even as unity in Christ remained. Cullman thus concludes that Acts shows us "there was no uniformity even in earliest Christianity."[66] Indeed, from the testimony of Acts we can conclude that from Pentecost the church was catholic, fulfilling the promise of a universal scope for God's people made to Abram so many years prior.

---

[64] God's instruction to "not call anyone ... unclean" (Acts 10:28) along with Peter's conclusion that "God ... accepts *from every nation* the one who fears him" (Acts 10:34-35) become programmatic for the Gentile mission.

[65] Loveday C. A. Alexander, "The Church in the Synoptic Gospels and Acts," in *The Oxford Handbook of Ecclesiology*, ed. Paul Avis (Oxford: Oxford University Press, 2018), 91.

[66] Oscar Cullman, *Unity Through Diversity*, trans. M. Eugene Boring (Philadelphia: Fortress, 1988), 29.

Redemptive-Historical Continuation: New Testament Epistles

The New Testament epistles belong to our own pivotal chapter of redemptive history bookended by Christ's ascension (accompanied by the gift of the Spirit at Pentecost) and his return at the eschaton (Acts 1:11). We have good reason to follow the conviction of Fahey that "even . . . in early New Testament texts, there was a keen awareness of the Church's 'catholicity,' something illustrated more by actions than by the use of the word. For early Christians catholicity was a lived reality, not a topic for theoretical speculation."[67] From this perspective, numerous passages from the epistles become candidates for demonstrating a biblical basis from which to speak of the church as catholic. Indeed, we find several references to the set of all believers across time and space (e.g., 1 Cor 10:32; Eph 3:21) that seem to have in view the church as a universal entity, as do certain passages that speak about Christ as the head of the whole church (e.g., Eph 5:23; Col 1:18). Additionally we might note passages that draw our attention to the scope of the church's mission among *all peoples* (e.g., Rom 1:16; 1 Tim 3:16), to the pervasiveness of gospel fruit among *all places* (e.g., Rom 1:8; Col 1:6), and to the election of God's people from among *all times* (e.g., Gal 6:16; Eph 1:4). But here we will focus on the Pauline epistles and on passages in which the church's nature as one of unified diversity comes particularly into focus. Though there are several qualified candidates, we will limit our study to three passages: 1 Corinthians 12, which emphasizes that the church is a body composed of *different parts* (and thus excludes uniformity); Galatians 3, which emphasizes that the church is made up of *different peoples from different times and different places* (and thus excludes exclusionism, sectarianism, and provincialism); and Ephesians 4, which emphasizes that the church's *diversity is marked by a profound unity* (and thus excludes pluralism).

1 Corinthians 12. In 1 Corinthians 12 the motif of unified diversity is pervasive. In 1 Corinthians 12:1-11 the particular manifestation of this unity-in-diversity is spiritual gifts, distributed by the Spirit for the common good (1 Cor 12:7, 11). At the end of the chapter (1 Cor 12:28-31) there is a clear

---

[67]Michael A. Fahey, "The Catholicity of the Church in the New Testament and in the Early Patristic Period," *The Jurist* 52, no. 1 (1992): 49.

return to the theme of gifts (and offices). But in 1 Corinthians 12:12-27 there is a broader reflection on the nature of the church, a section bookended by one of Paul's most characteristic ways of speaking about the church: that it is a body and the body of Christ (1 Cor 12:12, 27). Paul frequently uses body language to describe the church, though in each context he makes a slightly different point.[68] Clowney says what is common to these passages is that "the figure of the body . . . expresses the unity of the [one] messianic Servant with 'the many' as the servant people. . . . If the many are all reconciled in Christ's body, then the unity of their new position may be pictured as a body."[69]

What is unique about 1 Corinthians 12 is the emphasis on the *diverse* makeup of this united body.[70] The diversity is emphasized in three ways. First, Paul's discussion of the gifts begins with an emphasis on diversity derived from a triune unity: there are "different gifts" but the same Spirit, "different kinds of service" but the same Lord, and "different kinds of working" but the same God at work through them (1 Cor 12:4-6). First Corinthians 12:7-11 and 28-31 flesh this out by cataloging the diversity of gifts and offices that exists within the one body. Second, after Paul's assertion (1 Cor 12:13-14) that "we were all baptized by one Spirit so as to form one body" he adds the important aside that this was true whether they were "Jews or Gentiles, slave or free" and thus that, though each was given "one Spirit to drink," these distinctions make it clear that "the body is not made up of one part *but of many*." Third, Paul is not content in this passage to simply *assert* the reality that there must be "many parts [that] form one body" (1 Cor 12:12); rather, he also *illustrates* this reality in

---

[68]In Rom 12:4-5 the emphasis is on believers composing one body in Christ (also emphasized in Col 3:15); in 1 Cor 10:16-17 the emphasis is on the Eucharist representing that one body; and in Ephesians and Colossians the emphases (apart from Eph 2–4, which we will look at below) are on the reality that the universal church is the body of Christ (Eph 1:23; Col 1:24) and on the significance of Christ being its head (Eph 5:23; Col 1:18, 24; 2:19). For an interesting contrast of 1 Cor 12 and Rom 12, see Everett Ferguson, *The Church of Christ: A Biblical Ecclesiology for Today* (Grand Rapids, MI: Eerdmans, 1996), 95.

[69]Clowney, *The Doctrine of the Church*, 40-41.

[70]The fact that the diversity of the body is the primary emphasis of this passage is driven home by the observation of D. A. Carson, who notes that the best way to understand the transition from 1 Cor 12:3 to 1 Cor 12:4 is via an adversative *de* in 12:4, such that the argument might be paraphrased as "I want you to know that all who truly confess Jesus as Lord do so by the Holy Spirit, and thus attest his [common] presence in their lives; *but* that does not mean that there are no distinctions to be made among them." Quoted in Allison, *Sojourners and Strangers*, 169.

1 Corinthians 12:15-26. Paul leverages the image of a body's diverse makeup, from the foot to the ear to the eye to the "weaker . . . less honorable . . . [and] unpresentable" parts (1 Cor 12:22-23), in order to drive home the point that "God has placed the parts in the body, every one of them, just as he wanted them to be. If they were all one part, where would the body be? As it is, there are many parts, but one body" (1 Cor 12:18-20). Ferguson concludes that Paul "approached the body imagery in order to deal with the plurality of individual members who together are part of a corporate whole . . . [using] the human body succinctly to illustrate unity out of plurality, diversity of function, and the mutual bonds tying one to another."[71] The end result: "There should be no division in the body, but its parts should have equal concern for each other" (1 Cor 12:25).

It is important to consider the proper scope of the church that Paul has in view here, particularly whether this passage is speaking *only* about the local church or *also* about the universal church. Cullman acknowledges that there is a "proper exegetical objection" to be made that Paul only has members of the local church at Corinth in view.[72] But he sees the mention of the gift of apostleship (1 Cor 12:28) and the fact that the church in Corinth *primarily* in view in 1 Corinthians 12 is referenced at the beginning of the letter (1 Cor 1:2) in its relation to "*all* those *everywhere* who call on the name of our Lord Jesus Christ" as legitimizing the possibility that this chapter is *also* speaking about a broader expression of the church's unified diversity. David Watson concurs, noting that "although Paul used the body-metaphor in 1 Corinthians 12 to describe the healthy functioning of a *local* church, the basic principle of unity in diversity could well be extended to the many member churches within the one universal body of Christ."[73]

This passage thus highlights the ways that the church, both local and universal, is made up of different parts and yet is united by being one body in Christ. In other words, this passage demonstrates that the church is indeed catholic in nature, manifesting a unified diversity through the whole

---

[71]Ferguson, *Church of Christ*, 94-95.
[72]Cullman, *Unity Through Diversity*, 17.
[73]David Watson, *I Believe in the Church* (Grand Rapids, MI: Eerdmans, 1978), 344. This move is supported by recognizing that Paul makes a similar appeal to the body of Christ imagery in Colossians and Ephesians, where the primary emphasis is the universal church and only secondarily the local church.

of all times, peoples, and places. And particularly, 1 Corinthians 12 emphasizes the *diversity* part of that equation. As noted by Allison, the catholicity of the church envisioned here means that the church's "unity is not uniformity. The church does not insist that everyone be exactly the same; this denies . . . the diversity that is a legitimate part of true unity. . . . Rather, the unity with diversity toward which the church aspires is a much more robust harmony modeled after the interrelationships of the Father, Son, and Spirit."[74] Indeed, Cullman can say that "diversifying plurality is generated within unity. . . . [In 1 Cor 12:4-31] Paul shows clearly that the Holy Spirit creates unity not only in spite of diversity, but precisely *through* it."[75] Thus a proper reading of 1 Corinthians 12 helps us refine the content of biblical catholicity by recognizing that because the church is a body inherently composed of *different parts*, uniformity is at odds with a proper outworking of ecclesial catholicity as unified *diversity*.

Galatians 3. Galatians 3 is set within a broader argument that Paul is engaged in over the course of the entire letter. Paul sees nothing less than the truth of the gospel at stake, and views the Galatians' response to the issues raised in the letter as determinative of whether they will continue to rely on faith and be blessed or move to relying on works of the law and be cursed (Gal 3:9-10). But interestingly, some like Mark Dever have noted that "Paul, in Galatians, understood [the] question [of the church's catholicity] to be closely entwined with the very gospel itself."[76] Bavinck can say that while Galatians is certainly a warning against abandoning the gospel, it is also an example of "the apostles placing [the] unity and catholicity of the church in the foreground and issu[ing] serious warnings against all division . . . a widespread danger as early as the first century."[77] How can such a connection between the gospel and the catholicity of the church be made here? The answer is found particularly in examining Galatians 3:26-29.

There we see the biblical-theological backdrop of the promises made to Abraham once again playing a crucial role. Already in the letter Paul has made the case that "those who have faith are children of Abraham" (Gal 3:7),

---

[74] Allison, *Sojourners and Strangers*, 169.
[75] Cullman, *Unity Through Diversity*, 16.
[76] Mark E. Dever, "A Catholic Church," in *The Church: One, Holy, Catholic, and Apostolic*, ed. Richard D. Phillips, Philip G. Ryken, and Mark E. Dever (Phillipsburg, NJ: P&R, 2004), 77.
[77] Bavinck, "Catholicity of Christianity and the Church," 227.

the descendants he was promised so many years ago. This is because Abraham is, for Paul, "the man of faith" (Gal 3:9), having believed God and so been credited with righteousness (Gal 3:6; cf. Gen 15:6). In an incredible redemptive-historical summary, Paul says that "Scripture foresaw that God would justify the Gentiles by faith, and announced the gospel in advance to Abraham: 'All nations will be blessed through you'" (Gal 3:8). This all sets the stage for why Paul can affirm that "in Christ Jesus you are all children of God *through faith*" (Gal 3:26). The entry point into the true covenant community has always remained the same: faith. It is faith, the means God established for justification (of Gentiles, but also of Jews, exemplified in Abraham, the father of the Jews) back in Genesis, that now enables Jew and Gentile to be "baptized into Christ" and "clothed . . . with Christ" (Gal 3:27). These signs of belonging to Christ (Gal 3:29) come about through faith and thus lead to the conclusion that anyone who exhibits this faith is "Abraham's seed, and heirs according to the promise" (Gal 3:29; cf. Rom 3:30).

This universally available means of becoming a child of God is the great leveler of any distinctions between humans, summarized in Galatians 3:28: "There is neither Jew nor Gentile, neither slave nor free, nor is there male and female, for you are all one in Christ Jesus." As Timothy George observed, these categories cover "the fundamental cleavages of human existence," namely ethnicity, socioeconomic status, and gender.[78] The most significant of these, from a biblical-theological perspective, is the breakdown of the Jew/Gentile distinction in the covenant people of God. Speaking of Galatians 3:29, Badcock recognizes the audacity of the statement that "gentile Christians are spoken of as *Abraham's* descendants. Here Paul [leverages the] universality [found] in the foundational narratives of Judaism, in which Abraham is spoken of as the father of many nations, not just of one."[79]

How does all this relate to the church's catholicity? Dever understands the entirety of Galatians 3:26-29 as answering the question whether the church is indeed catholic. This is because, as Dever sees it, the question of the church's catholicity "is rooted in the very dispute that is at the center of

---

[78]Quoted in Bruce Milne, *Dynamic Diversity: Bridging Class, Age, Race and Gender in the Church* (Downers Grove, IL: IVP Academic, 2007), 33.
[79]Gary D. Badcock, *The House Where God Lives: Renewing the Doctrine of the Church for Today* (Grand Rapids, MI: Eerdmans, 2009), 33.

the New Testament from Acts on—the question of whether the church would be Jewish or would be multinational and multiethnic."[80] By Paul's argumentation in Galatians, if the church remains Jewish only then both the gospel and the church's catholicity have been compromised. Why? Because Paul insists that by teaching that salvation can be achieved by anything other than faith (in this case, through observing the law and particularly the Jewish rite of circumcision) these false teachers were denying both the gospel itself and the catholicity of the church that is rightly deduced from that gospel.[81] Not only is salvation by faith alone central to the gospel, but it is also central to the nature of God's people as a unified diversity through the whole of all times, peoples, and places. What relativizes ethnic background, socioeconomic status, and biological sex (among many other things) is the recognition that faith is the common entry point, and that this faith makes everyone, equally, children of God and heirs of his promises. In short, Dever rightly recognizes what Galatians 3 makes clear: "The church's catholicity is rooted in and bounded by the gospel's catholicity. Anytime, anywhere, anyone can be forgiven his or her sins by faith alone in the one and only Savior, our Lord Jesus Christ. That is the true catholic doctrine of the true catholic church."[82]

Dever draws out three very important implications of this insight. The first is that the catholicity of the church excludes racism.[83] By implication we could also say that this passage similarly rebukes sexism and classism (among other things): if all are one in Christ Jesus, there is no basis for favoritism or exclusionism of any kind. But Dever goes on to observe that catholicity cuts against any provincialism as well: "While the universal church exists in all cultures, it should be limited to none. The gospel is displayed when Christians of different cultures show themselves all preaching and believing the same gospel."[84] Indeed, we could say that provincialism particularly undercuts the "all places" aspect of catholicity, because

---

[80]Dever, "A Catholic Church," 77-78.
[81]Dever, "A Catholic Church," 78.
[82]Dever, "A Catholic Church," 92.
[83]He says "the universal nature of the true church seriously challenges our uniracial churches.... Our racially divided congregations—of any color—do not commend the gospel." Dever, "A Catholic Church," 89-90.
[84]Dever, "A Catholic Church," 88.

provincialism privileges one location rather than being open to what can be learned from others. Finally, Dever also makes clear that catholicity undercuts sectarianism: "The recognition of what we hold in common among true, faithful Christians must always be valued more highly and held more deeply than that which divides us."[85] Though other passages remind us that the church is marked by a manifold diversity, Galatians 3 makes clear that this diversity is never cause for exclusionism, provincialism, or sectarianism, for all undercut ecclesial catholicity.

Ephesians 4. Friedrich Heiler calls the book of Ephesians "the Magna Carta of the idea of the Universal Church."[86] Adams notes that "in Colossians and especially in Ephesians *ekklesia* is used in the singular for the worldwide community of believers, the 'universal church' . . . [demonstrating] the idea of the church as a universal body."[87] It is no surprise, then, that we would turn to Ephesians for insights into the nature of the church as catholic. And though we will focus most of our energies on Ephesians 4, the insights gleaned there stem from a larger argument that Paul makes throughout the letter.

Paul makes clear in this letter that the church, far from being a historical accident, is rather a central instrument in the accomplishment of God's cosmic kingdom purposes. In Ephesians 1 he emphasizes that the church has been part of God's plan "before the creation of the world" (Eph 1:4) and that it exists as an adopted, chosen people living for the praise of God's glory (Eph 1:5, 11, 12, 14). It is to the church that the mystery of God's will, "purposed in Christ [and] to be put into effect when the times reach their fulfillment" has been made known: "to bring *unity* to *all* things in heaven and on earth under Christ" (Eph 1:9-10). The church has Christ as its head and thus is his body, "the fullness of him who fills everything in every way" (Eph 1:22-23). In Ephesians 2 Paul claims that God's people are defined by the act of Christ "making peace, and in one body [reconciling] both [Jew and Gentile] to God through the cross" (Eph 2:15-16). Reconciliation to God

---

[85]Dever, "A Catholic Church," 89. As Ferguson has put it, "There is room within unity for a diversity that seeks to maintain unity; there is no place for a diversity born of party spirit." Ferguson, *Church of Christ*, 407.
[86]Quoted in Dulles, *Catholicity of the Church*, 39.
[87]Edward Adams, "The Shape of the Pauline Churches," in *The Oxford Handbook of Ecclesiology*, ed. Paul Avis (Oxford: Oxford University Press, 2018), 127.

was accompanied by reconciliation between humans, a destruction of "the dividing wall of hostility" creating "one new humanity out of the two," such that all are "fellow citizens . . . and members of [God's] household" together (Eph 2:14-15, 19). Because of Christ, both Jew and Gentile "have access to the Father by one Spirit" (Eph 2:18) and are "being built together to become a dwelling in which God lives by his Spirit." In Ephesians 3 Paul reflects on "the mystery . . . [regarding] the administration of God's grace . . . the mystery of Christ, which was not made known to people in other generations" (Eph 3:2-5). What is this redemptive-historical mystery? Ephesians 3:6: "that through the gospel the Gentiles are heirs together with Israel, members together of one body, and sharers together in the promise of Christ Jesus." Paul thus understood his own commission as "to make plain to everyone the administration of this mystery" so that "through the church, the manifold wisdom of God should be made known . . . according to his eternal purpose that he accomplished in Christ Jesus our Lord" (Eph 3:9-11).

Ephesians 4 can be understood as the culmination and advancement of the vision for the church set forth in Ephesians 1–3. As Gentiles called into the glories of covenantal communion with God and his people, Paul urges them to "live a life worthy" of that calling (Eph 4:1). Among other things, this means making "every effort to keep the unity of the Spirit through the bond of peace" (Eph 4:3). The theological underpinnings for this unity are set forth through a trinitarian framework; it is the triune God who has called the church to be one. There is, after all, only one body, just as there is only one Spirit to empower that body, one Lord to serve as head of that body, and one Father to sovereignly ordain and administer the plan of redemption for that body (Eph 4:4-6). This unity ought to manifest in the practice of one baptism and in the theological virtues of faith, hope, and love (Eph 4:2-5).[88]

The staggering nature of this unity is underscored by everything Paul has said in the first three chapters regarding the dividing wall of hostility between Jew and Gentile being destroyed by the wisdom of God in the gospel. But Ephesians 4:7 supplements this emphasis on unity with a corresponding emphasis on the *diversity* that remains amid this unity. Paul says, "But to

---

[88]Paul's words in 1 Cor 10:17 make clear that taking the Eucharist is also a sign of the church's unity. Thus both the sacrament of baptism and of the Lord's Supper become a way that the church's unity is displayed.

each one of us grace has been given as Christ apportioned it," emphasizing how each one is distinguished by the particular grace they are given by the gift-giving Christ (as Eph 4:8-10 showcases by making appeal to Ps 68:18). Ephesians 4:11 gives a more specific sense of what Paul has in mind: "So Christ himself gave the apostles, the prophets, the evangelists, the pastors and teachers." But the broader vision for the diversity of the church comes in seeing that it is the role of these officers "to equip his people for works of service, so that the body of Christ may be built up" (Eph 4:12). There is a vast diversity in the works of service that each believer will be called to, and yet they all contribute toward the goal of unified maturity: "[reaching] unity in the faith and in the knowledge of the Son of God and [becoming] mature, attaining to the whole measure of the fullness of Christ" (Eph 4:13). Ephesians 4:14-16 makes clear that every member of the body plays a role in moving the church from infant vulnerability to adult maturity. Indeed, with the full diversity of gifts, offices, and works of service that Christ has given, the church "will grow to become in every respect the mature body of him who is the head" (Eph 4:15). This consummate unity is achieved only through the interdependent and distinctive work of every member, which enables "the whole body . . . [to] grow and build itself up in love, as each part does its work" (Eph 4:16). Ferguson emphasizes that "the different functions in the body represent a diversity contributing to unity, for each member has a contribution to make to the growth of the whole."[89]

To take stock: the vision that emerges of the universal church in the book of Ephesians is one marked by diversity, especially the stunning diversity of Jew and Gentile making up one body. Timothy Gombis can thus survey these chapters and conclude that "[in] uniting a formerly divided humanity . . . God is building the multiracial, multiethnic, multigenerational church of Jesus Christ, which stands as a monument to his triumph over the powers of darkness."[90] While this is certainly true, the most distinctive thing that emerges from a survey of Ephesians is the note of profound *unity* that marks this diversified body, especially the depth of unity described in Ephesians 4:4-6. Küng can note the incredible tension that the book of Ephesians

---

[89]Ferguson, *Church of Christ*, 103.
[90]Timothy G. Gombis, *The Drama of Ephesians: Participating in the Triumph of God* (Downers Grove, IL: IVP Academic, 2010), 182.

maintains: amid "different peoples, different communities, different languages" there is a profound unity in Christ that prevails.[91] This is ultimately because it has always been God's wise plan in the gospel "to bring *unity* to all things in heaven and on earth under Christ" (Eph 1:10). Amid our proper emphasis on the church as a diversified entity, Ephesians 4 in particular reminds us that this diversity, from first to last, is *unified*. This rules out of bounds any proposals of catholicity that would give way to pluralism, for the church's diversity is always marked by a profound unity that only comes about in Christ by the Spirit through faith as proclaimed in the gospel.

Redemptive-Historical Consummation: Revelation

At the very end of redemptive history, we encounter the consummative vision of the church's catholicity. Here the scope of the God's covenant people through all times, peoples, and places is fully on display, for *all* of God's people finally dwell together in God's presence as it was in Eden before the fall (Rev 21:3; cf. Gen 3:8). The embryonic goodness of God's unified-yet-diverse creation is now expressed in its utter fullness; the incipient catholicity of God's people on display through God's covenantal dealings comes to full bloom in a consummative catholicity that has a greater breadth of diversity than was ever possible in Eden with its limited expression of human generations, cultural diversity, and geographical expansion.[92]

The book of Revelation is primarily where we encounter the church's catholicity on display at the consummation of redemptive history.[93] In Revelation 5 and 7 we particularly behold the manifold diversity that defines the one people of God. John's vision of the heavenly throne room testifies to this reality, for there he beholds the Lamb who is worthy to open the seals because his self-sacrifice "purchased for God persons from every tribe and language and people and nation" (Rev 5:9). This precious purchase cannot default, and so the multitude of those who stand before God's throne as the redeemed are indeed "from every nation, tribe, people and language" (Rev 7:9). Speaking of John's proclamation that God has made this catholic

---

[91] Quoted in Watson, *I Believe*, 346.
[92] The new heaven and new earth originally predicted in Is 65:17 is described in Rev 21–22 in a way that surpasses, rather than merely returns to, Eden.
[93] For more on the way Revelation functions within the larger canon, see Brian Tabb, *All Things New: Revelation as Canonical Capstone* (Downers Grove, IL: IVP Academic, 2019).

community "to be a kingdom and priests to serve our God, and they will reign on the earth" (Rev 5:10), Bruce observes that "those whom He redeems are constituted 'a kingdom and priests to our God'—language in which we recognize the echo of God's words to His people at Sinai. But now the kingdom of priests is no longer confined to one nation: it comprises men and women 'from every tribe and tongue and people and nation.'"[94] The fourfold description[95] of human diversity united in Christ should sound familiar: it is almost identical to the LXX translation of the Hebrew used in Genesis 10 to delineate humanity according to tribe, language, territory, and nation (Gen 10:5, 20, 31). If we recall our argumentation that Genesis 10–11, with its concern for the nations and its portrayal of the trajectory of the nations apart from God's redemptive work, sets the stage for the promise that "all the peoples would be blessed" (Gen 12:3), we recognize that this proto-catholic promise given to Abraham regarding the scope of God's covenant people comes to complete fulfillment at the end of the age.

Indeed, the universal scope of God's people was witnessed in the Law, promised by the Prophets, overheard in the Writings, anticipated in the ministry of Christ, enabled by the Spirit, and proclaimed by the apostles. But it is only at the eschaton that faith becomes sight, when "*all nations* will come and worship before [God]" (Rev 15:4) and "will walk by the light [of the Lamb]," and when "the glory and honor *of the nations* will be brought into [the eternal city]" (Rev 21:24, 26). The nature of God's people as a unified diversity through the whole of all times, peoples, and places, a nature veiled through much of redemptive history, will one day be fully and finally displayed as the nations in all their diversity are united in the healing provision that Christ has made (Rev 22:2). In fact, in words that echo Paul's recognition in Romans 9:24-25 that God's people had been "called not only from the Jews but also from the Gentiles" in answer to the promise of Hosea that God "will call them 'my people' who are not my people," we hear that God himself will utter the words once spoken only of Israel: "They will be

---

[94] F. F. Bruce, *God's Kingdom and Church* (London: Scripture Union, 1978), 56.
[95] This fourfold diversity pattern shows up six times in Revelation, with two of these instances positive (Rev 5:9; 7:9), two negative (Rev 13:7; 17:15) and two neutral (Rev 10:11; 14:6). This may indicate that John is using the fourfold description as a device to contrast a unified diversity through the whole that is God-honoring (true catholicity) with one that is in rebellion against God (Satanic counterfeit). Such a contrast is thematic in Revelation.

my *peoples*" (Rev 21:3).[96] The incredibly diverse *peoples* are eternally *one people* in Christ, such that Allison, echoing the imagery of 1 Peter 2 and Ephesians 2, can say that the church is composed of "members from all nationalities, ethnicities, races, [and] socio-politico-economic backgrounds . . . [as] stones that are joined together . . . [to form God's] holy temple, a dwelling place for God by the Spirit."[97] It is here that one of the most central and consistent promises throughout the canon, that God will call a people unto himself so that he can be their God and they can be his people (restated in Rev 21:3 and again in Rev 21:7), finally comes to fulfillment. When it does, the full scope of redemption will be displayed, grounded in the universal authority of Christ, who proclaims "I am making *everything* new!" and "I am the Alpha and the Omega, the Beginning and the End" (Rev 21:5-6).

Conclusion: The Church as Catholic

What may we conclude based on this inquiry into the biblical basis for confessing the catholicity of the church? First, it seems clear that the Scriptures do indeed provide a *warrant* for us to speak of the church as catholic. It is thus appropriate for us to understand the creedal confession of faith in the "catholic . . . church" as synthesizing and expressing the same judgment as Scripture, albeit in different terms. Indeed, the term *catholic* nicely describes the pattern of judgments found in Scripture regarding the *nature* of God's people as a unified diversity and the *scope* of God's people as through the whole of all times, peoples, and places. Hallig highlights how the breadth of redemptive history witnesses to the church's catholicity: "The fulfillment of the promise given to Abraham was realized in and through the story of Jesus and carried on by the church that is truly catholic in life and mission."[98] There is also a depth of the biblical witness to the church's catholicity, seen particularly in New Testament passages that deal with the nature and scope of the church. Thus Dever can say that "the New Testament . . . clearly

---

[96]Literal translation. *Laos* is rarely plural in the NT but is so here, not insignificant in light of our theme. Easley sees this as an emphatic underlining of the great ethnic diversity that will be on display in glory. See Kendell H. Easley, "The Church in Acts and Revelation: New Testament Bookends," in *The Community of Jesus*, eds. Easley and Morgan, 87.
[97]Allison, "Holy God and Holy People," 252.
[98]Hallig, *We Are Catholic*, 56.

speaks of a church that is not merely local, but universal and catholic. . . . It is this church—the universal church—and no one local church that has inherited the church's universal mission that Christ set out [for it]."[99] Indeed, once we connect the motif of unified diversity with catholicity, we see how the New Testament assumes that God's people will be increasingly marked by unity-in-diversity as the missional trajectory of the church works through all times, peoples, and places.

Second, it seems clear that Scripture provides a tremendous orientation to the proper *content* for the doctrine of the church's catholicity, establishing a biblical plumb line for evaluating doctrinal proposals down church-historical stream. As it is a "contested doctrine," we must continue to return to the Scriptures to adjudicate between differing visions of ecclesial catholicity. Scripture provides us with "guardrails" that prevent any doctrinal proposal regarding catholicity from deviating from the proper path. One guardrail prevents us from assenting to any vision of the church's catholicity that requires uniformity (seen particularly in 1 Cor 12); such uniformity compromises the reality that God's people represent a *diversity*. Another guardrail prevents us from embracing a vision of catholicity that allows for pluralism (seen particularly in Eph 4); this compromises the reality that God's people are *unified*. A third guardrail prevents us from holding to an understanding of catholicity that involves exclusionism, sectarianism, or provincialism (seen particularly in Gal 3); this compromises the fact that God's people are *through the whole of all times, peoples, and places*. In other words, we have seen that our provisional definition of catholicity as an attribute expressing the church's nature as a unified diversity through the whole of all times, peoples, and places is justified. Evaluating developments of the doctrine and proposals of catholicity that emerge from various ecclesial traditions by this biblical plumb line will be critically important for our work moving forward.

But for now, we can see that what is at stake in the catholicity of the church is no small matter in the biblical estimation. We can also see, in light of the fact that one day representatives from every nation, tribe, people, and language will fully commune with the triune God and with each other as a

---

[99]Dever, "A Catholic Church," 76-77.

whole people marked by an incorruptible unified diversity, that the biblical warrant for the doctrine of catholicity enables us to affirm with Bavinck that

> Christianity knows no boundaries beyond those which God himself has in his good pleasure established; no boundaries of race or age, class, or status, nationality, or language. . . . The Gospel is a joyful tiding, not only for the individual person but also for humanity. . . . [It is] a Gospel so rich [it] created a people of God that could no longer be contained within the boundaries of one nation and country.[100]

This is the good news of the church's catholicity according to the Scriptures.

---

[100] Bavinck, "Catholicity," 224.

Catholicity

The Development of a Doctrine

THE BIBLICAL WARRANT FOR SPEAKING of the church as catholic is far from the end of the (doctrinal) story. Indeed, while we have insisted that the primary desideratum of theology is that it be done "according to the Scriptures," this is not all we must say. The reason: as the doctrine of catholicity reminds us, we are not the first Christians to "take up and read." Indeed, there are *many* who have gone before us as a "great cloud of witnesses" (Heb 12:1), and we do well to hear their collective witness to the Word.[1] Historical theology offers us a vitally important step in our theological task, for it seeks to assess how the church has understood and lived in light of Scripture through the ages. With D. H. Williams we thus recognize that "there can be no faithful use of Scripture without recourse to Tradition"[2] and with Oberman that "Holy Scripture can only be [properly] interpreted in fellowship with the Brethren."[3] In other words, theology ought to be done in the communion of saints, and for our study this means

---

[1] Vanhoozer rightly says that theology ought to move *along the grain* of the biblical text—respecting and building on the prophets and apostles in a way that yields a *longer* obedience, and a *longer* understanding, in the same direction. See Kevin J. Vanhoozer, "May We Go Beyond What Is Written After All? The Pattern of Theological Authority and the Problem of Doctrinal Development," in *The Enduring Authority of the Christian Scriptures*, ed. D. A. Carson (Grand Rapids, MI: Eerdmans, 2016).

[2] D. H. Williams, *Retrieving the Tradition and Renewing Evangelicalism: A Primer for Suspicious Protestants* (Grand Rapids, MI: Eerdmans, 1999), 6.

[3] Heiko A. Oberman, *The Dawn of the Reformation: Essays in Late Medieval and Early Reformation Thought* (Edinburgh: T&T Clark, 1992), 296.

accounting for how the biblical content regarding the church's catholicity crystallizes over the course of church history into the *doctrine* of catholicity as God's people have read and interpreted God's Word.[4]

Since the time of Newman's famous *Essay*, it is uncontroversial to affirm his central insight: doctrine develops.[5] This simply recognizes that there is an inevitably *historical* element to what the church has come to understand and teach.[6] Amid this historical process we need to distinguish between doctrinal developments and doctrinal corruptions; both involve change, with the former representing a faithful and richer understanding of the implications of Scripture's discourse and the latter representing an unfaithful and more impoverished understanding of the same. Doctrinal developments accumulate in church tradition, faithfully setting out in a different idiom the "matter" of the biblical text by providing a more ordered and comprehensive view of it; doctrinal corruptions fail to do the same and are ultimately to be jettisoned.[7]

Amid the historical contingencies of such a process we do well to express with Williams that our "confidence in the authenticity of the message transmitted to us across the ages must be placed in the God of history who promised to lead us into all truth. . . . [This confidence is] in the Lord of the church, [trusting] that the essential tradition and Scripture are the sovereign work of the Holy Spirit operating in the . . . church."[8] Vanhoozer has termed this the pneumatically effective history of the written word: what

---

[4]Doctrine here is understood as "postcanonical expressions of the content of Christian belief." Rhyne R. Putman, *In Defense of Doctrine: Evangelicalism, Theology, and Scripture* (Minneapolis: Fortress, 2015), 27.

[5]Descriptively this is a very easy statement to make. For an excellent articulation of how to *evaluate* the development of doctrine, see Kevin J. Vanhoozer, "Improvising Theology According to the Scriptures," in *Building on the Foundations of Evangelical Theology*, ed. Gregg R. Allison and Stephen J. Wellum (Wheaton, IL: Crossway, 2015).

[6]We follow Putman in viewing doctrinal development as "the ongoing process of reconstructing and reordering doctrines into *systematic theologies* that offer both conceptual clarity and internal consistency . . . attempts to *contextualize* or 'translate' the substance of Christian teaching for new settings and new cultures . . . [and] the introduction of new *theological concepts and expressions*." Putman, *In Defense of Doctrine*, 31-32.

[7]The fact that doctrine develops is an insight derived from Scripture itself, for not only is there a doctrinal deposit to be guarded and handed on through the ages (Rom 6:17; 1 Cor 11:23; 15:3; 2 Thess 2:15; 3:6; 1 Tim 6:20; 2 Tim 1:14; Jude 3; Rev 3:3), but there is also a *fullness* of doctrine to be expounded by the church to the end of the age (Jn 16:13; Eph 1:18; 3:18; Col 1:9; 2 Pet 1:5).

[8]D. H. Williams, *Evangelicals and Tradition: The Formative Influence of the Early Church* (Grand Rapids, MI: Baker Academic, 2005), 35-36.

could be seen as an arbitrary history of interpretations looks different when viewed theologically, for it is understood as the fulfillment of Jesus' promise to send his Spirit to guide his followers into all truth (Jn 16:13).[9] As we begin our church-historical inquiry regarding the doctrine of the church's catholicity, we thus hold with Williams that "the church's Tradition and the traditioning process is indeed the work of God in the world. This means that we are related to Christ in a twofold way, in communion vertically through the Spirit and horizontally across the centuries through the consensual memory of the church. Both are necessary for the achievement of Christian orthodoxy."[10]

The Need for Church-Historical Precedent

The payoff of a church-historical investigation into the doctrine of the church's catholicity is twofold. First of all, it establishes a framework to determine the extent to which any particular proposal regarding the church's catholicity, as well as any understanding of that catholicity from a particular ecclesial vantage point, has precedent in church tradition. Such precedent would be important for any doctrine but is *particularly* significant when it comes to the doctrine of catholicity: after all, catholicity attempts to deal with connectedness to the whole, and thus a doctrinal proposal or ecclesial perspective on catholicity that has no forerunners in, or resonance with, the tradition would rightly be suspect. And yet we must guard against any conception that views church tradition monolithically, for (1) diverse perspectives and ecclesial vantage points have contributed to the tradition and (2) the church's catholicity remains a *contested* doctrine. Being aware of its history is the first step toward recognizing developments (and corruptions) of the doctrine that have occurred. A Reformational effort that seeks a biblical norming of the doctrine must be attentive to how tradition and confessional commitments *inevitably shape* our reading of Scripture while simultaneously insisting that these must *ultimately be shaped* by Scripture. This is to rightly understand tradition as a ministerial authority operating under the magisterial authority of Scripture; Scripture has the "final word,"

---

[9]See Vanhoozer, *Biblical Authority After Babel: Retrieving the Solas in the Spirit of Mere Protestant Christianity* (Grand Rapids, MI: Brazos Press, 2016), 143.
[10]Williams, *Retrieving the Tradition*, 217.

and yet continuity with the tradition (though multifarious and contested) is a good to be sought.

This chapter's second payoff is that, given the Free Church's largely poor track record of valuing church tradition, it is important that any proposal of Free Church catholicity demonstrate continuity with the main contours of that tradition. Newman is famous for his criticism that "to be deep in history is to cease to be a Protestant," going on to insist specifically that "many [Protestants] . . . speak of 'unity,' 'universality,' and 'Catholicity,' and use the words in their own sense and for their own ideas."[11] A compelling Free Church account of catholicity must demonstrate that it does not fall prey to Newman's concern; rather, it must show *connection to the church-historical whole* while also *offering distinctive insights toward a fuller-orbed doctrine of catholicity*. Indeed, in Williams's words, we are attempting to show that "to be 'deep in history' for [Free Church] Protestantism need not be and should not be oxymoronic."[12]

The Need for a Taxonomy of Catholicity

Catholicity is contested. This very fact means we need to be prepared to encounter a variety of understandings of what is primarily in view when we speak of the church as catholic. As we will see, the doctrine of catholicity demonstrates a general continuity through time while also experiencing developments as the contextual situation of the church changes and as a fuller reflection on the nature of the church occurs. In order to see both the consistency and the developments, we need a taxonomy of the differing conceptions of catholicity. Dulles starts us by outlining four ways the term has been used to characterize the church. First, he proposes his broadest category of catholicity as participating in wholeness, a "sharing in the universal community . . . that transcends the barriers of time and place" with its opposite descriptor being sectarian (#1 below).[13] Second, he posits catholicity as universality of locale, demonstrating worldwide dispersion as opposed to spatial limitation (#2 below). Third is catholicity as delineating what is true or

---

[11]Quoted in Williams, *Evangelicals and Tradition*, 11; See John Henry Newman, *An Essay on the Development of Christian Doctrine* (New York: Cosimo Classics, 2007), 182.
[12]Williams, *Evangelicals and Tradition*, 12.
[13]Avery Dulles, *The Catholicity of the Church* (Oxford: Oxford University Press, 1985), 185.

orthodox versus false or heretical (#5 below). Fourth, he presents an understanding of catholicity that emphasizes "visible continuity in space and time and visible mediation through social and institutional structures, such as creeds, sacraments, and the historic episcopate," in contrast to charismatic or mystical (read: invisible) conceptions of the church and a schismatic impulse (#6 below).[14] In addition to these, we have already seen from the introduction and our engagement with the biblical material that three more aspects should be added (#3, 4 and 7 below); three additional aspects will emerge over the course of our church-historical survey (#8–10 below). The taxonomy is provided here so that the aspects can be recognized in the church-historical survey and evaluated in the conclusion.

Table 2. A taxonomy of the church's catholicity

1	Holistic Catholicity: connected to the whole vs. sectarianism
2	Geographical Catholicity: embracing "all places" vs. provincialism
3	Missional Catholicity: reaching "all peoples" vs. exclusionism
4	Chronological Catholicity: commonality through "all times" vs. novelty
5	Orthodox Catholicity: doctrinal faithfulness vs. heresy or apostasy
6	Institutional Catholicity: visible mediation vs. invisible conceptions and schismatic impulse
7	Differentiated Catholicity: diverse identity and contribution vs. uniformity
8	Christological Catholicity: emphasis on christological connection vs. ecclesial minimalism
9	Liturgical Catholicity: sacramental continuity vs. ingenuity
10	Numerical Catholicity: greatest adherence vs. minority status

SKETCHING THE DEVELOPMENT OF CATHOLICITY: FIVE STAGES

This chapter examining five major stages of the development of the doctrine of catholicity can be understood as an inquiry into this question: "Why did [earlier] Christians regularly declare their belief in the . . . 'catholic church,' . . . what were they trying to affirm, and how should it be recovered as a means of ensuring a faithful ecclesiology?"[15] Indeed, in tracing out the

---

[14]Dulles, *Catholicity*, 185. Dulles actually provides a fifth definition that conforms to his Roman Catholic convictions: "the church which, organized in the world as society, is governed by the bishop of Rome . . . and by the bishops in communion with him." We will combine Dulles's fourth and fifth category into one, understanding the Church of Rome as embodying one particular instantiation of the sixth category (institutional catholicity).

[15]Williams, *Retrieving the Tradition*, 222.

church-historical story of the doctrine we are seeking to determine what a full-orbed doctrine of catholicity would involve, one that properly considers the contributions (and assesses the pitfalls) of the whole church. This is ultimately an attempt to parse out the logic of the gospel, specifically how we should understand *the scope* of the gospel's reception and *the nature* of the gospel-formed people (the church) as catholic. In this far-from-comprehensive survey we will emphasize breadth over depth in order to see the general contours of the doctrine's development and glimpse the main emphases that have emerged as God's people, reading Scripture and led by the Spirit, have confessed that Christ's church is, indeed, "catholic."

1. The early fathers. An important element of the biblical witness to catholicity is the "catholic spirit" of the apostles who wrote letters out of concern for the local churches (2 Cor 11:28; 2 Pet 1) and pastors (2 Tim 4) that would survive them. That same spirit manifested in churches taking an interest in the well-being of other churches (seen in Acts 15 and Rom 15) and in planting new churches throughout the known world (seen in Acts 13 and Col 1). Among the early fathers we find a strong continuation of this spirit, especially in church leaders concerned for God's people beyond the particular flock under their care. James Paget says that "the writings of the [early fathers] give us evidence of a growing conception of the Church as a universal body, in which a concern for churches other than one's own is evident."[16] This is witnessed very clearly in Clement of Rome (d. 99), whose first letter to the Corinthians demonstrates a supralocal pastoral concern. Clement reminds them that "all work harmoniously together, and are under one common rule for the preservation of the whole body. . . . [So] let our whole body, then, be preserved in Jesus Christ; and let every one be subject to his neighbor."[17]

But the first use of the term *catholic* in reference to the church comes from Ignatius of Antioch (d. 111) in his *Epistle to the Smyrneans*, where he, in the midst of a discussion about the Eucharist and baptism being overseen by bishops (or those authorized by bishops), notes that "wherever the bishop

---

[16]James Carleton Paget, "The Vison of the Church in the Apostolic Fathers," in *A Vision for the Church: Studies in Early Christian Ecclesiology in Honour of J. P. M. Sweet*, eds. Markus Bockmuehl and Michael B. Thompson (Edinburgh: T&T Clark, 1997), 196.

[17]Quoted in Earl D. Radmacher, *The Nature of the Church* (Portland, OR: Western Baptist Press, 1972), 24-25.

shall appear, there let the multitude of the people also be; even as, wherever Jesus Christ is, there is the catholic church."[18] Berard Marthaler argues, "Ignatius' point in this passage was that the local church community had reality, life, and power only to the extent that it formed part of the universal church in union with its spiritual head."[19] Jonker also notes the deep christological grounding, saying that for Ignatius "Christ is the true catholicity of the church, because the identity of the true church consists in its relationship to Christ."[20] Clowney finds here an example of how "the early church fathers used [catholicity] to express an important New Testament teaching: that the church as a whole is more than the local church,"[21] while Dana insists based on the majority of Ignatius's uses of *ecclesia* in reference to the local church that "primary in [his] thinking . . . was the notion of the church as a local assembly."[22]

The next usage, in what has come to be known as the *Martyrdom of Polycarp* (mid-second century), demonstrates again a local church concerned about the broader church. The epistle begins with a salutation: "The Church of God which sojourns at Smyrna, to the Church of God sojourning in Philomelium, and to all the congregations of the Holy and Catholic Church in every place."[23] As with Ignatius, we see the author demonstrating a connection between Christ and pastoral care: "[The] Lord Jesus Christ [is] the savior of our souls, the governor of our bodies and the shepherd of the catholic church throughout the world."[24] A supralocal concern is witnessed in Polycarp himself who, at the moment of his martyrdom, is portrayed as praying for "all the catholic church . . . throughout the world."[25] Williams,

---

[18] Angelo Di Berardino, ed. *We Believe in One Holy Catholic and Apostolic Church* (Downers Grove, IL: IVP Academic, 2010), 72. Here we see the beginnings of christological catholicity in this much quoted, but admittedly vague, statement by Ignatius. That there is a christological grounding of the church, and thus its nature as catholic, is almost universally recognized; parsing out the specifics of what is meant and the implications of the same has proven extremely difficult and contentious. Here we can only recognize that the christological component is central in the tradition yet clearly ambiguous. Any full-orbed account of catholicity must flesh out the christological connection, as a Free Church account of catholicity does by making much of Mt 18:20 in relation to Ignatius's foundational insight.
[19] Berard L. Marthaler, *The Creed* (Mystic, CT: Twenty-Third Publications, 1987), 314.
[20] W. B. Jonker, "Catholicity, Unity and Truth," in *Catholicity and Secession: A Dilemma?*, ed. Paul G. Schrotenboer (Kampen, Netherlands: J. H. Kok, 1992), 20.
[21] Edmund P. Clowney, *The Church* (Downers Grove, IL: InterVarsity Press, 1995), 91.
[22] Quoted in Radmacher, *Nature of the Church*, 26.
[23] Quoted in Radmacher, *Nature of the Church*, 28.
[24] Di Berardino, *We Believe*, 73.
[25] Quoted in Williams, *Evangelicals and Tradition*, 42.

in examining the usage of *catholic* in Ignatius and the *Martyrdom of Polycarp*, concludes that "profession of the church's catholicity grew out of the worship life of the local congregation and not out of statements framed by councils who were attempting to represent the mind of the whole church."[26] In short, catholicity in the earliest fathers concerned how the local church was connected to the whole and emerged from local reflections on the church's nature and scope.

Other early fathers contribute to a growing catholic sensibility. Irenaeus (130–202) says that "the Church, though dispersed throughout the whole world, even to the ends of the earth, has received from the apostles and their disciples this [one] faith . . . [and] as if occupying one house, carefully preserves it. It also believes these points [of doctrine] just as if it had only one soul, and one and the same heart. It proclaims them, teaches them, and hands them down, with perfect harmony, as if it possessed only one mouth."[27] Hippolytus (170–235) in his *The Refutation of All Heresies* connects catholicity to holiness for, after decrying various forms of sexual immorality, abortion, and exposure performed by certain professing Christian communities, he says, "After such audacious acts, they lose all sense of shame, yet still attempt to call themselves a catholic church!"[28] And Cyprian (200–258?) in his *On the Unity of the Church* uses the phrase "the Catholic Church" to challenge heretical groups in a way similar to Irenaeus: "Produce the origin of your churches; display the order of your bishops, running through succession from the beginning in such a way that the first bishop had as his teacher and predecessor some one of the apostles."[29] It is with Cyprian that a worldwide episcopate starts to be envisioned; whereas before bishops were referenced as the head of each local church, now there is a "unity we ought firmly to hold and assert . . . that we may also prove the episcopate itself to be one and undivided. . . . The episcopate is one, each part of which is held by each other for the whole."[30] In Cyprian's vision there is clearly an intermingling of unity and catholicity centered on the clergy: "The Church,

---

[26] Williams, *Retrieving the Tradition*, 224.
[27] Quoted in Gregg R. Allison, *Historical Theology: An Introduction to Christian Doctrine* (Grand Rapids, MI: Zondervan, 2011), 567.
[28] Quoted in Allison, *Historical Theology*, 567.
[29] Quoted in Radmacher, *Nature of the Church*, 32.
[30] Quoted in Radmacher, *Nature of the Church*, 32.

which is Catholic and one, is not cut or divided, but is indeed connected and bound together by the cement of the priests who cohere with one another."[31]

Taking stock of this first stage of catholicity's development, we can make the following observations. First, it is clear that the early fathers demonstrate a strong continuity with the catholic spirit manifest in the New Testament, testifying to the foundational nature of holistic catholicity (#1). Indeed, the first local churches are characterized by a strong sense of connection to the whole, exhibiting deep interrelationship and recognizing that their interdependence places obligations on them. This connection becomes difficult to maintain as the church expands geographically, but this expansion gives rise to a sense of geographical catholicity (#2): with Polycarp and Irenaeus the church's worldwide presence is emphasized, for the church is "in every place." Volf says that "the term *catholicity* acquired very early a geographic meaning"[32] while Dulles insists that the universal (vs. local) conception of the church "seems to be the primary meaning [of catholicity] . . . as used in a number of important texts from the early Fathers."[33]

The connectedness of these local churches is often expressed in terms of christological catholicity (#8): from Clement to Ignatius to Polycarp, the earliest fathers consistently emphasized that the churches are connected to the whole because of their common communion in Christ. This conviction leads to one of the most significant, if underdeveloped, church-historical insights regarding catholicity: wherever Jesus Christ is, there is the catholic church.[34] Sometimes this is cashed out in terms of an appeal to differentiated catholicity (#7): the local churches are related as diverse parts of one body, contributing distinct gifts and demonstrating a diversified unity throughout the world. Other times it is cashed out in terms of institutional catholicity (#6): the connection of these local churches is understood to be best demonstrated in the office of the bishop, which provides a strong sense of institutional continuity and liturgical legitimacy. Indeed, we see an increasing

---

[31]Quoted in Radmacher, *Nature of the Church*, 32.
[32]Miroslav Volf, *After Our Likeness: The Church as the Image of the Trinity* (Grand Rapids, MI: Eerdmans, 1998), 265.
[33]Dulles, *Catholicity*, 185.
[34]Irenaeus in his *Against Heresies* provides a similar formula except it is oriented around the Spirit of Christ: "Where the church is, there is the Spirit of God; and where the Spirit of God is, there is the church, and every kind of grace." Quoted in Jaroslav Pelikan, *The Christian Tradition: A History of the Development of Doctrine*, 5 vols. (Chicago: University of Chicago Press, 1971–1989), 1:156.

movement from differentiated to institutional catholicity as the patristic era marches on. Radmacher observes, based on the fact that the vast majority of Irenaeus's uses of *ecclesia* in *Against Heresies* refer to the universal (vs. local) church, that "whereas the earlier emphasis was upon the local *ekklesia* which was directly related to Christ, the head of the . . . *ekklesia*, the emphasis by the time of Irenaeus was upon the institutional unity of the visible, universal church."[35] Significantly, in just two centuries after the apostles we see five aspects of the church's catholicity (#1, 2, 6, 7, 8) attested by the early fathers.

2. *The era of the creeds and later fathers.* The next stage of development comes in the fourth century, which involved "a dramatic transition in the fortunes of the Church."[36] Indeed, a century that began with the "Great Persecution" under Diocletian ultimately saw two ecumenical councils and ended with the declaration of Christianity as the empire's official religion. Küng marks the significance: "Under the religious edict of 380 the '*ecclesia catholica*' became the only national religion. . . . Paganism and heresy became political crimes, 'catholicity' became orthodoxy, defended by law."[37] Louth says that in this time the "attempt to develop an 'ecumenical' understanding of the unity of the Church by assimilating it to the imperial institutions . . . was a considerable success."[38] This all had no small impact on the church's understanding of its catholicity.

One major contour of development in this period is the association of the term *catholic* with the notion of the true faith as contrasted with heresy, or orthodox catholicity (#5). So Lactantius (250–325) in his *The Divine Institutes* says that "Phrygians, Novatians, Valentinians, Marcionites, Anthropians, [and] Arians . . . have ceased to be Christians. They have lost the name of Christ and have assumed human and external names. It is *the catholic church alone* that retains true worship. This is the fountain of truth; this is the house of faith."[39] Pacian of Barcelona (310–391) observes how the notion of catholicity was developed for this exact purpose: "During

---

[35]Radmacher, *Nature of the Church*, 29.
[36]Andrew Louth, "Unity and Diversity in the Church of the Fourth Century," in *Doctrinal Diversity: Varieties of Early Christianity*, ed. Everett Ferguson (New York: Garland, 1999), 12.
[37]Quoted in Clowney, *The Church*, 91.
[38]Louth, "Unity and Diversity," 16.
[39]Quoted in Allison, *Historical Theology*, 570, emphasis added.

the time of the apostles . . . no one used to be called catholic. . . . But when, after the apostles, heresies had appeared . . . [so] did not the apostolic people require a name of their own, by which they would mark the unity of an uncorrupted people?"[40] Catholicity is conceived here as marking out the doctrinal boundaries of the gospel's true reception.

This notion of catholicity as doctrinal faithfulness is also expressed in the ecumenical creeds. There were of course forerunners to these creeds, summaries of the faith for use in local baptism rites. These forerunners clearly demonstrate that the concept of the church's catholicity was widely attested by the time of Nicaea (325).[41] And yet at Nicaea the formal creed crafted by the council failed to include any confession regarding the church generally or its catholicity specifically (the third article only states "We believe . . . in the Holy Spirit."). However, it is significant that the anathema that immediately follows the creed and proscribes views such as "there was [a time] when [the Son] was not" concludes with "these [views] the catholic and apostolic church anathematizes."[42] Thus Nicaea demonstrates an association of catholicity with apostolicity and the concept of doctrinal orthodoxy. Other post-Nicaea creeds show that the notion of the church's catholicity is becoming more prevalent. For instance, the Western Creed of Serdica (343) acknowledges, "This is what we have ourselves received and been taught, this is what we hold as the catholic and apostolic tradition and faith and confession."[43] By Constantinople in 381 the third article of the creed was much expanded, including not only a profession of belief in the church but also the accompanying ecclesial attributes: "We believe . . . in One Holy Catholic and Apostolic Church." Tracing the movement from the creed promulgated at Nicaea to the final form of the Nicene-Constantinopolitan

---

[40]Di Berardino, *We Believe*, 75-76.

[41]Significantly a baptismal confession from as early as the second century stated, "I believe . . . in the holy catholic church." Quoted in J. N. D. Kelley, *Early Christian Creeds*, 3rd ed. (London: Longman, 1972), 88. We also see the Jerusalem Creed, a forerunner to the Nicene Creed from as early as the third century, professes belief "in one holy catholic church" in connection to the Spirit. See Kelley, *Early Christian Creeds*, 184.

[42]D. H. Williams, ed., *Tradition, Scripture, and Interpretation: A Sourcebook of the Ancient Church* (Grand Rapids, MI: Baker Academic, 2006) 107.

[43]Williams, *Tradition, Scripture, and Interpretation*, 115. Similarly the regional council of Alexandria (362) proclaims "the following brief and clear statements are for every Christian," thus manifesting a catholic sensibility. See Williams, *Tradition, Scripture, and Interpretation*, 117.

Creed demonstrates how central the notion of the church's catholicity had become in fifty years.

Other ecumenical creeds demonstrate this same reality. The Early Roman Creed, an ancestor of the Apostles' Creed, only confessed faith in "the holy church." By the time the *textus receptus* of the Apostles' Creed emerged in the sixth century, the addition of "catholic" had occurred, but not the attributes of oneness and apostolicity that are attested in the Nicene Creed.[44] The Athanasian Creed (arising mid-fifth century), while not professing faith in the catholic church, nevertheless demonstrates once again a conception of catholicity particularly connected to doctrinal orthodoxy: "Whoever desires to be saved must above all things hold the catholic faith. . . . Now this is the catholic faith, that we worship one God in Trinity and Trinity in unity. . . . Unless one believes it faithfully and steadfastly, one will not be able to be saved."[45] Williams surveys the various creeds and summarizes that "the church's catholicity finds its voice in confessions which were already celebrated in individual churches throughout the Christian world."[46]

But Cyril of Jerusalem's (313–386) *Catechetical Lecture on the Nicene Creed* is a vibrant illustration of the fact that by this time catholicity had become quite multifaceted, not limited to one particular aspect of its content. This is evident in Cyril's vision of the church, which includes one of the most expansive expressions of its catholicity ever written. He says that the church "is called 'catholic' . . . because it extends all over the world, from one end of the earth to the other; and because it teaches universally and completely one and all the doctrines that ought to come to human knowledge."[47] Cyril goes on to say that it is also called catholic because "it brings into subjection to godliness the whole race of mankind, governors and governed, learned and unlearned; and because it universally treats and heals the whole class of sins, which are committed by soul or body, and possesses in itself every form of virtue which is named, both in deeds and words, and [it contains] every kind of spiritual gift."[48] Though Cyril

---

[44]See Williams, *Tradition, Scripture, and Interpretation*, 102.
[45]Williams, *Tradition, Scripture, and Interpretation*, 106.
[46]Williams, *Retrieving the Tradition*, 224-25.
[47]Di Berardino, *We Believe*, 74.
[48]Quoted in Marthaler, *The Creed*, 315.

points catechumens to the creed in order that they might "learn the faith and profess it; receive it and keep it" and thus witnesses to a doctrinal component of catholicity, it is clear that his conception of the ecclesial attribute goes way beyond marking out doctrinal boundaries.[49] Rather, as Williams puts it, Cyril emphasizes "that the catholic church is comprehensive in its message . . . [and holds] to everything necessary for the justification and sanctification of the believer."[50]

But there is another major development in the doctrine during this time, which Dulles describes in these terms: "The next major step . . . occurred in Northern Africa in the fourth and fifth centuries. Against the Donatists, who identified catholicity with the strict observance of the commandments, orthodox controversialists such as Optatus and Augustine held that catholicity meant communion with the Church spread over the whole world."[51] Here catholicity is concerned with the wholeness of worldwide fellowship rather than just doctrinal orthodoxy; in short, now schismatics in addition to heretics are conceived as outside the scope of the gospel's true reception. Clowney reminds us that groups like the Novatians and the Donatists were orthodox in theology; the professed problem was that they separated from the worldwide church and were restricted to one geographical area. Could they really claim to be (part of) the catholic church?[52]

Augustine (354-430) is illustrative of this development when he notes in his *On Faith and the Creed*, "We believe also in the holy church, intending thereby assuredly the catholic. . . . But heretics, in holding false opinions regarding God, do injury to the faith; while schismatics . . . in wicked separations break off from brotherly charity, although they may believe just what we believe. Therefore neither do the heretics belong to the church catholic . . . nor do the schismatics form a part of the same."[53] For Augustine, heresy *and* schism were anticatholic: the former because "the true faith, the right faith, the catholic faith . . . is not a bundle of opinions and prejudices . . . but founded on apostolic truth,"[54] the latter because "the church

---

[49]Williams, *Tradition, Scripture, and Interpretation*, 100.
[50]Williams, *Retrieving the Tradition*, 225.
[51]Dulles, *Catholicity*, 14.
[52]Clowney, *The Church*, 91.
[53]Di Berardino, *We Believe*, 75.
[54]Williams, *Retrieving the Tradition*, 226.

throughout the whole world is one, true, and catholic" and "the judgment of the whole world is reliable."[55] Augustine's notion of catholicity also involved christological and chronological aspects, for he notes in his *On the Catechizing of the Uninstructed* that "all the saints who lived upon the earth previous to the birth of our Lord Jesus Christ, although they were born antecedently, were nevertheless united under the Head with that universal body of which he is the Head."[56] Vincent of Lerins (d. 445), in addition to positing the "Vincentian canon" for which he is famous, also holds that catholicity requires brotherly love for, and fellowship with, the whole church.[57] He says, "He is the true and genuine Catholic who loves the truth of God, who loves the church, who loves the body of Christ, who esteems divine religion and the catholic faith above everything. . . . He will believe that and that only which he is sure the catholic church has held universally and from ancient time."[58] As Steinacker observes, in Vincent we see catholicity solidifying into its medieval conception, particularly as "the idea of universality . . . is coupled with that of continuity . . . [and thus] catholicity refers to identity maintained through the ages."[59]

Taking stock, it is clear that the doctrine of catholicity in this time takes on more complexity. Cyril is in many ways illustrative: his understanding of catholicity involves not only geographical (#2) and orthodox (#5) aspects but also differentiated (#7) and missional (#3) aspects. Williams can thus say that with Cyril we arrive at an understanding of catholicity that is truly expansive in scope: "It is a wholeness of faith that offers the complete counsel of God to all people in all times and places."[60] The creeds showcase the rise of orthodox catholicity (#5), leading Pelikan to note that for the fathers,

---

[55]Di Berardino, *We Believe*, 66.
[56]Quoted in Allison, *Historical Theology*, 571. Here we see the origin of *totus Christus*, one of the most significant manifestations of christological catholicity. For an excellent overview of its content and difficulties, see Kevin J. Vanhoozer, "Hocus Totus: The Elusive Wholeness of Christ," *Pro Ecclesia* 29 no. 1 (2020): 31-42.
[57]The canon relates to catholicity, for Vincent says, "In the Catholic Church itself, all possible care must be taken, that we hold that faith which has been *believed everywhere, always, by all*. For that is *truly and in the strictest sense 'Catholic,'* which, as the name itself and the reason of the thing declare, *comprehends all universally.*" Quoted in John R. Willis, ed., *The Teachings of the Church Fathers* (San Francisco: Ignatius Press, 2002), 95.
[58]Di Berardino, *We Believe*, 76-77.
[59]Quoted in Volf, *After Our Likeness*, 265.
[60]Williams, *Retrieving the Tradition*, 225.

"Catholicity was a mark both of the true church and of the true doctrine, for these were inseparable.... To identify orthodox doctrine, one had to identify its locus, which was the catholic church, neither Eastern nor Western, but universal throughout the civilized world."[61] The fact that these creeds and the councils they stemmed from were "ecumenical" showcases an emphasis on holistic (#1) and missional (#3) dimensions.

But the fourth and fifth centuries also demonstrate that not only does catholicity become more complex; it also becomes more contested. The Donatist controversy particularly unveiled the contested nature of catholicity. Dulles holds that "by the middle of the fourth century [catholicity] begins to take on a more precise meaning ... [referencing] the great Church in opposition to dissenting Christian groups."[62] The problem with this increasingly institutional emphasis (#6), as the Reformation will go on to make clear, is that one church's anticatholic schismatic is another church's truly catholic purifier. In the face of schism, attempts are made to posit certain criteria for catholicity, such as Vincent's conditions of holding that which demonstrates universality, ubiquity, and antiquity. While the question of *who exactly* it is that fulfills these catholic criteria turns out to be much harder than first supposed, the instinct points to an increasing recognition that catholicity properly involves the scope of all times (antiquity, #4), all peoples (universality, #3), and all places (ubiquity, #2). We thus see a gamut of conceptions of catholicity on display in the later patristic era; indeed, some form of holistic, geographical, missional, chronological, orthodox, institutional, differentiated, and christological aspects (#1–8) are represented and begin to blend into a premedieval synthesis. In short, catholicity becomes more dynamic and, simultaneously, more contested.[63]

3. *The medieval "consensus."* With the medieval era (roughly 500–1500), we enter a period of greater consensus regarding catholicity (though the depth of that consensus ultimately proved quite shallow). Radmacher

---

[61]Pelikan, *Christian Tradition*, 1:334.
[62]Dulles, *Catholicity*, 14.
[63]Part of that contestation came from non-Chalcedonian churches, such as the Coptic church. The fact that some churches did not adhere to the Chalcedonian definition of Christ as one person with two natures demonstrates why the orthodox dimension alone is not sufficient to mark out ecclesial catholicity.

describes the circumstances leading to a desire for greater ecclesial stability and doctrinal agreement: "Ancient Christianity faced a confusion of views in interpreting its fundamental facts. There needed to be a common faith . . . [which] was steadily productive of a catholic consciousness, an instinct for unity for all Christian[ity]."[64] This catholic consensus was thought to be built on the foundation of the apostles (Scripture) and the fathers (tradition). Such an understanding informed expressions of the church's catholicity, as seen in Boethius's (477–524) *On the Catholic Faith*: "This catholic church, then, spread throughout the world, is known by three particular marks: whatever is believed and taught in it has the authority of the Scriptures, or of universal tradition, or at least of its own and proper usage [of these]."[65] Gregory the Great's (540–604) *Moral Discourse on Job* shows forth a vision of the church as uniform and unchanging: "The churches, although many, make up one catholic church, diffused through the whole world."[66] In teaching on the parable of the laborers, he says, "Our founder . . . has a vineyard, namely the universal Church, which, from Abel the just to the last of the elect who will be born at the end of time, brings forth saints as a vine puts out young shoots."[67]

But one of the most significant developments in the doctrine of catholicity during the medieval period in the West was the increasingly exclusive association of the Roman Church with the catholic church. So with Alcuin (735–804) we see the designation "Roman" enter alongside the creedal attributes when he says, "We take our stand firmly within the borders of the apostolic doctrine and of the holy Roman church, following [its] established authority and clinging to [its] sacred doctrine, introducing nothing new and accepting nothing apart from what we have in [its] catholic writings."[68] Hincmar of Reims (806–882) demonstrates a similar conflation: "The catholic, apostolic, and holy Roman church . . . has given birth to us in faith, fed us with catholic milk, nourished us with breasts full of heaven until we were ready for solid food, and led us by her orthodox discipline to perfect

---

[64]Radmacher, *Nature of the Church*, 39.
[65]Pelikan, *Christian Tradition*, 1:333.
[66]Pelikan, *Christian Tradition*, 1:334.
[67]Quoted in Nicholas Lash, *Believing Three Ways in One God: A Reading of the Apostles' Creed* (Notre Dame, IN: University of Notre Dame Press, 1993), 87.
[68]Quoted in Allison, *Historical Theology*, 573.

manhood."[69] Thus in the medieval era what is meant by the "catholic church" is largely an uncontroversial identity with the Roman institution.

An additional emphasis in this (fleeting) moment of doctrinal consensus was on the threefold scope of the church through all times, people, and places. Guitmond of Aversa (d. 1094) notes that "[Catholicity consists in what has been taught] everywhere over a long period of time. . . . The universal faith of the church [was] not recent, not a matter of this or that man, but of the whole world."[70] James of Viterbo (1255–1307) similarly defined catholicity as being "through the entire world . . . [and] from the beginning of the world through its end."[71] The scholastics also assumed the given doctrine of the church's catholicity as a connection to the whole of all times, peoples, and places.[72] Aquinas is characteristic in his exposition of the Apostles' Creed: "The Church is Catholic, i.e. universal, first with respect to place, because it is everywhere in the world. . . . Secondly, the Church is universal with respect to the state of men, because no one is rejected, whether master or slave, male or female. . . . Thirdly, it is universal with respect to time . . . because this Church began from the time of Abel and will last to the end of the world."[73] Thomas emphasizes the threefold scope because he "sees catholicity as freedom from all the limits of particularity. Because it possesses this property the Church . . . is able to transcend the frontiers of place and time and to include people of every kind and condition."[74]

Of course, the Great Schism between East and West that had built for centuries, broke open in 1054, froze over at the Council of Florence, and was cemented by the sack of Constantinople in 1453, was the fly in the ointment of the medieval "catholic consensus" and complicated the picture of the church in the Middle Ages as exhibiting doctrinal uniformity.[75] But even in the West the picture of the Roman church as a unified whole was

---

[69] Quoted in Allison, *Historical Theology*, 573.
[70] Quoted in Pelikan, *Christian Tradition*, 2:217.
[71] Quoted in Pelikan, *Christian Tradition*, 3:99.
[72] This is largely because "the doctrine of the Church as developed by Cyprian and Augustine was [understood as] quite complete; thus, the Scholastics have very little to say about it." Radmacher, *Nature of the Church*, 43.
[73] Quoted in Dulles, *Catholicity*, 181.
[74] Dulles, *Catholicity*, 15.
[75] Eastern Orthodox views of catholicity fall beyond the scope of this project. Dulles summarizes the Eastern view as centering on orthodox catholicity (#5), but one can easily see it places just as strong of an emphasis on institutional (#6) and liturgical (#9) aspects. See Dulles, *Catholicity*, 185.

harder to support than is often admitted. One example of dissent initiated on behalf of the catholic church is found in the Waldensian movement, which refused to recognize the pope as the head of the catholic church and initiated a lay ministry of hearing confession and even administering the sacraments. Wycliffe (1328–1384) provides another example of doctrinal diversity in this era; he held, in Allison's words, an "idea of the church as composed of the elect [which] meant that membership in the empirical Catholic Church provides no guarantee that people are truly saved or members of the [catholic] church . . . not even for its own Pope."[76] Hus (1369–1415) built on Wycliffe's definition of the church as "the universality of the predestinate" by claiming that "every pilgrim ought faithfully to believe the holy, catholic church" while arguing one could be a member of the catholic church without being in the Roman Church.[77] These reforming rumblings and differing conceptions of the church as catholic demonstrated what the Reformation would soon make clear: catholicity was still very much contested.

Taking stock, Pelikan summarizes that in the heyday of Christendom "declarations of loyalty to the catholic tradition . . . [demonstrated the] assumption that it was a unified whole, resting on the consensus of the orthodox teachers of the church . . . [so that Bede] spoke of 'the unanimous consensus of all in the catholic faith' . . . [and Alcuin could] refer to 'the total unanimity of the catholic church . . . shining brightly through the whole world.'"[78] This assumption proved to be much too simplistic, as recognized by Nicolas of Cusa (1401–1464). On the one hand, Nicolas states in his *Catholic Concordance* that "[it is through] concordance [that] the church is called 'catholic' in conformity with Christ. . . . [Indeed,] all Christian doctrine and any constitution or tradition ought to be such that it is in consensus with the universal church."[79] And yet, Nicolas also recognized in his work *On Learned Ignorance* that there was much legitimate theological

---

The classic expression of the Eastern view is found in John Meyendorff, *Catholicity and the Church* (Crestwood, NY: St. Vladimir's Seminary Press, 1983).
[76] Allison, *Historical Theology*, 576.
[77] Quoted in Williams, *Retrieving the Tradition*, 227.
[78] Pelikan, *Christian Tradition*, 3:9-10. Dulles's summary is similar: "In the Middle Ages there was no major shift. Bonaventure, Albertus Magnus, and Thomas Aquinas follow the patristic authors, especially Augustine." Dulles, *Catholicity*, 15.
[79] Pelikan, *Christian Tradition*, 3:99.

diversity in the catholic church: "So long as we are here on earth as pilgrims, the truth of our faith cannot consist in anything else but the Spirit of Christ . . . so that there might be diversity in concordance in the one Jesus."[80] Though we see here a recognition of legitimate doctrinal diversity (and thus an emphasis on differentiated catholicity, #7), we can summarize that the medieval era demonstrates an emphasis on catholicity as doctrinal uniformity (orthodox catholicity, #5) and institutional continuity with Rome (institutional catholicity, #6). These enabled, to the medieval mind, a connection to the whole church in all places, among all peoples and through all times (catholicity, #1–4). It would take what Dulles calls "the first great crisis of catholicity" to demonstrate that the criteria of who *genuinely* belonged to this catholic church and who *rightly* stood in the catholic tradition were passionately contested.[81]

4. Reformational insights. We begin with Pelikan's assessment that "the Protestant Reformation of the sixteenth century made a decisive contribution to the development of the doctrine of the Catholicity of the church. . . . It was because of the Reformation that in the West the doctrine of Catholicity, and the Catholicity of doctrine, came to be defined, and hence also circumscribed, with a particularity that had not been deemed necessary before."[82] Indeed, the conflict between Rome and the Reformers became the refining fire of a doctrine that had never been critically assessed and changed the status quo of the doctrine all the way to our own time. Particularly, varied conceptions of catholicity were wielded in different ways for the largely polemical purpose of demonstrating that the Roman Catholic or Protestant Church had the greatest claim to catholicity.[83] At this critical juncture the veneer of consensus regarding catholicity gave way to renewed theological reflection on the creedal attribute amid many contested claims.

---

[80]Pelikan, *Christian Tradition*, 3:99.
[81]Dulles, *Catholicity*, 15. Aulén notes that "the Reformation was the most profound rupture in the life of Christendom." Gustaf Aulén, *Reformation and Catholicity*, trans. Eric H. Wahlstrom (Philadelphia: Muhlenberg Press, 1961), v. The legitimate objection that the Great Schism rivals the Reformation as Christendom's deepest rupture (contra Aulén) and as the first crisis of catholicity (contra Dulles) need not detain us.
[82]Pelikan, *Christian Tradition*, 4:245.
[83]Reinhard Hütter argues that "the real business of the church of the Reformation was . . . its struggle with its counterpart, the Roman Catholic Church. The issue at stake for both sides was and is true catholicity." Reinhard Hütter, *Bound to Be Free: Evangelical Catholic Engagements in Ecclesiology, Ethics, and Ecumenism* (Grand Rapids, MI: Eerdmans, 2004), 78.

Calvin and certain Roman Catholic leaders along with the decrees of Trent will be used to illustrate.

Protestant case study: Calvin. John Calvin (1509–1564) is perhaps the clearest embodiment of Reformation catholicity. Of all the Reformers he demonstrated one of the sharpest visions of the church's centrality in God's redemptive economy, earning him the epithet "the churchman of the Reformation."[84] Calvin didn't just have a robust doctrine of the church's catholicity; he also demonstrated a deep catholicity of doctrine and practice.[85] But here we are particularly concerned with Calvin's understanding of what it means that the church is catholic, an understanding that emerged amid an extremely tumultuous ecclesial scene. Inevitably Calvin's notions of the church and its catholicity were developed against the backdrop of what he perceived as grievous errors and abuses of the Roman church that created an extremely dangerous situation for the whole church. In answer to Rome's exclusive claim to catholicity, Calvin pointed to the inherent dangers of remaining within the Roman Catholic communion. He conceded that breaking away from Rome was not desirable but insisted that it was not the Protestants who were the schismatics *but the Roman Catholics themselves* when they abandoned the apostolic foundation, the tradition of the Fathers, and the faithful remnant of the medieval church. It was the apostasy of Rome that forced the lamentable Protestant departure after repentance and reform became impossible prospects, enabling Hesselink to conclude that "Calvin, like Luther, left the Roman Church because he felt he was forced out of it in his desire to be faithful to the gospel."[86] Kelly summarizes Calvin's entire project in this way: "Calvin thought that he was reforming and purifying the remnants of the church back to her original catholicity by recalling her to the voice of her Lord and Savior."[87]

---

[84] I. John Hesselink, "Calvin's Theology," in *The Cambridge Companion to John Calvin*, ed. Donald K. McKim (Cambridge: Cambridge University Press, 2004), 87.

[85] By his catholicity of doctrine, we mean the way Calvin sees his teaching and his church as in the stream of catholic tradition (i.e., the Great Tradition). By his catholicity of practice, we mean the ways Calvin labored to maintain connection with the whole church. Indeed, his work seeking a common mind among the Reformers and guiding the Reformation toward reform rather than schism serves as testimony to Calvin's catholic spirit. Hesselink says, "None of the reformers had . . . a larger vision of [the church's] catholicity . . . [for] no one in the sixteenth century worked as tirelessly toward achieving its unity." See Hesselink, "Calvin's Theology," 87.

[86] Hesselink, "Calvin's Theology," 88.

[87] Douglas Kelley, "The Catholicity of Calvin's Theology," in *Tributes to John Calvin: A Celebration of His Quincentenary*, ed. David W. Hall (Phillipsburg, NJ: P&R, 2010), 215.

While Calvin's ecclesiology is often misunderstood as *primarily* concerned with the "invisible" church, in point of fact Calvin insists that the church is the primary "*external* means . . . by which God invites us into the society of Christ and holds us therein."[88] This visible means of grace is central in Calvin's mind; he says "there is no other way to enter into life unless this mother conceive us in her womb, give us birth, nourish us at her breast, and . . . keep us under her care and guidance."[89] For Calvin the invisible church of all the elect who are united to Christ by faith is made visible (imperfectly) in the twofold marks of the church: "Wherever we see the Word of God purely preached and heard, and the sacraments administered according to Christ's institution, there, it is not to be doubted, a church of God exists."[90]

Calvin's doctrine of catholicity emerges out of his larger ecclesiological framework. In the *Institutes*, explicit discussion of the doctrine of catholicity is limited to the section where Calvin asks what the relationship between the church and the creed is. In the first edition (1536) the confession is rather elaborate and puts emphasis on the *invisible* church:

> We believe the holy catholic church—that is the whole number of the elect . . . whether dead or still living; of the living, in whatever lands they live, or wherever among the nations they have been scattered—to be one church and society, and one people of God. Of it, Christ . . . is Leader and Ruler. . . . Now this society is catholic, that is universal, because there could not be two or three churches. But all God's elect are so united and conjoined in Christ that, as they are dependent on one head, they also grow into one body.[91]

By the second edition (1539) Calvin tilts more toward the *visible* church, noting that "the universal church is the multitude gathered from all nations, which, dispersed from place to place, yet agrees in the one truth of the divine doctrine and is kept together by the bond of the same religion. In it the singular churches, which are distributed through city and country . . . are

---

[88]John Calvin, *Institutes of the Christian Religion*, trans. Ford Lewis Battles, ed. John T. McNeill (Louisville, KY: Westminster John Knox, 2001), 1011, emphasis added.
[89]Calvin, *Institutes*, 1016.
[90]Calvin, *Institutes*, 1023.
[91]Quoted in Klaas Runia, "Catholicity in the Reformed Confessions and in Reformed Theology," in Schrotenboer, *Catholicity*, 61.

so comprised that each one of them legitimately bears the name and authority of the church."[92] By the final edition (1559), there is a much briefer statement that synthesizes the invisible/visible tension and emphasizes union with Christ. Calvin says the church as "catholic" means that "there could not be two or three churches unless Christ be torn asunder—which cannot happen."[93] Calvin connects catholicity to unity and to Christ, saying "all the elect are so united in Christ that as they are dependent on one Head ... [they are] knit together as are the limbs of a body."[94] Here Calvin sees catholicity as a descriptor of all the elect, the whole of those united to Christ from among all times, peoples, and places. He builds on conceptualities in the tradition while anchoring them in God's electing decree; it is only the church grounded here that can be unquestionably said to be "one, holy, catholic and apostolic."

We also find Calvin's doctrine of catholicity on display in the *Catechism of the Church of Geneva* (1545). To the question "What is the meaning of the attribute catholic or universal?" the answer is, "By it we are taught that, as there is one head of all the faithful, so all ought to unite in one body, so that there may be one Church spread throughout the whole earth, and not a number of Churches."[95] We also see it in Calvin's interaction with Jacopo Sadoleto, a priest who wrote to Calvin's Geneva with the express goal of winning them back to the Roman Catholic fold. In his *Reply to Sadoleto* (1539) Calvin inists that "the Church ... is the society of all the saints ... which, spread over the whole world, and existing in all ages, yet bound together by one doctrine and the one Spirit of Christ, cultivates and observes unity of faith and brotherly concord. With this Church we deny that we have any disagreement. Rather, as we revere her as our mother, so we desire to remain in her bosom."[96] Calvin here claims continuity with the catholic tradition, asserting that, contrary to Sadoleto's accusations, "our agreement with antiquity is far closer than yours. ... All we have attempted

---

[92]Quoted in Runia, "Catholicity," 61-62.
[93]Calvin, *Institutes*, 1014.
[94]Calvin, *Institutes*, 1014.
[95]John Calvin, *Theological Treatises*, trans. and ed. J. K. S. Reid (Louisville, KY: Westminster John Knox, 2001), 103.
[96]John Calvin, Jacopo Sadoleto, and John C. Olin, *A Reformation Debate: Sadoleto's Letter to the Genevans and Calvin's Reply*, ed. John C. Olin (Grand Rapids, MI: Baker Book House, 1976), 55-56.

has been to renew the ancient form of the Church ... which the Apostles instituted ... [and was found] in the age of Chrysostom and Basil, among the Greeks, and of Cyprian, Ambrose, and Augustine among the Latins."[97] Calvin says it is Rome that sacrifices catholicity at the altar of Roman exclusivity and innovation, noting that "we have not acted without the concurrence of the ancient Church.... [Indeed] we are armed not only with the energy of the Divine Word, but with the aid of the holy Fathers also.... [such that] the ancient Church is clearly on our side, and opposes you."[98]

Roman Catholic case study: Select leaders and Trent. Jacopo Sadoleto (1477–1547) wrote to the Genevans in hopes of winning them back to the Roman Church. He addressed them as "brethren in Christ" and with the opening salutation: "Peace to you and with us, that is, with the Catholic Church, the mother of all, both us and you."[99] Sadoleto expresses the view that had built much steam over the medieval period: that the Roman institution was to be identified directly with the catholic (i.e., true) church. This assumption is behind his question of which is more pleasing to God and expedient for salvation: "believing what the Catholic Church throughout the whole world, now for more than fifteen hundred years [has taught] ... or [following] innovations introduced within these twenty-five years by crafty ... men?"[100] At one point his understanding of catholicity becomes explicit when he says, "The Catholic Church is that which in all parts, as well as the present time in every region of the world, united and consenting in Christ, has been always and everywhere directed by the one Spirit of Christ; in which Church no dissention can exist; for all its parts are connected to each other, and breathe together."[101] Rome's catholic identity rightly leads to its catholic aspirations in Sadoleto's mind; he notes that "for this the Catholic Church always labors: our concord and unity in the same Spirit, that all men, however divided by space or time, and so incapable of coming together as one body, may yet be both cherished and ruled by one Spirit, who is always and everywhere the same."[102]

---

[97]Calvin, Sadoleto, and Olin, *Reformation Debate*, 56.
[98]Calvin, Sadoleto, and Olin, *Reformation Debate*, 65-68.
[99]Calvin, Sadoleto, and Olin, *Reformation Debate*, 23.
[100]Calvin, Sadoleto, and Olin, *Reformation Debate*, 34-35.
[101]Calvin, Sadoleto, and Olin, *Reformation Debate*, 35.
[102]Calvin, Sadoleto, and Olin, *Reformation Debate*, 41.

Similar sentiments are expressed by another prominent Roman Catholic leader of the later sixteenth century, Robert Bellarmine (1542–1621). One of Rome's staunchest defenders and a key contributor to anti-Protestant polemical theology, he makes it clear in no uncertain terms that only Rome is catholic because "only the Roman Church has spread over the whole world and through all times; heretical communities spread only at certain times and in certain countries."[103] For Bellarmine, the catholic church is "a union of the same Christian faith, bound by confession and the communion of the same sacraments under the dominion of legitimate pastors and chiefly of the one Vicar of Christ on earth."[104] Such an understanding had no room for Protestants to participate in catholicity; they had rejected, in the words of Ignatius Loyola (1491–1556), "the true spouse of Jesus Christ, our holy mother, our infallible and orthodox mistress, the Catholic Church, whose authority is exercised over us by the hierarchy."[105]

But it was with the Council of Trent (1545–1563) that Roman conceptions of catholicity solidified not just as exclusively Roman but also as explicitly anti-Protestant. The council tackled many of the pressing issues that needed addressing in the Roman Church, from reforming longstanding clerical abuses to repudiating Protestant calls for the reform of doctrine. Justo González thus says of Trent that while it took important steps to reform the life and worship of the church, its greatest legacy became the way it committed Catholicism to being virulently anti-Protestant and linked up catholicity with doctrinal uniformity for the next four hundred years.[106] Trent offered an understanding of catholicity that incorporates much of what we have seen in the tradition so far and, ironically, even see in many Protestant conceptions. For instance, the council speaks of the church's catholicity by drawing attention to the scope of all times, peoples and places. In one place it says that "unlike states of human institution . . . she is not confined to any one country or class of men, but embraces within the amplitude of her love

---

[103]Quoted in Johann Auer, *The Church: The Universal Sacrament of Salvation* (Washington, DC: The Catholic University of America Press, 1993), 424.
[104]Quoted in Runia, "Catholicity," 58.
[105]Henry Bettenson and Chris Maunder, eds., *The Documents of the Christian Church*, 3rd ed. (Oxford: Oxford University Press, 1999), 272.
[106]Justo L. González, *The Story of Christianity: The Early Church to the Present Day* (Peabody, MA: Prince Press, 2007), 120.

all mankind."[107] In another decree it says that within the catholic church are "all the faithful who have existed from Adam to the present day, or who shall exist, in the profession of the true faith, to the end of time."[108] But ultimately Trent's anti-Protestant polemic committed it to a primarily *institutional* understanding of catholicity. For one, the "the sects of heretics" were unable to justify their catholicity because of their geographical limitation and minority status. Roger Haight can say here that "universality [for Trent] means that no salvation can be found outside [the Roman] church. . . . [holding] that something so universal must be true, while something local . . . is not."[109] Ultimately Protestants couldn't be catholic because they had broken communion with Rome and its bishops (especially the pope, who is understood to maintain "Petrine succession"), a communion understood as necessary to being part of the catholic church. Such communion was essential because, as the catechism of the council made clear: "The Savior appointed Peter head and pastor of all the faithful, when he committed to his care the feeding of all the sheep, in such ample terms that he willed the very same power of ruling and governing the entire Church to descend to Peter's successors."[110] Catholicity thus conceived sets the backdrop for the oath of allegiance which Pope Pius IV called for in his bull *Injunctum Nobis* (1564): "I acknowledge the holy Catholic Apostolic Roman Church for the mother and mistress of all churches; and I promise and swear true obedience to the Bishop of Rome, successor of St. Peter, Prince of the Apostles, and Vicar of Jesus Christ."[111]

Assessment. We see the Reformation crisis unveil a fundamental disagreement about the catholicity of the church. On the Reformational side we saw how Calvin grounds catholicity christologically (#8), making much of the fact that the church is united to Christ by faith and thus makes up his body. Calvin holds that this body can't ultimately be torn asunder because it is impossible for Christ to be so treated; the implication is that catholicity is strongly connected to unity and thus can largely be

---

[107] Quoted in Roger Haight, *Christian Community in History*, vol. 2 (New York: Continuum, 2005), 268-69.
[108] Quoted in Haight, *Christian Community*, 2:269.
[109] Haight, *Christian Community*, 2:269.
[110] Quoted in Stephen W. Sykes, "The Papacy and Power: An Anglican Perspective," in *Church Unity and the Papal Office: An Ecumenical Dialogue on John Paul II's Encyclical Ut Unum Sint*, ed. Carl E. Braaten and Robert W. Jenson (Grand Rapids, MI: Eerdmans, 2001), 62.
[111] Quoted in Runia, "Catholicity," 58.

understood through the aspect of differentiated catholicity (#7). Of course, Calvin and other Reformers with him also followed a strand of the Augustinian emphasis (largely assumed in the medieval period) that the church's catholicity marks out a fellowship inclusive of all places, peoples, and times (#2-4). As for institutional catholicity (#6), Calvin and the Reformers were not willing to follow Rome's understanding of it; rather, they emphasized that the visible, local church was an essential means of grace and the place where the full catholicity enjoyed by the invisible church grounded in election became manifest (if imperfectly). Ultimately the Reformers held that doctrinal faithfulness (orthodox catholicity, #5), specifically faithfulness with regard to the gospel as the church's "greatest treasure," was a more central and significant aspect of catholicity than any other. Calvin never failed to emphasize the importance of preserving the "good deposit" of orthodox doctrine (vs. Roman innovations and corruptions) passed down in the catholic tradition through the ages. Clowney says that the Reformers consistently responded to Roman polemics "by pointing to another dimension of catholicity: its extension in time. . . . [The Reformation] could claim continuity with the early catholic church, a continuity that had been severed by the false teachings and corrupt practices of Rome. For Luther and Calvin, the preaching of the apostolic gospel defined the true church. Apart from gospel orthodoxy, Rome's claim to catholicity was meaningless."[112] Indeed, Jonker can even claim that "the Reformation. . . . contended that the norm for true catholicity could not be sought in mere geographical and temporal universality, nor in the general acceptance of the doctrines of the Church, but only in the adherence to the Word of God."[113] In other words, for the Reformers, the creedal note of apostolicity always qualified catholicity. This was the key to achieving their aim: reforming the catholic church by recovering the genuinely catholic (i.e., apostolic) tradition.

On the Roman Catholic side, we saw a shared emphasis on the threefold scope of catholicity: the church spoken of in the creed was one that existed through the whole of all times, peoples, and places (#2–4). Bellarmine among others emphasized sacramental continuity as marking out the

---

[112]Clowney, *The Church*, 91-92.
[113]Jonker, "Catholicity," 21.

catholic church (liturgical catholicity, #9). A significant part of Rome's polemic against the Reformers contributed to the emergence of numerical catholicity (#10) as a proposed aspect of catholicity. Clowney says of this doctrinal innovation, "The apologists of the Counter-Reformation added numerical preponderance; the Catholic Church was the true church for it enclosed the largest number of members."[114] But particularly significant in terms of Rome's anti-Protestant polemic was the spatial dimension, for as Clowney notes, "Augustine's argument [against the Donatists] was used again against the Reformers. . . . [Rome asked:] how could the Reformers claim to represent the church catholic when only the Roman Catholic Church was spread around the world?"[115] The Donatist *redux* demonstrated Rome's central claim against the Reformation: Protestant provincialism (vs. Rome's geographical expansion) revealed that Protestants, like the Donatists, were schismatics worthy of condemnation for rending the one church. Institutional catholicity (#6) thus became more and more central to the Roman Catholic conception; indeed, both orthodox catholicity (#5) and christological catholicity (#8) were ultimately understood to be dependent on it. By Trent's end a huge difference of opinion had emerged as to which church stood in the catholic stream and how a particular church was properly connected to the whole (holistic catholicity, #1).

5. Modern contributions. Here space constraints prevent anything but a survey of certain developments of the doctrine of catholicity in the modern period. Two case studies will be utilized to do so. First we will examine Roman Catholic developments, particularly focused on the significance of Vatican II for contemporary Roman conceptions of catholicity. Finally we will survey some of the contributions of the ecumenical movement toward a more dynamic doctrine of catholicity.

Roman Catholic developments. In the Roman Catholic tradition the emphases of Trent largely carried all the way through to the twentieth century before encountering the *aggiornamento* and *ressourcement* efforts of Vatican II (1962–1965). What occurred at Vatican II that led to the thawing of the hardened institutional conception of catholicity established at Trent, and what new conception emerged? Beyond the fact that the likes of Henri

---

[114]Clowney, *The Church*, 91.
[115]Clowney, *The Church*, 91.

de Lubac and Yves Congar exercised particular influence on the ecclesial documents produced by Vatican II (e.g., *Dei Verbum, Lumen Gentium*), we can conclude with Ruddy that "the council was essentially an ecclesiological one, setting forth Catholicism's self-understanding through a recovery of the fullness of the Christian tradition [*ressourcement*] and a response to the sign of the times [*aggiornamento*]."[116] A particular emphasis of this "updating" involved articulating an "ecclesiology of communion and catholicity" that fluctuated between an emphasis on the universal and the local church.[117]

This is nowhere more evident than in *Lumen Gentium* (henceforth *LG*). Several very important statements are made there regarding the Roman Catholic understanding of the church's catholicity. First it is acknowledged that "all men are called to belong to the new people of God. Wherefore this People, while remaining one and unique, is to be spread throughout the whole world and must exist in all ages, so that the purpose of God's will may be fulfilled."[118] That purpose is expressly that Jesus "might be Teacher [i.e., Prophet], King, and Priest of all, the Head of the new and universal people of the sons of God. For this [purpose] God finally sent His Son's Spirt as Lord and Lifegiver."[119] From this theological foundation "it follows that among all the nations of earth there is but one People of God, which takes its citizens from every race. . . . For all the faithful scattered throughout the world are in communion with each other in the Spirit."[120] It goes on: "This attribute of universality which adorns the People of God is that gift of the Lord whereby the Catholic Church tends efficaciously and constantly to recapitulate the whole of humanity with all its riches under Christ the head in the unity of his Spirit. In virtue of this catholicity each part brings its particular gifts to the others and the whole Church, so that the whole and the parts are enriched by the mutual sharing of gifts and the striving of all for fullness of unity."[121]

---

[116]Christopher Ruddy, *The Local Church: Tillard and the Future of Catholic Ecclesiology* (New York: Crossroad, 2006), 46.
[117]Ruddy, *Local Church*, 46.
[118]John H. Leith, ed., *The Creeds of the Church*, rev ed. (Richmond, VA: John Knox Press, 1973), 463.
[119]Leith, *Creeds*, 463.
[120]Leith, *Creeds*, 463-64.
[121]Quoted in Dulles, *Catholicity*, 183.

But the most significant developments concerning catholicity involve Rome's relationship to other Christian communions. Speaking of the catholic unity of God's people, *LG* surprises with its statement that "there belong to it or are related to it in various ways, the [Roman] Catholic faithful *as well as all those who believe in Christ.*"[122] Vatican II ultimately declared that the one, holy, catholic, and apostolic church was "constituted and organized in the world as a society [and] *subsists* in the Catholic Church, which is governed by the successor of Peter and by the bishops in union with that successor."[123] Lest we hear in this demarcation of the catholic church the same exclusionary language of Trent, we should remember that the *est* of the original draft was replaced with *subsistit*, indicating a movement toward a broader position on catholicity.[124] Such a hope is fanned, if only faintly, by the next statement: "Many elements of sanctification and of truth can be found outside of [Rome's] visible structure. These elements [are] gifts [that] properly belong to the Church of Christ [and] possess an inner dynamism toward Catholic unity."[125] When we recall that Vatican II was the first time Protestants were officially referred to by Catholics as "brethren" (though "separated"), we recognize a palpable sense of *rapprochement* impossible in yesteryear. Dulles acknowledges that Vatican II predicated catholicity to the Church of Christ rather than the Roman Church (though, as we saw, the council declared that the Church of Christ "subsists in" the Roman Church) and left open the possibility of a second tier catholicity for non-Roman churches.[126] For the council catholicity is "cautiously ecumenical rather than narrowly confessional," and is understood "not as a monotonous repetition of identical elements but rather as reconciled diversity."[127] This is evident in the *Catechism of the Catholic Church*, which quotes Paul VI: "Let us be very careful not to conceive of the universal Church as the simple sum, or . . . the more or less anomalous federation of essentially different particular churches. In the mind of the Lord the Church is universal by vocation and

---

[122]Leith, *Creeds*, 465, emphasis added.
[123]Leith, *Creeds*, 460, emphasis added.
[124]This movement was confirmed in many ways by *Ut Unum Sint* (1995), an encyclical of Pope John Paul II that largely demonstrated an appreciation for ecumenism and an openness to other Christian communions.
[125]Leith, *Creeds*, 460.
[126]Dulles, *Catholicity*, 21.
[127]Dulles, *Catholicity*, 21, 24.

mission, but when she puts down her roots in a variety of cultural, social, and human terrains, she takes on different external expressions and appearances in each part of the world."[128] This is quite a change from the uniformity emphasized at Trent.

Ecumenical developments. The ecumenical movement has been defined as "the quest of Orthodox, Roman Catholic, Anglican, Old Catholic, and most Protestant churches for reconciliation, and the restoration of their visible unity in faith, sacramental life, and witness in the world."[129] The movement surged in the twentieth century and has been one of the most significant contributors to the development of the doctrine of the church's catholicity, and this because, as Hendrikus Berkhof has put it, "catholicity is . . . the purpose and fruit of ecumenicity."[130] Albert C. Outler explains how the mindset of the ecumenical movement relates to catholicity:

> It is axiomatic in modern ecumenism that the recomposition of unity aims at the *fullness* of Christian community. . . . The Christian family is incurably diverse; this is one of the plainest lessons of church history. But because of its common confession of Jesus Christ as Lord and Savior, it also aspires to be a genuine comm*unity*. Thus, the goal of true ecumenism is unity-in-creative-diversity and a natural diversity that lives gracefully within the compass of authentic unity.[131]

The movement, which draws in diverse communions from all over the world, thus has major implications for how we think about the church as catholic today.

The World Council of Churches, and specifically the Faith and Order commission, has played the lead role in facilitating this ecumenical movement.[132] Two of the WCC's assemblies have been particularly significant for developing an ecumenical understanding of the church's catholicity. One of these is the third assembly, New Delhi (1961), where a strong

---

[128] *The Catechism of the Catholic Church*, 2nd ed. (Vatican: Libreria Editrice Vaticana, 2000), 221.
[129] Thomas E. FitzGerald, *The Ecumenical Movement: An Introductory History* (Westport, CT: Praeger, 2004), 1.
[130] Quoted in Runia, "Catholicity," 74.
[131] Quoted in Donald F. Durnbaugh, "Free Churches, Baptists, and Ecumenism: Origins and Implications," in *Baptists and Ecumenism*, ed. William Jerry Boney and Glenn A. Igleheart (Valley Forge, PA: Judson Press, 1980), 3.
[132] The Lausanne Conference of 1974 and the subsequent Lausanne Movement provides an evangelical parallel, one specifically focused on the task of world evangelization.

interrelationship between church unity and catholicity is identified. The assembly report sets forth its understanding of the "organic unity that we seek" as a unity "being made visible as *all in each place* who are baptized into Christ Jesus and confess him as Lord and Savior are brought by the Holy Spirit into one fully-committed fellowship, holding the one apostolic faith, preaching the one Gospel, breaking the one bread, joining in common prayer, and having a corporate life reaching out in witness and service *to all* and who at the same time are united *with the whole Christian fellowship in all places and all ages*."[133]

While catholicity was in the backdrop of New Delhi's emphasis on (diversified) unity, at the fourth assembly, Uppsala (1968), it takes center stage. The assembly report begins with a section titled "The Holy Spirit and the Catholic Church" and notes that

> God makes catholicity available to men through the ministry of Christ in his Church. The purpose of Christ is to bring people of all times, of all races, of all places, of all conditions, into an organic and living unity in Christ by the Holy Spirit under the universal fatherhood of God. This unity is not solely external; it has a deeper, internal dimension, which is also expressed by the term 'catholicity.' Catholicity reaches its completion when what God has already begun in history is finally disclosed and fulfilled.[134]

The emphasis is now on a (unified) diversity, and it recognizes that there is an internal dimension to church unity (not just an external dimension) that catholicity, an organic connectedness to the whole, marks out. The comprehensive theological vision of catholicity at Uppsala is summarized well by Feurth: "The ecclesiological framework within which the notion of catholicity was set . . . [understands] the Church on earth, preeminently [as] a *koinonia*, a participation in God. . . . Even though the Church lives now in a state of division, her unity and her catholicity are assured by the faithful presence of Christ and his Spirit. Therefore, her catholicity has both a Christological and pneumatological basis."[135] According to the Uppsala report,

---

[133]Quoted in Carl E. Braaten and Robert W. Jenson, eds., *In One Body Through the Cross: The Princeton Proposal for Christian Unity* (Grand Rapids, MI: Eerdmans, 2003), 21-22, emphasis added.
[134]Quoted in Dulles, *Catholicity*, 183-84.
[135]Patrick W. Feurth, *The Concept of Catholicity in the Documents of the World Council of Churches 1948-1968* (Rome: Editrace Anselmiana, 1973), 254.

catholicity is a gift given by God through Christ in the Spirit, and "since it has been given this gift, the Church *is* catholic, but at the same time, no church can claim to *be* catholic. The Church is constantly on the way to *becoming* catholic. Catholicity is a task yet to be fulfilled."[136]

Since Uppsala, other WCC documents have consolidated the ecumenical understanding of catholicity. In *Confessing the One Faith* (Faith and Order Paper 153) it is recognized that the "catholic nature of the Church is realized and expressed in a great diversity of Christian life and witness among all peoples in space and time."[137] In *The Church: Toward a Common Vision* (Faith and Order Paper 214) the scope of catholicity is highlighted: "The Church is catholic because of the abundant goodness of God. . . . [For] through the life-giving power of God, the Church's mission transcends all barriers and proclaims the Gospel to all peoples."[138] A section from the ninth assembly (Porto Alegre, 2006) titled "Called to Be the One Church" emphasized that "the catholicity of the Church expresses the fullness, integrity, and totality of its life in Christ through the Holy Spirit in all times and places. This mystery is expressed in each community of baptized believers in which the apostolic faith is confessed and lived, the gospel is proclaimed, and the sacraments are celebrated."[139] It goes on, "Each church fulfils its catholicity when it is in communion with the other churches. . . . The catholicity of the Church is expressed most visibly in sharing holy communion and in a mutually recognized and reconciled ministry."[140] Notice the emphasis on orthodox catholicity (#5), institutional catholicity (#6), and liturgical catholicity (#9) as central in churches being connected to a diversified whole (#1, 7).

Assessment. As we look across these developments in the modern period, several themes emerge. The first is that we see a consistent emphasis across

---

[136]Quoted in Miriam Haar, "The Struggle for an Organic, Conciliar and Diverse Church: Models of Church Unity in Earlier Stages of the Ecumenical Dialogue," in *Ecumenical Ecclesiology: Unity, Diversity, and Otherness in a Fragmented World*, ed. Gesa Elsbeth Thiessen (London: T&T Clark, 2009), 56.

[137]*Confessing the One Faith*, Faith and Order Paper 153 (Geneva: WCC Publications, 1991), 88-89.

[138]*The Church: Toward a Common Vision*, Faith and Order Paper 214 (Geneva: WCC Publishing, 2013), 14.

[139]Quoted in John St-Helier Gibaut, "Catholicity, Faith and Order, and the Unity of the Church," *Ecumenical Review* 63, no. 2 (July 2011): 183.

[140]Quoted in Gibaut, "Catholicity," 183.

the board on the scope of catholicity as inclusive of all places, peoples, and times (#2–4). The aspect of inclusive mission is particularly emphasized by the ecumenical movement, building on the Protestant missions emphasis of the nineteenth century. The movement also made Roman polemical claims to exclusive catholicity based on worldwide distribution unconvincing, since now many more churches than the Roman one had "gone global."

For the Roman Catholic tradition, the catholic essence of the church is Christ himself, and it is certainly not alone here: each tradition has emphasized the centrality of christological catholicity (#8). But while for the Reformed tradition (witnessed in Calvin) this centers on union with Christ by faith, for Catholicism christological catholicity often means an emphasis on christological "fullness," with the church understood as part of the *totus Christus*. With Vatican II the Roman Catholic tradition also begins emphasizing a "communion theology," viewing the church in more sacramental (rather than institutional) terms. This led to a stronger emphasis on the liturgical aspect of catholicity (#9), for the church's catholicity is thought to be best expressed in terms of a eucharistic communion legitimated by bishops, offered by priests, and received by laypeople. But we must also recognize that institutional catholicity (#6) was not repudiated but rather reworked: *LG*, among other documents, seemed to posit various *degrees* of catholicity and ecclesiality, with the Roman institution at the center. The ecumenical movement found in sacramental communion (liturgical catholicity, #9) its greatest expression of the church's catholic unity, while it found in institutional catholicity (#6) its greatest hindrance to the same. But by far the largest convergence of these traditions (and others) was toward an increased emphasis on differentiated catholicity (#7). Reformational, Roman Catholic, and ecumenical traditions alike all increasingly recognized that "the opposite of catholicity is not locality or diversity, but uniformity"[141] and that catholicity is best understood "as a dynamic unity in diversity."[142] It is only amid such a development that the sentiment of Aulén is even possible: "It is obvious that no communion which takes the

---

[141]Ruddy, *Local Church*, 47, 49.
[142]Walter Kasper, "'Credo Unam Sanctam Ecclesiam'—the Relationship Between the Catholic and the Protestant Principles in Fundamental Ecclesiology," in *Receptive Ecumenism and the Call to Catholic Learning: Exploring a Way for Contemporary Ecumenism*, ed. Paul. D. Murray (Oxford: Oxford University Press, 2008), 79-80.

content of the confession seriously can attach the catholicity of the church to any one specific communion."[143]

Conclusion: Toward A Faithful, Fuller Doctrine of Catholicity

What may we conclude from this limited church-historical investigation into the development of the doctrine of the church's catholicity? First, we can largely conclude with Dulles that the doctrine clearly demonstrates a "richness of [its] traditional concept . . . relative stability through time . . . and gradual shifts made to accommodate new situations."[144] Indeed, our survey has shown that the doctrine of catholicity hands on the "good deposit" of its biblical foundation: the pattern of judgments found in Scripture regarding the *nature* of God's people as a unified diversity and the *scope* of God's people as through the whole of all times, peoples, and places is crystalized and faithfully communicated through the ages via the confession that the church is "catholic." The doctrine maintains a "faithful" continuity through the modulations of church history, and yet becomes "fuller" as the pneumatically affected "great cloud of witnesses" grows; as the scope of the gospel's reception has increased, so has our understanding of the nature of the gospel-shaped people as catholic. We can thus say that there are many proper developments in the doctrine, proper because they are in keeping with Scripture's testimony while further elucidating its ultimate concerns amid new historical and cultural contexts in such a way that they become part of, and contribute toward, the fullness of the church's tradition.

Another thing we may conclude is that we can refine the proposed taxonomy in an important way: scratching numerical catholicity (#10) from our list as an example of a doctrinal *corruption* rather than a doctrinal *development*. We have seen that the notion of catholicity as emphasizing greatest adherence comes much later in the church-historical story and comes about amid the largely polemical context of Roman/Protestant conflict. Such a view not only lacks support in Scripture (consider the implications of Jesus' statement in Lk 18:8) and earlier tradition, but is also recognized by multiple ecclesial traditions further downstream as a false

---

[143] Aulén, *Reformation and Catholicity*, 178.
[144] Dulles, *Catholicity*, 10.

path for properly understanding the church's catholicity. In other words, the whole church recognized via the *consensus fidelium* that catholicity as numerical superiority failed to provide a faithful and fuller understanding of the ultimate implications of Scripture's discourse regarding the scope and nature of the church and, in fact, represented an unfaithful and thinner understanding of the same. It was a development of the doctrine to recognize this corruption.

All the other aspects of catholicity expressed in the taxonomy, while certainly interrelated, are distinct and, as proper developments, help ensure that the doctrine of catholicity is as full-orbed as possible. This doesn't mean that every aspect is of equal significance or that every ecclesial vantage point on catholicity must give equal emphasis to all (now nine) categories; in fact, by prioritizing and relating the aspects in different ways, each ecclesial tradition will inevitably bring out particular insights for the whole church to consider. But by maintaining the legitimacy of each aspect, and by seeking in the task of doctrinal synthesis to be as integrative as possible, proposals regarding the church's catholicity are more likely to remain faithful to the tradition while contributing to its fullness. And by referring to common categories we can better see how catholicity is understood and enacted by the various ecclesial traditions and better work toward greater doctrinal consensus between them.

It is my contention, then, that proposals regarding how best to understand the church's catholicity will be most compelling when they are *integrative* of as many of the aspects that have emerged over the church-historical trajectory as possible, articulating their proper prioritization and interrelationship. What should guide these proposals? First, as a Reformational effort to see Scripture function as the *norma normans* of theology, we could ask which of the categories has the greatest support and grounding in the biblical witness. As we saw in the last chapter, there is indeed strong biblical warrant for the doctrine of the church's catholicity. That warrant oriented around both the *scope* of God's people through redemptive history and the *nature* of that gospel-shaped people. It might be argued that in terms of the scope the Scriptures put a relatively equal emphasis on the "all times" (#4), "all peoples" (#3), and "all places" (#2) aspects, thus leading us to equally prioritize them. Similarly it might be argued that in terms of the nature of the church as catholic there is more explicit support for the christological aspect (#8) than for the liturgical aspect (#9). This doesn't mean the latter aspect is *not* supported by Scripture, only that it might not be as *well* supported. Ultimately the tasks of exegetical and biblical theology will be vital in adjudicating such claims.

Second, as an effort to interpret Scripture in the communion of saints and learn from their collective insights, we could ask which of the categories are given the *strongest emphasis* in the tradition.[145] Here the task of historical theology plays the lead role. Based on our findings here, we can make several observations toward this end. One would be that while holistic catholicity (#1) provides the initial orientation and vital foundation in the earliest days of the church, that aspect alone became insufficient as church history marched on, for ultimately much more needed to be said about *how* we are connected to the whole and *what* exactly that whole is. Another observation is that christological catholicity (#8) emerges from our study as quite central, playing a particularly significant role at the bookends of church history and demonstrating a presence in nearly every ecclesial tradition when it comes to accounting for the church's catholicity. While this does much to commend it as a foundational aspect for any attempts to parse out what it means that the church is catholic, it must also be recognized that much of what is meant by it, following Ignatius's formula that "where Jesus Christ is, there is the catholic church," is not always clear; a compelling account of catholicity would need to further spell out Christ's relationship to the church as catholic. Another observation is that there is a "golden thread" that runs through the story of the doctrine's development: at every stage and in every ecclesial tradition, from Cyril to Augustine to Aquinas to Calvin to Bellarmine to Vatican II, there is a common recognition that the scope of God's people includes all times, peoples, and places (#2–4). A compelling proposal must build on this common insight while seeking to reconcile the agreement regarding the *scope* of catholicity (the quantitative elements) with the substantial disagreement regarding the *nature* of catholicity (the qualitative elements). Still another observation is that at the "points of crisis" for catholicity (the Great Schism, the Reformation, etc.) orthodox catholicity (#5) and

---

[145] With Melanchthon we thus seek a doctrine of catholicity "supported by the witness of all time, of all ages." Quoted in Dulles, *Catholicity*, 182.

institutional catholicity (#6) seem to come into particular conflict with one another, especially as it relates to the question of which church stands in proper relation to the whole (holistic catholicity, #1) and in continuity with the catholic tradition of the church through the ages (chronological catholicity, #4). Compelling proposals must make sense of this tension and find ways to potentially overcome it.

From these observations we can say that our provisional definition of catholicity as expressing the church's unified diversity through the whole of all times, peoples, and places is further justified as a starting point in part because it is capable of further filling out as we integrate the various aspects of catholicity witnessed in church history and categorized in the taxonomy. For instance, we might begin by recognizing holistic catholicity (#1) as the *spirit* of catholicity: this marks out churches that seek to connect with the universal church and to combat a spirit of sectarianism. We can also recognize widespread agreement regarding the *scope* of this universal church: geographical, missional, and chronological aspects of catholicity (#2–4) ensure that the church as catholic is conceived as inclusive of "all places," "all peoples," and "all times" in a way that rules out provincialism, exclusionism, and novelty. But chronological catholicity (#4) also functions to emphasize *continuity with the catholic tradition*, a tradition established in the ancient rule of faith manifest in the creeds of the undivided church. Differentiated catholicity (#7) emphasizes that the *unity* of the church is not manifest in uniformity but in a divinely ordained diversity, with each member contributing its distinctive gifts and graces. Liturgical catholicity (#9) emphasizes that the *holiness* of the church is manifest in a common sacramental expression whereby the community is set apart by its distinctive gospel practices. Orthodox catholicity (#5) emphasizes that the *apostolicity* of the church provides the "guardrails" of catholicity such that its diversity is properly unified around the gospel and its first-order doctrinal entailments (here a proper dogmatic rank becomes important). The remaining two aspects emphasize that catholicity must be *visible* (institutional catholicity, #6) and *theologically grounded* (christological catholicity, #8). Now we turn to explore how these various dimensions are integrated in Episcopal (chapter three) and Free Church (chapter four) accounts of the church's catholicity.

Engaging Anglican Accounts of Catholicity

THIS CHAPTER IS AN EXERCISE in what Roger Haight has called comparative theology, the goal of which "is to show the richness, vitality, and creativity of the whole church as it moves through history adjusting to new times, places, and cultures. . . . The object of study [is] the whole church, but from the sixteenth century forward the church will always be constituted by the churches."[1] The fact that after the Reformation "the church" exists as "the churches" has tremendous import for understanding the church's catholicity and, as we have recognized, continually highlights the contested nature of that catholicity.

This chapter will particularly require that we exhibit what David Buschart has called "theological hospitality." That is, we will seek to "present the history, theological method and selected beliefs of the traditions in a way that accurately represents them as understood by people who stand within these traditions."[2] Indeed, this stance of generous hospitality (vs. polemical judgment) actually stems from our confession of the church's catholicity, for as Bird has noted, "Catholicity is recognizing that God is at work in other places and in other churches, drawing men and women to himself and drawing them together under the banner of Jesus Christ."[3] This does not mean that we must refrain from any criticism; rather, it means that as we

---

[1]Roger Haight, *Christian Community in History*, vol. 2 (New York: Continuum, 2005), vii.
[2]W. David Buschart, *Exploring Protestant Traditions: An Invitation to Theological Hospitality* (Downers Grove, IL: IVP Academic, 2006), 27.
[3]Michael Bird, *Evangelical Theology* (Grand Rapids, MI: Zondervan, 2013), 738.

seek to evaluate the contributions of any particular stream of the Christian tradition (especially a stream not our own), we operate from "the humble recognition that all traditions of Christianity contain an admixture of truth and error, of wisdom and weakness. The fact that one's own . . . tradition contains some error . . . [while] other traditions contain some truth and wisdom means that potentially [ours] can grow, fill gaps and learn constructive lessons from them."[4]

Why Engage Episcopal Accounts of Catholicity?

Why should a project dedicated to articulating a *Free Church* theological account of the church's catholicity dedicate an entire chapter to engaging accounts from an *Episcopal* vantage point? In answer we can say, first of all, that this is a proper response to Volf's observation that the vast majority of reflection on the church's catholicity to date has been from an Episcopal vantage point. To articulate an understanding of catholicity without first taking into account the insights of the Episcopal tradition would not only be foolish; it would also be *uncatholic*. A Free Church account of catholicity must not only be attentive to Scripture and the doctrine's church-historical development; it must also engage other ecclesial traditions' accounts of catholicity.

The second reason for this chapter stems from an insistence that no one ecclesial tradition can have a monopoly on catholicity.[5] The church's catholic character undercuts all attempts to equate a particular church with the whole, and thus we follow Vanhoozer in expressing "the necessity of involving the *whole* church in the project of theology" and holding that "no single denomination 'owns' catholicity . . . [for] catholicity is no more the exclusive domain of [Episcopal Churches] than the gospel is the private domain of evangelicals."[6] Because we contend with Williams that "no single communion can . . . be the sole possessor of the *catholica*," we recognize this

---

[4]Buschart, *Exploring Protestant Traditions*, 28.
[5]Yoder says, "someone who polemically claims 'the ecclesiastical institution of which I am a member is catholic as the others are not' has put . . . valuational spin on the language." John Howard Yoder, *The Royal Priesthood: Essays Ecclesiastical and Ecumenical*, ed. Michael G. Cartwright (Scottdale, PA: Herald Press, 1998), 304.
[6]Kevin Vanhoozer, *The Drama of Doctrine: A Canonical-Linguistic Approach to Christian Theology* (Louisville, KY: Westminster John Knox, 2005), 158.

applies first to *our own tradition* and that, therefore, we do well to acknowledge our own blind spots while looking to benefit from the riches of others, holding that they, too, are part of the one catholic church seeking to better understand and live in light of that catholicity.[7]

The third reason for this chapter stems from an attempt to observe what might be called the golden rule of comparative theology: attend to the insights of others as you would have them attend to your own. In the second half of this project, we will be making the claim that there is a significant contribution the Free Church tradition still has to make to a fuller-orbed doctrine of the church's catholicity. Until that contribution is made, the catholic church is more impoverished. But if we desire for that contribution to be heard, we must first do the work of hearing the insights of traditions that have already made a significant contribution themselves. Indeed, catholicity demands nothing less, and attentiveness to the insights of other ecclesial traditions not only prepares the way for greater reception of one's own insights, but also reveals blindspots that have prevented a fuller-orbed doctrine of the church's catholicity from being articulated and enacted.

What Do We Mean by Episcopal Accounts of Catholicity?

But before we turn to the Anglican contribution, we must first clarify what we mean by "Episcopal accounts of catholicity," of which Anglicanism provides a subset. In the introduction we referred to Volf's insight that the Episcopal and Free Church traditions, broadly conceived, are best understood in contrast to one another, especially around the question whether ordained ministers, particularly bishops, belong to the *esse* of the church. The differing answers to this question ultimately reveal a "bottom up" (Free Church) versus "top down" (Episcopal) pattern of ecclesial authority that leads to conceptions of the church's catholicity as deriving "from below" (Free Church) versus "from above" (Episcopal). We insisted that this involves more than questions of polity (church *order*) but ultimately centers on questions of the church's *nature*, for the disagreement between the traditions isn't just over how the church should be governed; it is, more centrally, over how the church, and its catholicity, are conceived and constituted.

---

[7]D. H. Williams, *Evangelicals and Tradition: The Formative Influence of the Early Church* (Grand Rapids, MI: Baker Academic, 2005), 42.

This is ultimately because the disagreement concerns the nature and pattern of ecclesial *authority*. If authority is the "power of say so," the power to give orders within a particular *domain* over which one is authorized, then here we are after the question of how authority properly manifests within the domain of the church. The Free Church authors of *The Catholicity of Protestantism* understood how central this question was to their disagreement with the Episcopal tradition. They ask, "*On what authority* . . . do we base our claim that this or that doctrine is part of the Gospel and therefore true? It is not too much to say that if all the divided parts of Christendom could agree on the answer to that question, our divisions might be speedily healed."[8] They go on to acknowledge there are "vast differences" between the two traditions regarding the authority of tradition and its implications for proper church order.[9] Indeed, it seemed to them "impossible" for the Free Churches "to state any doctrine of authority which would be accepted by the Roman Catholics, Old Catholics, Orthodox, and Anglo-Catholics."[10] It was thus no surprise to them that their understandings of catholicity were worlds apart.

Consequently, parsing out Episcopal accounts of the church's catholicity, and the ways they are distinct from Free Church accounts of the same, necessarily involves tracing the pattern of ecclesial authority these traditions see as in keeping with the church's nature. This is not merely to delineate a particular polity; it is rather to articulate the ecclesiological convictions undergirding *why* such a polity is authorized and *how* such a polity relates to God and God's Word. It is, in other words, to set forth *a theological account of ecclesial authority*, and, more specifically, an account of how such authority is transferred from Christ the Lord of the church to the community and ministers of the church. We are thus investigating the means by which Christ *properly* rules the church and any implications this has for the church's catholicity.

An Episcopal account of the church's catholicity flows from a pattern of ecclesial authority that is largely top down. Littlejohn summarizes the position thus:

---

[8]R. Newton Flew and Rupert E. Davies, eds., *The Catholicity of Protestantism: Being a Report Presented to His Grace the Archbishop of Canterbury by a Group of Free Churchmen* (London: Lutterworth Press, 1950), 115, emphasis added.
[9]Flew and Davies, *Catholicity of Protestantism*, 132.
[10]Flew and Davies, *Catholicity of Protestantism*, 133.

[Christ] entrusted [the apostles] alone with His authority to lead His Church and minister to it. He did not simply entrust the Church as such with the same commission and gift, for them to delegate to such authorities as they would constitute. And, as this authority was given only into the apostles' hands, none others could receive it but from their hands. Thus it was necessary that all subsequent ministers must receive authority directly from the apostles or their successors. Historically speaking, this succession took the form of the bishops, upon which form the Catholic, Orthodox, and Anglican all insisted on maintaining.[11]

Authority resides with the bishops, regarded as successors in the line of apostolic authority. Much is made of Paul laying hands on Timothy as one called to guard the good deposit (2 Tim 1:6, 14) and authorizing Titus to "appoint elders in every town" (Titus 1:5); more is made of the authority invested in the apostles (Jn 20:23) and those seen to be their successors. While it is widely acknowledged that the New Testament does not distinguish the office of bishop from that of elder, the emphasis is placed on the emerging distinction between the offices in the second century. An Episcopal account of ecclesial authority thus traces the pattern from God to the apostles to bishops in apostolic succession to those the bishops vest with their authority (clergy) to, finally, the laity. Properly following this line of authority becomes critical for any church to participate in the whole, that is, to be properly deemed "catholic."

Why Anglicanism?

But if there are multiple streams within this broader Episcopal tradition, this prompts the question: Why engage *Anglicanism* versus other highly qualified candidates that, in certain cases, might embody an even *more robust* expression of Episcopal catholicity? For instance, Roman Catholicism offers essentially the oldest conception of catholicity on the church-historical block.[12] Eastern Orthodoxy would be another obvious choice. Lutheranism might also be a candidate, though in some segments of it, bishops, as such, are nonexistent.[13]

---

[11]W. Bradford Littlejohn, *The Mercersburg Theology and the Quest for Reformed Catholicity* (Eugene, OR: Pickwick, 2009), 110.
[12]The Eastern Orthodox would, of course, object to this particular characterization.
[13]Kärkkäinen notes that "Scandinavian and other European Lutheran churches are episcopal ... whereas most American ones have not had bishops" and holds that "Luther and Lutheranism after him demonstrate two lines of argumentation concerning the church's constitution of its ministry: one from below and one from above." Veli-Matti Kärkkäinen, *An Introduction to*

It can only be said here that space constraints prevent us from engaging these ecclesial traditions in detail, though these traditions have much to contribute to a fuller understanding of the church's catholicity.

So then, what has Canterbury to do with Schleitheim? That is, what does the Anglican tradition have to do with the Free Church? Three things. First, they share a *common history*. Rupp explains that "the most important of all tensions in English religion [is] the antiphon often tragic but always fruitful between the Establishment and historic Dissent."[14] Anglicanism has largely maintained an Episcopal conception of the church's catholicity as constituted from above (that is, via a bishop in historic succession) while simultaneously demonstrating a lengthy track record of interaction with the Free Church tradition (in a way not true of Roman Catholicism and Eastern Orthodoxy). These traditions have shared a history since the Reformation that has significantly impacted them both. Indeed, while the Free Church tradition came to define itself in the midst of an Anglican-dominated ecclesial scene and largely in response to its claims, Sykes believes their contact was mutually defining, saying that "by the mid-seventeenth century the Church of England was developing an apologetic self-understanding over against independency and presbyterianism, as representative of left-wing Protestantism."[15]

Second, they share a *theological proximity*. The traditions exhibit large areas of agreement, even though there has been significant conflict between the two and even as substantial disagreements remain. Indeed, Anglicanism can be understood as the Episcopal tradition closest to the Free Church tradition in that there are shared Protestant convictions, especially among the Evangelical stream of Anglicanism, not to be found among Roman Catholicism or Eastern Orthodoxy. Sykes recognizes that Anglicans' "long history of permitting lay involvement in church government means that they cannot fully share the theologies of the episcopate advanced in Orthodox or Catholic circles."[16] This "distance" from Catholic and Orthodox churches means greater proximity, in some sense, to the Free Church tradition.

Ecclesiology: Ecumenical, Historical & Global Perspectives (Downers Grove, IL: IVP Academic, 2002), 41, 43.
[14]Gordon Rupp, *Protestant Catholicity: Two Lectures* (London: Epworth Press, 1960), 53.
[15]Stephen Sykes, *Unashamed Anglicanism* (Nashville: Abington Press, 1995), 82.
[16]Sykes, *Unashamed Anglicanism*, 187.

Third, they demonstrate an *ecclesial distinction*. The Church of England provides a particularly enlightening foil for the Free Church tradition because its brand of Episcopalism is nationally oriented under royal supremacy. Thus the Anglican Church, at least historically, has manifested some of the most direct contrasts with the Free Church tradition's identity as congregationally constituted, conscientiously nonconformist, and corporally local. In many ways the Free Church came to articulate and refine these ecclesial convictions in response to what were understood as abuses and false paths demonstrated by the Anglican Church. Thus the more we come to understand about Anglicanism and its conception(s) of catholicity, the more we will be prepared to glimpse the distinctive contribution the Free Church tradition has to make.

What Is Anglicanism?

But then another question emerges: What exactly do we mean by *Anglicanism* here? Anglican theologian Gerald Bray has admitted the initial difficulty, saying that "few branches of the Christian church have as much difficulty defining themselves as the Anglican one has."[17] Amid this problem Sykes provides an initial orientation: "The Anglican Communion is one family or federation of Provinces within the One, Holy, Catholic and Apostolic Church. The Provinces of the Anglican Communion are legally autonomous, but morally interdependent."[18] What is it unites these autonomous provinces (currently numbering at 41) under an "Anglican" identity? It is not, as Sykes explains, that they function as "a united Church or even a number of Churches controlled by an authoritative body." Rather, their common bond is threefold: their "communion with the see of Canterbury," their common history having "emerged from the Church of England," and their common "doctrines and practices [that] approximate closely to those of that Church."[19] Significantly Pickering adds that "all Anglican

---

[17]Gerald L. Bray, "Why I Am an Anglican and an Evangelical," in *Why We Belong: Evangelical Unity and Denominational Diversity*, ed. Anthony L. Chute, Christopher W. Morgan, and Robert A. Peterson (Wheaton, IL: Crossway, 2013), 65.
[18]Sykes, *Unashamed Anglicanism*, ix.
[19]W. S. F. Pickering, "Sociology of Anglicanism," in *The Study of Anglicanism*, ed. Stephen Sykes, John Booty, and Jonathan Knight, rev ed. (Minneapolis: Fortress, 1998), 405. It should be noted that this is only one account of what binds Anglicans together. Another way to express this bond is by highlighting the four "instruments of unity": the archbishop of Canterbury, the Lambeth

Churches have accepted a Catholic concept of church order, namely, one based on the historic episcopacy. The claim of apostolic succession means that the Church of England traces its ecclesiastical formation back to the early Church."[20] We recognize, then, that Anglicanism sits within the larger Episcopal tradition delineated above, even as there is disagreement within the Anglican Communion regarding the proper expression of Episcopal ecclesial authority. For our purposes we will focus primarily on the Church of England, not because it is necessarily representative of all provinces (indeed, the global diversity within the Communion would ensure this is likely *not* the case), but because of the formative role this Church has played within Anglicanism and the fact that it is the Church of England with which the Free Church tradition has had the most significant dialogue and debate through the years.[21]

But to discuss Anglican catholicity, we must first grasp what is distinctive in Anglican *ecclesiology*. Despite claims to the contrary, uttered even from the church's own archbishops in arguing that Anglicanism is simply "catholic Christianity," Sykes insists that "it cannot be the case that there is no Anglican ecclesiology."[22] Every church, communion, and ecclesial tradition has an ecclesiology, and when it comes to Anglicanism Philip Thomas can say that "since its beginnings, [it] has been forged on the anvil of ecclesiological controversy,"[23] while Avis insists that "it is the doctrine of the Church . . . rather than the doctrine of salvation . . . that has been the driving force of historic Anglicanism."[24] To unearth Anglican catholicity requires unearthing the Anglican understanding of the church because, as Sykes says, "there is dispute between the denominations about what the catholicity of the Church signifies, and if . . . Anglicans have a view worth

---

Conference, the Primates' Meeting, and the Anglican Consultative Council. Others (such as those connected to the GAFCON movement) would emphasize a more confessional, synodical, and missional form of union. Still others would place more emphasis on common practices that unite Anglicans, such as use of the Book of Common Prayer.

[20]Pickering, "Sociology of Anglicanism," 408.

[21]Pickering says, "The Anglican Communion cannot be understood ecclesiastically and socially apart from a thorough comprehension of the Church of England, its mother." Pickering, "Sociology of Anglicanism," 411.

[22]Quoted in Paul Avis, *The Anglican Understanding of the Church*, 2nd ed. (London: SPCK, 2013), 22.

[23]Quoted in Avis, *Anglican Understanding*, 22.

[24]Avis, *Anglican Understanding*, 22.

considering on this matter, we must . . . [first offer] an Anglican doctrine of the Church."[25]

While it may be true that there is a common Anglican ecclesiology at root, we must also heed Avis's statement that "Anglicans have never fully agreed about what sort of Church theirs is and should be. There has been no single dominant Anglican ecclesiology."[26] This stems not only from the global diversity of the Anglican Communion, but also from the fact that there are at least three major schools within Anglicanism, often identified as Anglo-Catholic ("high church"), evangelical ("low church"), and liberal ("broad church"). Bray holds that it is to the Oxford Movement "that we owe the modern concept of Anglicanism, because they were determined to construct a distinctive theology and ecclesiology that could stand on a par with those of Rome and the Eastern churches as a third branch of catholic Christianity."[27] Indeed, it is primarily high-church Anglicans, from the seventeenth-century "Caroline divines" to the nineteenth-century "Tractarians," that stressed the apostolic succession of Anglican bishops.[28] By contrast, low-church Anglicans often "believe that the [Episcopal] structures are a convenience—adopted for practical reasons but not imposed by divine authority, and therefore open to revision."[29] The presence of these schools alongside each other throughout Anglican history has led many to note that "it may well be that comprehensiveness, that is, the ability to absorb extremes and at the same time be the milieu for debate without giving rise to disunity, is the overriding virtue of Anglicanism."[30]

It is the differences of opinion between these streams regarding the essentiality of the episcopate for the church that is most pertinent to sounding out Anglican catholicity. Peter Toon provides a very helpful categorical analysis of this in terms of the *esse* (being), *bene esse* (well-being), and *plene esse* (fullness of being) of the church. Anglo-Catholics hold that the historic episcopate is of the *esse* (being) of the church, claiming "that the episcopate *guarantees* the church. . . . [and that] the church derives all her authority

---

[25]Sykes, *Unashamed Anglicanism*, 109.
[26]Avis, *Anglican Understanding*, 23.
[27]Bray, "Why I Am an Anglican," 70.
[28]Buschart, *Exploring Protestant Traditions*, 123.
[29]Bray, "Why I Am an Anglican," 68-69.
[30]Pickering, "Sociology of Anglicanism," 412.

from the Lord Jesus Christ through the divinely ordained means of the historical episcopate. Only bishops, who are in this apostolic succession of persons and doctrine, and the priests that they ordain, have authority and grace to celebrate the Eucharist as an effectual sacrament of grace."[31] Next is the position Toon says is claimed by evangelical and liberal churchmen alike, namely that the episcopate is of the *bene esse* (well-being) of the church. They thus recognize as churches those communions that do not maintain the historic episcopate and argue for it largely based on "the value of an ancient and long succession of persons and doctrine in time and through space . . . [bringing] the greatest good to the church of God in terms of value and usefulness."[32] Finally, Toon offers his own position: the historical episcopate belongs to the church's *plene esse* (fullness of being). This is out of the conviction that "the high claim of *esse* is erroneous and that the low claim of *bene esse* is inadequate."[33]

Avis holds that this disagreement points to one of the most distinctive things about Anglican ecclesiology, for "the Anglican Communion is the only world family of churches, universally maintaining the apostolic succession of the episcopate, that does not believe . . . that it is *the one true Church*, the whole church, the only church. . . . [Indeed] it is an article of faith . . . for Anglicans that their churches 'belong to' or are 'part of' the one, holy, catholic, and apostolic church."[34] Sykes says there is a "long, consistent and distinguished tradition in the Church of England which insists that . . . trinitarian non-episcopal Churches really participate in the One, Holy, Catholic and Apostolic Church of Christ. That affirmation . . . is compatible with a judgment that different Churches may be in various states of error, of varying degrees of seriousness, in relation to particular doctrines."[35]

Last, for the purposes of comparing Anglicanism with the Free Church tradition, it is important to observe the significance of the Church of England's establishment and its understanding of the proper relation between

---

[31]Peter Toon, "Episcopalianism," in *Who Runs the Church? Four Views on Church Government*, ed. Steven B. Cowan (Grand Rapids, MI: Zondervan, 2004), 36-37.
[32]Toon, "Episcopalianism," 37.
[33]Toon, "Episcopalianism," 37.
[34]Paul Avis, "Anglican Ecclesiology," in *The Oxford Handbook of Ecclesiology*, ed. Paul Avis (Oxford: Oxford University Press, 2018), 240.
[35]Sykes, *Unashamed Anglicanism*, 135.

church and state.³⁶ In language that is quite strange to Free Church ears, Bray can proclaim that "the English Reformation was the victory of the laity over the clergy, because ultimate authority for the church's life and doctrine was vested in the king and Parliament, not in the bishops."³⁷ Haight recounts that the 1534 Act of Supremacy served "to mark the threshold crossed by the withdrawal from Roman authority and institution, as well as the official wedding of church and state."³⁸ Norris can even insist that "what set the English church apart was precisely the principle of and the fact of royal, as opposed to papal, supremacy. The English Reformation was seen to be the work of the 'godly prince'... [who ordered] the spiritual as well as the temporal affairs of the kingdom.... Monarch and bishop stood or fell together, as James I asserted, and Charles I and his archbishop demonstrated."³⁹ This presupposes a *corpus Christianum*, for "the rationale behind all talk of royal supremacy rests on the assumption of the coextensiveness of the commonwealth and the Christian church."⁴⁰

Anglican Catholicity

Henry Chadwick has observed that "an Anglican is ordinarily defined as a Christian who, through his or her diocesan bishop, is in communion with the see of Canterbury. That presupposes a certain idea of catholicity... [for] the archbishop of Canterbury embodies a tradition which precedes the Reformation.... [while] at the same time Anglicans know that the Reformation left a lasting mark on their Church."⁴¹ Chadwick's sentiment sums

---

[36] Here we explicitly speak of the Church of England rather than the broader Anglican Communion because the vast majority of member churches in the communion are nonestablished and have never been. In fact, in our postcolonial context, most Anglican provinces today do not look to the English sovereign as a source of unity.
[37] Bray, "Why I am an Anglican," 88.
[38] Haight, *Christian Community*, 2:207. But Hinchliff is right to note that "the English religious establishment of the sixteenth century was built upon the relationship between Church and state that had already existed in the Middle Ages." Peter Hinchliff, "Church-State Relations," in *Study of Anglicanism*, Sykes, Booty, and Knight, 392.
[39] Richard A Norris, "Episcopacy," in *Study of Anglicanism*, Sykes, Booty, and Knight, 334. Haight agrees: "the king's position [as] head of the church is one of the most distinctive characteristics of this ecclesiology." Haight, *Christian Community*, 2:176.
[40] Haight, *Christian Community*, 2:177.
[41] Henry Chadwick, "Local and Universal: An Anglican Perspective," *The Jurist* 52, no. 1 (1992): 515.

up well why Anglicans often identify as "Reformed *and* catholic." But upon further investigation this "certain idea of [Anglican] catholicity" is harder to get at than it might first seem, if only because, as Bruce Kaye has said, "the word 'catholic' has had a varied and often controversial history in Anglicanism."[42] In other words, catholicity has been much contested in Anglicanism as well.

Foundational contributions. We begin by considering sources that have made an indelible mark on Anglican conceptions of catholicity. This requires going all the way back to the Reformation because, as Mark Chapman makes clear, "from the very beginnings of the Church of England, which was founded on the 'containment' of the church within national boundaries, the problem of the catholicity of the church has repeatedly come to the fore."[43] By interfacing with certain historical sources, ecclesial schools, and influential theologians, we will see how "the particularities of Anglican history . . . help to explain the contested nature of catholicity [within it]."[44] Our interest is particularly in how bishops are conceived as relating to catholicity.

Historical sources. In returning to the sixteenth century, we do well to recall the polemical environment in which theology was being done and churches were advertising their catholic bona fides. Avis reminds us that "in the sixteenth and seventeenth centuries Anglicans defended their continuity with the pre-Reformation Church, rebutted charges of schism, and refuted the claims of the papacy. Thus they emphasized the catholicity of the Church of England, as a church that lacked no essential part of catholic faith and order."[45] This defense came at a time when "catholic was somewhat self-consciously used to mean all Christians in distinction from those churches under the jurisdiction of the Church of Rome."[46] Here too was the assumption of every Reformation Church: there is a catholic church not coextensive with the Roman Church, and we are a distinct member of it.

---

[42]Bruce Kaye, "Reality and Form in Catholicity," *Journal of Anglican Studies* 10, no. 1 (June 2012): 3.
[43]Mark D. Chapman, "William Reed Huntington, American Catholicity, and the Chicago-Lambeth Quadrilateral," in *The Lambeth Conference: Theology, History, Polity and Purpose*, ed. Paul Avis and Benjamin M. Guyer (London: Bloomsbury, 2017), 84.
[44]Mark D. Chapman, "Catholicity and the Future of Anglicanism," in *The Hope of Things to Come: Anglicanism and the Future*, ed. Mark Chapman (London: Mowbray, 2010), 107.
[45]Paul Avis, "What Is 'Anglicanism'?," in Sykes, Booty, and Knight, *Study of Anglicanism*, 462.
[46]Kaye, "Reality and Form," 3.

While papal authority was rejected with Henry VIII's 1534 Act of Supremacy, and while it was assumed that bishops would continue to exercise authority in the newly independent Church of England, it was not immediately clear what role they would play in maintaining its participation in the catholic church. Avis, for one, is convinced that "while the historic episcopate was preserved in the English Reformation it was not regarded as of the essence of the church or as constitutive of her catholicity. . . . The catholicity of the church for the English Reformers did not reside in the succession of its bishops but in continuity of true doctrine."[47] Here there is much in common with the Lutheran and Reformed camps, since catholicity was being "defined in relation to truth, not to the universal jurisdiction of the hierarchy or of the pope. Inward possession of truth was set above the outward imposition of unity. . . . For the Reformers—and here the English divines are merely representative—universality is only equivalent to catholicity when it is joined with truth. Unity must be in verity."[48] Yet the Church of England was unique among the Reformed churches in that "the form of polity that [was] adopted qualified what it might mean to be a catholic church: it was always the 'contained catholicity' of a national church. And it was that form of polity that was eventually exported to the other churches of the Anglican world."[49] While Luther was largely disinterested in church order and Calvin attempted to enact a polity that became the foundation for Presbyterian government, across the channel "bishops—and with them the distinction of office between bishops and presbyters—were simply a given of the English reform."[50]

The English Reformation thus came to be understood as a via media between the *theology* of the Reformation and the *form* of Western Christendom: reformed in faith yet catholic in order. Kater draws the threads together nicely: "Defining the identity of the Church of England as a national body required that it remain faithful to the implicit *universality* of a

---

[47]Paul Avis, *Anglicanism and the Christian Church: Theological Resources in Historical Perspective* (Minneapolis: Fortress, 1989), 33-34.
[48]Paul Avis, *The Church in the Theology of the Reformers* (Atlanta: John Knox Press, 1980), 130.
[49]Mark D. Chapman, Sathianathan Clarke, and Martyn Percy, "Introduction," in *The Oxford Handbook of Anglican Studies*, ed. Mark D. Chapman, Sathianathan Clarke, and Martyn Percy (Oxford: Oxford University Press, 2015), 4.
[50]Norris, "Episcopacy," in Sykes, Booty, and Knight, *Study of Anglicanism*, 333.

catholic heritage. But its constant wrestling to define *the faith* and the *structure* of that heritage reminded it that catholicity also applies to its teachings and its institutions." He goes on: "The early Anglican apologists assumed that these two meanings of catholicity—'universal' and 'correct' or 'sound'—belonged together. 'Correct' doctrine was the faith professed by the 'universal' company of believers; and its *truth*, guarded by the bishops to assure its faithfulness, was attested in part by its *universality*."[51] To the polemical question asked by Roman Catholics as to where the Anglican Church was prior to the sixteenth century, the answer often came back, "Where was your face before you washed it?"[52] Continuity through time, common church structures, and a conviction that the Reformation was recovering the ancient purity of doctrine (jettisoning Roman accretions) thus laid the foundation for Anglican conceptions of catholicity.

These notions are found in the foundational documents of the all-important sixteenth century. In article 8 of the *Thirty-Nine Articles* we hear that "the Three Creeds, *Nicene* Creed, *Athanasius's* Creed, and . . . *Apostles'* Creed, ought thoroughly to be received and believed: for they may be proved by most certain warrants of Holy Scripture."[53] When the church is explicitly discussed in article nineteen the creedal attributes are assumed and the church is marked out in language very close to the Augsburg confession: "The visible Church of Christ is a congregation of faithful men, in which the pure Word of God is preached, and the Sacraments be duly administered according to Christ's ordinance."[54] A certain understanding of the church's catholicity seems to lie behind article thirty-four, where we find the statement that "it is not necessary that Traditions and Ceremonies be in all places one, and utterly like; for at all times they have been divers, and may be changed according to the diversities of countries, times, and men's manners, so that nothing be ordained against God's Word."[55] This implicitly allows for a diversity of liturgical and ministerial practice among the churches.

---

[51]John L. Kater Jr., "Whose Church Is It Anyway? Anglican 'Catholicity' Re-examined," *Anglican Theological Review* 76, no. 1 (Winter 1994): 48.
[52]Avis, *Anglicanism and the Christian Church*, 64.
[53]G. R. Evans and J. Robert Wright, eds., *The Anglican Tradition: A Handbook of Sources* (Minneapolis: Fortress, 1991), 231.
[54]Evans and Wright, *Anglican Tradition*, 235.
[55]Evans and Wright, *Anglican Tradition*, 240.

Another resource to consider is John Jewel's *Apologie* (1564), where we see perhaps the earliest treatment of the church's catholicity from an Anglican perspective. Jewel notes that "we believe that there is one Church of God, and that the same is not shut up . . . into some one corner or kingdom, but that it is catholic and universal, dispersed throughout the whole world."[56] Here we see geographical and missional catholicity signaled along with the assumption that the universal church is made up of many churches. But Andre Gazal points out how significant chronological catholicity is for Jewel as well. He notes that "among the three marks of catholicity comprising the Vincentian canon the controlling one for Jewel is antiquity. While the number of people believing the faith has, and continues, to vary . . . it is the faith itself whose content has been defined and determined in antiquity that remains constant, and therefore serves as the principal basis of catholicity."[57] Thus for Jewel "the essence of catholicity is the unalterable constancy of the ancient faith" because "the Scriptures, the first four general councils, the writings of the church fathers, and example of the primitive church . . . [formed] a body of truth whose common possession characterized catholicity, namely biblical truth as interpreted and applied by the early church."[58] Chapman says that Jewel is an example of "the 'temporal' catholicity implicit in the English Reformation. Catholicity is understood through a return to the past rather than as something conferred by any visible institution in the present."[59]

As we close out our survey of the "early formularies" of Anglicanism, we agree with Chapman and company in their assessment that "despite its claim to catholicity . . . there was no clarification in any of the early formularies of the Church of England as to precisely what such catholicity could mean. What was clear, however, was that . . . the catholicity of the church had to be based on something other than fellowship with the church overseas."[60] So Anglican catholicity is not Roman catholicity, and perhaps not a Reformed

---

[56] Quoted in Haight, *Christian Community*, 2:215.
[57] Andre Gazal, "Reforming Catholicity in Tudor England: John Jewel's Doctrine of the Universal Church," in *Reforming the Catholic Tradition: The Whole Word for the Whole Church*, ed. Joseph Minich (Leesburg, VA: Davenant Institute, 2019), 38.
[58] Gazal, "Reforming Catholicity in Tudor England," 39.
[59] Chapman, "Catholicity," 112.
[60] Chapman, Clarke, and Percy, "Introduction," 4.

or Lutheran catholicity. But what is it exactly? This question would continue to arise in the battle for the very heart and soul of the Anglican Church. Kater observes that "in fact [the] Anglican understanding of 'catholicity' as . . . [observing] the 'faith once delivered to the saints' was sorely tried from the beginning. When recalcitrant Puritans steadfastly refused the early Anglican Reformers' efforts to create a national consensus, the Church of England attempted to legislate uniformity—'catholicity'—by controlling and even forbidding 'non-conformist' worship."[61] This part of the story we will need to pick up in the next chapter as the Free Church voice emerges.

For now, we turn to one more significant historical source: the Chicago-Lambeth Quadrilateral established at the Lambeth conference of 1888. Turnbull tells us that the quadrilateral was intended "as a basis for the reunion of the Churches. It dealt primarily with the first-order issues of the catholicity of the Church, the universal principles of faith—a confession of faith—upon which Christian unity can be based."[62] The statement sets forth four requirements for churches wishing to pursue "home reunion":

> 1. The Holy Scriptures of the Old and New Testaments, as "containing all things necessary to salvation," and as being the rule and ultimate standard of faith.
> 2. The Apostles' Creed, as the baptismal symbol; and the Nicene Creed, as the sufficient statement of the faith. 3. The two sacraments ordained by Christ himself—Baptism and the Supper of the Lord. . . . 4. The historic episcopate, locally adapted in the methods of its administration to the varying needs of the nations and the peoples called of God into the unity of his Church.[63]

It is the fourth element that does the most to reveal the connection between bishops and catholicity to the Anglican mind. Chapman notes that "the inclusion of the 'historic episcopate' into the Quadrilateral elevated one distinctive version of the doctrine of episcopacy into part of the definition of worldwide Anglicanism."[64] One way of interpreting the quadrilateral is to argue that in it "episcopacy was elevated into the essence of the Church: churches with other forms of oversight could not be embraced by Anglicans

---

[61]Kater, "Whose Church Is It Anyway?," 49.
[62]Richard Turnbull, *Anglican and Evangelical?* (London: Continuum, 2007), 38.
[63]Quoted in Mary Tanner, "The Ecumenical Dimension of the Lambeth Conference," in Avis and Guyer, *Lambeth Conference*, 360.
[64]Chapman, "William Reed Huntington," 103.

as true churches unless they accepted the historic episcopate (by which most meant apostolic succession, even if they did not explicitly say so)."[65] Other, less exclusionary, interpretations point to places like the Lambeth "Appeal to All Christian People" of 1920, which called for "all the separated groups of Christians to . . . [reach] out towards the goal of a reunited Catholic Church . . . [that is] a Church, genuinely Catholic, loyal to all Truth, and gathering into its fellowship 'all who profess and call themselves Christians,' within whose visible unity all the treasures of faith and order, bequeathed as a heritage by the past to the present, shall be possessed in common, and made serviceable to the whole Body of Christ."[66] The Lambeth statements demonstrate the still ambiguous nature of catholicity within Anglicanism, especially regarding the relation of bishops to catholicity.

Theological schools: Anglo-Catholic and evangelical. One place we see the contested nature of Anglican catholicity particularly expressed is a midtwentieth century dialogue initiated by the Archbishop of Canterbury Geoffrey Fisher, who invited a group of Anglo-Catholics and a group of evangelical Anglicans (along with a group of Free Church theologians, examined in chapter 5) to respond, in part, to this question: "What is the underlying cause . . . of the contrast or conflict between the catholic and protestant traditions?"[67] The Anglo-Catholics, drawing on elements of the Anglican tradition through the centuries but especially on the nineteenth-century Oxford Movement,[68] gave their response in *Catholicity* (1947).[69] They expressed suspicion of any views of the church's catholicity shared between evangelical Anglicans and the Lutheran/Reformed Churches. Catholicity, they believed, concerns more than receiving the apostolic gospel proclaimed

---

[65]Mark D. Chapman, *Anglicanism: A Very Short Introduction* (Oxford: Oxford University Press, 2006), 121.
[66]Quoted in Tanner, "Ecumenical Dimension," 365.
[67]Flew and Davies, *Catholicity of Protestantism*, 5.
[68]Space constraints prevent us from dealing with the historical particulars of the Oxford Movement, but here we note that its expressions, from John Keble's sermon on "National Apostasy" to John Henry Newman's tract *Remarks on Certain Passages in the Thirty-Nine Articles*, laid the foundations for the contemporary Anglo-Catholic school and impacted the nature of the Lambeth articles discussed above. Kater summarizes that "the leaders of the Oxford Movement considered that a truly catholic episcopate . . . is the cornerstone that guarantees the faithfulness of a truly catholic English church and people." Kater, Jr., "Whose Church Is It Anyway?," 51.
[69]Gregory Dix, ed., *Catholicity: A Study in the Conflict of Christian Traditions in the West* (London: Dacre, 1947).

in word and demonstrated in sacrament; it involves "the many-sided unity of the apostolic Tradition" as a "primitive 'totality' or 'wholeness.' . . . To be a Christian [is] to belong to the one Body, to hold the one apostolic faith, to share in one visible series of sacramental rites, to be under the rule of one apostolate."[70] The rule of the one apostolate continues through bishops in historic succession, for "the apostles were commissioned by our Lord, and had authority to rule, to teach, and to ordain. . . . [Now] their functions remain in their successors . . . [for] the whole Church."[71] In their view "the problem of reunion is that of the recovery of the 'wholeness' of Tradition," and a large part of what is missing from that 'wholeness' concerns "the *historic Episcopate* [and] the recovery of the true place of the Bishop in the Church . . . as the guardian and exponent of the faith, as the bond of sacramental unity, and as an organ of the Body of Christ in true constitutional relation to the presbyters and people."[72] While they acknowledge that such a wholeness is "far from involving cast-iron uniformity," they insist that "it is for those who at present are without certain elements in Catholic faith and order to receive them . . . in the conviction that they are true."[73] In short, there is no true catholicity without receiving the episcopate.

In contrast, the Anglican evangelical expression of catholicity placed less of an emphasis on the episcopate, as seen in their response to the archbishop's question provided in *The Fullness of Christ* (1950).[74] For them to be catholic is "to stand for the *wholeness* of truth . . . [bearing] testimony to the *whole* truth against partial . . . versions of it. The opposite of catholic is not 'protestant' but one-sided and sectarian."[75] Because catholicity is a reminder of the church's wholeness, it can't be identified with any one conception of ministerial authority. Instead, "the visible Church is . . . defined in terms of the means of grace, not of institutional and ministerial order, because it is through [these] that the visible community nourishes and preserves within it the mystical fellowship which is the deepest essence of the Church's nature."[76]

---

[70]Dix, *Catholicity*, 15.
[71]Dix, *Catholicity*, 13.
[72]Dix, *Catholicity*, 17, 54-55.
[73]Dix, *Catholicity*, 15, 55.
[74]S. F. Allison, ed., *The Fullness of Christ: The Church's Growth into Catholicity* (London: SPCK, 1950).
[75]Allison, *Fullness of Christ*, 14, emphasis added.
[76]Allison, *Fullness of Christ*, 33.

This is not to deny that "the historical continuity of the Church in every age with the Church of the apostles is a reality of immense importance" and that "the continuity through the ages and its unity throughout the Church can be most significantly expressed through continuity of episcopal ordination."[77] In these assertions the group's *Anglican* identity is clear. But their *evangelical* identity leads them to recognize that "the *essential* marks of this continuity are continuous preaching of the gospel and administration of the sacraments in the Church rather than the continuous succession . . . of the episcopal form of ministry."[78] They conclude: "We may not say that episcopacy is constitutive of the visible Church in the same way as the Word and sacraments are. Nor can we say that God cannot and does not, in a divided Church, raise up and use other forms of ministry for the effectual ministration of his word and sacraments."[79] This is because, in their understanding, the doctrine of the priesthood of all believers "denies the view that the [ordained] ministry is a privileged caste . . . able to pass on [its] powers by ordination even without the consent of the Church. . . . Ordination is the act of Christ in his Church, setting apart certain of its members to act representatively on behalf of Christ and the Church."[80] Here is a Reformational understanding of church and ministry, and therefore an understanding of catholicity as continuity in the gospel proclaimed in word, enacted in sacrament, and guarded by doctrinal orthodoxy.

Contemporary contributions

The work of Michael Ramsey. We turn now to three contemporary theologians to see how notions of Anglican catholicity have been synthesized downstream. Perhaps no other Anglican theologian has addressed the question of Anglican catholicity as thoroughly as the Archbishop of Canterbury Michael Ramsey (1904–1988) in his magisterial *The Gospel and the Catholic Church* (first edition 1936). As a representative of the Anglo-Catholic school who was nonetheless critical of certain extremes he saw in the Oxford Movement, Ramsey sought to bridge the gap between Anglo-Catholic and evangelical schools. This is seen even in the title of his work,

---

[77] Allison, *Fullness of Christ*, 33, 66.
[78] Allison, *Fullness of Christ*, 33, 66.
[79] Allison, *Fullness of Christ*, 33, 66.
[80] Allison, *Fullness of Christ*, 35.

which indicated his attempt to show that the gospel (the typical emphasis of the evangelical school) and the church (the typical emphasis of the Anglo-Catholic school) were not competing principles but integrally related. His goal was to expound "the Church as part of the Gospel of Christ crucified" largely in answer to what he saw as one of the most critical questions for Anglican catholicity: "Is Episcopacy merely a convenient form of Church government, or has it some deeper meaning in the Gospel of God?"[81] His conclusion is that "the structure of the Catholic Church has great significance in the Gospel of God, and ... apostolic succession is important on account of its *evangelical* meaning."[82] In short, the gospel and the (catholic) church are, to Ramsey's mind, analytically related.

Ramsey understands catholicity in some sense as a unified diversity through the whole, saying, "From the deeds of Jesus in the flesh there springs a society which is one in its continuous life. Many kinds of fellowship in diverse places and manners are created by the Spirit of Jesus, but they all ... [are] part of the one life of the one family in every age and place. ... In later language [this] Church is called ... 'Catholic' (living one universal life)."[83] But the emphasis quickly falls on church order as the way the gospel is expressed and catholicity is recognized, for "the structure of Catholicism is an utterance of the Gospel."[84] Specifically, Ramsey views episcopacy as, among other things, "a development which grew in the Gospel and through the Gospel, and which expresses the Gospel and can be belittled only at the expense of the Gospel."[85] It even seems that for Ramsey episcopacy is a *necessary* conduit for the gospel; he notes that "the church's full and continuous life in grace does depend upon the succession of bishops, whose work ... [is] bound up with the whole Body."[86] Not surprisingly, Ramsey ultimately affirms "that the Episcopate is of the *esse* of the universal Church" because "the growth of all Christians into the measure of the stature of the fulness of Christ means their growth with all the saints in the unity of

---

[81]Michael Ramsey, *The Gospel and the Catholic Church* (Cambridge, MA: Cowley Publications, 1990), vi.
[82]Ramsey, *Gospel and the Catholic Church*, vii.
[83]Ramsey, *Gospel and the Catholic Church*, 44-45.
[84]Ramsey, *Gospel and the Catholic Church*, 54.
[85]Ramsey, *Gospel and the Catholic Church*, 57.
[86]Ramsey, *Gospel and the Catholic Church*, 83.

the one Body, and of this unity the Episcopate is the expression."[87] Anglicanism has a mission when it comes to seeking unity among the divided churches, a mission centered on its bishops because "the Episcopate succeeded the Apostolate as the organ of unity and continuity. Its meaning is seen in the rites of ordination and in the ordering of the Eucharist. Every ordination and every Eucharist is the act of Christ in his one Body, and the Episcopate expresses this fact in outward order. . . . Hence all Christians need the restoration of the one Episcopate."[88] Here is an understanding of catholicity that places a premium upon the episcopate as the source of the church's catholicity because it is the structural expression of the unifying gospel, demonstrating its apostolic authority even today.

The work of Paul Avis. Another significant contemporary voice is that of Paul Avis, a theologian who has published scores of works dealing with Anglican ecclesiology, including an examination of the church's catholicity in Anglican perspective. At various points Avis defines catholicity generally, saying things like, "Catholicity refers to the universal scope of the Church as a society instituted by God in which all sorts and conditions of humanity, all races, nations and cultures, can find a welcome and a home."[89] But Avis moves beyond merely defining the *scope* of catholicity to actually articulating what catholicity *is*, qualitatively. For him catholicity is ultimately a way of speaking about "the communion of local churches with the universal Church today."[90] He explains that such catholicity as communion centers on "the unity, continuity and sacramentality of the Church," and this because these were the core elements "expressed in the ecclesial forms or structures that emerged between the New Testament writings and the first Ecumenical Councils. . . . These forms were the canon of Holy Scripture, the ecumenical Creeds, the threefold ordained ministry with an episcopate in ordered succession, and the liturgical structure of the Eucharist."[91] Thus for Avis catholicity necessarily involves continuity in word, sacrament, creed, liturgy, and ministry, explaining that "the Church of Christ is a single, visible,

---

[87]Ramsey, *Gospel and the Catholic Church*, 84-85.
[88]Ramsey, *Gospel and the Catholic Church*, 223.
[89]Avis, *Anglican Understanding*, 84-85.
[90]Avis, *Anglican Understanding*, 38.
[91]Paul Avis, *The Vocation of Anglicanism* (London: Bloomsbury T&T Clark, 2016), 105.

historical and ordered community.... Its structures include the threefold ministry... in historical continuity and provision for conciliarity or synodality in governance."[92]

In some sense Avis holds that Anglican catholicity is no different from Catholic or Orthodox catholicity because with them "the Anglican tradition's adherence to episcopacy is in the interests of its own catholicity of order and an expression of its intended faithfulness to the early undivided church."[93] In fact, this leads Avis to even say that "it is... paradoxical that Anglicanism cannot now affirm its catholicity by identifying itself with any other extant tradition that also preserved intact the ancient structures of Catholicism, particularly the historic episcopate."[94] It *should* be able to affirm its catholicity by identifying with "either of the two main catholic, episcopal, pre-Reformation traditions," and yet it cannot, revealing that "we are bound... to conclude that *the appeal to catholicism is necessary but not sufficient to define Anglican ecclesial identity.*"[95] Indeed, Anglican catholicity is distinct in that, while it defends its own claim to catholicity by appealing to an episcopate in historic succession, it *does not require the same for other churches to be connected to the catholic whole*. On this point Avis is clear, saying that "like Rome and the Orthodox, together with the Reformation Churches who would emphatically defend their own catholicity, Anglicanism stands by its claim to belong to the catholic Church, *but it does this without unchurching other claimants.*"[96] This is because Anglicans understand that "though outwardly divided, the catholic Church consists of all Christians united to Christ in the Holy Spirit through faith and baptism and ordered in their various communities under the ministry of word, sacrament and pastoral oversight."[97]

Avis concludes that this is the case by making an important distinction between catholicity and apostolicity, holding that while "apostolicity is the dimension of *depth* in the Church, its extension in time [and] forward momentum in mission.... Catholicity is the dimension of *breadth* in the

---

[92] Paul Avis, "Catholic and Reformed?," *Ecclesiology* 12, no. 2 (2016): 140.
[93] Avis, *Anglicanism and the Christian Church*, 353.
[94] Avis, *Anglican Understanding*, 51-52.
[95] Avis, *Anglican Understanding*, 51-52.
[96] Avis, *Anglican Understanding*, 52, emphasis added.
[97] Avis, *Anglican Understanding*, 81-82.

Church, its extension in space, its aspiration to universality."[98] In other words, "apostolicity has to do with the authenticity of the Church; its faithfulness to its apostolic foundation; the reality of the apostolic mission in . . . the Church today. . . . Catholicity has to do with fullness and completeness; the inclusivity of the Church; the presence of the whole Church in the local churches."[99] Avis connects episcopacy to both of these, insisting that Anglicans value "episcopal ordination in historic succession and in communion with the college of bishops of the universal Church. . . . as an aspect of the catholicity and apostolicity of Anglicanism."[100] But it is only *an aspect*; Avis recognizes that episcopacy "is a sign *but not a guarantee* of apostolicity and catholicity."[101] Even though it remains "a non-negotiable platform of Anglicanism" it is not a *requirement* for apostolicity or catholicity.[102] Rather, it is to be commended to non-Episcopal churches *as churches* to assist them in attaining a *fuller* apostolicity and catholicity.

Here, Avis's disagreement with Ramsey is evident. Avis, while commending much of Ramsey's work, ultimately deems it as an exercise in polemical theology, noting that "the course of the argument is predetermined by Ramsey's acceptance of the principle that there can be no abstraction of Christ and the gospel from the church and its structures. . . . To claim that without the apostolic succession, we cannot have the gospel in its wholeness, is special pleading and smacks of legitimation of ideology."[103] Avis holds with Ramsey that gospel and church are deeply intertwined, even saying that Ramsey's "general model of the relation of the gospel and the church does indeed give us a principle of order, of transmitted authority, of apostolicity."[104] But, Avis insists, "it does not establish . . . that that can be achieved *in only one way*. It is one thing to say that the episcopate can *bear witness* to the corporate dimension of the gospel: it is quite another to reverse this and claim that the gospel *entails* the episcopate."[105] Avis insists that *this* is what

---

[98] Avis, *Anglican Understanding*, 92, emphasis added.
[99] Avis, *Anglican Understanding*, 92.
[100] Avis, *Anglican Understanding*, 89.
[101] Avis, *Anglican Understanding*, 89, emphasis added.
[102] Avis, *Anglican Understanding*, 89.
[103] Avis, *Anglicanism and the Christian Church*, 307.
[104] Avis, *Anglicanism and the Christian Church*, 308.
[105] Avis, *Anglicanism and the Christian Church*, 308, emphasis added.

is distinctive of Anglican catholicity: "The Anglican Church's adherence to episcopacy is in the interests of her own catholicity of order . . . but it does not imply any adverse judgment on the ministries of other communions."[106] To the question "What has the historic episcopate to do with catholicity?" Avis is clear: "Catholicity should not be defined solely by reference to holy order, nor reduced to it. . . . Anglicans have maintained that ordination in the historical episcopal succession *enhances* the catholicity of the Church and *helps* to constitute it."[107] This is why Avis rejects Ramsey's claim that "the historic episcopate was essential to the very existence of the Church . . . [and] that no ecclesial body that lacked it could be fully recognized as a Christian Church."[108] Instead, Avis hopes to arrive at catholicity by another way, noting "the ecumenical theology of communion (*koinonia*) makes it possible for Anglicans to endorse the principle that Ramsey was arguing for—the intrinsic connections between the historic episcopate and the catholicity of the Church—without appearing to unchurch other, non-episcopal communions."[109]

The work of John Webster. The late John Webster (1955–2016) was a theologian whose work is not often discussed as an example of *Anglican* theology, and Webster's work only rarely moves into territory dealing with church order. But there is one important exception: his "The Self-Organizing Power of the Gospel of Christ: Episcopacy and Community Formation" (2001). Webster begins with a nod to Ramsey's "most potent and celebrated" attempt to parse out the relationship between gospel and church order, noting that he will be taking up Ramsey's line of inquiry but indicating in advance that "[my] conclusions are rather different from those which Ramsey reached."[110] In another essay, Webster recognized that "the threefold order [of ministry] enjoys quasi-axiomatic authority in most Anglican institutional practice and liturgical provision, having often been identified as a prime instrument of the Church's unity, catholicity, and apostolicity."[111] Webster laments that this threefold order, and particularly the historical episcopate, has so often

---

[106] Avis, *Anglicanism and the Christian Church*, 308.
[107] Avis, *Anglican Understanding*, 85, emphasis added.
[108] Avis, *Anglican Understanding*, 85-86.
[109] Avis, *Anglican Understanding*, 86.
[110] John Webster, "The Self-Organizing Power of the Gospel of Christ: Episcopacy and Community Formation," in *International Journal of Systematic Theology* 3, no. 1 (March 2001), 69.
[111] John Webster, "Ministry and Priesthood," in Sykes, Booty, and Knight, *Study of Anglicanism*, 332.

been defended on *historical* grounds (and that quite inadequately, in his view) and in a *polemical* manner. He specifically critiques

> those serene Anglican accounts of the history and practice of episcopal ministry in which the emergence of the monarchical episcopate is shown to be an entirely natural and unproblematic development from the earliest Christian impulse. The naiveté of such accounts is not merely their reliance on the apologetic power of historical reconstructions, but their incapacity to envisage the history of episcopacy as political and ideological.[112]

That is, in Webster's view episcopacy is so often commended in Anglican circles because it is held that "in the charmingly deceptive phrase beloved of Anglican apologists . . . 'from the earliest times' the order of the church has been normatively mono-episcopal and that the structure and content of the office has exhibited a high degree of stability"; to this sort of presentation of the story Webster offers a blunt rebuke: "It hasn't."[113]

Webster believed that Ramsey was right to expound episcopacy's relation to the gospel. With Ramsey, Webster seeks a theology of episcopacy "by dogmatic description, not by historical defence . . . [for] a ministry of oversight is a necessary implication of the church's confession of the gospel."[114] Such an account "sets the office and its exercise in the light of the christological, pneumatological and ecclesiological principles of the gospel."[115] This is an inquiry into the dogmatics of church order, the task of which "is to inquire into the entailments of the gospel for the structure of the church as political society; in the matter of episcopacy, such a dogmatics inquires into whether episcopal order is (minimally) fitting or (maximally) necessary to the life of a community at whose centre lies the gospel of Jesus Christ."[116] Accounts that see episcopacy as *necessary* for the church need evangelical reform. This is especially so of accounts arguing something to the effect that "at his ascension Jesus Christ . . . resigns his office in favour of human ministers, and that henceforth the church is the real centre of ministerial agency."[117]

---

[112]Webster, "Self-Organizing Power," 82.
[113]Webster, "Self-Organizing Power," 70.
[114]Webster, "Self-Organizing Power," 70.
[115]Webster, "Self-Organizing Power," 82.
[116]Webster, "Self-Organizing Power," 69-70.
[117]Webster, "Self-Organizing Power," 74.

To avoid accounts of church order that don't "usurp the work of Christ or the Spirit, or the work of the whole church in witnessing to that work," Webster proposes that the key distinction is "between *episcope*, a ministry of oversight, and particular, contingent orderings of the episcopal office."[118] This is because, on the one hand, "oversight is a necessary implication of the gospel through which the church is brought into being and which it is commissioned to proclaim."[119] Thus ministerial office has the vital task "of overseeing the unity and authenticity of the testimony of the church, and so of being caught up into Christ's own formation of his community. In this sense, *episcope*, oversight, is the basic ministry of the church."[120] But, on the other hand, Webster insists that such a claim "is quite other than a defence of . . . a threefold order of ministry headed by a regional episcopate, or of an 'historic episcopate' . . . nor, on the other hand, does it necessarily entail a synodical or congregational episcopate. Such orderings are *adiaphora*."[121] Notice that Webster is conceiving here of at least three different expressions of *episcope*, noting that to insist on any of them as essential to the church's being is out of step with "an evangelical dogmatics of order . . . [that requires] a sharp distinction between episcopacy as a given norm for the church's ministry and any particular contingent ordering of the episcopal office in a given context."[122]

With that key distinction highlighted, Webster is now freed to ask, "What shape of episcopal ministry will *best* serve . . . the rule of Christ in the visible community of the gospel?"[123] In arguing for an Episcopal outworking of *episcope*, Webster appeals to the unity and apostolicity of the church. With regard to unity he observes that "the office of bishop *indicates* the unity of the church, testifying in a public manner to the oneness of the people of God as it is set out in the gospel. Episcopal office is thus a focused, public and institutional place through which attention can be turned to the given unity of the people of God through Spirit, baptism and confession."[124] He then notes that "the ministry of oversight . . . is closely

---

[118]Webster, "Self-Organizing Power," 77, 81.
[119]Webster, "Self-Organizing Power," 81.
[120]Webster, "Self-Organizing Power," 77.
[121]Webster, "Self-Organizing Power," 81.
[122]Webster, "Self-Organizing Power," 71.
[123]Webster, "Self-Organizing Power," 78, emphasis added.
[124]Webster, "Self-Organizing Power," 79-80.

related to the church's apostolicity. Apostolicity has less to do with transmission and much more to do with identity or authenticity, with the 'Christianness' of the church's teaching and mission."[125] And because any particular form of ministry "cannot guarantee authenticity" it implies that "episcopal office is not some sort of condensation of apostolicity, or some means of securing the apostolic character of the whole church."[126] Webster summarizes by suggesting that "the office of oversight is best understood as a function of the unity and apostolic character which the church has by virtue of its election, gathering and sanctification, and its empowerment to know and speak the gospel."[127] In passing he indicates that because "the function of *episcope* is to indicate the church's unity and apostolicity" it "therefore [also indicates] its catholicity," not expanding on this comment but merely drawing from it that "[ministerial] office cannot be simply reinvented at will."[128] He concludes that "episcopal order is indicative of the 'self-organizing' power of the gospel."[129]

Consolidating and Evaluating Anglican Catholicity

What can we conclude regarding Anglican catholicity as a representative of Episcopal catholicity from this brief survey? Certainly one thing we can conclude is that there is no singular "Anglican catholicity"; as with every ecclesial tradition, catholicity is a (much) contested notion within Anglicanism. This contested nature is seen in the current global diversity of the Anglican Communion and in the historical development of the ecclesial tradition, such that what Turner has said regarding authority and *episcope* we can similarly say regarding catholicity: "During the course of their history, Anglicans have believed that the link between [catholicity] and episcopacy is a necessary aspect of the very being of the church (e.g., Kenneth Kirk), that the link is ancient and effective but not necessary (e. g., Thomas Cranmer) or that the link represents an aspect of the church still in need of reform (e.g., various Puritans who nonetheless remained members of the

---

[125] Webster, "Self-Organizing Power," 80.
[126] Webster, "Self-Organizing Power," 80.
[127] Webster, "Self-Organizing Power," 81.
[128] Webster, "Self-Organizing Power," 81.
[129] Webster, "Self-Organizing Power," 82.

Church of England)."¹³⁰ Today it is witnessed most starkly in the ongoing debate between Anglo-Catholic and evangelical schools regarding whether bishops are of the *esse* or *bene esse* of the church. If the former, a church's catholicity stands or falls on whether it has bishops in apostolic succession; if the latter, a church's catholicity is better guarded and perhaps enhanced by the presence of such bishops.

But this is not to say that we can't, to some extent, consolidate the notion of Anglican catholicity and articulate a potential center of it. When we consult the taxonomy provided in the previous chapter, one thing that is immediately evident is that Anglicanism consistently attests to multiple senses of catholicity, mirroring the entire Christian church in that regard. Indeed, all nine conceptions of catholicity are attested in one way or another, and this in and of itself speaks to a deeply catholic ethos. Holistic catholicity (#1) is assumed in the stance of the English Reformers from the very beginning: the Church of England viewed itself as connected to the whole and abhorred schism and a sectarian spirit (though Roman Catholics objected here). Geographical (#2) and missional (#3) catholicity are not only attested by the makeup of the (global) Anglican Communion itself, but the scope of the church among all places and all peoples is testified to by Anglican theologians from Jewel to Avis. Avis has gone on to show that the global scope of Anglicanism testifies to differentiated catholicity (#7), insisting that every province has a distinct contribution to make to the whole. And it is Avis that has drawn attention to resources in the tradition that emphasize liturgical catholicity (#9), arguing that Anglicanism can understand catholicity as sacramental communion because the church is "one visible series of sacramental rites."¹³¹ Here Lutheran theologian Günther Gassman believes that the Anglican Communion gives powerful "ecclesiological and institutional expression to the notion of catholicity by understanding itself as a communion of national churches, rooted in full sacramental communion and manifested in common deliberation at the Lambeth Conferences."¹³² This is, no doubt, a multifaceted and robust catholicity.

---

¹³⁰Philip Turner, "Episcopal Authority in a Divided Church: On the Crisis of Anglican Identity," *Pro Ecclesia* 8, No. 1 (Winter 1999): 37.
¹³¹Avis, *Anglican Understanding*, 86.
¹³²Günther Gassmann, "The Church—Local and Catholic: A Lutheran Perspective," *The Jurist* 52, no. 1 (1992): 521.

But the constant of Anglican catholicity, we would argue, is its strong and consistent emphasis on catholicity as primarily chronological (#4), holding that the church is catholic when it is connected to the church of "all times," especially the early church in its undivided state. Nearly every discussion of Anglican catholicity emphasizes the importance of the Church of England's preceding the Reformation and continuing to maintain the tradition that has been handed down from saints who have walked before. From the *Thirty-Nine Articles* to the Lambeth Quadrilateral, the ecumenical creeds have been commended as a proper expression of the rule of faith and are understood as providing a concrete connection to the church through the ages (especially because they are backed by "most certain warrants of Holy Scripture"). Yet it is here that we see the largest chasm in Anglican conceptions of catholicity, for while the evangelical school largely interprets this connection through time as stemming from *orthodox catholicity* (#5), a continuity of true doctrine centered on the gospel, the Anglo-Catholic school largely interprets this connection through time as stemming from *institutional catholicity* (#6), a visible mediation through common structures and ministry orders. At the heart of this debate is substantial disagreement about what enables participation in christological catholicity (#8); for evangelicals it is faith in the gospel and participation in the means of grace manifest in word and sacrament, while for Anglo-Catholics it is communion with a diocesan bishop (in apostolic succession) serving under an archbishop.

It is no secret that there are severe problems plaguing the Anglican Communion today, and these problems raise the question: Has the episcopate been sufficient to guard the catholicity of the church in Anglicanism? Chapman and company confess that "although the Anglican Communion remains bound together through each bishop being in communion with the Archbishop of Canterbury, many bishops are no longer in full communion with each other."[133] They go on to ask, "Is Anglicanism, as a global Communion . . . 'catholic' in the sense . . . [of having] a clear set of authority structures and [a] sense of communion across space and time? Or is it 'catholic' only because it happens to be so geographically dispersed and globally influential?"[134] Peters gets to the root of the problem in saying that

---

[133]Chapman, Clarke, and Percy, "Introduction," 9.
[134]Chapman, Clarke, and Percy, "Introduction," 11.

"the seeming weakness of this Anglican ecclesiology, and what appears to validate . . . the unpopularity of catholicity in the Anglican Communion, is that each province is autonomous and, thereby, local. This has often led each province to choose the amount of catholicity that they desire from the other Anglican provinces and perhaps also from other Christian churches and traditions."[135] Thomas agrees that the underlying problems stem from the tension between the universal and the local, noting that "because the Anglican view of the Church seeks to do justice both to a vision of the Church in its universal dimension and to the reality of the Church in its local manifestations . . . it is difficult to envisage a systematic treatment of its teaching."[136] In other words, the Anglican tradition and its attempts to articulate the catholicity of the church reveal the need for additional theological resources to be brought to bear, resources that can inform how one understands the church's *universality* as manifesting *locally*. Both evangelical and Anglo-Catholic schools testify to this need, and, we will argue, it is the Free Church tradition that best stands to meet it.

The evangelical Anglican school, we might say, *leaves room* for a Free Church account of the church's catholicity by refusing to hold that bishops belong to the *esse* of the church and in its recognition that catholicity means being attentive to the insights of *all* ecclesial traditions. Here we recall Webster's case that episcopacy was a particularly fitting expression of both the *unity* and the *apostolicity* of the church. Where Webster was not as detailed was in arguing that it was also a particularly fitting expression of the *catholicity* of the church. His argumentation leaves room for the possibility that other forms of church order, other manifestations of *episcope*, might do a better job of expressing the church's catholicity, its wholeness as a unified diversity among all times, peoples, and places. In fact, Webster's articulation of Anglican catholicity would seem to indicate that what he called "synodical and congregational episcopates" are to be embraced alongside episcopacy if they can be shown to be church orders that serve the church's gospel faithfulness through the whole of redemptive history.

---

[135] Greg Peters, "Confessions, Creeds, and Reformed Catholicity—an Anglican Perspective" (paper presented at the national conference of the Evangelical Theological Society in a session titled "Confessions, Creeds, and Catholicity," Denver, November 13–15, 2018), 4.

[136] Philip H. E. Thomas, "Doctrine of the Church," in Sykes, Booty, and Knight, *Study of Anglicanism*, 261.

But the Anglo-Catholic school, we might say, *needs* a Free Church account of the church's catholicity as a form of what Webster has termed "evangelical reform" because it insists, despite the scope of gospel reception being among all times, all peoples, all places, and all ecclesial traditions (including those without bishops), that bishops belong to the *esse* of the church and that, therefore, there is no need to be attentive to others' insights because they are not *ecclesial* insights. Here there is inconsistency: a strong affirmation of the catholicity of the church is coupled with a refusal to heed insights gleaned from the whole church. Ramsey's own statement showcases the problem. He admits that "the Episcopate will be perverted unless it knows itself as nothing in isolation and as significant only as an organ of the one Body, which, by the healthy relation of all its parts, sets forth the Gospel."[137] This would seem to imply that these other parts of the body have something to contribute. Ramsey admits the same: "The tests of a true development are whether it bears witness to the Gospel, whether it expresses the general consciousness of the Christians, and whether it serves the organic unity of the Body in all its parts. These tests are summed up in the Scriptures . . . [which have] a special authority to control and to check the whole field of development on life and doctrine."[138]

If this is true, we could ask why congregational episcopates are ruled out of bounds as a gospel-testifying, unity-serving, and catholic-oriented development. Ramsey believes that the threefold ministry is a development "which speaks of the Gospel and the one Body, so that the Bishop by his place in the one Body bears that essential relation to the Gospel which the Apostle bore before him" and that this is a "form of ministry which the whole New Testament creates [as] the more evangelical way."[139] But this invites the question: Is it the *only* evangelical way? Ramsey says that "every act of grace is the act of the whole Church; and Bishop, presbyters, and people exercise their share in the one priesthood of Christ."[140] It seems fair to conclude, then, that Episcopal and Free Church traditions emphasize the primacy of either the bishop or the people, and because they each have a share in the royal

---

[137]Ramsey, *Gospel and the Catholic Church*, 63-64.
[138]Ramsey, *Gospel and the Catholic Church*, 64.
[139]Ramsey, *Gospel and the Catholic Church*, 69.
[140]Ramsey, *Gospel and the Catholic Church*, 84.

priesthood made possible by Christ, neither one should be excluded as an illegitimate expression of gospel order within the one body. In fact, it is the very doctrine of the church's catholicity that insists that this not be done. As Ramsey himself admits, "The Gospel of God. . . . is not something Roman or Greek or Anglican; rather does it declare to men their utter dependence upon Christ by setting forth the universal Church in which all that is Anglican or Roman or Greek or partial or local in any way must share in an agonizing death to its pride."[141] This is a catholic word indeed.

Conclusion: Episcopal Catholicity Alone Is Not Catholic Enough

We have seen that Anglican catholicity, as a representative of Episcopal catholicity, is contested. Attempts to synthesize Episcopal notions of catholicity often do not produce a common denominator but rather leave conflicting positions in tension, unresolved. This demonstrates that the resources within the Episcopal tradition alone are insufficient for offering a full-orbed doctrine of the church's catholicity. Why is this? It is our contention that such a doctrine will not be arrived at until the theological insights of *all* the ecclesial traditions are brought to bear; only the *whole* church can account for the *wholeness* of the church in a way that is faithful to the *whole* witness of Scripture and integrative of the doctrinal developments that emerge across the *whole* of church history. Avis recognizes this:

> It is important to stress [the] point that catholicity is concerned with completeness, universality and hospitality because, of all the notes of the Church, catholicity is the one that has been most prone to be hijacked for sectarian purposes, not least within Anglicanism. . . . Catholicity simply cannot be allowed to become the private prerogative of any one part of the Church because by definition it has to do with the whole.[142]

In other words, it is the temptation of every ecclesial tradition to "hijack catholicity" for its own purposes, and the only defense against this temptation is to really listen to other traditions and the insights they have been gifted with.

---

[141]Ramsey, *Gospel and the Catholic Church*, 66.
[142]Avis, *Vocation of Anglicanism*, 152.

In this chapter we have heard important testimony regarding the church's catholicity from the Anglican tradition as a stream of the larger Episcopal tradition. Zahl's words summarize that testimony well: "The threefold order of ministry that culminates in the order of bishops is intended to sustain and safeguard the church's catholicity . . . [which] consists in its preaching of the pure Word of God and its faithful administration of the two Bible or 'gospel' sacraments."[143] This is an insight that is both reformed and catholic. It is *reformed* because, as Avis has said,

> the concept of the Church fundamental to the thought of the reformers (including of course the Anglicans)—namely, that only the gospel was of the *esse*—had profound implications for the doctrine of [apostolic] succession and with it the key concept of catholicity. . . . [For] the gospel of truth was held to be sufficient to secure the catholicity of the Church. The Reformers believed . . . that the Church was one, holy, catholic and apostolic, but . . . [with] the gospel itself [as] the decisive and dominant criterion.[144]

But it is also *catholic* because it understands the episcopate as "an office the exercise of which could . . . protect the church's gospel and Bible . . . [and] hence the Church's 'Catholic' identity."[145]

Yet there was another voice in the mid-twentieth century dialogue that Archbishop Fisher invited: the Free Church voice, which insisted that "the scriptural teaching of the work of the Holy Spirit seems . . . to be continually imperiled by various 'catholic' utterances about episcopacy. . . . The gifts of the Holy Spirit promised in the New Testament are [also] given to [Free Churches]."[146] This voice held that "wherever there is contact with Christ there is grace, grace overflowing, grace sufficient for all the manifold ministries of the Church of Christ. It should therefore be impossible . . . to declare that 'the historic episcopate is the *essential* channel through which sacramental grace flows out to the Church.'"[147] These statements made in conversation with Anglicanism require us to articulate a Free Church vision of catholicity.

---

[143]Paul Zahl, "The Bishop-Led Church," in *Perspectives on Church Government: Five Views of Church Polity*, ed. Chad Owen Brand and R. Stanton Norman (Nashville: Broadman & Holman, 2004), 228.
[144]Avis, *Church in the Theology of the Reformers*, 128.
[145]Zahl, "Bishop-Led Church," 230.
[146]Flew and Davies, eds., *Catholicity of Protestantism*, 142.
[147]Flew and Davies, eds., *Catholicity of Protestantism*, 142, emphasis added.

Free Church Catholicity Explored
Examining Reformational Manifestations

WE NOW TURN OUR SIGHTS toward an articulation of Free Church catholicity. Many, including not a few representatives of the Anglican tradition, have contributed to the sense that Free Church catholicity might be a contradiction in terms. We only need to note Ramsey's characterization of congregationalism "with its belief . . . in the autonomous local community which is in itself the Church, existing wherever two or three are gathered together in Christ's name . . . choosing and authorizing its own ministers" as disturbingly lacking "one note of the primitive Church—the note of a continuous, visible, historical society, upon which the local community depends, inwardly and outwardly, in all its sacramental acts. . . . [It omits] the universal Church . . . [and it has] borne incomplete witness to the 'One, Holy Catholic and Apostolic Church.'"[1] In short, it insufficiently expresses the gospel because it lacks catholicity.

In light of this claim regarding a lack of Free Church catholic consciousness, Williams has issued a call to retrieve the riches of church tradition primarily to "suspicious Protestants," of whom "those communions . . . designated as Free Church" are particularly conspicuous.[2] But has

---

[1] Michael Ramsey, *The Gospel and the Catholic Church* (Cambridge, MA: Cowley Publications, 1990), 196.
[2] D. H. Williams, *Retrieving the Tradition and Renewing Evangelicalism: A Primer for Suspicious Protestants* (Grand Rapids, MI: Eerdmans, 1999), 1.

it always been this way? Has the Free Church tradition always manifested a neglect and even a suspicion of catholicity as an attribute of the church? Or have there been pockets within it that have, even if as a minority report, *appreciated* catholicity? Have there been attempts to integrate the doctrine with Free Church ecclesiology? If so, which sources might we retrieve in further refining a doctrine of Free Church catholicity and delineating its yet untapped contribution to the catholic whole? It is to these questions that we turn here, exploring where catholicity shows up within the church-historical contours of the Free Church tradition as it emerged in the sixteenth and seventeenth centuries during the Protestant Reformation and its immediate afterglow.

The significance of these questions should not be overlooked. If a solid case can be made that Free Church catholicity is no oxymoron and actually has a contribution to make toward further development of the doctrine, some degree of precedent for Free Church catholicity needs to be established. This is particularly because the living legacy of the Free Church might be summarized under the banners of sectarianism and independence, both flagrant opposites of catholicity. Avis is right when he says that "the invoking of autonomy and the claiming independence are hardly the language of Zion. More appropriate in the speech of Christians and churches is the rhetoric of communion, consultation, bearing one another's burdens and interdependence."[3] The Free Church tradition has a largely *sectarian* reputation, and with it arguably a repudiation of any claim to catholicity; this must be shown to be a wrong path, and one that the tradition can indeed turn back from. This is the prescription Bird calls for: "The concept of 'independent' churches is an oxymoron. One cannot be 'independent' of other churches any more than one can be independent of Christ. . . . [Thus] the ecclesiological solipsism of many [Free] churches today needs to be countered with a healthy dose of catholicity."[4]

The task of this chapter is quite modest. We don't have to show that the *whole* Free Church tradition has been characterized by a deep-seated catholicity. Instead, all we have to demonstrate here is that *some* of its streams

---

[3]Paul Avis, *Vocation of Anglicanism* (London: Bloomsbury T&T Clark, 2016), 186.
[4]Michael Bird, *Evangelical Theology* (Grand Rapids, MI: Zondervan, 2013), 738.

have placed a premium on the church's catholicity and seen it as fully compatible with Free Church ecclesial convictions.[5]

SPEAKING OF THE FREE CHURCH

But before we proceed, we must revisit a critical question: What do we mean by the Free Church tradition? In the introduction we acknowledged both the *difficulty* of delimitating the tradition's boundaries and the *helpfulness* of understanding the Free Church as a distinct ecclesial tradition made up of diverse-yet-interconnected streams. Following Littell's contention that "the place to begin [defining the tradition] is with [its] view of the church" we identified three Free Church ecclesial marks.[6] We argued that we can speak of the Free Church tradition in a coherent way and that we can look back in church history and see a common "family resemblance" amid the distinct streams that make up this broader tradition.

This raises the question: When did the Free Church tradition *begin*? Though there is much debate within the tradition on exactly this question, here we hold that the Free Church tradition as such begins amid the watershed event of Reformation. Yes, there have been manifestations of a Free Church *ethos* through church history because it is "a type *sui generis* which . . . keeps arising again and again, in every century, taking on similar shapes."[7] And yet, we recognize that the Free Church *tradition* stems from the Reformation because it is, above all else, a "segment of the Protestant Christian heritage."[8] Williams is right that with the Reformation "historical patterns of ecclesiology. . . . [stemming from] the conviction that the church is not an institution on account of its structure or external rites, but [on account of] the faithful" become

---

[5]This exploration will follow D. H. Williams in his conviction that "since most of the descendants of the Free Church phenomenon on the European continent or in England are Trinitarian, I am deliberately omitting the antinomian and anti-trinitarian elements of the sixteenth century that have been also referred to by historians as manifestations of the 'Free Church.'" Williams, *Retrieving the Tradition*, 2.

[6]Franklin H. Littell, "The Historical Free Church Defined," *Brethren Life and Thought* 50, nos. 3-4 (Summer-Fall 2005): 53. The three marks were being congregationally constituted, conscientiously nonconformist, and corporately local.

[7]John H. Yoder, "The Believers' Church Conferences in Historical Perspective," *The Mennonite Quarterly Review* 65, no. 1 (January 1991): 12-13.

[8]James Leo Garrett Jr., "Preface," in *The Concept of the Believers' Church: Addresses from the 1968 Louisville Conference*, ed. James Leo Garrett Jr. (Scottdale, PA: Herald Press, 1969), 5.

more definitively expressed in the ecclesial tradition we now know as the Free Church.[9]

What Do We Mean by Free Church Accounts of Catholicity?

Recall that in chapter three we expressed what was meant by "Episcopal accounts of catholicity" primarily by examining Anglican notions as distinct-yet-representative of it. We have insisted that to identify how catholicity is conceived differently between the Episcopal and Free Church traditions we have to move beyond questions of church *order* (polity) to questions of the church's *nature* and the pattern of ecclesial authority understood as in keeping with that nature. This involves tracing out their distinctive *theological accounts of ecclesial authority*, especially investigating how authority is transferred from Christ to the community and its ministers. In chapter three, we described and then illustrated through the Anglican tradition how an Episcopal account of the church's catholicity flows from a pattern of ecclesial authority that is largely "top down." Now we will briefly describe how the Free Church account of the church's catholicity flows from a pattern of ecclesial authority that is largely "bottom up."

This Free Church pattern appeals to parts of the New Testament witness that demonstrate all of God's people engaging in the constitution and regulation of congregational life.[10] A Free Church account of ecclesial authority takes its lead from this portion of the biblical testimony in tracing a proper pattern of ecclesial authority as flowing from God to the apostles to the gathered congregation and, finally, to ministers (including bishops/elders/pastors and deacons) who derive their authority from Christ as expressed through the congregation. Note that the installation and ordination of

---

[9]Williams, *Retrieving the Tradition*, 2.

[10]For instance, much is made of how the book of Acts sets corporate deliberation on display (such as Acts 1 noting the involvement of 120 persons in selecting a replacement for Judas, Acts 6 portraying the whole Jerusalem congregation as involved in choosing "proto-deacons," and Acts 15 testifying to "all the people" playing a role even in the Jerusalem Council), of how Paul addresses whole congregations in the majority of his letters and calls on the whole church to exercise responsibility with regard to regulating the Lord's Supper (1 Cor 11:22, 27) and exercising discipline (1 Cor 5:5), and of places the doctrine of the "priesthood of all believers" (1 Pet 2:9; Heb 10:19, Rev 1:6) flows out of the conviction that every one of God's people has the Spirit of God (1 Cor 7:40).

ministers and their relation to the apostles becomes a key area of differentiation from the Episcopal tradition. Both traditions believe that maintaining a proper line of ecclesial authority is an important part of keeping with the whole and thus being properly deemed "catholic"; they vary significantly on whether ministerial authority is derived from Christ via his apostles from below (the gathered local church) or from above (bishops in apostolic succession). The Free Church tradition consistently emphasizes that the gathered congregation is the proper conduit for ecclesial authority and thus serves as the locus of catholicity.

Tracing this pattern brings up an important question of clarification: What of the Presbyterian tradition?[11] Should it be considered part of the Free Church tradition, a variation of the Episcopal tradition, or a distinct third tradition? It turns out that it very much depends on which Presbyterians you ask and what segments of Presbyterianism you examine. In Presbyterian polity, ecclesial power is understood to reside *in both* a representative assembly above the local church (a presbytery, then a synod or general/national assembly) and the local congregation itself (expressed in its session of elders). This would seem to make the Presbyterian tradition a potential mediating position between the Episcopal and Free Church traditions.[12] But when we inquire about the *pattern* of how such ecclesial authority is derived, significant differences within the Presbyterian tradition emerge.[13] Some

---

[11]Cowan explains that "in presbyterianism, the local church is ruled by a group of elders . . . who are chosen by the congregation. Members of the sessions from several local churches in a geographical region are also members of the *presbytery* which has ruling authority over their several churches. In turn, at least some members of each presbytery are also members of a general assembly which governs the entire denominational body." Cowan goes on to distinguish this from congregationalism where "the elders have no authority or jurisdiction outside their own local church." Steven B. Cowan, "Introduction," in *Who Runs the Church? Four Views on Church Government*, ed. Steven B. Cowan (Grand Rapids, MI: Zondervan, 2004), 13-15.

[12]So Robert Reymond, who believes that Presbyterianism holds "the perfect middle" and concludes that "each court in Presbyterianism . . . necessarily [has] its own intrinsic authority peculiar to itself, for . . . Christ has in fact authorized ascending levels of courts." See Robert Reymond, "The Presbytery-Led Church," in *Perspectives on Church Government: Five Views of Church Polity*, ed. Chad Owen Brand and R. Stanton Norman (Nashville: Broadman & Holman, 2004), 125.

[13]Taylor acknowledges that some Presbyterian systems "have a more hierarchical system whereby ecclesiastical power flows from the higher courts of the church to the lower courts. . . . [Others] hold to more of a 'grassroots' presbyterianism whereby ecclesiastical power flows from lower courts of the church to the higher courts." L. Roy Taylor, "Presbyterianism," in Cowan, *Who Runs the Church?*, 74.

describe the pattern in ways that emphasize the "bottom-up" trajectory.[14] Others describe the pattern in ways that are predominantly "top-down."[15] Still others try to maintain something like a pattern of "simultaneously bottom-up and top-down," but it is hard to see exactly how this works and even whether such a position is coherent.[16] When we ask about *how* this authority comes to the local congregation and the supra-local presbytery/ synod, and what to do in cases where these two *loci* of ecclesial authority conflict, it seems that one must default back to either a "bottom-up" or "top-down" pattern. Because of this intramural debate regarding the proper pattern of ecclesial authority, in this project we will not include Presbyterianism within the Free Church tradition.

Concern for Catholicity in the Early Free Church Tradition

We turn now to our primary task: exploring expressions of catholicity in the early Free Church tradition. Kärkkäinen sets our parameters: "Anabaptism and later Baptist movements were on the one hand forerunners of later Free churches and on the other hand the . . . part of the Protestant Reformation that wanted to go further than the Magisterial Reformers went."[17] To these we will also add the Congregational movement because the emerging Free Church tradition is shaped significantly by both sixteenth-century Continental Anabaptism and seventeenth-century English Separatist Puritanism (of which both "Baptists" and certain "Independents" were counted). Fiddes speaks of all these groups as constituting a "fourth strand of the Reformation" alongside Lutheran, Reformed, and Anglican.[18] George Williams concurs that "the Radical Reformation . . . is one that is as distinctive as Lutheranism,

---

[14]American Presbyterianism tends to exhibit this. For instance, the *PCA Book of Church Order* states, "The power which Christ has committed to His Church vests in the whole body, the rulers and those ruled, constituting it a spiritual commonwealth. This power, as exercised by the people, extends to the choice of those officers whom He has appointed in His Church." Quoted in L. Roy Taylor, "A Presbyterian's Response," in Cowan, *Who Runs the Church?*, 164.
[15]Scottish Presbyterianism tends to exhibit this. Reymond points to Samuel Rutherford as an example of someone who expresses a top-down conception.
[16]Berkhof is probably the best example here. See Louis Berkhof, *Systematic Theology*, new ed. (Grand Rapids, MI: Eerdmans, 1996), 583-84.
[17]Veli-Matti Kärkkäinen, *An Introduction to Ecclesiology: Ecumenical, Historical & Global Perspectives* (Downers Grove, IL: IVP Academic, 2002), 61.
[18]Paul Fiddes, "A Fourth Strand of the Reformation," *Ecclesiology* 13, no. 2 (2017): 153.

Calvinism, and Anglicanism, and it is perhaps comparably significant in the rise of modern Christianity."[19] Meanwhile, D. H. Williams holds that, despite the reputation of the Radicals as being anticatholic and deeply sectarian, "careful studies of certain free church communions demonstrate that there was in their earlier days a greater awareness of just how indebted they were to the catholicism of the early church. . . . The historic impetus of free church Christianity, on the whole, was not anticreedal and certainly not antichurch."[20] This chapter serves as an attempt to vindicate this claim by finding such testimony to Free Church catholicity.

The sixteenth-century continental context: Anabaptism. We begin here because we agree with Durnbaugh's assessment that "the Free or Believers' Church movement starts with the Anabaptists."[21] We must acknowledge that Anabaptism was, as Finger characterizes it, "extraordinarily diverse . . . rich in tales both heroic and horrific."[22] Part of the movement's diversity stems from its differing locales, originating "from three relatively independent sources—Swiss, South German-Austrian and Dutch—and also a Polish stream with some Italian provenance."[23] Additionally, it was common for Catholics and magisterial Protestants to group the whole lot of religious mystics, militant revolutionaries, rationalist antitrinitarians, and centrist reformers indiscriminately under the despicable label *Anabaptists*. It is the last of these groups, the one we might call the "conservatives" of the Reformation's left wing, that we are concerned with in this study. It is this group, which Littell describes as those who sought to "gather . . . a 'true church' upon the apostolic pattern as they understood it," where an appreciation for catholicity is most likely to be found in the earliest Free Church heritage.[24]

The challenge of establishing any concern for catholicity among the Anabaptists is well known. Such a task is often viewed as no more than a fool's

---

[19]Quoted in Irvin Buckwalter Horst, *The Radical Brethren: Anabaptism and the English Reformation to 1558* (Nieuwkoop, Netherlands: B. De Graaf, 1972), 25.

[20]D. H. Williams, "Preface," in *The Free Church & the Early Church: Bridging the Historical & Theological Divide*, ed. D. H. Williams (Grand Rapids, MI: Eerdmans, 2002), ix.

[21]Donald D. Durnbaugh, ed., *Every Need Supplied: Mutual Aid and Christian Community in the Free Churches, 1525-1675* (Philadelphia; Temple University Press, 1974), 16.

[22]Thomas N. Finger, *A Contemporary Anabaptist Theology: Biblical, Historical, Constructive* (Downers Grove, IL: InterVarsity Press, 2004), 17.

[23]Finger, *Contemporary Anabaptist Theology*, 17.

[24]Franklin H. Littell, *The Origins of Sectarian Protestantism: A Study of the Anabaptist View of the Church* (New York: Macmillan Company, 1964), xvii.

errand in light of comments such as those of Anabaptist Sebastian Frank, who confessed, "I believe that the outward Church of Christ . . . because of the breaking in and laying waste by antichrist right after the death of the Apostles, went up into heaven, and lies concealed in the Spirit and in truth. I am thus quite certain that for fourteen hundred years now there has existed no gathered Church nor any sacrament."[25] The reputation of sixteenth-century Anabaptists as anticatholic exists not just in our own time (thanks, in part, to continued misunderstandings of their reforming efforts) but also existed in theirs. It was known that "Anabaptists were pretty certain that all other groups would inherit not the kingdom of God but his fierce wrath for their intractable stubbornness in rejecting the truth that they . . . had found. Their conviction [was] that they [alone] were the true church."[26]

An important part of understanding why Anabaptist expressions were frequently sectarian stems from recognizing that their experience was so often one of persecution and even martyrdom by the very churches that claimed to be following Christ and standing in the tradition of the one, holy, catholic, and apostolic church. Gordon Rupp states that the Anabaptists were consistently "persecuted by Protestant and Catholic alike, denigrated and caricatured by [those who claimed] orthodoxy, [and unfairly] discredited by their own extremists. . . . [They experienced] a higher proportion of martyrs than any other Reformation movement."[27] It was reasonable to conclude, as some Anabaptists did, that if such gruesome persecution and martyrdom of those professing Christ (and unwilling to retaliate on the basis of a New Testament ethic) came at the hands of those claiming to be part of the catholic church (whether Catholic or Protestant), then such catholicity, whatever it might be, had nothing to do with true, apostolic Christianity.

---

[25]Quoted in Kärkkäinen, *Introduction to Ecclesiology*, 61.
[26]Walter Klaasen, "A Fire That Spread: Anabaptist Beginnings," *Christian History Magazine* 4, no. 1 (1985): 8.
[27]Gordon Rupp, *Protestant Catholicity: Two Lectures* (London: Epworth Press, 1960), 25-26. Rupp recounts the "examination" of Anabaptist Hans Hut, which began with "so called friendly interrogation and going on to examination under torture, first the weights and then the rack, and to [death] from burns received while trying to escape. [This is] a grim reminder of the war crimes of Protestant civil war . . . amid which these haunted, hunted men presented a shocking, challenging emblem of the simplicity of the apostolic Church." Rupp, *Protestant Catholicity*, 27.

It is also important to see that the consistency of this early Anabaptist experience led to the situation where they could rarely, if ever, produce formal creeds or elaborate theological treatises, for, as Lumpkin says, "On account of ceaseless persecution and oppression, they had little opportunity to write extensively of their faith. A sense of organizational strength, out of which creedal expression naturally comes, was not permitted to develop."[28] This is not to deny that this was often accompanied by a general predisposition against creeds as a false substitute for Scripture and a potential hindrance to the Spirit leading God's people to interpret Scripture aright. But it is to insist that a lack of such expressions relative to other Reformation movements should not be counted against them, for such a luxury was never theirs to leverage.

So, where should we look for Anabaptist views on the church's catholicity? The consistent answer has been their views and assumptions regarding the church. Littell has said "in a treatment of the Anabaptists, the doctrine of the church affords the classifying principle of first importance."[29] Some scholars in Anabaptist studies note that "from the writings of the sixteenth century Anabaptists in Switzerland, Germany, and the Netherlands we receive the overwhelming impression and conviction that they were *ecclesio-centric*. . . . The Church of Believers was basic and significant. Their views of other aspects of salvation such as sin, regeneration, Christian living, etc., were influenced by their concept of the church."[30] And for the same reasons that Calvin expressed a deep appreciation for catholicity without always using the term, so we must be on the lookout for expressions of Anabaptist catholicity without necessarily expecting the word *catholic* to appear.

Select Anabaptist Expressions

We will use Leo Laurense's article "The Catholicity of the Anabaptists" for our orientation. It is one of the only studies ever dedicated to the subject,

---

[28]William L. Lumpkin and Bill J. Leonard, eds., *Baptist Confessions of Faith*, second rev. ed. (Valley Forge, PA: Judson Press, 2011), 18. The Schleitheim Confession of 1527 is a significant exception.

[29]Littell, *Origins of Sectarian Protestantism*, xvii.

[30]P. K. Regier, ed., *Proceedings of the Study Conference on the Believers' Church* (Newton, KS: Mennonite Press, 1955), 85.

likely because of the challenge he acknowledges at its beginning: "A search [for] source materials to find [catholicity attested here] leads to disappointment, for it is scarcely to be found at all among the Anabaptist writers of the sixteenth century."[31] But, Laurense insists, not all hope is lost if "the concept of catholicity [is] placed in the [context] of ecclesiology . . . [for] the ultimate significance of sixteenth-century Anabaptism lies in its concept of the Church."[32] Laurense believes that an implicit catholicity can be found in the way that the Anabaptists followed the logic of the creed in stressing the work of the Holy Spirit in creating and sustaining the church. With this emphasis in view "a more dynamic church comes into being and the church receives a more catholic character. . . . [For] if catholicity is synonymous with fulness, it may be said that the Anabaptists have expressly viewed themselves as catholic, and have seen the guarantee of their catholicity in the working of the Spirit, and not primarily in the office, the order, or the confession."[33]

This emphasis on the Spirit's common work in the lives of believers and in gathering those believers as the church is thus understood as a potential touchstone for catholicity. The fact that the Spirit had, from Abraham to the Zurich Reformers, set apart a people to be holy meant that such a transformation from death to life, from worldliness to godliness, was a common bond of those who were truly God's people. Thus Laurense argues that though "Anabaptism held the *sola fide, sola gratia,* and *sola scriptura* in common with the Reformation . . . it [maintained] that these are not . . . the ultimate. The faith [has to] comprehend the whole of life, and only that faith which comprehends the whole of life is catholic. [Therefore] only that church which inculcates this in its being as the church is catholic in Anabaptist thought."[34] Menno Simons expressed this desire to go beyond the outward magisterial marks of the church when he hints at where the catholic church can truly be found: "Let it be unto you a certain rule—namely, where the Spirit, Word, sacraments, and life of Christ are found, there the Nicene

---

[31]Leo Laurense, "The Catholicity of the Anabaptists," *Mennonite Quarterly Review* 38, no. 3 (July 1964): 266.
[32]Laurense, "Catholicity of the Anabaptists," 266.
[33]Laurense, "Catholicity of the Anabaptists," 267.
[34]Laurense, "Catholicity of the Anabaptists," 270.

article is pertinent, I believe in one holy, Christian church, the communion of saints."[35]

Similarly a classic Anabaptist manual of faith and the closest to a treatise on Christian doctrine as emerged from early Anabaptism, Peter Riedeman's *Rechenschaft*, speaks of the church as "an assembly of the children of God who have separated themselves from all unclean things."[36] This call for holy separation from the world doesn't necessarily imply a deep sectarianism, as indicated by the fact that the *Rechenschaft* not only provided a copy of the Apostles' Creed at its start, but is actually based on its pattern. Though the article on the "One Holy, Christian Church" refrains from confessing the church explicitly as catholic, it indicates that connection to the whole of God's people is something the Spirit brings about. The text notes, "We confess that God through Christ has chosen and accepted a people for himself, a people without stain. . . . Such a community or church is gathered together by the Holy Spirit. . . . [as] an assembly of the children of God."[37] The confession's closing statement hints at an inclusive catholic scope: "We wish with all our heart that all people would be built into a holy house with us."[38] It is the common work of the Spirit that is understood to bring about a whole church of all people.

Another key to understanding the sense of Anabaptist catholicity is recognizing that it is the gathered community as a visible church that would be the center of any such concern. Laurense comments that "Anabaptism did not try to [answer] the question of catholicity by positing an invisible church, thus [spiritualizing] the church concept. The point of departure was and remained the church that assembled around the Word and Sacrament, the gathered church. There Christ was in the midst . . . even though it be a pneumatic presence."[39] Laurense thus concludes that for the Anabaptists "the *katholica* was present in the congregation. Thus [they] can assent at least to the second part of the well known pronouncement . . . 'For where Jesus

---

[35] Quoted in Alfred T. DeGroot, "A People Under the Word: Historical Background," in Garrett, *Concept of the Believers' Church*, 191.
[36] Lumpkin and Leonard, *Baptist Confessions of Faith*, 40-41.
[37] John J. Friesen, ed., *Peter Riedemann's Hutterite Confession of Faith* (Scottdale, PA: Herald Press, 1999), 76-77.
[38] Friesen, *Peter Riedemann's Hutterite Confession*, 170.
[39] Laurense, "Catholicity of the Anabaptists," 270-71.

Christ is, there is the catholic church.'"⁴⁰ Here we can cite the Dordrecht Confession (1632), for even though it comes a century later, it demonstrates the trajectory of early Anabaptist theology. This confession says, "We believe in ... a visible Church of God, consisting of those who ... have truly repented, [have] rightly believed ... are rightly baptized, [have been] united with God in heaven, and [have been] incorporated into the communion of saints on earth."⁴¹ It is expressed that this church is "a habitation of God through the Spirit, built on the foundation of the apostles and prophets, of which 'Christ Himself is the chief cornerstone'—the foundation on which His church is built."⁴² The catholic scope of this visible Church is hinted at in articles four and five, which say that Christ "purchased redemption for the whole human race ... [becoming] the source of eternal salvation to all who from the time of Adam to the end of the world shall have believed in Him and obeyed Him.... [This message is] to be proclaimed ... to all nations, peoples, and tongues ... having thus excluded none from ... eternal salvation."⁴³ Article nine makes it clear that Christ as the "faithful and great Shepherd, the Bishop of our souls was sent into the world ... so as to make out of many one; thus collecting ... out of all nations a church in His name."⁴⁴ Here we can see that a chronological, geographical, and missional catholicity is implicit.

So, did certain Anabaptists express at least a degree of catholicity? Laurense answers with a yes, provided we are willing to allow the Anabaptists to express their distinctive understanding of what that would mean. He notes cautiously that "the Anabaptists certainly wanted to belong to the *Una Sancta Catholica*, but with their own view of the church and of the world."⁴⁵ For the early Anabaptists, true catholicity, according to Laurense,

> involved participating in the one people of God by being filled by the one Spirit to be joined with the one Body of Christ through the ages, using the church of the apostles as a primary reference point, desiring the restitution of that church ... demonstrating evidence of reformed life and doctrine ...

---

⁴⁰Laurense, "Catholicity of the Anabaptists," 270-71.
⁴¹John H. Leith, ed., *The Creeds of the Church*, rev. ed. (Richmond, VA: John Knox Press, 1973), 299.
⁴²Lumpkin and Leonard, *Baptist Confessions of Faith*, 67.
⁴³Leith, *Creeds*, 296.
⁴⁴Leith, *Creeds*, 300.
⁴⁵Laurense, "Catholicity of the Anabaptists," 277.

keeping in view the limits of the church expressed in faithful discipline, and manifesting in a vision for the church on mission reaching a lost humanity with the gospel.[46]

This is not catholicity as it was conceived in Wittenberg, Geneva, or Canterbury; it was *certainly* not catholicity as it was conceived in Rome. But it is enough to lead George Williams to argue that the Anabaptists exhibited what he calls a "sectarian ecumenicity." For him it is no small thing that their "practice of . . . believers' baptism and the concomitant rigorous exercise of the ban did not theologically isolate [them] from due concern for other Christians . . . [or preclude] the possibility of salvation *extra ecclesiolam*."[47] Indeed, Williams concludes that "in an age of mounting nationalism and dynastic absolutism . . . the Radical Reformation recovered on an intentionally sectarian basis of gathered churches the catholicity of explicit faith."[48]

The seventeenth-century British context: Separatist Puritanism. Timothy George holds that, despite clear differences between their visions for church reform, "the Anabaptist vision of the Church . . . [finds] Free Church parallels in radical puritan, separatist and Baptist modalities."[49] If sixteenth-century Continental Anabaptism was where the Free Church tradition was born, the seventeenth-century British context was where it entered its most formative stage. This is why Donald Ashmall can describe Free Churches as "those communions which came out of the Puritan movement in England. . . . [carrying] a strong strain of Calvinist theology within their

---

[46]Laurense, "Catholicity of the Anabaptists," 278-79.

[47]George Huntston Williams, "Sectarian Ecumenicity: Reflections on a Little Noticed Aspect of the Radical Reformation," *Review and Expositor* 64, no. 2 (Spring 1967): 154.

[48]Williams, "Sectarian Ecumenicity," 159. For perhaps the strongest expression of Anabaptist catholicity see the life and work of Balthasar Hubmaier (1480-1528). Hubmaier, despite his embrace of radical reform, never lost sight of his connectedness to the Great Tradition. He was "among those who endeavored to keep the catholic vision in full view. . . . [calling for Anabaptists] to recognize the universal faith that unites all Christians from the days of the apostles to the present . . . and which is shared in common by believers throughout the whole earth." Curtis W. Freeman, James Wm. McClendon Jr., and C. Rosalee Velloso da Silva, eds., *Baptist Roots: A Reader in the Theology of a Christian People* (Valley Forge, PA: Judson Press, 1999), 4. Hubmaier's dedication to searching the Scriptures, appealing to the fathers, leveraging medieval insights, working with other Reformers, respecting certain legacies of Roman Catholicism, and calling for a universal council to resolve contemporary doctrinal disputes demonstrates a catholic spirit admittedly rare among the Radical Reformers.

[49]Timothy George, "The Sacramentality of the Church: An Evangelical Baptist Perspective," in *Pro Ecclesia* 12, no. 3 (Summer 2003): 310.

heritage, accompanied by a pervasive conviction that questions of ecclesiology are more than incidental to the Christian enterprise."[50] James Maclear can similarly say, "The free church form . . . was molded in the unique environment of religious multiplicity which Puritan divisions produced . . . [and was] shaped by certain axioms of Puritan thought and piety. Indeed . . . Puritanism both produced the problem and suggested the alternatives out of which the final free church concepts emerged."[51]

What exactly we mean by "Puritanism" is notoriously difficult to pin down. Wallace gives us a start by noting its catholic character: "Puritan theology was an episode in the larger story of international Reformed theology . . . [that made] no break with the principle creeds of the ancient church, retaining belief in the doctrines of the Trinity and the two natures of Christ."[52] Coffey and Lim hold that Puritanism was (1) a type of Protestantism that heavily emphasized *sola fide*, *sola gratia*, and *sola Scriptura*, (2) linked particularly with the Calvinist stream of the Reformation, (3) a distinct form of Reformed Protestantism given its cultivation in the English context, (4) prone to branch beyond the Church of England into different streams, including Presbyterian, Congregational, and Baptist and (5) international in scope and influence.[53]

Separatism is thus best understood as a distinct stream of the larger Puritan movement. B. R. White says that "for many it was but a short step from impatient Puritanism within the established Church to convinced Separatism outside it."[54] Macclear also insists on Separatism's continuity with Puritanism, calling these groups "the Puritan sects" or "left-wing Puritanism"; others have found the designation of "Radical Puritans" the most accurate.[55] This reinforces a point we made in the last chapter, which

---

[50]Donald H. Ashmall, "Spiritual Development and the Free Church Tradition: The Inner Pilgrimage," *Andover Newton Quarterly* 20, no. 3 (January 1980): 141-42.

[51]James Fulton Maclear, "The Birth of the Free Church Tradition," *Church History* 26, no. 2 (June 1957): 99.

[52]Dewy D. Wallace Jr., "Puritan Polemical Divinity and Doctrinal Controversy," in *The Cambridge Companion to Puritanism*, ed. John Coffey and Paul C. H. Lim (Cambridge: Cambridge University Press, 2008), 206.

[53]John Coffey and Paul C. H. Lim, "Introduction," in Coffey and Lim, *Cambridge Companion to Puritanism*, 2-6.

[54]B. R White, *The English Separatist Tradition from the Marian Martyrs to the Pilgrim Fathers* (London: Oxford University Press, 1971), 84.

[55]Maclear, "Birth of the Free Church Tradition," 104, 120.

is that the Free Church tradition is shaped largely by the ecclesiological issues that emerged in an Anglican-dominated context. So John Coffey reminds us that "the story of Dissent can only be told in conjunction with the story of the Church of England. . . . What we call Puritanism was imbricated with Anglicanism. . . . Much of early Protestant Dissent was not dissent *from* the Church of England, but dissent *within* it and on its behalf. . . . Only after much struggle and various contingencies did Church and Dissent become rival ecclesiastical blocs."[56] Understanding this backdrop is vital if we are to grasp how Baptist and Congregational groups that "broke away" from the Church of England can be said to express a catholic spirit.

Baptist Manifestations

George Williams holds that "Baptists might be considered the very model of the Believers' Church . . . [drawing as they do] upon a number of historic impulses toward the pure church of true believers."[57] But the Baptist tradition, as Lumpkin notes, draws on more "historic impulses" than just those of the Radical Reformation: "In one sense, all of the Protestant confessions, beginning with the Lutheran Confession of Augsburg in 1530, stand in the background of the Baptist [movement], but those of Anabaptism and English Separatism are immediate forerunners."[58] When we recall that "Calvinism was the dominant theology of the Separatists" we also recognize how formative the Reformed tradition was for the early Baptist movement, especially the strand running from Geneva.[59] Briggs can summarize that "seventeenth century Baptists were essentially Reformed or Calvinistic Christians who admitted believers, on the declaration of their faith in baptism, into congregationally ordered churches."[60] Bingham also emphasizes the

---

[56]John Coffey, "Church and State, 1550–1750: The Emergence of Dissent," in *T&T Clark Companion to Nonconformity*, ed. Stephen J. Pope (London: Bloomsbury, 2013), 48.
[57]George Huntston Williams, "A People in Community: Historical Background," in Garrett, *Concept of the Believers' Church*, 117.
[58]Lumpkin and Leonard, *Baptist Confessions of Faith*, 16.
[59]Lumpkin and Leonard, *Baptist Confessions of Faith*, 14.
[60]John Briggs, "The Influence of Calvinism on Seventeenth-Century English Baptists," *Baptist History and Heritage* 39, no. 2 (Spring 2004): 10. This description would remain true, to some extent, of what were known as "General Baptists," those who were more Arminian in their theological outlook. This is partly because, we will recall, Arminian views in the seventeenth century were still understood as views (albeit increasingly unpopular ones) *within the Reformed faith*.

ecclesiological proximity of Baptists to other strands of the Reformation, noting that Baptists shared "theological affinities and relational networks . . . [with] paedobaptistic congregationalists or independents"; that is, they were "a baptistic variation on the more mainstream congregational movement developing on both sides of the Atlantic."[61]

Baptist confessions. The Baptist tradition has a reputation for being "noncreedal," but as we will see, this is in fact a later development (and a negative one at that). To the contrary, Timothy George says, "Baptists in particular [have] been prolific in promulgating confessions, both as public declarations of their own faith and as a means of testing the true faith in others."[62] Indeed, Leon McBeth emphasizes that early "Baptists often used their confessions not so much to proclaim 'Baptist distinctives' (though they did use them in this manner to some extent), but instead to show how similar they were to other orthodox Christians of their day."[63] These early confessions thus reveal an implicit catholicity by demonstrating both "the same themes which were central in the theology of the great reformers of the sixteenth century"[64] and "a concern for doctrinal continuity with patristic Christianity . . . primarily in echoes of Nicaeno-Constantinopolitan Trinitarianism and Chalcedonian Christology,"[65] even if they didn't explicitly affirm catholicity or articulate how the church's catholicity was to be understood.

Though there were earlier confessions that are embraced as a part of the Baptist heritage and demonstrate some degree of catholic sensibility, it is with the First London Confession (first edition 1644, second edition 1646) that an *implicit* Baptist catholicity emerges.[66] By 1644 seven Particular Baptist churches in London who already exhibited an informal association began drawing up a formal confession, primarily for apologetic purposes.

---

[61]Matthew C. Bingham, *Orthodox Radicals: Baptist Identity in the English Revolution* (Oxford: Oxford University Press, 2019), 4, 8.
[62]Timothy George, "The Priesthood of All Believers," in *The People of God: Essays on the Believers' Church*, ed. Paul Basden and David S. Dockery (Nashville: Broadman Press, 1991), 89.
[63]Quoted in Timothy George, "The Reformation Roots of the Baptist Tradition," *Review & Expositor* 86, no. 1 (Winter 1989): 11.
[64]George, "Reformation Roots," 11.
[65]Steven R. Harmon, *Towards Baptist Catholicity: Essays on Tradition and the Baptist Vision* (Eugene, OR: Wipf & Stock, 2006), 72.
[66]Lumpkin says that "perhaps no Confession of Faith has had so formative an influence on Baptist life as this one." Lumpkin and Leonard, *Baptist Confessions of Faith*, 140.

It is significant that this influential confession drew directly on one of the earliest confessions of English Separatism, the so-called True Confession of 1596. The Particular Baptists identified with much of its content and with the motivation of these earlier confessors, who wrote "for the clearing of our selves from those unchristian slanders of heresy [and] schism."[67] The fact that the True Confession was used as a basis for the First London Confession indicates a common Separatist heritage and an emerging Baptist catholic spirit (after all, the authors of the True Confession were paedobaptist). The authors of the First London Confession embraced a more catholic stance in using the True Confession for their apologetic and didactic purposes, adding certain distinctives (e.g., baptism was "to be dispensed only upon persons professing faith") while coming up short of *explicitly* affirming the church's catholicity.

That honor is reserved for the Particular Baptist Second London Confession (first edition 1677; second edition 1689) and the General Baptist Orthodox Creed (1679). That both confessions fully embrace the creedal language of catholicity attests that as the Baptist tradition became more established, it became increasingly explicit in its affirmation of the church's catholic nature. This is particularly compelling in light of the fact that relations with the Church of England worsened significantly after the restoration of the monarchy in 1660. Lumpkin explains that "the renewal of persecution brought dissenting groups nearer to one another and especially brought Baptists and Congregationalists nearer to Presbyterians. . . . It was important that Dissenters form a united front, which might be demonstrated by a show of doctrinal agreement. . . . [And] the best proof of this agreement on essential matters was . . . the Westminster Confession."[68] That the Westminster Confession (1646) became the new rallying point for dissent is clear from the fact that it was adopted (with changes due to congregational convictions) by the Congregationalists at the Savoy Conference of 1658 (subsequently issuing the Savoy Declaration) and made the basis of the Baptist Second London Confession.[69]

---

[67] Lumpkin and Leonard, *Baptist Confessions of Faith*, 78, language updated.
[68] Lumpkin and Leonard, *Baptist Confessions of Faith*, 216.
[69] The Second London Confession also freely borrows from the Savoy Declaration to articulate a doctrine of the church, demonstrating a common Free Church heritage. The possibility that this borrowing is an intentional act of catholic consciousness is supported by the fact that, as Birch

In the preface to the 1677 edition of the Second London Confession the authors make clear their agreement "in all the fundamental articles of the Christian religion . . . [as expressed in] orthodox confessions [that] have been published to the world on behalf of the protestants in diverse nations and cities. . . . [Indeed], in consent with the Holy Scriptures . . . [we hereby declare] our hearty agreement with them, in that wholesome protestant doctrine."[70] Though they relied heavily on the form and substance of Westminster, they were also not afraid to deviate from its lead, especially in its discussion of the church and its sacraments.

Here we will focus more on what is in common between the confessions, particularly the fact that the Second London Confession follows Westminster in fully embracing creedal language in article twenty-six, "On the Church." There it states that "the Catholic or universal Church which, with respect to the internal work of the spirit and truth of grace, may be called invisible, consists of the whole number of the elect, that have been, are, or shall be gathered into one, under Christ the head thereof; and is the spouse, the body, the fullness of Him that filleth all in all."[71] As with Westminster, there follows an insistence not to constrain the church's catholicity to the invisible church alone: "All persons throughout the world, professing the faith of the Gospel . . . may be called visible saints; and of such ought all particular congregations to be constituted."[72] Christ's direct lordship over the church is emphasized, for "the Lord Jesus Christ is the head of the Church, in whom . . . all power for the calling, institution, order, or government of the Church, is invested in a supreme and sovereign manner."[73] Undoubtedly a catholic spirit pervades this section, seen in statements like this: "Each church and all the members of it are bound to pray continually for the good and prosperity of all the Churches of Christ, in all places, and

---

has said, "by joining together under the banner of theological orthodoxy, represented by the Confessions, the early Baptists intended to show they stood in the stream of historic, orthodox Christianity as true churches of Christ." Ian Birch, "'The Counsel and Help of One Another': The Origins and Concerns of Early Particular Baptist Churches in Association," *The Baptist Quarterly* 45, no. 1 (January 2013): 21.

[70] Timothy George and Denise George, eds., *Baptist Confessions, Covenants, and Catechisms* (Nashville: Broadman & Holman, 1999), 52.
[71] George and George, *Baptist Confessions*, 85.
[72] George and George, *Baptist Confessions*, 85.
[73] George and George, *Baptist Confessions*, 85.

upon all occasions to further it, (every one within the bounds of their places and callings, in the exercise of their gifts and graces)."[74] An ethos of collaboration and even of formal association is encouraged, noting "in cases of difficulties and differences . . . it is according to the mind of Christ that many churches hold communion together, do by their messengers meet to consider and give their advice in or about that matter . . . to be reported to all the Churches concerned."[75]

On the General Baptist side, the Orthodox Creed expresses a similar catholic ethos. Perhaps the greatest expression of such comes in its catholicity of doctrine: not only does it present itself as a "creed" (vs. the confessions cited above), but it explicitly endorses and reproduces the three ancient creeds (Nicene, Athanasian, and Apostles'), noting that they "ought thoroughly to be received and believed . . . [because] they may be proved by most undoubted authority of Holy Scripture and are necessary to be understood of all Christians. . . . [as] a means to prevent heresy in doctrine and practice . . . containing all things in a brief manner that are necessary . . . to our salvation."[76] Article twenty-nine continues to embrace creedal language in its discussion of "the invisible Catholic Church of Christ" where it is affirmed that "there is one holy catholic church . . . made up of the whole number of the elect that have been, are, or shall be gathered, in one body under Christ, the only Head thereof."[77] Following the earlier confessions, the Orthodox Creed also goes on to affirm that "the catholic Church [is also] visible" arguing that "the visible church of Christ on earth is made up of several distinct congregations, which make up that one catholic church or mystical body of Christ."[78] This then leads into a discussion of the marks by which "the true spouse of Christ" is known: the Word of God rightly preached, the sacraments truly administered "according to Christ's institution and the practice of the primitive church," and "discipline and government duly executed, by ministers or pastors of God's appointing and the

---

[74] George and George, *Baptist Confessions*, 87.
[75] George and George, *Baptist Confessions*, 87.
[76] George and George, *Baptist Confessions*, 120. The catholic nature of this confession is also driven home by the fact that the Orthodox Creed uses language from article eight of the *Thirty-Nine Articles* almost verbatim.
[77] George and George, *Baptist Confessions*, 114.
[78] George and George, *Baptist Confessions*, 114.

church's election."[79] Though it is called "to reform according to God's Holy Word" in the places it has erred, the confession is clear that "from such [a] visible church . . . no man ought, by any pretense whatever, schismatically to separate."[80]

Baptist connections. But the catholicity of the early Baptist tradition isn't something we only *hear* in the confessions; it is something that we also *see* in the connections that existed between Baptist churches which partnered together in formal and informal ways. This is because, as Ian Birch notes, "From the early 1640s Baptist ecclesiology, although determined by separatist and congregational principles, did not regard independence of the local gathered congregation as the ideal ecclesiological stance."[81] As one example of this tendency toward association, we can look at representatives from at least three Particular Baptist churches in Abington, which established an Agreement of Certain Churches in 1653. This agreement recognized the need for intercongregational concern and cooperation in mission, saying that "true churches of Christ ought to acknowledge one another to be such and to hold a firm communion each with [the] other in point of advice in things remaining doubtful to any particular church . . . as also in giving and receiving in case of want and poverty of any particular church . . . and in consulting and consenting (as need shall require and as shall be most for the glory of God) to the joint carrying on of the work of the Lord that is common to the churches."[82]

Another association, that of Midland Baptist churches, set forth in 1655 an agreement that "[we] do mutually acknowledge each other to be true churches and that it is [our] duty to hold a class communion each with [the] other according to the rule of his word and so be helpful each to [the] other as God shall give opportunity and ability. . . . [We] are faithfully to hold such communion each with [the] other and to endeavor to be helpful each to [the] other."[83] This included five practical outworkings: (1) giving advice on matters of controversy one particular church couldn't settle alone (according to the pattern of Acts 15), (2) addressing the material poverty of any one

---

[79]George and George, *Baptist Confessions*, 114.
[80]George and George, *Baptist Confessions*, 114.
[81]Birch, "Counsel and Help," 4.
[82]Quoted in Birch, "Counsel and Help," 7, updated language.
[83]Quoted in Birch, "Counsel and Help," 12-13, language updated.

church as it might arise (according to the pattern of Rom 15:26), (3) providing gifted ministers to churches that lacked pastoral leadership (with Barnabas in Acts 11:22 appealed to in support), (4) undertaking any work that the churches might have in common (according to the pattern of 2 Cor 8:19), and (5) watching over one another as common members of the body of Christ, especially to maintain "purity of doctrine [and] exercise of love" (according to the teaching of 1 Cor 12:12, 29).[84]

These associations did not wield any formal authority over local congregations but were viewed as advisory. As such, they make clear "the organic, instinctive impulse towards networking that is characteristic of translocal Baptist ecclesiology" at this time, indicating that "from a simple and practical necessity of mutual assistance [there] developed a theology of association among early Particular Baptists."[85] Birch concludes that "it is evident that early Particular Baptist ecclesiology functioned at two levels, local and universal. The body of Christ could equally be the local congregation as well as the translocal communion of churches. . . . While the local congregation is not deficient in anything that is required for it to be a local manifestation of Christ's body, yet the single congregation cannot function in isolation from other believers in the universal body of Christ to which it is essentially joined."[86] He continues, "It seems that in the thinking of the early Baptists the universal church, as the body of Christ, was not comprised of the aggregate of local congregations here and there, but rather the local congregation is a manifestation of the one universal church of Christ on earth and in heaven."[87]

Baptist manifestations. We now move to Congregational manifestations of catholicity in light of Littell's recognition that "radical puritans" of seventeenth-century Congregationalism (which was paedobaptist) ought to be viewed as the "other wing" of the emerging Free Church tradition, complementing the party that insisted on credobaptism as a necessary

---

[84]Birch, "Counsel and Help," 13, language updated.
[85]Birch, "Counsel and Help," 13.
[86]Birch, "Counsel and Help," 17.
[87]Birch, "Counsel and Help," 18. For a case study of a catholic Baptist, see G. Stephen Weaver, Jr., *Orthodox, Puritan, Baptist: Hercules Collins (1647–1702) and Particular Baptist Identity in Early Modern England* (Bristol, CT: Vandenhoeck & Ruprecht, 2015).

outworking of Free Church ecclesiology.⁸⁸ In many ways the Congregational voice is an extremely significant one in terms of articulating a more robust conception of catholicity from a Free Church vantage point. This is because, as David Priestly has observed, "the confession that the church is 'the communion of saints' was taken quite literally by . . . Congregationalists; hence they deserve investigation as a seventeenth-century English believers church."⁸⁹ Priestly highlights Congregationalism's value of "cooperativeness" as a particularly strong indication of its implicit catholicity, noting that while "no authority was vested in any inter-congregational office or agency . . . the Independents made no pretence of *absolute* congregational autonomy . . . [for] each church sought to be subject to Christ . . . [and] should a church be unable to discern the mind of Christ on an issue. . . . It was to call on the neighbouring churches to send their elders and experienced brethren to advise them."⁹⁰ This was in addition to the movement's catholic instinct that its "voluntarist convictions . . . [were] deduced from Scripture and *elaborated out of the church's traditions*."⁹¹ In short, Congregationalism was, from its origins, another attempt to work out a faithful ecclesiology from Scripture and in dialogue with the whole church.

Congregational confessions. Here we must limit our focus on the English expression of Congregationalism found most definitively in the Savoy Declaration (1658).⁹² In the extensive preface the statement is made that "amongst all Christian States and Churches, there ought to be vouchsafed a forebearance and mutual indulgence unto Saints of all persuasions, that keep unto, and hold fast the necessary foundation of faith and holiness, in all matters extrafundamental, whether of Faith or Order."⁹³ In the confession

---

⁸⁸Franklin H. Littell, "The Claims of the Free Churches," *The Christian Century* 78, no. 14 (April 5, 1961): 417-18.
⁸⁹David T. Priestly, "Believers' Assembly or Believers Church: A Seventeenth-Century Rationale for Congregational Polity" in *The Believers Church: A Voluntary Church*, ed. William H. Brackney (Kitchener, Ontario: Pandora Press, 1998), 13.
⁹⁰Priestly, "Believers' Assembly or Believers Church," 22-23, emphasis added.
⁹¹Priestly, "Believers' Assembly or Believers Church," 24, emphasis added.
⁹²Of course, the colonial equivalent, with its similar emphases yet distinct character, is found in the Cambridge Platform of 1648. This document, which stated the view of New England Congregationalist churches on proper church government, along with the Westminster Confession, was used as a basic template for Savoy.
⁹³Henry Bettenson and Chris Maunder, eds., *The Documents of the Christian Church*, 3rd ed. (Oxford: Oxford University Press, 1999), 330.

there is once again a large-scale incorporation of Westminster's categories and language; the key area of departure regards ecclesiology. When it comes to the chapter on the church, the first statement regarding "the catholic or universal church, which is invisible" follows Westminster word for word. But from there Savoy departs, emphasizing that "the whole body of men throughout the world, professing the faith of the gospel and obedience unto God by Christ according to it . . . are, and may be called the visible catholic church of Christ; although as such it is not entrusted with the administration of any ordinances, or have any officers to rule or govern in, or over the whole body."[94] So while Savoy follows suit in emphasizing first the invisible nature of the catholic church and then the visible nature of the same, it seeks to correct Westminster's statement that "unto this catholic visible church Christ hath given the ministry, oracles, and ordinances of God" by insisting that only particular, local churches are capable of exercising proper ministerial oversight and administering the sacraments aright.

After the doctrinal exposition there follows a section titled "The Institution of Churches, and the Order Appointed in Them by Jesus Christ," which further specifies how their polity differs from the Presbyterian divines. Articles four and five emphasize that

> to each of these churches thus gathered, according to his mind declared in his Word, he hath given all that Power and Authority, which is any way needful for their carrying on that Order in Worship and Discipline. . . . These particular Churches thus appointed by the Authority of Christ, and entrusted with power from him . . . [are] the seat of that Power which he is pleased to communicate to his Saints . . . so that as such they receive it immediately from himself.[95]

While these articles emphasize the sufficiency of each local church to govern their own affairs, article twenty-six makes it clear that this is never at the cost of mutual cooperation and interdependence with other churches, noting that "in case of Difficulties or Differences, either in point of Doctrine or Administrations . . . it is according to the mind of Christ that many Churches holding communion together, do by their messengers meet in a

---

[94]Gerald Bray, ed., *Documents of the English Reformation 1526–1701* (Cambridge: James Clarke, 2004), 538.
[95]Bettenson and Maunder, *Documents*, 330, language updated.

Synod or Council, to consider and give their advice.... Howbeit these Synods ... are not enstrusted with any Church-Power, or with any jurisdiction over the Churches themselves."[96] This is their testimony to a Congregational ecclesiology that never compromises catholicity.

Congregational case study: John Owen. John Owen (1616–1683) represents the epitome of Puritans as "Reformed Catholics." He was both "a champion of Reformed orthodoxy" and at the same time "profoundly learned, at ease with both the wider theological tradition of Western catholic thought ... and contemporary theological literature, Protestant, Catholic and heretical."[97] Owen was a theologian who "while acknowledging the confessional normativity of the Reformation ... identified [himself] with the church of all times and all places, using the cumulative wisdom of the ages to develop a theological synthesis."[98] But, simultaneously, Owen has the reputation of being a staunch defender of Congregationalism as a proper outworking of Puritan convictions. Van Vlastuin and Kapic can even refer to Owen as a "father of congregationalism," noting that he "stood at the forefront of the evangelical vision of the local church as the predominant form of church governance."[99] Knapp says that once Owen read John Cotton's *Keys of the Kingdom* and embraced Congregational convictions, he consistently emphasized "that the local congregation is the only true form of earthly church instituted by the Lord. Every other church structure and government is a creation of man and consequently carries no binding force upon the believer."[100]

But even here Owen's catholicity informed his congregationalism. Trueman concludes that Owen's "commitment to Independency was not the equivalent of a narrow sectarianism," arguing that Owen, even in his articulation of congregational convictions, was "well schooled in the history of

---

[96] Bettenson and Maunder, *Documents*, 331, language updated.
[97] Carl Trueman, *John Owen: Reformed Catholic, Renaissance Man* (Aldershot, UK: Ashgate, 2007), 2.
[98] Willem van Vlastuin and Kelly M. Kapic, "Introduction, Overview and Epilogue," in *John Owen Between Orthodoxy and Modernity*, ed. Willem van Vlastuin and Kelly M. Kapic (Leiden: Brill, 2019), 14.
[99] van Vlastuin and Kapic, "Introduction, Overview and Epilogue," 13, 26. Owen's playing a key role in drafting the Savoy Declaration mentioned earlier is just one example of his influence on Congregationalism.
[100] Henry M. Knapp, "John Owen, on Schism and the Nature of the Church," *The Westminster Theological Journal* 72, no. 2 (Fall 2010): 349.

theology, reading and citing a large number of patristic and medieval texts with approval, and engaging in dialogue with the same, in order to produce ... theology ... marked by historical integrity and, on the whole, respect, albeit critical respect, for the church's theological tradition."[101] Far from being "novel and innovative" as he was accused of by many of his Anglican interlocutors, and not a few of his Presbyterian ones, it was rather that "Owen's concern throughout his career was to articulate and defend the faith which he regarded as once and for all delivered to the saints; and that involved not only a commitment to the scripture principle but [also] a careful listening to, critical interaction with, and judicious appropriation of the church's theological, exegetical, and polemical traditions."[102] For Owen, this led him to congregational conclusions that became part and parcel of the emerging Free Church tradition.

Owen held to a threefold understanding of the church's nature and linked each of these to the church's catholicity in a specific way. He says that a person "belongs to the *church catholic* who is united to Christ by the Spirit, and none other. And he belongs to the *church general visible* who makes profession of the faith of the gospel, and destroys it not by any thing of a just inconsistency with the belief of it. And he belongs to a *particular church* who, having been in due order joined thereunto, hath neither voluntarily deserted it nor been judicially ejected out of it."[103] Van Vlastuin observes that Owen's first instinct is to identify the catholic church as "absolutely invisible in its mystical form, or spiritual saving relation unto the Lord Christ and its unity with him."[104] He then speaks, second, of the "visible catholic church of Christ" as "the whole body of men throughout the world, professing the faith of the gospel and obedience unto God by Christ according to it."[105] But Owen's congregational convictions lead him to clarify that this visible catholic church "is not entrusted with the administration of the ordinances, [nor does it have] officers to rule ... over the whole body."[106] Instead, that

---

[101] Trueman, *John Owen*, 4, 11.
[102] Trueman, *John Owen*, 123-24.
[103] Quoted in Knapp, "John Owen, on Schism," 350.
[104] Quoted in Willem van Vlastuin, "John Owen as a Modern Theologian: A Comparison of Catholicity in Cyprian and Owen," in van Vlastuin and Kapic, *John Owen Between Orthodoxy and Modernity*, 168.
[105] Quoted in van Vlastuin, "John Owen as a Modern Theologian," 168-69.
[106] Quoted in van Vlastuin, "John Owen as a Modern Theologian," 169.

privilege is reserved only for particular congregations as manifestations of the visible catholic church.

Most surprising is Owen's argument that congregationalism actually provides the strongest support for the church's genuine catholicity. Owen held that the catholic church found expression in many different churches at different times and in different places, even exhibiting different doctrinal stances and liturgical practices (so long as these did not compromise the gospel). In fact, van Vlastuin can say that "Owen's fundamental attitude is to be open and positive towards every assembly of two or three people who are gathered in the name of Christ."[107] He held this attitude, in part, because he believed, according to Knapp, "that the congregational polity advocated for by Independents was the true pathway to biblical unity. By reducing the goal of unity to the scriptural essentials of mutual faith and love, Owen thought that individual congregations could find true communion" and manifest a purer catholicity.[108] Because evangelical unity (and catholicity) comes only by way of fidelity to Christ in his Word, Owen argued, the Separatist departure from the state church due to conscience was not sectarian or schismatic and had the potential to witness to a greater manifestation of catholic unity.

However, this catholicity also made demands on a particular church, according to Owen. In *The True Nature of a Gospel Church* (1689) he argues that local congregations are "obliged into mutual Communion among themselves, which in their consent, endeavor and conjunction in and for the promotion of the Edification of the Catholic Church, and therein their own, as they are Parts and Members of it."[109] For Owen, congregations that denied their connection to the whole were in grave danger because "the Church which confines its Duty unto the Acts of its own Assemblies, cuts itself off from the external Communion of the Church Catholick," a situation in which Owen believes it would not "be safe for any Man to commit the Conduct of his Soul to such a Church."[110] This stems from the fact that "No Church . . . is so Independent . . . [as to be able to] observe the Duties it owes to the Lord Christ

---

[107] van Vlastuin, "John Owen as a Modern Theologian," 173.
[108] Knapp, "John Owen, on Schism," 357.
[109] Quoted in John H. Y. Briggs, "The Changing Shape of Nonconformity, 1662–2000," in Pope, *T&T Clark Companion*, 4.
[110] Quoted in Briggs, "Changing Shape of Nonconformity," 4.

and Church Catholick . . . without conjunction with others."[111] In fact, Owen is quick to recognize that when a "particular Church . . . extends not its Duty beyond its own Assemblies and Members . . . [and confines] its Care and Duty unto its own Edification," it has lost "the principal end of its Institution" because it is "neglective of all due means of the Edification of the Church Catholick . . . [and is therefore] Schismatical."[112] In short, Owen's defense of congregationalism never compromises congregational interdependence derived from the church's catholic nature.

Owen was engaged in much polemical debate; being the foremost defender of the Independent party made that inevitable. But amid the debates, Owen's catholic spirit shines through in many ways. His desire was for unity and brotherly love between Christians to become more manifest. He says at one point, "I confess I would rather, much rather, spend all my time and days in making up and healing the breaches and schisms that are amongst Christians than one hour in justifying our divisions, even [when] they are capable of a fair defence."[113] He goes on to say, "A reconciliation amongst all Protestants is our duty, and practicable. . . . When men have laboured as much in the improvement of the principle of forbearance as they have done to subdue other men to their opinions, [true] religion will have another appearance in the world."[114] His opinions of other churches (save the Roman Church) were often judicious: he judged that the Church of England was "as sound and healthful a part of the Catholic church as any in the world" and was even happy to say, "I embrace the doctrine of the church of England, as declared in the Thirty-nine Articles, and other approved public writings of the most famous bishops and other divines thereof."[115] Despite the fact that Owen held "the national church is an unbiblical concept" and denied that "such a church was ever instituted on earth by Christ, or by the apostles in his name," he was "unwilling to refuse completely all communion with the established churches."[116] Because of their union with Christ by faith, Owen

---

[111] Quoted in Briggs, "Changing Shape of Nonconformity," 4.
[112] Quoted in Briggs, "Changing Shape of Nonconformity," 4.
[113] Quoted in Knapp, "John Owen, on Schism," 354.
[114] Quoted in Knapp, "John Owen, on Schism," 354.
[115] Quoted in van Vlastuin, "John Owen as a Modern Theologian," 172, and in Lee Gatiss, "Anglicanism and John Owen," *Crux* 52, no. 7 (Spring 2016): 51.
[116] Knapp, "John Owen, on Schism," 350-51.

maintained that a love of all the faithful must exist among "all members of the church catholic, however divided in their visible profession by any differences among themselves, or differenced by the several measures of gifts and graces they have received."[117] This is indeed a catholic spirit.

CONCLUSION: FREE CHURCH CATHOLICITY AS REFORMATIONAL CATHOLICITY

Any survey of sixteenth-century Continental Anabaptism and seventeenth-century English Separatism will inevitably reveal that portions of these streams of the Free Church tradition, even large portions, manifest a thoroughly sectarian and anticatholic stance. Our task here was to investigate whether it can be established that at least a minority within these streams articulated a more explicit appreciation of the church's catholicity and sought to manifest a more catholic spirit than the rest of their Radical brothers and sisters. The answer that this chapter provides to that question is a resounding yes. We join with Briggs in his evaluation of English Separatism that "while some Dissenters were undoubtedly sectarian, others. . . . [demonstrated that] the rationale for their separation from the national church was occasioned by their desire to reclaim the true catholicity and apostolicity of the church, in which 'the Crown Rights of the Redeemer' were truly respected without fear of state interference."[118] And we argue based on Laurense's analysis that even Anabaptism, perhaps the most sectarian of the movements studied here, occasionally demonstrates capacity for a "catholic spirit" to manifest.

How should we understand these expressions that have placed a premium on the church's catholicity and understand it to be fully compatible with Free Church ecclesial convictions? My answer is that we should understand them as efforts to bring about a *genuine reformation* of the catholic church as they understood the need. St. Amat describes how the Free Church tradition differed in its approach to the means and ends of reform:

> The Anabaptists and later the Baptists were equidistant from magisterial Protestantism . . . [primarily in offering] an alternative in the Reformation period that differed sharply from the "old Christendom," the *Corpus Christianum*, the idea that church and state form a single "Christian Body." They

---
[117]Quoted in Knapp, "John Owen, on Schism," 346.
[118]Briggs, "Changing Shape of Nonconformity," 4.

tried ... to replace [this] ... coercive sociopolitical synthesis, with the *Corpus Christi*, "the Body of Christ" [understood as] a voluntary nonpolitical community of discipleship.[119]

Their hope that the church could be reformed according to Scripture stemmed from their conviction that the true church, unlike the one they frequently saw in their day, "transcended national boundaries and local cultures. ... [and was] not simply a subdivision of society ... [but was rather] a disciplined community made up of baptized believers unrestricted in their missionary concerns by territorial limitations."[120]

The efforts of the Radical Reformers have often been described as not just seeking *reformatio*, but ultimately *restitutio*: a restitution of the New Testament, or apostolic, church. Certainly some manifestations of this *restitutio* are best described as anticatholic. But other manifestations can be understood as having a catholic spirit motivating them. In fact, we might say that the Anabaptists and English Separatists were, at their best, pursuing a *reformatio* via *restitutio*. To judge this as anticatholic is to ignore the insights of two Roman Catholic theologians. The first is that of Hans Küng when he recognizes that "one can only know what the Church should be now if one also knows what the Church was originally. This means knowing what the Church of today should be in light of the gospel. ... [It] must return to the place from which it proceeded; must return to its origins, to Jesus, to the gospel."[121] The second is that of Edward Schillebeeckx when he says that certain errors and rotten manifestations of the church require what he calls "development by demolition" before the proper (re)building project can begin.[122] For the full work of reform to move forward, one can't remain in the demolition stage; but for the reforming effort to *ultimately* be successful, one may have to start there.

The findings of this chapter suggest that at least a subset of the Free Church tradition as it manifested among Anabaptists and English Separatists ought to be considered a full-fledged contributor to the project of the

---

[119]C. Penrose St. Amat, "Reformation Views of the Church," in Basden and Dockery, *People of God*, 221-22.
[120]St. Amat, "Reformation Views of the Church," 222.
[121]Quoted in Paul Avis, *The Church in the Theology of the Reformers* (Atlanta: John Knox Press, 1980), 219.
[122]Quoted in Avis, *Church in the Theology of the Reformers*, 223.

Protestant Reformation, which has been described as "less about starting a new church than retrieving the ancient and true church."[123] The claim has rightly been made that the Reformation was, at its best, an inherently catholic movement. Carl Braaten and Robert Jenson passionately argue that catholicity largely characterizes the original intent of the Magisterial Reformers, insisting that they "did not set out to create a new church. They aimed to reform a church that lived in continuity with the church the Creed calls 'one, holy, catholic and apostolic' . . . to return to the Scriptures and ancient church tradition, [and] to increase rather than decrease the church's catholicity."[124] Braaten makes a similar case: "The Reformers made their protest against Rome on behalf of the whole church, out of love and loyalty to the truly catholic church. . . . The Reformation was a movement of protest for the sake of the one church."[125] These sentiments can also describe some of the earliest representatives of the Free Church tradition, from the character of the Anabaptists to the confessions of the Baptists to the connections of the Congregationalists. This "fourth strand of the Reformation" aligns with a larger Reformational movement that Vanhoozer has rightly described as having "a high regard for catholic tradition as long as such catholicity is not defined by Rome rather than Romans (i.e., the gospel)."[126]

In the case of the early Free Church tradition, though, they protested not just the catholicity of Rome, but also of Wittenberg, Geneva, and Canterbury, all for the sake of the catholic church. This is why George can say that the best of the Free Church has sought, with the rest of the Reformers, "to reconstruct a purified form of catholic Christianity, a real life and blood community of faith that would bear the 'marks of the true church.' . . . The *notae* do not replace the traditional Nicene attributes, but they rather call into question the unity, catholicity, apostolicity, and holiness of every congregation which claims to be a church, thus subjecting it to an outward,

---

[123]Kevin J. Vanhoozer, "A Mere Protestant Response," in *Was the Reformation a Mistake? Why Catholic Doctrine Is Not Unbiblical*, by Matthew Levering (Grand Rapids, MI: Zondervan, 2017), 229.

[124]Carl E. Braaten and Robert W. Jenson, eds., *The Catholicity of the Reformation* (Grand Rapids, MI: Eerdmans, 1996), vii-viii.

[125]Carl E. Braaten, *Mother Church: Ecclesiology and Ecumenism* (Minneapolis: Fortress, 1998), 12.

[126]Vanhoozer, "Mere Protestant Response," 229.

empirical examination."[127] Such an endeavor is no Free Church novelty; it is a Protestant cornerstone. Avis insists that "full weight should be given to the 'catholic intention' of the Reformers. . . . The fact is that the Reformers believed that their work was to save the catholic Church. But . . . to save the Church they had to first save the gospel."[128] T. F. Torrance argues similarly that the Reformation trumpeted the supremacy of God's Word over all human traditions and saw its task as "repentant rethinking of all tradition face to face with the revelation of God in Jesus Christ."[129]

The Free Churches of the sixteenth and seventieth centuries, at least to a certain extent, were after these same ends. They embody Avis's criteria for Reformation catholicity because they (1) manifest a coherent body of Reformation theology (particularly ecclesiology), (2) interact with, appreciate, and criticize the broader Christian tradition, and (3) make a serious claim to preserve catholicity in its essentials.[130] They hold unswervingly to the conviction that true catholic unity only comes about under canonical authority and the common reign of Christ by the Spirit. These churches demonstrated a Reformational concern for the whole church and provided a powerful witness that the Free Church tradition has much to contribute toward a faithful, fuller doctrine of catholicity. While it would take further development of the tradition to demonstrate a more robust and coherent understanding of the church's catholicity from a Free Church vantage point (the topic of our next chapter), for now we conclude that there is much at the fountainhead of the Free Church tradition to be retrieved for its renewal and the benefit of the catholic church.

---

[127] George, "Sacramentality of the Church," 314.
[128] Avis, *Church in the Theology of the Reformers*, 216.
[129] Quoted in Avis, *Church in the Theology of the Reformers*, 225.
[130] Avis, *Church in the Theology of the Reformers*, 217.

FIVE

Free Church Catholicity Expounded
Assessing Contemporary Proposals

FREE CHURCH CATHOLICITY EMERGED in the foundational sixteenth-century Continental and seventeenth-century British contexts. But how has it been articulated and defended downstream? Is Free Church catholicity "a thing of the past" or does it manifest in contemporary Free Church expression? And if so, in what way? It is to these questions we now turn, examining the most robust attempts to articulate the *what* and the *how* of Free Church catholicity amid the British and American contexts in the twentieth and twenty-first centuries. We will then assess and consolidate these attempts, along with the Reformational Free Church voices examined in the last chapter, in order to move toward a fuller-orbed account of the church's catholicity from a Free Church vantage point. Our criteria for assessment will involve determining how *faithful* such accounts are to the biblical warrant for the doctrine, how *coherent* they are as expressions of Free Church ecclesial convictions, and how *integrative* they are of the various aspects of catholicity that emerge in its church-historical development. To anticipate, by and large what we will find is a tendency to either neglect a robust enough notion of the church's catholicity (failing to exhibit Free Church *catholicity*) or express such catholicity in a manner ultimately inconsistent with Free Church ecclesial convictions (failing to exhibit *Free Church* catholicity).

BROAD FREE CHURCH CATHOLICITY

We begin with representatives of "broad Free Church catholicity," by which we mean those from a Free Church tradition *other* than the Baptist one.

Proposals of Baptist catholicity have become quite abundant in the last twenty years, but before this relative plethora of Baptist proposals, theologians in the broader Free Church tradition articulated a sense of catholicity that we need to examine first.

The work of the Free Church Federal Council. The Free Church Federal Council (which includes Methodist, Baptist, Presbyterian, and Congregational churches, among others, in England and Wales) was formed in 1940 with the union of the National Council of the Evangelical Free Churches (founded in 1896) and the Federal Council of the Evangelical Free Churches (founded in 1919). It operated as a way for nonestablished churches to partner in endeavors of mutual interest, and it inherited previous efforts to articulate a Free Church understanding of the church and its catholicity. Its most important contribution to forwarding an understanding of Free Church catholicity came when certain of its members were invited to participate in the mid-twentieth century dialogue initiated by Archbishop of Canterbury Geoffrey Fisher (discussed in chapter 3). Alongside a group of Anglo-Catholics and a group of evangelical Anglicans, this group of Free Church theologians was invited to respond to the question, "What is the underlying cause . . . of the contrast or conflict between the catholic and protestant traditions?" The results of their deliberation were published in 1950 as *The Catholicity of Protestantism*.[1] The authors, who explicitly endorse the work of the Free Church Federal Council and quote its doctrinal statement at length, wrote with the expressed intent of offering "a positive statement of the catholicity of Protestantism," especially to clarify "the very points where our main tradition has been most misunderstood."[2]

Indeed, the writing is in many ways a direct appeal to "those in the older communions who would unchurch us, or deny our ministries and sacraments" to consider in a manner reminiscent of Acts 15 whether

> if God has poured out His Spirit on our communions, if in all of them the fruit of the presence of the Holy Spirit is manifestly given to us . . . if our alleged "irregularies" or "invalidities" have not barred us from the grace of our Lord who

---

[1] R. Newton Flew and Rupert E. Davies, eds., *The Catholicity of Protestantism: Being a Report Presented to His Grace the Archbishop of Canterbury by a Group of Free Churchmen* (London: Lutterworth Press, 1950).
[2] Flew and Davies, *Catholicity of Protestantism*, 5.

undoubtedly meets us in our Eucharists, and crowns our proclamation of the Word by drawing men and women all over the world out of darkness into light, who is there . . . that can deny to us the mark of catholicity.[3]

The authors decry how their churches are perceived as noncatholic because

> belief in the one Holy, Catholic, and Apostolic Church is integral to the faith of Protestantism. . . . [Indeed] the whole Reformation movement may be fairly described as an attempt to take seriously the New Testament doctrine of the Church, actual, visible and catholic. . . . This applies both to the Lutheran and Calvinist wings . . . and also to the radical movement of the Anabaptists.[4]

In short, they argue, if Free Churches are Protestant, then Free Churches are catholic.

Appealing to Ignatius's use of the term, the authors state that "the primary sense of catholicity . . . is the presence of the living Christ, recognized, adored and obeyed."[5] This alone "secures the catholicity of the church" because "for St. Ignatius, for the Reformers, and for us, to be 'in Christ' is to be in the Church."[6] They go on to articulate that catholicity "means 'wholeness' or 'totality'" and that the church's catholicity derives from "the 'wholeness' of the Gospel. . . . Only that Church, or communion, or tradition, is in the full sense catholic which possesses the 'wholeness' of the Gospel, and such 'wholeness' can be derived only from our Lord Jesus Christ, His message of the Kingdom of God, [and] His work of salvation."[7]

They then make two important clarifications regarding this "wholeness of the gospel" as constitutive of the "wholeness (catholicity) of the church." First, they clarify that "there is no communion on earth which is *fully* catholic, for no communion possesses, *in the full and absolute sense*, the 'wholeness' of the Gospel. For . . . this 'wholeness' is eschatological, fully realized . . . in the world to come."[8] In good Free Church fashion, they insist that no ecclesial tradition and no individual church can claim to *possess* the

---

[3]Flew and Davies, *Catholicity of Protestantism*, 20.
[4]Flew and Davies, *Catholicity of Protestantism*, 91.
[5]Flew and Davies, *Catholicity of Protestantism*, 21.
[6]Flew and Davies, *Catholicity of Protestantism*, 21-22.
[7]Flew and Davies, *Catholicity of Protestantism*, 23.
[8]Flew and Davies, *Catholicity of Protestantism*, 23, emphasis added.

wholeness of the gospel; churches derive their catholicity from the gospel, but having the gospel does not mean churches are *fully* catholic, *fully* "whole." This is why they can say "we do not find the 'wholeness' of the Gospel fully realized in the primitive Church. . . . [Thus] we find it difficult to allow the almost universal prevalence of episcopacy in its various forms at the end of the second century [as] a proof that a particular form of it is an integral part of the 'wholeness' of the Gospel."[9] Here, at the crux of their disagreement with the Episcopal tradition, they argue that "it is the truth of the Gospel and the life in accord with the Gospel which count, not the episcopal succession."[10]

The other important clarification is that they believe there are indicators as to whether a church can justify its claim to being catholic. They write that "no communion can lay claim to 'wholeness' which does not believe in the Word of God contained in the Holy Scriptures, the catholic Faith, the One, Holy, Catholic and Apostolic Church, the Gospel Sacraments . . . [and] the Christian ministry. But to a communion which does so believe the title catholic may not be denied."[11] Here it is important to note that while these Free Church theologians deny that the Episcopal office (*episcopos*) is necessary for catholicity, they would not deny that some form of oversight (*episcope*) is. The authors thus hold that the catholicity of Protestantism requires the following features to justify claims to catholicity: (1) proclamation of the Word of God found in Scripture and centered on the gospel, (2) adherence to church tradition (manifest in the creeds) that expounds the gospel, (3) participation in the universal church by virtue of the gospel, (4) baptism and the Lord's Supper as sacramental expressions of the gospel, and (5) ministerial oversight that guards the gospel. In fact, they argued that the Reformation was necessary precisely because "certain [of these] elements, vitally necessary to the 'wholeness' of the Church, were grievously lacking in the Church of their day."[12] Thus, these Free Church theologians held that "it was the very concern for the genuine 'wholeness' of the true faith which evoked the Confessions of the sixteenth and seventeenth centuries," including those

---

[9] Flew and Davies, *Catholicity of Protestantism*, 24-25.
[10] Flew and Davies, *Catholicity of Protestantism*, 27.
[11] Flew and Davies, *Catholicity of Protestantism*, 23.
[12] Flew and Davies, *Catholicity of Protestantism*, 28.

of the Anabaptists, Baptists and Congregationalists.[13] There is here clear testimony that Free Church catholicity is Reformational catholicity, although the question still remains: Is Free Church catholicity a *distinct species* of Protestant catholicity?

The work of Miroslav Volf. When it comes to the question of Free Church catholicity, it is hard to overestimate the contribution of Miroslav Volf. His 1992 article "Catholicity of 'Two or Three': Free Church Reflections on the Catholicity of the Local Church" was significant in flagging the lacuna concerning Free Church catholicity. The article, which engages the Episcopal tradition as expressed by Joseph Ratzinger (Catholic) and John Zizioulas (Orthodox), became the fount for his much fuller account of Free Church catholicity provided in *After Our Likeness: The Church as the Image of the Trinity*.[14] The book can be understood as Volf's effort to answer his own question of whether Free Church catholicity is *indeed* a contradiction in terms.[15]

In *After Our Likeness*, Volf chooses as his starting point the contested nature of catholicity, observing that "all churches want to be catholic, though each in its own way. This is the paradox of catholicity on this side of God's new creation. Though it stands for totality (*holos*), it is always based on a certain particularity. No church is catholic purely and simply; each is catholic *in a certain way*. Thus . . . arises the dispute concerning catholicity."[16] Volf also recognizes that the dispute is strongest between "the episcopal churches and Free Churches [which] have stood at opposite extremes" because they "seem to have diametrically opposed understandings of catholicity, which are rooted deeply in their respective ecclesial identities."[17] To those in the broader Episcopal tradition, "the Free Church understanding of unity, of holiness, of apostolicity is problematic precisely because it is uncatholic."[18] Meanwhile, the Free Church tradition has "simultaneously

---

[13]Flew and Davies, *Catholicity of Protestantism*, 33.
[14]In fact, many aspects of chapter 7, "The Catholicity of the Church" are taken from his earlier article.
[15]While Volf writes that the ultimate goal of *After Our Likeness* was "to spell out a vision of the church as an image of the triune God," we will focus in this chapter only on the portions of his argument most germane to articulating the what and the how of Free Church catholicity. Miroslav Volf, *After Our Likeness: The Church as the Image of the Trinity* (Grand Rapids, MI: Eerdmans, 1998), 2, 7.
[16]Volf, *After Our Likeness*, 259.
[17]Volf, *After Our Likeness*, 259, 261.
[18]Volf, *After Our Likeness*, 259.

denied [catholicity] to the Catholic Church.... [because it] refuses to accept its own particularity, and thus denies (full?) catholicity to other churches."[19]

But there is at least some common ground, for Volf recognizes that both traditions believe "the discussion of catholicity always involves the fundamental question of the relationship between *unity* and *multiplicity*."[20] Volf appeals to Aristotle's discussion of "a whole" in his *Metaphysics* to draw out that by a whole (or a totality) we mean a differentiated unity, and thus that "any church claiming catholicity must include multiplicity in its unity and must be the one church in that multiplicity."[21] The problem of catholicity remains because "the various understandings of catholicity differ in the *degree* of unification and differentiation they either require or permit.... [which] depends on [a] respective basic ecclesiological decision."[22] The payoff, for Volf, comes in recognizing that "one can meaningfully criticize particular understandings of catholicity as totalitarian [the Free Church criticism of the Episcopal tradition] or individualistic [the Episcopal criticism of the Free Church] only *in a perspectival way*."[23]

An understanding of Free Church catholicity thus requires, according to Volf, a careful articulation of Free Church ecclesiology versus its ecclesiological opposite. Volf provides his understanding of the same in a summary statement that is worth quoting at length:

> Every congregation that assembles around the one Jesus Christ as Savior and Lord in order to profess faith in him publicly in pluriform fashion, including through baptism and the Lord's Supper, and which is open to all churches of God and to all human beings, is a church in the full sense of the word, since Christ promised to be present in it through his Spirit as the first fruits of the gathering of the whole people of God in the eschatological reign of God. Such a congregation is a holy, catholic, and apostolic church. One might rightly expect such a congregation to grow in unity, sanctity, catholicity, and apostolicity, but one cannot deny to it these characterizing

---

[19]Volf, *After Our Likeness*, 260.
[20]Volf, *After Our Likeness*, 261.
[21]Volf, *After Our Likeness*, 262.
[22]Volf, *After Our Likeness*, 262.
[23]Volf, *After Our Likeness*, 262.

features of the church, since it possesses these on the basis of the constitutive presence of Christ.[24]

Notice how central confession of faith is to Volf's ecclesial definition. Volf can say that "by confessing faith in Christ through celebration of the sacraments, sermons, prayer, hymns, witnessing, and daily life, those gathered in the name of Christ speak the word of God both to each other and to the world. This public confession of faith in Christ through the pluriform speaking of the word is *the central constitutive mark of the church*."[25] Based on this understanding, Volf sees ecclesial identity tied up with personal faith corporately expressed, for "the basic condition of ecclesiality . . . coincides with the basic condition of salvific grace, which consists in the faith of the heart and the confession of the mouth (Rom 10:10)."[26]

But what makes this a *Free Church* notion of the church and its catholicity? The answer comes in recognizing that for Volf "an indispensable condition of ecclesiality is that the people assemble *in the name of Christ*. Gathering in the name of Christ is the precondition for the presence of Christ in the Holy Spirit, which is itself constitutive for the church."[27] Volf confesses that in this regard he joins a "long tradition by taking Mt 18:20 as the foundation not only for determining what the church is, but also for how it manifests itself externally as a church."[28] Christ's promise leads Volf to conclude that "where two or three are gathered in Christ's name, not only is Christ present among them, but a Christian church is there as well, perhaps a bad church, a church that may well transgress against love and truth, but a church nonetheless."[29] Such an understanding leads Volf to express thoroughly Free Church convictions: "There is no church as-such 'above the local assembled congregation'; it is only to be found 'in, with and beneath' it."[30] Only local congregations can gather in Christ's name as indicated by its pluriform confession (including sacramental observance),

---

[24]Volf, *After Our Likeness*, 158.
[25]Volf, *After Our Likeness*, 150. So critical is this mark that Volf can say, "The church is . . . [constituted] by the assembled people confessing Christ. Those who confess Christ *are* the church."
[26]Volf, *After Our Likeness*, 150-51.
[27]Volf, *After Our Likeness*, 145.
[28]Volf, *After Our Likeness*, 135-36.
[29]Volf, *After Our Likeness*, 136.
[30]Volf, *After Our Likeness*, 138, quoting Otto Weber to make his point.

and so only local congregations have Christ's promise to be among them *as a church*. In sum: "If Christ is present among the people, you've got the church."[31] This overrules the claim that bishops are necessary for a church since "the church is . . . constituted by the Spirit of Christ *from below* rather than from above."[32]

But we should also notice how Volf's definition of the church relates to catholicity through the language of the church's "openness." Volf makes it clear that "the *openness* of every church toward all other churches [is] an indispensable condition of ecclesiality. . . . To be a church. . . . it must acknowledge all other churches, in time and space, as churches, and must at least be open to diachronic and synchronic communication with them."[33] Such ecclesial openness connects, for Volf, back to the centrality of confession for ecclesiality, and that because "the requirement of openness . . . emerges from the character of the confession of faith that makes a church into a church. Such a confession is an event in which a congregation appropriates the confession of all churches of God."[34] If confession is constitutive for the church, Volf holds, then in some sense "*every* church must be constituted by the *same* confession. Confession of faith not only distinguishes the church from the nonchurch, it simultaneously connects every church with all other churches."[35] A common confession of Christ serves as the ecclesial core, and if an assembly doesn't have a confession in common with other churches and thus the capacity for openness toward them, there's reason to think that that assembly is not a true church.

What, then, is catholicity to the Free Church mind? It is indeed "the catholicity of two or three" or "the catholicity of the local church." Here Volf recognizes that the tradition faces what he calls a dilemma of catholicity: "Although only the local church can be catholic, in fact it is precisely the local church that seems unable to be catholic," especially because "every church is [understood as] autonomous . . . [and] may fall

---

[31]Miroslav Volf, "The Nature of the Church," *Evangelical Review of Theology* 26, no. 1 (January 2002): 68.
[32]Volf, *After Our Likeness*, 152.
[33]Volf, *After Our Likeness*, 156-57.
[34]Volf, *After Our Likeness*, 157.
[35]Volf, *After Our Likeness*, 154.

prey to local particularism."[36] The answer to the dilemma, Volf believes, comes in "examining how the catholicity of the local church arises from the 'manifold grace of God' (1 Peter 4:10)."[37] In expounding this, Volf cites the 1611 *Declaration of Faith of the English People* in its claim that "every . . . congregation, though they be but two or three, have CHRIST given them, with all the means of their salvation. . . . [These] are the Body of CHRIST . . . and a whole Church."[38] This insight at the fountainhead of the Free Church tradition implies that "every church has the whole Christ along with all the means of salvation and is for that reason not part of the church [nor the whole church], but rather is a *whole* church and is in this sense catholic . . . [where] catholicity means *the wholeness of a congregation or church based on the presence of the whole Christ*."[39]

For Volf, then, "the catholicity of the church is constituted by the presence of Christ through the Spirit" and "a local church can be catholic only by way of a [christological] connection with an ecclesiological whole transcending it."[40] That whole, to Volf's mind, isn't primarily the *invisible* church but rather the *eschatological* one, and the payoff is that "the catholicity of a local church . . . [is] an anticipation of the still outstanding gathering of the whole people of God. . . . [and] of the eschatological catholicity of the people of God in the totality of God's new creation."[41] To sum up: Volf believes a local church is catholic when it (1) demonstrates an openness to all churches and all peoples as exhibited in a common confession of Christ, (2) understands itself as one assembly of God's people (among many) constituted by Christ's presence through the Spirit, (3) recognizes that the fullness of catholicity will not occur until all God's people are gathered together in the eschaton, and yet (4) continues to labor for greater unity with and connectedness to other churches who are similarly "already-and-not-yet" holy, apostolic, and catholic.[42]

---

[36]Volf, *After Our Likeness*, 270.
[37]Volf, *After Our Likeness*, 270.
[38]Volf, *After Our Likeness*, 271, language updated. Volf also quotes John Smyth in this regard: "Every true visible Church hath title to [the] whole Christ and all the holy things of God."
[39]Volf, *After Our Likeness*, 271.
[40]Volf, *After Our Likeness*, 271.
[41]Volf, *After Our Likeness*, 272.
[42]Volf, *After Our Likeness*, 259, 267.

Baptist Free Church Catholicity

If anyone has sought to address the lacuna that Volf identified in 1992, it would be theologians exploring "Baptist catholicity." Baptist catholicity is a particular species of Free Church catholicity, and one that has tremendous capacity to inform the larger enterprise. Toward that end we will begin by examining the attempts of postliberal[43] Baptist theologian Steven Harmon to articulate the sense in which Baptists are (or at least should be) catholic. We then move on to examine attempts by evangelical Baptist theologian Jonathan Leeman to do the same.[44]

The work of a postliberal Baptist: Steven Harmon. Though several postliberal Baptists could be considered here,[45] it is Steven Harmon who has perhaps done more than any other contemporary Baptist theologian to argue that Baptist catholicity is not only not a contradiction in terms but is something that should be retrieved for the renewal of the Baptist tradition. His groundbreaking work, *Towards Baptist Catholicity* (2006), initiated

---

[43]Ronald Michener is helpful here in summarizing that postliberal theology "stresses the narrative of scripture along with the community of church and its practices" and can be identified by five basic characteristics: (1) nonfoundationalist in its epistemology, (2) intratextually oriented to the story of Jesus' life, the story of Scripture, and the story of the church, (3) socially centered rather than individually focused, (4) respectful of plurality and diversity without affirming unbridled pluralism, and (5) ecumenically focused and sensitive to the catholic community of faith now and through church history. See Ronald T. Michener, *Postliberal Theology: A Guide for the Perplexed* (London: Bloomsbury T&T Clark, 2013), 4-9.

[44]Here we follow Timothy Larsen, who holds that evangelicals are (1) orthodox Protestants, (2) of the revivalist tradition, (3) who have a preeminent place for the Bible, (4) stress reconciliation with God through Christ's cross work, and (5) emphasize the work of the Holy Spirit to bring about individual conversion, an ongoing life of fellowship and service, and participation in the great commission. Timothy Larsen, "Defining and Locating Evangelicalism," in *The Cambridge Companion to Evangelical Theology*, ed. Timothy Larsen and Daniel J. Treier (Cambridge: Cambridge University Press, 2007), 1.

[45]One prominent candidate would be Curtis W. Freeman, whose *Contesting Catholicity: Theology for Other Baptists* (Waco, TX: Baylor University Press, 2014) offered a full-scale proposal for Baptist catholicity, one framed as both diagnosis and therapy: diagnosis of the sickness that "many Baptists and other Free Church Christians are suffering from" (autonomous sectarianism) and prescription of the cure required (recovered catholicity). Specifically, his work explores whether Baptist catholicity can be made possible "by embracing a mode of being in which contestation and catholicity are not opposites but are instead complementary and necessary for the church to be the church." Freeman, *Contesting Catholicity*, ix. Freeman's vision of Baptist catholicity holds "the conviction that the gathered communities are visible manifestations of the church catholic. Such an approach is both quantitatively catholic, because it participates with the *consensus fidelium* in mystical and historical continuity with the faith of the apostolic church, and qualitatively, in that it joins voices with the apostolic witness to the Bible as the unfolding story of the triune God." Freeman, *Contesting Catholicity*, 128.

great interest in Baptist catholicity (along with a plethora of reviews across the ecclesial spectrum), and his second volume, *Baptist Identity and the Ecumenical Future* (2016), builds on earlier insights. Harmon's primary intention is to argue "that the reconstruction of the Baptist vision . . . requires a retrieval of the ancient ecumenical tradition that forms Christian identity" and that this "envisioned retrieval of catholicity in the worship, doctrine, teaching, and life of Baptist churches is rooted in a recovery of the surprisingly catholic ecclesial outlook of the earliest Baptists."[46]

In *Towards Baptist Catholicity*, Harmon places a strong emphasis on catholicity as centering on church liturgy and practices and seeks to commend the earliest Baptist ecclesial vision with its manifestly catholic character to a tradition that he believes has largely lost its way. He further defines his project by delineating seven identifying marks of a catholic Baptist theology: (1) explicitly recognizing tradition as a source of theological authority, (2) pursuing a place in Baptist ecclesial life for the ancient ecumenical creeds as key expressions of the larger Christian tradition, (3) giving attention to liturgy as the primary context in which Christians are formed by tradition, (4) locating the authority of tradition in the community and its formative practices, (5) advocating a sacramental theology, (6) engaging tradition as a resource for contemporary theological construction, and (7) encouraging a thick ecumenism.[47] Harmon goes to great lengths to argue in ways that he hopes will be compelling to Baptists that "the universal church is the larger community of all the saints through all the ages that also possesses a derivative authority, subordinate to the Scripture, to which Baptists . . . must listen as they seek to think and act Christianly."[48] At the end of the volume Harmon characterizes catholicity in a more specific way as "describing the fully orthodox pattern of faith and practice that distinguished early catholic Christianity from Gnosticism, Arianism, Donatism, and all manner of other heresies and schisms" adding that it "has to do with a *qualitative* fullness of faith and order that is visibly expressed in one Eucharistic fellowship."[49]

---

[46]Steven R. Harmon, *Towards Baptist Catholicity: Essays on Tradition and the Baptist Vision* (Eugene, OR: Wipf & Stock, 2006), xix.
[47]Harmon, *Towards Baptist Catholicity*, 7-16.
[48]Harmon, *Towards Baptist Catholicity*, 37.
[49]Harmon, *Towards Baptist Catholicity*, 204.

In *Baptist Identity and the Ecumenical Future* Harmon continues his appeal to Baptists but now with a larger audience also in view. The work is motivated by the belief that "catholic renewal of Baptist life [is] necessary to the movement of the whole church toward the ecumenical future" and that "the ecumenical quest for the full visible unity of the church . . . [can't] be fulfilled apart from a mutually receptive ecumenical engagement between Baptist communities and the churches from which they are separated."[50] In short, Baptists need the catholic church and the catholic church needs Baptists. This is particularly because, as Harmon argues, "Baptists have their own distinctive ecclesial gifts to offer the church catholic, without which . . . [other churches] are something less than fully catholic themselves," particularly highlighting the Baptist proclivity to guard against coercion, their emphasis on God's freedom in salvation, their clarity regarding the pilgrim nature of the church, their insistence on the need for personal faith matched with communal responsibility, their suspicion of how over-realized eschatology can distort ecclesiology, and their commitment to proclaim and live under the rule of Christ over the church as testified in Scripture.[51]

Harmon has had the opportunity at various points to clarify and refine his proposal in light of reviews of his work. One of those places is in an appendix to *Baptists and the Christian Tradition* (2020), where he emphasizes that in both the works mentioned above he attempted to make the case "that seeking the visible unity of the church at present calls for fuller cultivation of . . . catholicity within our divided churches rather than moving to another church we might believe already possesses that catholicity to a greater degree than our own."[52] He goes on to reiterate that "one of the distinctive ecclesial gifts that Baptists have to share with the rest of the church is the way they do theology as a relentlessly pilgrim community that resists all overly realized eschatologies of the church," by which he means that they locate their "ecclesial ideal . . . somewhere ahead of us rather than in any past or present instantiation of the church."[53]

---

[50]Steven R. Harmon, *Baptist Identity and the Ecumenical Future* (Waco, TX: Baylor University Press, 2016), 9, 18.
[51]Harmon, *Baptist Identity*, 15-16.
[52]Steven R. Harmon, "Baptists, Bapto-Catholic Baptists, and the Christian Tradition," in *Baptists and the Christian Tradition: Toward an Evangelical Baptist Catholicity*, ed. Matthew Y. Emerson, Christopher W. Morgan, and R. Lucas Stamps (Nashville: B&H Academic, 2020), 364.
[53]Harmon, "Baptists, Bapto-Catholic Baptists, and the Christian Tradition," 371.

In another place, Harmon clarifies that the project of cultivating Baptist catholicity involves Baptists "reclaim[ing] the Nicene faith and other expressions of ancient catholicity for the sake of their future, [holding] that such retrieval is not alien to Baptist identity but very much in continuity with the surprisingly catholic ecclesial outlook of the early Baptists."[54] Harmon argues that the problem for most Baptists is not "a *quantitative* understanding of the catholicity of the church, according to which there is a universal church to which all believers belong and that transcends visible local congregations."[55] The problem lies much more in whether Baptists will, or even can, embrace a *qualitative* understanding of catholicity, which concerns what he calls a "fullness of faith and order that is visibly expressed in one Eucharistic fellowship."[56] Harmon examines the letters of Ignatius to draw out what he calls "four marks of qualitative catholicity—incarnational Christology, sacramental realism, visible unity, and the ministry of oversight."[57] Harmon then appeals to Melanchthon to make the argument that "the 'catholicity of the Reformation' stood in continuity with the patristic conviction ... that the quantitative inclusion of all Christians in the catholicity of the church is inseparable from a qualitatively catholic pattern of faith and practice that characterizes this church and its members."[58] The question, for Harmon, is whether Baptists can embrace such a view of catholicity as primarily having a qualitative sense and centering on a catholic pattern of faith and order that is much more ancient (and Roman) than modern (and Baptist).

In response to critical reviews and the concern registered by Paul Avis in the forward to *Towards Baptist Catholicity* about "whether authority is an underdeveloped and therefore unresolved issue," Harmon took on what he saw as two central questions that needed to be clarified: "Precisely why should Baptists embrace catholicity as essential to their identity? And by what authority would they do so?"[59] To the first question he answers, "The

---

[54]Steven R. Harmon, "The Nicene Faith and the Catholicity of the Church: Evangelical Retrieval and the Problem of Magisterium," in *Evangelicals and Nicene Faith: Reclaiming the Apostolic Witness*, ed. Timothy George (Grand Rapids, MI: Baker Academic, 2011), 76.
[55]Harmon, "Nicene Faith and the Catholicity," 76.
[56]Harmon, "Nicene Faith and the Catholicity," 76.
[57]Harmon, "Nicene Faith and the Catholicity," 78.
[58]Harmon, "Nicene Faith and the Catholicity," 79.
[59]Steven R. Harmon, "Why Baptist Catholicity, and by What Authority?," *Pro Ecclesia* 18, no. 4 (Fall 2009): 386.

catholic wholeness currently wanting in Baptist ecclesial life . . . is . . . a *qualitative* fullness of faith and order that is visibly expressed in one Eucharistic fellowship. Baptists need this sort of catholicity first and foremost because it will help their churches form more faithful disciples of Jesus Christ."[60] The second question, Harmon admits, is "a much more crucial and infinitely more problematic question: what would authorize a catholic pattern of Baptist faith and practice? In other words, where is the magisterium that could reliably guide Baptists toward catholicity?"[61] In attempting an answer, Harmon gestures toward a "MacIntyrean construal of the authority of tradition as the authority of the *communio sanctorum* in its contestation of the tradition" and holds that such a construal "could be read as an argument for a 'magisterium of the whole,' in which [every voice is] heard and weighed along with other ecclesial voices."[62] But Harmon acknowledges that problems remain, for

> without greater specificity in its location of ecclesial authority, the theory lacks adequate safeguards against the very thing it seeks to avoid: self-chosen patterns of faith and practice by independent individuals and autonomous congregations in the configuration of a "selective catholicity" . . . [one] that, as Paul Avis perceptively pointed out . . . embraces certain ancient marks of catholicity but ignores the episcopal office and its historical role as the ecclesial location of teaching authority that authorizes the other marks of catholicity.[63]

Harmon holds that these concerns are connected to "the larger question of how one determines which elements of catholicity Baptists can embrace without betraying their Baptist identity. To ask such questions is to inquire about the location of magisterial authority in Baptist life."[64] And it is clear based on Harmon's conclusions that he sees these questions as live and very much unresolved.

The work of an evangelical Baptist: Jonathan Leeman. The emphasis on Baptist catholicity is not only found on the more liberal (or, in this case,

---

[60] Harmon, "Why Baptist Catholicity?," 386.
[61] Harmon, "Why Baptist Catholicity?," 388.
[62] Harmon, "Why Baptist Catholicity?," 388-89.
[63] Harmon, "Why Baptist Catholicity?," 388-89.
[64] Harmon, "Why Baptist Catholicity?," 389-90.

postliberal) side of the theological spectrum; evangelical Baptists have also engaged these issues, at times criticizing the likes of Harmon, not because they advocate a recovery of catholicity, but because they do so from what are viewed as less-than-faithful theological starting points (and some would say, ironically, not particularly catholic ones).[65] While there have been several voices exhibiting a (commendable) desire to cultivate a catholic spirit among more conservative Baptists, often the questions of what exactly is meant by the church's catholicity and how ecclesial authority intersects the creedal attribute have largely been left unaddressed. But the difficult question of how ecclesial authority might relate to catholicity from a Free Church vantage point is particularly taken up by one evangelical Baptist: Jonathan Leeman. Leeman has dedicated much of his career to pursuing a version of Harmon's question: Why Free Church catholicity and by what authority? His proposal, which operates from distinctly Free Church convictions and seeks to be faithful to the witness of Scripture above all else, is pregnant with possibilities for a proper confession of the church as catholic from a Free Church vantage point.

Leeman (with Dever) makes it very clear where he believes Scripture places the locus of ecclesial authority: "Jesus gave authority to the local assembly called a church (Mt 16:13-20; 18:15-20; Heb. 13:7; 1 Peter 5:1-5)"[66] Leeman defines such a local church as "a group of Christians who regularly

---

[65] In this regard see Nathan A. Finn, "Contesting *Catholicity*: Some Conservative Reflections on Curtis Freeman's Theology For 'Other Baptists,'" *Southeastern Theological Review* 6, no. 2 (2015): 151-70. The Center for Baptist Renewal has perhaps done more to explore the what and how of Baptist catholicity in an evangelical register than any other group. The work of the center has been spearheaded by two theologians, Matthew Emerson and Lucas Stamps, who have done much to assess Baptist conceptions of the church and its catholicity and propose how Baptist catholicity might be enacted today. Space constrains prevent us from engaging their proposal, but to be commended are their efforts to cultivate "a uniquely *Baptist* catholicity [that] seeks to situate the Baptist vision within this broader body of Christ" while hoping that "as we call the church to greater faithfulness to Scripture (as we understand it in terms of Baptist distinctives) . . . [we will] learn from other traditions . . . [and] especially . . . what many have called the 'Great Tradition' of Christian reflection on the gospel and its triune God." See Matthew Y. Emerson, Christopher W. Morgan, R. Lucas Stamps, "Baptists and the Christian Tradition: What Hath Nicaea to Do with Nashville?," in *Baptists and the Christian Tradition*, eds. Emerson, Morgan, and Stamps, 3.

[66] Mark Dever and Jonathan Leeman, "Preface," in *Baptist Foundations: Church Government for an Anti-Institutional Age*, ed. Mark Dever & Jonathan Leeman (Nashville: B&H Academic, 2015), xviii.

gather in Christ's name with the power of the keys to affirm the gospel and one another's citizenship in the gospel through the ordinances."[67] To Leeman's thinking it is fitting that ecclesial authority is entrusted by Christ to the local assembly because it is only there that it is possible to "preach the gospel [while possessing] the keys of the kingdom for binding and loosing through the ordinances . . . [declaring] who does and does not belong to the kingdom. [The church thus] exercises oversight. And exercising such affirmation and oversight *meaningfully* means gathering regularly and getting involved in one another's lives."[68] The universal church as such cannot enact the sacraments or make a declaration about someone's kingdom standing. These require "the ability to *gather in Jesus' name*" which "presupposes an agreement with one another about the good news of Jesus, as well as an agreement that the [others] possess genuine faith in the good news about Jesus. . . . [Thus] the very heart and substance of church authority [is found in] two or three . . . agreeing that we're talking about the same good news [and] agreeing that we're all his followers."[69] Such ecclesial authority is "most manifest in our church's decisions about the *what* and the *who* of the gospel. . . . It's about [proper] confessions and confessors."[70]

Understanding Matthew 16, 18, and 28 as connected through the keys representing Jesus' authority entrusted to the church (with Mt 18:20 playing a controlling role), Leeman argues that "the *gathering* represents the authority of Christ. . . . A church is a church ultimately because of the authority of Christ and his declaration that he would identify himself with *gatherings*."[71] From this stating point, Leeman argues that the local church is best understood as an *embassy* because it represents Christ's rule on earth; indeed, "Jesus Christ's universal Lordship gets exercised *there*—among *them*" as indicated in places like Matthew 16:19 and by the pervasive use of the term *ecclesia* to mark out the church.[72] Like an embassy representing a kingdom

---

[67]Jonathan Leeman, *Political Church: The Local Assembly as Embassy of Christ's Rule* (Downers Grove, IL: IVP Academic, 2016), 364.
[68]Dever and Leeman, "Preface," xviii.
[69]Jonathan Leeman, "A Baptist View of the Royal Priesthood of All Believers," *The Southern Baptist Journal of Theology* 23, no. 1 (Spring 2019): 128.
[70]Leeman, "Baptist View of the Royal Priesthood," 130-31.
[71]Jonathan Leeman, *One Assembly: Rethinking the Multisite & Multiservice Church Models* (Wheaton, IL: Crossway, 2020), 23-24, emphasis added.
[72]Leeman, *Political Church*, 23.

in a particular place, "the church is an authoritative body . . . a political or authority-structured thing. And just as the idea of a kingdom typically invokes the idea of a land or a place, so Jesus choses a word for the people of this kingdom that necessarily invokes the idea of place—an assembly."[73] Leeman holds that "through preaching and the ordinances, Jesus publicly identifies himself with us in the gatherings: 'I am there among them,' he said. He tied his authority to the gatherings. So it's there we affirm our allegiance to him and our accountability to one another."[74] In short, "the church gathering is where Christ's kingdom becomes visible and active. . . . It is the 'geography' of Christ's kingdom."[75]

So how does this local church as embassy relate to the universal church in Leeman's thinking? Leeman says that the "assembly of a church demonstrates, proves, embodies, illustrates, incarnates, makes concrete, makes palpable and touchable and hearable and seeable the unity we possess in the gospel."[76] Unity with whom? Unity with Christ and with all others who are in Christ, who also gather in other local assemblies. In this way "the gathering manifests the universal church. . . . The gathering makes [that] Church present, and . . . it enables the members to discover, see, and recognize themselves together as *a* church and as *the* church."[77] Leeman entertains the objection, "Doesn't Christ's kingdom rule unite all Christians everywhere?" by answering, "Yes, it does: invisibly. What a local church does is make that rule visible. It expresses or manifests his kingdom rule in a way that everyone—insiders and outsiders—can actually see with their eyes and hear with their ears. This happens when a group of Christians physically gather together, agree upon the gospel to be preached, undertake a naming ceremony (baptism), and then enjoy a regular family meal that both affirms the gospel and their unity (the Lord's Supper)."[78] Because the universal church cannot gather, Leeman argues, it can't exercise kingdom authority as the local church can.

What implications does all this have for a Free Church doctrine of the church's catholicity? Here Leeman doesn't speak with the same degree of

---

[73]Leeman, *One Assembly*, 53.
[74]Leeman, *One Assembly*, 41.
[75]Leeman, *One Assembly*, 41-42.
[76]Leeman, *One Assembly*, 23.
[77]Leeman, *One Assembly*, 23.
[78]Leeman, *One Assembly*, 45.

regularity and confidence. He refers to the term *catholic* as meaning simply "worldwide or universal" and cites the church's catholicity as "our recognition of other churches."[79] He writes out of an explicit concern that "our church intuitions need to become more catholic—more appreciative of our partnership with other churches."[80] Leeman laments that in the Free Church tradition especially there is "too much *independence* . . . and not enough *inter-dependence,* not enough catholicity. And that lack of catholicity, that over-exuberant independence, is its own kind of divisiveness or factionalism, relative to other churches."[81] Leeman uses "interdependence" or "integration" more frequently than "catholicity" (seeing them as interchangeable) and notes that "local churches possess independence . . . because they possess authority for representing Christ, pronouncing a confession, and initiating the Great Commission. . . . [While] the interdependence of local churches is founded in the fact that they share the same Christ, the same confession, and the same Commission."[82] In fact, for Leeman the church's catholicity is actually what drives it to gather locally, for "gathering as a local assembly is the very first imperative to the indicative of the unity we possess as members of the universal church."[83] We gather locally *because* our (universally shared) Christ, confession, and commission drive us to.

Leeman puts a tremendous focus on what he views as the *implications* of the church's catholicity, in part because he sees the New Testament constantly spelling out the implications of our common bond in Christ. Leeman believes that the universal church

> should "show up" in every church's disposition to partner with other churches. . . . The New Testament churches shared love and greetings (Rom 16:16; 1 Cor 16:19; 2 Cor 13:13; etc.). They shared preachers and missionaries (2 Cor 8:18; 3 John 5-6a). They supported one another financially with joy and thanksgiving (Rom 15:25-26; 2 Cor 8:1-2). They imitated one another in Christian living (1 Thes. 1:7; 2:14; 2 Thes. 1:4). They cared for one another

---

[79]Leeman, *One Assembly*, 100.
[80]Leeman, *One Assembly*, 101.
[81]Leeman, *One Assembly*, 102.
[82]Jonathan Leeman, "A Congregational Approach to Catholicity: Independence and Interdependence," in Dever and Leeman, *Baptist Foundations*, 375-76.
[83]Leeman, *One Assembly*, 23.

financially (1 Cor 16:1–3; 2 Cor 8:24). They prayed for one another (Eph 6:18). And more.[84]

Leeman argues that "authority remains with people who can literally shake hands in agreement with one another because they are gathered together.... Born-again hearts don't need global structures or city structures. But they do need a global and city mindset, one that both affirms God's work through other churches and shapes how we do ministry."[85] Leeman can even say, "I don't want [ministers] to build the structures of a bishopric.... But I want [them] to adopt the mentality of a bishop—someone devoted to the good and growth of the churches and pastors in [their] region. I want [them] to be ... catholic pastor[s]."[86] For Leeman, a good embassy is going to have concern for other embassies (even from other eras) that represent the same king and kingdom, wanting to learn from them, support them, and partner with them for the greater good.[87] Leeman thus makes an important contribution to grounding Free Church catholicity in the local church on the basis of the authority Christ has entrusted to even just two of three who gather ecclesially in his name.

Consolidating Free Church Catholicity

Here we will assess the various proposals surveyed in the last two chapters and consolidate their greatest insights in order to move toward a more robust articulation of Free Church catholicity than any one of them provides. Our criteria for assessment involves determining how *faithful* such accounts are to the biblical warrant for the doctrine, how *coherent* they are as expressions of Free Church ecclesial convictions, and how *integrative* they are of the various aspects of catholicity that emerge in its church-historical development. By and large what we found in surveying the various proposals is a tendency either to neglect a robust enough notion of the church's catholicity (failing to exhibit Free Church *catholicity*) or to express such catholicity in a manner inconsistent with Free Church ecclesial convictions (failing to

---

[84]Jonathan Leeman, "The Church: Universal and Local," The Gospel Coalition, accessed April 12, 2021, www.thegospelcoalition.org/essay/the-church-universal-and-local/.
[85]Leeman, *One Assembly*, 103-4.
[86]Leeman, *One Assembly*, 126.
[87]Jonathan Leeman, *Don't Fire Your Church Members: The Case for Congregationalism* (Nashville: B&H Academic, 2016), 167.

exhibit *Free Church* catholicity). Believing that a more robust account of Free Church catholicity requires faithfulness to both the "catholic" and "Free Church" parts of the equation, I will close with a brief summary of what I believe might represent such an account under the banner of "Free Church catholicity as local catholicity."

The need for Free Church catholicity. We begin with those proposals that, in short, have not offered a robust enough vision of what the church's catholicity involves. At the very fountainhead of the Free Church tradition, it seems clear that the Anabaptist forefathers fall in this category. While it is true that an implicit catholicity can (at times) be found in the way that the Anabaptists sought to follow the logic of the creed (intentionally or unintentionally) in stressing the work of the Holy Spirit in creating and sustaining the catholic church, there is little explicit theological reflection on the nature of catholicity as an ecclesial attribute. Anabaptists typically did not value broader engagement with the Great Tradition, often holding that its contents detracted from the singular task of reviving apostolic Christianity. For them, the gathered community as a visible church was central, and occasionally a sense of chronological, geographical, and missional catholicity is derived from the fact that faithful local churches have gathered in all times, among all peoples, and in all places. But catholicity as such was of little concern, if only because all the churches that claimed to be the faithful manifestation of the catholic church were committed to their demise.

Something similar could be said for evangelical Baptists downstream. Unlike the sixteenth-century Anabaptists, they have a much greater recognition of the importance of catholicity for a proper understanding of the church. Many evangelical Baptists recognize the problem: the Baptist tradition (and, by extension, the Free Church tradition) has largely neglected catholicity (while emphasizing autonomy) and thus has become isolated and insular. They understand that part of what will address the movement's ills is a recovery, a retrieval, of catholicity, often looking to the Baptist confessions, connections and theologians of a previous era for models to do just that. But amid all the claims for renewal via retrieval, an explicit doctrine of the church's catholicity is either missing or is significantly underdeveloped. Leeman particularly argues that local churches are interdependent and should partner in various ways for the promulgation of the gospel. This is, of course, true; but how this is grounded in a proper understanding of the church's catholicity remains unclear. In short, Kärkkäinen's assessment seems to still very much apply: "The Free Churches have traditionally insisted on the primacy of the local churches almost to the exclusion of the *concept* of the universal church."[88] Kärkkäinen recognizes that "if one starts with the priority of the local church in keeping with the general tone of Free church ecclesiology, then the universal church is [merely] the sum of all local churches."[89] Catholicity, properly understood, is much more than this; and the change these theologians long to see in their tradition will require moving beyond this "mere catholicity" to articulating what it means, from a Free Church vantage point, to affirm the catholicity of the church in all its fullness.

The need for Free Church catholicity. Now we turn to those proposals that expressed catholicity in a manner not fully consistent with Free Church ecclesial convictions. First we consider the seventeenth-century English Separatists, both Baptist and Congregational. That these movements manifested a robust appreciation for and understanding of the church's catholicity there can be no doubt: from the Second London Confession to the Savoy Declaration, from the Orthodox Creed to the Baptist connections, the church's catholicity was often front and center. But here we ask, Was the sense of catholicity articulated a distinctly *Free Church* notion of the doctrine? We recall that much of what was expressed in the later seventeenth-century confessions was largely imitative of Westminster, and that out of the (not-unimportant) motivation to gain greater ecclesial respectability and even avoid persecution by the state. Baptists especially used their confessions not so much to proclaim "Baptist distinctives" but to show how similar they were to other orthodox Christians of their day, and the doctrine of catholicity was an obvious resource to employ in that endeavor. And as we observed in the last chapter, Baptists were not afraid to deviate from Westminster's lead where their ecclesial convictions called for the same, especially in any discussion of the church and its sacraments. So we ask, Why did Baptists not do the same when it came to expressing what they meant

---

[88]Veli-Matti Kärkkäinen, *An Introduction to Ecclesiology: Ecumenical, Historical & Global Perspectives* (Downers Grove, IL: IVP Academic, 2002), 138, emphasis added.
[89]Kärkkäinen, *Introduction to Ecclesiology*, 138.

by the church's catholicity? Seventeenth-century Baptists and Congregationalists sought to consistently work out and apply the principles of the Reformation in a Puritan framework, but this was a gradual process. The Free Church tradition was still quite young, and insights gleaned from Anabaptists of a previous generation were verboten (to be identified with the Anabaptists in seventeenth-century England was *not* a step toward credibility). In this sense, seventeenth-century Baptists and Congregationalists were in the early stages of articulating their *distinct* expression of Reformational Puritanism, and thus offered less than a fully *Free Church* doctrine of the church's catholicity.

We might also observe that the theologians who wrote *The Catholicity of Protestantism* exhibit a similarly *underdeveloped* doctrine of Free Church catholicity due to an *overidentification* with a broader Protestant catholicity. The authors of *The Catholicity of Protestantism* brilliantly defend the fact that Free Church catholicity is, before all else, Reformational catholicity. While this is an important point, it doesn't go far enough in articulating how Free Church catholicity is actually best understood as a *distinct form* of Reformational catholicity. The fact that the Free Church Council was inclusive of all nonestablished churches meant that to speak with one voice they needed to articulate a broadly Protestant perspective on the church's catholicity, one that was less committed to the particular pathway that the Anabaptists and English Separatists had taken (pursuing a *reformatio* via *restitutio*, and deviating from the magisterial pathway that left intact the marriage of church and state). The emerging Free Church ecclesial tradition made common cause with the magisterial Reformers in protesting the catholicity of Rome, but it also went on to protest that of Wittenberg, Geneva, and Canterbury, all for the sake of the catholic church. The authors of *The Catholicity of Protestantism* largely miss this and settle for equating Free Church catholicity with an amorphous Reformational catholicity, one that is merely non-Roman and non-Anglo-Catholic.

The problem also crops up in postliberal Baptist articulations of Free Church catholicity. There is no doubt that Harmon and others have done vitally important work in demonstrating that early Baptist history is deeply informed by the creedal confession of catholicity, and they have similarly done much to cast vision for how important retrieving such a vantage point is for the renewal of Baptist ecclesiology and practice today. They picture that Free Church catholicity is in vital dialogue with the tradition while always being willing to contest the tradition based on the authority of Scripture. They bring attention to the need for further understanding how liturgy and sacrament provide important points of "catholic contact" for Baptists to consider, and they rightly encourage Baptists to join in a receptive ecumenism out of a catholic spirit. But amid all these important emphases the question remains: How *Baptist* (or, for our purposes, *Free Church*) are these proposals? That is, how true would we say that such proposals are to the central ecclesial convictions of the Free Church tradition? One wonders whether Baptists, even of a more catholic spirit, resonate with Harmon's call for "full Eucharistic fellowship" with all churches. One wonders whether the commendation of pursuing a universal visible unity (often with hints that the pope would serve as the best candidate to oversee this global "communion of communions") ends up betraying the Baptist distinctives of being a pilgrim people and contesting over-realized eschatologies. In short, it doesn't seem clear that postliberal Baptist proposals of catholicity are, at present, sufficiently grounded in distinctly Free Church ecclesial convictions.

Conclusion: Free Church Catholicity as Local Catholicity

There is one perspective that we have not yet engaged in this assessment: that of Miroslav Volf, whose proposal of "the catholicity of two or three" comes closest to offering a sufficiently robust notion of catholicity (engaging the biblical witness and the church's tradition while in substantial ecumenical dialogue) from a distinctly Free Church vantage point. Volf's account is impressive, but still leaves us with questions. For instance, how do we account for the dimension of *institutional catholicity* from a Free Church vantage point, especially given the central role it plays in the Episcopal tradition and the prevalence of this dimension in large swaths of the Christian tradition? What dimensions are to be *privileged* in a Free Church account, and on what basis? Is a Free Church account of catholicity capable of integrating *all* of the dimensions? And, to return to that ever-pressing problem: *By what authority* would such an account be commended to the catholic church for its consideration in developing a fuller-orbed doctrine of catholicity? Volf has helped us to move toward a more robust Free Church account of catholicity, but we still have yet to arrive at one.

So where do we go from here? First, Free Church theologians need to heed Gordon Rupp's call for us "to take stock of our common heritage, Puritan, Evangelical, Nonconformist, in the light of biblical theology."[90] We must remember that as Protestants we embrace the slogan *ecclesia semper reformanda est* (the church is always being reformed). We evaluate our tradition and its theology at the bar of God's Word. We recognize that there is corruption in every theological tradition, hence the need to return to the Word for reformation. And yet, not every corruption is inevitable: some are historically contingent, not inherent to the tradition's theological DNA. Hence the important reminder that "in the history of any tradition of the Church catholic there are periods of depravation of which its heirs have cause to be ashamed. They will say: please do not judge us by these moments of error which sully the original purity of our inheritance."[91]

We are making a case that the relative neglect of catholicity in the Free Church tradition is a corruption of *this* type, and we have surveyed the biblical warrant for catholicity, the church-historical development of the doctrine, and the proposals of catholicity emerging from the bookends of the Free Church tradition to make the case that Free Church catholicity is *not* a contradiction in terms. Even though it is perhaps the newest tradition to the "catholic table," it has produced some promising proposals for better understanding the nature of the catholicity that we confess, proposals that need to be further refined so that the Free Church tradition and the broader catholic church may benefit. We said in chapter two that the doctrine of catholicity is complex; after surveying the biblical witness and the many developments that have occurred in two thousand years of God's people reading God's Word in an attempt to better understand what we mean when we confess that the church is catholic, it is clear there are many aspects that a robust account of catholicity needs to account for and integrate. We also said that by prioritizing and relating the various aspects (we identified nine in our final taxonomy) in different ways, each ecclesial tradition brings out

---

[90]Gordon Rupp, *Protestant Catholicity: Two Lectures* (London: Epworth Press, 1960), 53.
[91]Flew and Davies, *Catholicity of Protestantism*, 82.

particular insights for the whole church to consider. It is now time to glimpse what distinctive contribution the Free Church tradition has to make, building on, yet going beyond, the proposals surveyed in the last two chapters. It is time to articulate a fuller-orbed and genuinely Free Church account of the church's catholicity.

To do so, we must recall from chapter one that the term *catholic* nicely describes the pattern of judgments found in Scripture regarding the *nature* of God's people as a unified diversity and the *scope* of God's people as through the whole of all times, peoples, and places. Indeed, once we connected the prevalent biblical motif of unified diversity with catholicity, we saw how the New Testament builds on and clarifies the Old Testament in teaching that God's people will be marked by increasing unity-in-diversity as the missional trajectory of the church's gospel witness works through all times, peoples, and places. Particularly we saw that Scripture provides us with important "guardrails" for any proposal of how to understand the doctrine of ecclesial catholicity. One guardrail prevents us from assenting to any vision of the church's catholicity that requires uniformity (seen particularly in 1 Cor 12); this compromises the reality that God's catholic people represent a *diversity*. Another guardrail prevents us from embracing a vision of catholicity that allows for pluralism (seen particularly in Eph 4); this compromises the reality that God's catholic people are *unified*. A third guardrail prevents us from holding to an understanding of catholicity that involves exclusionism, sectarianism, or provincialism (seen particularly in Gal 3); this compromises the fact that God's catholic people are *through the whole of all times, peoples, and places*.

In chapter two we argued that proposals regarding how best to understand the church's catholicity will be most compelling when they are *integrative* of as many of the aspects that have accumulated over the church-historical story as possible, articulating their proper prioritization and interrelationship. We argued that such prioritization and integration should be guided, first, by a Reformational effort to see Scripture function as the *norma normans* of theology, asking which of the categories has the greatest support and grounding in the biblical witness. We argued, second, that such an effort should be undertaken as an enterprise of interpreting Scripture in the communion of saints and learning from their collective insights, asking which of the categories are given *more emphasis* in the tradition. Then we argued that a compelling proposal will work to reconcile the relative agreement across ecclesial traditions regarding the *scope* of catholicity (the quantitative elements) with the substantial disagreement regarding the *nature* of catholicity (the qualitative elements). Finally, we argued that compelling proposals will help us better understand why at the "points of crisis" for catholicity the dimensions of orthodox catholicity (#5) and institutional catholicity (#6) seem to come into particular conflict with one another, especially as it relates to the question of which church stands in proper relation to the whole (holistic catholicity, #1) and in continuity with the catholic tradition of the church through the ages (chronological catholicity, #4). Compelling proposals also help us potentially overcome these points of crisis and work toward greater unity among the catholic church.

We also concluded in chapter two that our provisional definition of catholicity as expressing the church's unified diversity through the whole of all times, peoples, and places is justified as a *starting point* in part because it is capable of further filling out as we integrate the various aspects of catholicity witnessed in church history and categorized in the taxonomy. We recognized that holistic catholicity (#1) connotes the *spirit* of catholicity, a stance of connectedness to the universal church and a willingness to combat sectarianism. We also recognized widespread agreement regarding the *scope* of this universal church expressed in geographical, missional, and chronological aspects of catholicity (#2–4), ensuring that the church as catholic is conceived as inclusive of "all places," "all peoples," and "all times" in a way that rules out provincialism, exclusionism, and novelty. But we went on to say that chronological catholicity (#4) also emphasizes *continuity with the catholic tradition*, a tradition foundationally established in the ancient rule of faith manifest in the creeds of the undivided church. We saw that differentiated catholicity (#7) highlights that the *unity* of the church is not manifest in uniformity but in a divinely ordained diversity, with each member contributing its distinctive gifts and graces. We claimed that liturgical catholicity (#9) emphasizes the *holiness* of the church and is manifest in a common sacramental expression whereby the community is set apart by its distinctive gospel practices, while orthodox catholicity (#5) emphasizes that the *apostolicity* of the church provides the "guardrails" of catholicity such that its diversity is properly unified around the gospel and its first-order doctrinal entailments. The remaining two aspects, we said, emphasize that catholicity must be *visible* (institutional catholicity, #6) and *theologically grounded* (christological catholicity, #8), and we noted that a compelling proposal for properly understanding the church's catholicity will articulate how these deepest dimensions of catholicity relate and reinforce one another.

In the last two chapters, we have examined how the Free Church tradition in its Reformation and contemporary expressions has understood the church and its catholicity. Our survey has confirmed that the three *defining marks* provided in the introduction are indeed helpful in understanding what we mean by the Free Church tradition defined theologically (vs. being conceived as simply nonestablished). We said, first, that churches in the Free Church tradition are *congregationally constituted*, holding that their ecclesiality is established "from below" in the voluntary gathering of God's faith-filled, priestly people. Second, churches in the Free Church tradition are *conscientiously nonconformist*, emphasizing the necessary "otherness" of the church and rejecting Constantinian arrangements out of a conviction that the church's distinctiveness is best preserved when it is nonestablished, kept from state interference, and identified with the *corpus Christi* (body of Christ) rather than the *corpus Christianum* (body of Christendom). And third, churches in the Free Church tradition are *corporately local*, insisting on the primacy of the local, visible church that convenes under the authority of Christ by the power of the Spirit for covenanted fellowship marked by Word, sacrament, and ministerial oversight, seeking conformity to the pattern of Scripture and God's greater glory.

Now, in addition to these marks, we are in a better position to articulate three *ecclesiological convictions* that must be applied in bringing about a distinctively Free Church doctrine of the church's catholicity, two of which are shared with the broader catholic church and one of which is distinct to the Free Church tradition. One such ecclesiological conviction, shared with the catholic church, would undoubtedly be a redemptive-historical claim that perhaps *the most fundamental thing God is doing in the gospel is gathering a people for himself.* Yoder articulates this prime conviction thus: "The work of God is *the calling of a people*, whether in the Old Covenant or the New. The church is then not simply the bearer of the message of reconciliation.... [It is] a new social wholeness [which] is itself the work of God."⁹² In other words, the Free Church tradition never wants to shortchange the fundamental description that we find of the church in Scripture: it is the *people* of God, a *community* of the redeemed. It wants to maximize the creedal confession that the church is "the communion of saints."

A second ecclesiological conviction, shared with the catholic church, is that *the magisterial ecclesial authority is Christ alone* as head of the church (Col 1:18) and shepherd and overseer of his people (1 Pet 2:25). Here Yoder very much speaks for the tradition in saying, "If [our] locus ... is Jesus Christ, it would seem ... [reasonable] to declare inadmissible the attribution of authoritative character to any particular historical development and to recognize, as the only legitimate judge, *Christ himself* as he is made known through Scripture to the congregation of those who seek to know him and his will."⁹³ Because Christ himself is the *Episkopos* (Bishop) who shepherds his people, this relativizes the authority of any *episkopos* (or any other ministerial ecclesial authority, for that matter) that oversteps the proper bounds of ministerial oversight. Augustus Strong notes that the government of the church can thus be understood as an "absolute monarchy," with each member and the church as a whole under the rule of Jesus Christ as its head.⁹⁴ John Owen has said much the same by proclaiming that "all authority in and over the church is vested in [Christ] alone."⁹⁵

Yet Owen simultaneously points us to a third Free Church ecclesiological conviction, one that is distinctive to this tradition, by going on to say that the *means* by which Christ rules the church is the congregational meeting, for "a *visible professing church* ... avoweth [its] authority from Christ ... [and] is the way which Christ hath ordained to render his kingdom visible or conspicuous."⁹⁶ This conviction might be summarized thus: *the highest ministerial ecclesial authority is the local assembly of God's faith-filled people.* Indeed, to return to Strong's claim that the church is an absolute monarchy,

---

⁹²John Howard Yoder, *The Royal Priesthood: Essays Ecclesiastical and Ecumenical*, ed. Michael G. Cartwright (Scottdale, PA: Herald Press, 1998), 74, emphasis added.
⁹³Yoder, *Royal Priesthood*, 221-22.
⁹⁴Augustus Hopkins Strong, *Systematic Theology* (Philadelphia: The Judson Press, 1907), 903.
⁹⁵John Owen, *The True Nature of a Gospel Church and Its Government*, ed. John Huxtable (London: James Clarke, 1947), 42.
⁹⁶John Owen, *The Works of John Owen*, vol. 15, ed. William H. Gould (Edinburgh: T&T Clark, 1862), 323-26.

he also simultaneously insists that each believer is called to obey Christ and thus is responsible for the well-being of Christ's bride; hence the church can also be understood as an "absolute democracy."[97] The fullest picture of the church thus only comes together when we hold these poles in tension: the church is, more accurately, a Christocracy-Democracy, one where Christ rules through the rule of the gathered people of God.

The claim that Christ's rule over the church is most concretely expressed in the congregational gathering has vast implications for our understanding of the church's very nature and, thus, its catholicity. The promise that Christ himself is present by the Spirit in the formal assembly of God's believing people (Mt 18:20) is properly worked out, to the Free Church mind, in the fact that ministerial ecclesial authority is to be found most centrally in the collective gathering of royal priests (1 Pet 2:9; Heb 10:19; Rev 1:6) who are equally endowed with the Spirit of God (Acts 2; 1 Cor 2:12; 7:40). Often expounded through a particular outworking of the doctrine of the priesthood of all believers, the Free Church notion of the church centers on the visible, local congregation and accents the way that the New Testament again and again emphasizes full congregational involvement in the church's affairs. Such distributed ecclesial authority is grounded in the "democratization of the Spirit" hoped for by Moses (Num 11:29), promised by the prophets (Ezek 36:27; Joel 2) and demonstrated at Pentecost (Acts 2); if each member of Christ's body has been given the Spirit then the church should be *corporately* seeking the mind of Christ (1 Cor 2:16). This shared ecclesial authority does not exclude the legitimacy of other ministerial authorities (e.g., ordained ministers or associational conventions); on the contrary, it establishes the ability of the collective membership to appoint, partner with, and submit to such authorities as the congregation sees fit.

Here we find the very principles undergirding a distinctively Free Church notion and outworking of the church's catholicity, because a Free Church account of the church involves a pattern of ecclesial authority that is "bottom up." The variance between the Episcopal and Free Church traditions as to whether ecclesial authority is derived from Christ via his apostles from below (via the gathered congregation) or from above (via

---

[97]Strong, *Systematic Theology*, 903.

bishops in apostolic succession) inevitably leads to very different conceptions of the church's catholicity because they provide different understandings of the *locus* of that catholicity. For its part, the Free Church tradition, in consistently emphasizing that the gathered congregation is the proper conduit for ecclesial authority, holds that the *local church* is the proper locus of catholicity.

It is this local orientation that provides the unique vantage point regarding the integration of the various aspects of catholicity, for it emphasizes that Christ's presence by his Spirit in the ordered, faith-filled community gathered around Word and sacrament under oversight constitutes *each local church* as a catholic church. This theological account of the church leads the Free Church tradition to understand how the qualitative aspects of catholicity relate to its quantitative aspects in a unique way, specifically because the unified diversity of God's people becomes visibly manifest in all times, peoples, and places thanks to Christ's presence promised *in every locale* where the community gathers. Thus catholicity, according to a distinctly Free Church account, is always a "local catholicity," meaning that in our attempt to *locate* the catholicity of the church and understand what we mean by this creedal attribute, we look not to the aggregate of all the saints in an invisible church, nor to a visible (and supposedly universal) translocal institution, nor even to the eschatological gathered church of all times and peoples, but rather to local church gatherings of all peoples at all times in all places.

Free Church catholicity as "local catholicity" thus emphasizes that *each local church* is an ambassadorial, visible institution under oversight (#6) connected to the whole of *all other local churches* (#1) through all times, peoples, and places (#2–4) via a common christological connection (#8) promised to diverse-yet-unified believing communities of even just "two or three" (#7) that are ordered around Word (#5) and sacrament (#9); each local church thus manifests the one catholic church spoken of in the tradition and testified to in Scripture. Such an account emphasizes that locality and catholicity are mutually dependent: only a *local* catholicity ensures that the various qualitative aspects of catholicity *fully* manifest through the *whole* scope of the gospel's reception delineated in the quantitative aspects. Such a Free Church account insists that the catholicity of the church envisioned in Scripture and expounded in tradition only comes into its fullness when the universality of the church is understood as a unified diversity through the *multifarious* whole, when there is a unity in ever-increasing, *localized* diversity. Such an account ultimately holds that there is no fulsome catholicity without sufficient locality (and adds, as we shall see, that there is no fulsome locality without sufficient catholicity).

If indeed genuine catholicity is local catholicity, the Free Church tradition stands in the best position to articulate what that means and to share those insights with the catholic church. Briggs asks whether "the Free Churches in recent history [have] properly deployed their freedom in the interests of . . . the [catholic] Church of Jesus Christ?"[98] It would seem that the answer to date is no. That must change. We must now move to further unpacking Free Church catholicity as local catholicity and its implications for the catholic church, particularly by continuing our dialogue with the Episcopal tradition, that the whole body of Christ may benefit.

---

[98]John H. Y. Briggs, "The Changing Shape of Nonconformity, 1662–2000," in *T&T Clark Companion to Nonconformity*, ed. Stephen J. Pope (London: Bloomsbury, 2013), 24.

Free Church Catholicity Embodied
Locating Catholicity

THE VERY FACT that there are multiple ecclesial traditions in the one, holy, catholic, and apostolic church assures us that no ecclesial tradition has a monopoly on catholicity. Though the doctrine of the church's catholicity remains contested, we can rule out of hand *exclusive* claims to catholicity as both overreaching and not particularly catholic in spirit. A corollary of this is that any attempt to set forth a full-orbed doctrine of catholicity should be done in dialogue with other ecclesial traditions. If it is true, as Avis has said, that "the vocation of Anglicanism is to witness to and serve the *catholicity* of the Church" and that this "is true of *all churches*" because "to realize the four creedal marks is necessarily the vocation of *all manifestations or traditions* of the Church," then it follows that each ecclesial tradition ought to listen attentively to the others when they articulate what is meant, from that tradition's standpoint, in confessing the church as catholic.[1] We have observed that, on the whole, it is the Episcopal traditions that have made the most substantial contributions to the doctrine to date. But now it is time we take up Kenneth Scott Latourette's question posed to the 1968 Louisville conference: "What is the distinctive function of [Free

---

[1]Paul Avis, *The Vocation of Anglicanism* (London: Bloomsbury T&T Clark, 2016), 181, emphasis added.

Churches] in the Church Universal?"[2] More specifically, what insights into catholicity does the Free Church tradition have to offer for the benefit of the catholic church?

WHY WE NEED COMPLEMENTARY ACCOUNTS OF CATHOLICITY

Catholicity isn't just contested; it is also complex. In fact, we might say that *one* of the reasons the doctrine is so contested is because it is so *multifaceted*. Our church-historical survey identified nine aspects of ecclesial catholicity, and attempts to relate and prioritize these aspects reveal that speaking about the church's catholicity is no simple task. But the complexity is heightened by the fact that confessing *the church* also has complexity, for as Colm O'Grady has so aptly put it, "The more one tries to understand the Church the more one realizes how ultimately unintelligible it is. . . . [For] it is the mysterious unity of a human and a divine, a temporal and an eternal, an earthly and a heavenly reality."[3] Haight recognizes that this difficulty is compounded by the fact that "the subject matter of an adequate ecclesiology must be the whole church. . . . [But] one only belongs to the whole Christian church from a specific standpoint, that is, in and through a particular church. Therefore . . . [a] tension arises when one tries to deal with the whole church from a particular tradition."[4] That "tension" might be summarized as attempting to make sense of the complex whole from a particular angle, inevitably emphasizing some things to the neglect of others. Leeman has specifically brought attention to the fact that ecclesial traditions tend to give more emphasis to either the local or the universal church, even noting that we inevitably "view the relationship between the universal and local church— between the one church and the many congregations—in a manner that suits [our] denominational affiliations."[5] More positively, we might say that the doctrine of the church and its catholicity proves the need for what Vanhoozer calls "Pentecostal plurality," for many ecclesial traditions are

---

[2]Kenneth Scott Latourette, "A People in the World: Historical Background," in *The Concept of the Believers' Church: Addresses from the 1968 Louisville Conference*, ed. James Leo Garrett Jr. (Scottdale, PA: Herald Press, 1969), 241.
[3]Colm O'Grady, *The Church in Catholic Theology: Dialogue with Karl Barth* (London: Geoffrey Chapman, 1969), 279.
[4]Roger Haight, *Christian Community in History*, vol. 2 (New York: Continuum, 2005), 216-17.
[5]Jonathan Leeman, *One Assembly: Rethinking the Multisite & Multiservice Church Models* (Wheaton, IL: Crossway, 2020), 72.

needed to do full justice to the catholic nature of the church.[6] Part of how we embrace a collaborative mindset and avoid the abuses of emphasizing certain dimensions of the church and its catholicity over others is by dialoguing with other ecclesial traditions, recognizing that both the church and its catholicity are best understood in terms of various interrelated dimensions that require *all* the ecclesial traditions to fully parse out.

The dimensions of the church. While many "dimensions" of the church have been recognized in its history, here we can only briefly attend to three that most directly impact our understanding of the church's catholicity: the local and universal dimensions,[7] the visible and invisible dimensions, and the militant and triumphant dimensions. Clowney helpfully expresses that these are really three *distinctions* in how we speak of the church: the local/universal distinction of *space*, the visible/invisible distinction of *perspective*, and the militant/triumphant distinction of *time*.[8]

First, the local/universal tandem is a distinction of *space*. The local church is fully the church in one place, yet each local church is part of a larger whole that transcends any one place. It is a contextualization of this translocal whole, representing the universal church and making it concrete. George is right to note that "it is not a mark of sound churchmanship . . . to play off the universal church against the local church, or vice versa."[9] Rather, we should see these as complementary ways to understand the one church: in its local expression or in its universal scope. In short, the church is *both* local and universal (i.e., translocal).

This is connected to, second, the visible/invisible tandem as a distinction of *perspective*, particularly our own versus God's on the one church. It functions primarily as an acknowledgment of our fallible perception: we can only see the visible church and may make errant judgments regarding it, but God

---

[6]Kevin Vanhoozer, *Biblical Authority After Babel: Retrieving the Solas in the Spirit of Mere Protestant Christianity* (Grand Rapids, MI: Brazos Press, 2016), 223.
[7]Here we use the language of "universal" in a way that should not be conflated with "catholic." Indeed, we will be making the case that the church in both these dimensions, which might otherwise be stated as local and translocal, is to be described as catholic. Catholicity is, as this study is attempting to show, more than universality (but not less).
[8]See Edmund P. Clowney, *The Doctrine of the Church* (Philadelphia: Presbyterian and Reformed, 1974), 73.
[9]Timothy George, "Is Jesus a Baptist?," *First Things*, August 12, 2013, www.firstthings.com/web-exclusives/2013/08/is-jesus-a-baptist.

sees perfectly the church as it actually is (ultimately something *not visible* to us). For Calvin and the other Reformers, belonging to the invisible church was virtually inseparable from participating in the visible church, for the visible church is the place where God employs his chosen means to evoke and sustain faith: the hearable Word and seeable sacraments.

Third, the militant/triumphant tandem is a distinction of *time*. This distinction enjoys the broadest agreement across ecclesial traditions (the disagreement being over whether there is a church "penitent," that is, whether purgatory exists). The church triumphant is the church of the eschaton, where faith has become sight and prayer has become praise. The church militant is the church still struggling against principalities and powers. There is only one church, but depending on the timeframe we have in view we speak of it as either having arrived or still *in via*.

If we put each of these distinctions in dialogue, what emerges are eight distinct "combinations" of ways to confess the church. Half of these deal with the church triumphant, and here we recognize that there is no contesting eschatological catholicity; everyone holds that at the eschaton the catholicity of the church will be on full display and that *believing* the church is catholic will no longer be required.[10] This leaves us with four combinations dealing with the church militant, one of which is a false category (there is no such thing as the *invisible*, local, militant church). Therefore, we are left with three pertinent combinations for confessing the (militant) church that have direct bearing on how we confess its catholicity.

First is the church as *visible and local*, the church as an *assembly* of God's people in a particular place. Every ecclesial tradition confesses the local church (often expressed as a "particular church"), but what is meant differs significantly across the traditions. Second is the church as *invisible and universal*, the church as an *aggregate* of God's people inclusive of all peoples and places. This is the category confessed in the creed as "the communion of saints." Every ecclesial tradition confesses this understanding of the church. Third is the militant church as *visible and universal or translocal*,

---

[10]This is why Volf's emphasis on the eschatological nature of catholicity isn't much help in navigating the current ecclesial disagreements. To say the eschatological gathering of the church is the sine qua non of catholicity puts its locus beyond our current experience and possibly indicates that *true* catholicity is only a future reality.

the church as an *institution* that goes beyond any particular locale. The Roman Catholic Church and denominational bodies provide examples of this on a global scale, while national assemblies, presbyteries, and dioceses provide examples of this on a national or regional scale. This is a contested category with significant disagreement between ecclesial traditions as to the legitimacy of confessing these sorts of groups as *church*.[11] We conclude that the Scriptures do permit us to speak of the church as an institution beyond the local gathering as visible and translocal in a certain sense (see, for example, Acts 9:31; 1 Cor 10:32; 12:28),[12] but here we raise the question: Though Scripture authorizes us to be able to speak of the church as visible and translocal in some way, should that be *primarily* what we have in mind when we confess the church and its catholicity? The Free Church tradition consistently argues to the contrary: the *primary* way we should confess the church and speak of its catholicity is by *thinking locally*, insisting that this is where the catholic church is *located*. The complexity of confessing the church's catholicity comes, in part, from delineating which of these three senses of the militant church ecclesial traditions tend to put more weight on when they confess the church as catholic. Volf argues that "the theologically decisive question involves the catholicity of concrete, visible churches," and we would agree.[13]

---

[11]This disagreement is evident even within the Anglican tradition, our primary Episcopal dialogue partner. Graham Cole has argued, citing H. W. Griffith-Thomas, that the standard Anglican view expressed in the *Thirty-Nine Articles* understands the church in exactly the threefold manner just articulated: the church is local (congregative), general (aggregative), and universal (inclusive). Cole engages the work of Anglicans Broughton Knox and Donald Robinson (synthesized in what has been called the "Knox-Robinson ecclesiology"), which calls into question the legitimacy of the church as a translocal institution. Knox and Robinson's concern is similar to that of many Free Church theologians: that *ecclesia* should only be used to designate the local gathering of the church (whether on earth, in heaven around Christ, or at the eschaton) and thus it is illegitimate to call institutions such as "the Anglican Church" a *church*. See Graham Cole, "The Doctrine of the Church: Towards Conceptual Clarification," in *Church, Worship and the Local Congregation*, ed. B. G. Webb (Homebush West, New South Wales: Lancer, 1987).

[12]Cole agrees, but argues that our term *church* has suffered from "theological inflation" due to its imprecise overuse, and that this could be remedied by more frequently employing the construct of "the people of God" as broader and better comporting with the creedal confession of the one, holy, catholic, and apostolic church. Cole points out the need for spelling out how *ecclesia* is a subset of the people of God and offers the possibility that "the church is a meeting of the people of God." Cole, "Doctrine of the Church," 3, 7.

[13]Miroslav Volf, *After Our Likeness: The Church as the Image of the Trinity* (Grand Rapids, MI: Eerdmans, 1998), 270.

The dimensions of catholicity. The complexity of confessing the church as catholic is deepened by the fact that there aren't just dimensions to the church; there are dimensions to the church's catholicity itself. This is clear when we ask certain questions seeking analytical clarity regarding the content of catholicity. One such question would be, Is catholicity primarily quantitative or qualitative (or equally both)? Another would be, How does the creedal attribute of catholicity interface with the other creedal attributes and with the Reformational marks of a true church? A third would be, How can the various aspects of catholicity that we have seen witnessed to in Scripture and over the course of church history be properly prioritized and related?

Attempting to answer these questions leads us to see that catholicity is best understood as having interrelated yet distinct dimensions. This is clear from even some basic reflections on the nature of the creedal confession: "I believe . . . [in] one, holy, catholic and apostolic church." First, we recognize that this is indeed a *confession*, that is, something that requires faith. Here George has said well that: "as a reality beyond our ken, this universal church is not at our disposal. . . . When we confess that we 'believe the church,' we are bearing witness to its reality. We mean to say that we believe that it exists; that we ourselves by God's grace have been placed within it, along with all others who 'bow their necks under the yoke of Jesus Christ' (Belgic Confession, art. 28)."[14] Second, we recognize that such a confession of faith is required in the case of both the visible, local church as well as the invisible, universal church. It requires faith, not to *see* the local church, but to *believe* that it is actually connected to a larger whole, that it is a manifestation of the one, universal church. This means that both *quantitative* and *qualitative* dimensions will be required, with the quantitative marking out the *scope* of the universal church and the qualitative marking out the *nature* of the church as it manifests locally. Third, we recognize that because this confession of faith is *continually contested* due to competing claims regarding which group or groups are catholic, marks of a true (catholic) church are required this side of glory. Here the burning question of the Reformers comes to the fore: Amid what was understood as an abandonment of the apostolic gospel and the catholic faith of the one, holy church through the

---

[14]Timothy George, "The Sacramentality of the Church: An Evangelical Baptist Perspective," in *Pro Ecclesia* 12, no. 3 (Summer 2003): 313.

ages, where was the church confessed in the creed *to be found*? Their answer was in local churches that bear the marks of a true church, and we must understand how these marks are properly related to the attribute of catholicity, or how catholicity can be *confirmed*. Finally, we recognize that one day this confession of faith will give way to sight, for there is also an eschatological dimension to our confession of the church as catholic. In fact, there is a great mystery at the heart of our confession of the church: the church is *already* one, holy, catholic, and apostolic; at the same time it is *not yet* one, holy, catholic, and apostolic; in fact, the church is *on the way* to being one, holy, catholic, and apostolic; but *one day* it will be *fully* one, holy, catholic, and apostolic. We could thus say the confession of the church's catholicity, as with all of the creedal attributes, is simultaneously "already," "not yet," "on the way," and "one day."

These reflections lead us to conclude that we can think about catholicity in four distinct senses, what we might call the four dimensions of catholicity. The first is the widely accepted sense of *quantitative* catholicity. This is the "not yet" dimension that deals with the *scope* of catholicity, a scope that is incomplete because it increases over the course of redemptive history as the church's gospel increasingly goes forth at all times, among all peoples, and to all places. This corresponds to what Dulles has called the "breadth of catholicity," connected as it is to the way the ever-expanding mission of the church has enabled a greater and greater extent of ecclesial communion to occur.[15] This dimension highlights the inclusive and expansive nature of the church, a fullness that increases as the church encounters and incorporates greater and greater degrees of diversity. It corresponds to the "all" of the Great Commission and rebukes expressions of the church that favor a certain time, people, or place over others. It integrates geographical, missional, and chronological aspects of catholicity (#2–4) leading to greater and greater degrees of differentiated catholicity (#7), for as the church increasingly manifests among all times, peoples, and places, it demonstrates ever-increasing amounts of (unified) diversity.

But the dimension of quantitative catholicity is interconnected with, and even dependent on, a second widely recognized dimension: *qualitative*

---

[15] Avery Dulles, *The Catholicity of the Church* (Oxford: Oxford University Press, 1985), 68.

catholicity.¹⁶ This is the "already" dimension that deals with the *nature* of catholicity. It is this dimension Volf has in view when he says that catholicity "is a *proprietas* of the church, its essential characteristic, which (together with other essential characteristics) expresses the essence of the church with which it is identical."¹⁷ This dimension doesn't grow or change over the course of redemptive history; it fully characterizes the church (however expansive) from Pentecost to parousia. Additionally, unlike quantitative catholicity, which can be witnessed (i.e., we can *see* the church's expansion happening), qualitative catholicity is something we can only grasp by faith. It is also the dimension at the heart of ecclesial disagreement about catholicity. In this project, we have understood it as speaking of the *nature* of God's people as a *unified diversity*: the church of all times, peoples, and places is marked by a manifold diversity as it is united in Christ (#8). In this we follow Congar's thinking: "The Catholicity of the Church . . . is the *dynamic universality of her unity*, the capacity of her principles of unity to assimilate, fulfil and raise to God in oneness with [Christ] all men."¹⁸ Here Koskela's observation is apt: "[Catholicity] reflects, in many ways, a theologically robust account of [the church's] diversity."¹⁹

But these two dimensions alone don't do justice to the fullness of the church's confession of its catholicity because they haven't yet encapsulated the "on the way" and "one day" dynamic. For that we need to add two more dimensions, one of which we might call *consummative* catholicity. This is the "one day" dimension that deals with the *fulfillment* of catholicity. It references the eschatological fullness of the church as catholic, the fact that after Christ's return the church's catholic nature will be on full display as quantitative catholicity comes to completion and qualitative catholicity no longer

---

¹⁶Here Congar is representative: "There cannot be quantitative Catholicity without qualitative, this being the necessary cause of the former. If the Church is indeed able and destined to extend over the whole world, it is in virtue of the universal assimilative *capacity* of her constituent principles." Yves Congar, *Divided Christendom: A Catholic Study of the Problem of Reunion*, trans M. A. Bousfield (London: Centenary Press, 1939), 93-94.
¹⁷Volf, *After Our Likeness*, 261.
¹⁸Congar, *Divided Christendom*, 94-95, emphasis added. This emphasis on qualitative catholicity leads Congar to see that the grounding of catholicity is "essentially Trinitarian and Christological. . . . The Catholicity of [the Church's] Head is the principle cause of the Catholicity of the Church." Congar, *Divided Christendom*, 95, 98.
¹⁹Douglas M. Koskela, "Holiness and Catholicity: A Fruitful Tension for the Wesleyan Tradition," *Wesleyan Theological Journal* 49, no. 1 (Spring 2014): 73.

requires faith to be grasped (and the Reformational marks to be confirmed). In short, it is the catholic nature of the church triumphant. Volf emphasizes that consummative catholicity informs our understanding of the church's catholicity now, saying "the church is catholic because the Spirit of the new creation present within it anticipates in it the eschatological gathering of the whole people of God."[20]

Significantly, Volf holds that there is "widespread consensus" regarding the "eschatological maximum" of catholicity; it is what he calls the "historical minimum" of catholicity where much dispute remains, noting that it is "questions concerning the optimal form of historical catholicity and its minimum . . . [that are] of crucial importance in ecumenical relations."[21] Indeed, while there is virtually no disagreement regarding consummative catholicity, there is significant disagreement regarding this fourth dimension of catholicity, what I am calling *inaugurated* catholicity. This is the "on the way" dimension that deals with catholicity's *enactment*. It gets at the degree to which churches currently embody and express a connectedness to the whole (#1), contributing toward greater quantitative catholicity, living out their qualitative catholicity, and anticipating their consummative catholicity. This dimension can be understood as existing in different degrees within different churches, and thus is something churches can grow in over time as they become more of who they already are in Christ. And, as we will see in more detail later, this dimension of catholicity is particularly expressed in the orthodox, institutional, and liturgical aspects of catholicity (#5, 6, 9), aspects that are closely related to the Reformational marks and the other creedal attributes confirming the catholicity of a church.[22] In short, this dimension moves from the indicative to the imperative of catholicity. Gibaut says of this that while "catholicity . . . belongs to the church's nature by the power of the Spirit . . . the demand of catholicity is for the church to become what it is."[23]

To take stock: confessing the church's catholicity is complex, and hence the particular understandings of the church's catholicity from various

---

[20]Volf, *After Our Likeness*, 268.
[21]Volf, *After Our Likeness*, 269.
[22]For more here see G. C. Berkouwer, *The Church* (Grand Rapids, MI: Eerdmans, 1976), 128-30.
[23]John St-Helier Gibaut, "Catholicity, Faith and Order, and the Unity of the Church," *Ecumenical Review* 63, no. 2 (July 2011): 183.

ecclesial vantage points are contested. This is largely because each ecclesial tradition tends to emphasize certain dimensions of both the church and its catholicity over others. But a full-orbed understanding of the church's catholicity requires that each dimension of the church and its catholicity are accounted for, and thus it will take a diversity of ecclesial traditions to get more fully at what ecclesial catholicity means and entails. Our claim is that currently this holistic understanding is hindered by the relative lack of Free Church contributions to the doctrine. This is especially true concerning the sense in which the local church is catholic and the way that such "local catholicity" maximizes the statement that the church is catholic, that is, marked by a unified diversity in Christ through the whole.

An Episcopal Account of Locality's Relationship to Catholicity

We said earlier that no ecclesial tradition, including the Episcopal tradition, has a monopoly on catholicity. Now we must also insist that no ecclesial tradition has a monopoly on locality, or the visible/local dimensions of the church discussed above. Though it is a signature emphasis of Free Church ecclesiology to expound the nature of the church as primarily a local assembly, this is by no means to insist that other ecclesial traditions do not have robust accounts of the church as local. In fact, we can cite tremendous reflections on the local church and its relation to catholicity from the broader Episcopal tradition.[24] But ultimately the Free Church tradition insists that "local catholicity" will be insufficiently developed if we hear from the Episcopal tradition alone. Why? It is not that they do not have a conception of the church as local, but that this conception is *insufficiently* local because it places the locus around the bishop and his *translocal* diocese. This is, to the Free Church mind, not simply organizing locality in a different way, but

---

[24]One such example would be Jean Marie Tillard's work *L'Église locale: Ecclésiologie de communion et catholicité* (Paris: Cerf, 1995). The critical move in Tillard's work is described by Ruddy: "Tillard joins a qualitative catholicity to a theology of the local church to argue that the church of God is inseparably local and catholic.... [The church] is catholic precisely because it is local: the fullness of the divine gift given at Pentecost takes root only in the diverse cultures, geographies, and histories of humanity." Christopher Ruddy, *The Local Church: Tillard and the Future of Catholic Ecclesiology* (New York: Crossroad, 2006), 68. Ruddy then summarizes the import of Tillard's work: "In short, locality does not compete with catholicity, but instead expresses it fully." Ruddy, *Local Church*, 68-69.

failing to recognize the truth that the local church is constituted as an assembly of even just two or three believers in Christ's name. We are thus making the case that the Free Church tradition provides the *most consistent* account of the local dimension of the church, and that this account *maximizes* the church's quantitative catholicity and *spotlights* the church's qualitative catholicity by insisting that every ecclesial assembly, even of just two or three, is catholic. To justify this claim, we will look at Anglican notions of the local church's relation to catholicity and argue that, when compared to a Free Church account of the same, it shortchanges both the "local" and "catholicity" parts of "local catholicity" by *failing to be sufficiently local* and by *privileging unity over catholicity*.

First, let's examine what is meant by the local church in Anglican ecclesiology. We begin by recognizing that locality, too, is contested. Faith and Order Paper 181 recognizes this when it says that "the term 'local church' is used differently by different traditions. For some traditions the 'local' church is the local congregation of believers gathered in one place to hear the Word and celebrate the sacraments. For others, 'local' or 'particular' church refers to the bishop with the people around the bishop, gathered to hear the Word and celebrate the sacraments."[25] Jeremy Morris further clarifies the discrepancy between traditions by setting forth four models of what is meant by "local" when referring to a particular church, all of which "can be traced through Christian history."[26] They are the following: (1) the congregation as a community of "gathered believers" assembling in one place (the Free Church conviction), (2) the parish as a "community church" marked out by a jurisdictional boundary distinguishing it from other parishes, (3) the diocese as a "regional church" focused on the exercise of *episcope* by a bishop, and (4) the "national church" as an ecclesial conglomerate based on a common cultural-linguistic and historical-geographical identity.[27] Morris mentions that province, communion, denomination, and connection are additional ways to mark out the local church but concludes that these, along with the national church model, fail "to do sufficient justice to the concept of place to qualify for inclusion in

---

[25] *The Nature and Purpose of the Church: A Stage on the Way to a Common Statement*, Faith and Order Paper 181 (Bialystok, Poland: Orthdruk, 1998), 33.
[26] Jeremy Morris, "The Unity We Seek: Prospects for the Local Church," in *The Unity We Have and the Unity We Seek*, ed. Jeremy Morris and Morris Sagovsky (London: T&T Clark, 2003), 96.
[27] Morris, "Unity We Seek," 96-97.

a consideration of local ecclesiology."²⁸ Morris defends the diocese model as sufficiently local on the basis of its "*potential* for gathering together all the worshipping people [of the diocese] in one place," but to the Free Church mind the diocese, especially of a larger variety, would seem to fall into Morris's category of failing to be sufficiently local.²⁹

So what constitutes the local church in the Anglican tradition? In some sense, that answer depends on who you ask, as Bray openly acknowledges that in Anglicanism "authority is dispersed in such a way that it is hard to say what the basic unit of the church is. Some claim that it is the parish; others say that it is the diocese, the national church, or even the Anglican Communion as a whole.... That such varied views on the locus of authority are possible shows how subtle the structures of Anglicanism are."³⁰ This "subtlety" allows for one person to claim that the local church is the parish, while another says it is the diocese; Peters can even say that in Anglicanism "each *province* is autonomous and, thereby, local."³¹ Phillip Thomas, while recognizing the importance of the church having "local expression," says that in Anglicanism "'particular and national Churches' hold the responsibility for shaping their corporate existence in accordance with the precepts of Scripture but within the context of their own local environment. [It is in these that] the universal Church must take on a particular identity."³² Here we raise the question: how "local" can a "national" or "provincial" church be, and what is lost when all that is meant by "local" is something like "not global"? In fact, a Free Church theologian might even insist here that if everything is local, ultimately nothing is.

More promising is the possibility that the *parish* may represent something of an Anglican equivalent to the local congregation, truly representing the local church in Anglicanism. But Morris makes clear that this is a false

---

[28] Morris, "Unity We Seek," 97.
[29] Morris, "Unity We Seek," 97, emphasis added.
[30] Gerald L. Bray, "Why I Am an Anglican and an Evangelical," in *Why We Belong: Evangelical Unity and Denominational Diversity*, ed. Anthony L. Chute, Christopher W. Morgan, and Robert A. Peterson (Wheaton, IL: Crossway, 2013), 75-76.
[31] Greg Peters, "Confessions, Creeds, and Reformed Catholicity—an Anglican Perspective" (paper presented at the Evangelical Theological Society, Denver, November 13-15, 2018), 4, emphasis added.
[32] Philip H. E. Thomas, "Doctrine of the Church," in *The Study of Anglicanism*, ed. Stephen Sykes, John Booty, and Jonathan Knight, rev ed. (Minneapolis: Fortress, 1998), 252.

path, for "the canons of the Church of England offer a sobering corrective to those inclined to see the parish as the fundamental unit of the Church's ministry, for it is there evident that the real focus of local unity is the diocesan bishop."[33] Indeed, this bishop-centric orientation is evidenced by Rowan Williams who, according to Cary, explains Anglicanism as "an ecclesial polity that represents a via media between localism and centrism . . . [having] a non-centralized, episcopally oriented polity . . . [that] highlights the nature of the church as 'a network of mutual dependence and mutual acknowledgement.'"[34] This echoes in certain ways the sentiment of Ramsey when he said that the episcopate is not "something 'Anglican' or 'Roman' or 'Greek,' but . . . the organ of the one people of God before and behind all that is local or sectional."[35] Pobee can even conclude that "Anglicanism is committed to episcopacy as the focus of identification of the local church and in the fellowship and harmony of the family of God."[36] This is why Chadwick can observe that "an Anglican is ordinarily defined as a Christian who, through his or her diocesan bishop, is in communion with the see of Canterbury. That presupposes a certain idea of catholicity."[37] While that may be true, it also presupposes a certain idea of locality, and it is one that Free Churches would deem inadequate. When the *local* assembly of believers has been swallowed up by a *translocal* bishop due to an emphasis on his connections to the broader church, something seems amiss. Radmacher expresses the concern well when he sees it as a continuation of trends emerging at the end of the patristic era, when "there gradually developed a trend toward external unity. . . . [For] hand in hand with [the] growth of the episcopacy was the blossoming of the universal consciousness and *practical disappearance of the concept of the local congregation* as related to Christ."[38] The conception of the local church as centered on the bishop is, to the Free

---

[33] Morris, "Unity We Seek," 97.
[34] Jeffrey W. Cary, *Free Churches and the Body of Christ: Authority, Unity, and Truthfulness* (Eugene, OR: Cascade, 2012), 147-48.
[35] Michael Ramsey, *The Gospel and the Catholic Church* (Cambridge, MA: Cowley Publications, 1990), 84.
[36] John S. Pobee, "Non-Anglo Saxon Anglicanism," in Sykes, Booty, and Knight, *Study of Anglicanism*, 453.
[37] Henry Chadwick, "Local and Universal: An Anglican Perspective," *The Jurist* 52, no. 1 (1992): 515.
[38] Earl D. Radmacher, *The Nature of the Church* (Portland, OR: Western Baptist Press, 1972), 39, emphasis added.

Church mind, insufficiently local by failing to put the locus on the assembly of even just two or three believers.

But this is related to a second concern, which is that this inadequate understanding of the local church leads to a consequence of largely privileging the *unity* of the church over its *catholicity* (especially by conflating the two rather than keeping them properly distinguished). This is *not* to say that there is no Anglican catholicity, or that its conception is not particularly robust; on the contrary, we argued in chapter three that Anglicanism demonstrates a deeply catholic ethos and manifests a multifaceted catholicity that finds its center in chronological catholicity, emphasizing its connectedness to the church of all times and especially to the church of the first five centuries through embrace of its creeds, liturgy, canon law, and offices. Rather, it is to say that by centering the local church on the bishop and thus privileging the translocal over the local, *an emphasis on unity over diversity begins to manifest.* As a via media between localism and centrism (a la Williams), it may demonstrate this tendency less than, say, the Roman Catholic tradition. But to the Free Church mind, the problem (perhaps counterintuitively) remains: when one's ecclesial tradition is not sufficiently local, it is not sufficiently catholic (particularly because it has traded in the fullness of catholicity for a unity that borders on uniformity).

We see this problem succinctly in the way Ramsey links up the church's unity and its catholicity (and its apostolicity?) to bishops: "The Episcopate succeeded the Apostolate as the organ of unity and continuity."[39] Chadwick is close to affirming the same when he says that though "the claim is not being made that the episcopate is of the being of the church" it must be acknowledged that "unity and universality are of the church's very being. . . . And the episcopal ministry in due succession and apostolic commission is the immemorial tradition of the catholic church . . . and therefore is also a providential instrument of [these] marks of the church as a visible society in history."[40] The point of contention with the Free Church tradition is particularly brought out by Avis, for even though he reassures that "Anglicans have not insisted on the historic episcopate as a precondition for

---

[39]Ramsey, *Gospel and the Catholic Church*, 223.
[40]Quoted in Paul Avis, *The Anglican Understanding of the Church*, 2nd ed. (London: SPCK, 2013), 89.

recognition of another Church as a true Church," nevertheless "they do continue to regard the historic episcopate as an *essential* aspect *of the Church's catholicity* and therefore as a prerequisite for visible unity, including the reconciliation of ordained ministries."[41] The episcopate is understood as essential because, as Avis says elsewhere, "the catholicity of Anglicanism rests on its continuity of worship. . . . [and] on the retention of the three-fold order of bishops, priests and deacons in the historic succession."[42] Zahl agrees, also connecting Anglican catholicity and ordination: "Anglicans of all schools of thought . . . have understood the *episkopoi* or bishops to be symbolic guardians of unity and also of continuity." This is because "only the bishop has the authority . . . to ordain presbyters and deacons. In the bishop's unique ordaining power lies the validity of the church. . . . Thus bishops on any reading embody the continuity of the church, as well as its unity. Episcopacy is thus the form of church government by which bishops represent the true catholicity, continuity, and Christianness of the Christian family."[43] Rowan Williams could also be cited, arguing that ordained ministry "focuses the church's catholicity."[44] Cary summarizes Williams's position on the relation of bishops to unity and catholicity: "The bishop's authority is primarily an authority to unify . . . [while apostolic] succession relates directly to the task of the bishop to 'unveil the catholicity of the local church' . . . [and for this] 'he cannot depend for his ordination only on the local and contemporary, he must visibly belong in a community extended in space and time and beyond the local.'"[45]

We witnessed this tendency to emphasize unity over catholicity even in the work of a more evangelical Anglican like Webster. Webster says that "the office of bishop *indicates* the unity of the church, testifying in a public manner to the oneness of the people of God. . . . Episcopal office is thus a focused, public and institutional place through which attention can be turned to the given unity of the people of God through Spirit, baptism and

---

[41] Avis, *Anglican Understanding*, 88-89, emphasis added.
[42] Paul Avis, "What Is 'Anglicanism'?," in Sykes, Booty, and Knight, *Study of Anglicanism*, 472.
[43] Paul Zahl, "The Bishop-Led Church," in *Perspectives on Church Government: Five Views of Church Polity*, ed. Chad Owen Brand and R. Stanton Norman (Nashville: Broadman & Holman, 2004), 228.
[44] Quoted in Cary, *Free Churches*, 143.
[45] Cary, *Free Churches*, 143, 145.

confession."⁴⁶ He can also say that "it is to . . . unity, established and formed by the gospel, that the ministry of oversight directs its own attention and the attention of the whole church"⁴⁷ and that "Episcopal office serves the unity of the church as it takes form in the congregation of the redeemed."⁴⁸ This all might be quite true; but if so it should be recognized that when Webster says that "the function of *episcope* is to indicate the church's unity and apostolicity" and then adds, with no further comment, "[and] therefore [it also indicates] its catholicity," not enough work has been done to recognize the *distinction* between the unity and the catholicity of the church and to ask whether it might be that other manifestations of ministerial authority have something to contribute as well.⁴⁹ Others could be cited as evincing the same oversight regarding oversight.⁵⁰

Here the local church is only incorporated into the church's catholicity because of its connection to a bishop in apostolic succession. The translocal nature of that bishop and the emphasis on his connection with the broader church combined with a neglect of the genuine diversity that local churches represent as they manifest at all times, among all peoples, and within all places leads to a privileging of unity over catholicity. While unity emphasizes the *oneness* of the gospel-formed people, catholicity emphasizes the *diversity* of that gospel-formed people as it manifests among all churches. Continually distinguishing these two creedal attributes and ensuring they are related but not conflated is vital.⁵¹ Without sufficiently local catholicity (and the diversity that accompanies

---

⁴⁶John Webster, "The Self-Organizing Power of the Gospel of Christ: Episcopacy and Community Formation," *International Journal of Systematic Theology* 3, no. 1 (March 2001): 79.
⁴⁷Webster, "Self-Organizing Power," 79.
⁴⁸Webster, "Self-Organizing Power," 79.
⁴⁹Webster, "Self-Organizing Power," 81.
⁵⁰Peter Toon would be another example. He argues that the historic episcopate belongs to the church's *plene esse* (fullness of being), holding that the episcopate "provides the embodiment of the gospel in church order in two ways. First, it provides the effectual sign of unity. . . . Second, it includes the principle of apostolicity. The episcopally ordained ministry is sent to represent Christ to his church and is representative of his church. It provides the guardianship of the Word and sacraments, of the faith, and of the flock of Christ. The historical episcopate is thus an effectual sign of the relation of Christ to his church, for it shows forth his authority within his church." Peter Toon, "Episcopalianism," in *Who Runs the Church? Four Views on Church Government*, ed. Steven B. Cowan (Grand Rapids, MI: Zondervan, 2004), 38. Here we ask, But what of catholicity?
⁵¹Here Congar is on point when he says catholicity is "the quality of the Church through which its . . . multiplicity enters into harmony with its . . . unity." Quoted in Josef Neuner, "The Idea of

it), unity easily morphs into uniformity, and with Lukas Vischer the Free Church tradition insists that "unity does not mean uniformity. The church . . . of the New Testament is marked by a multiplicity of expressions of the gospel. Unity need not do away with differences."[52] With Tillard we insist that unity and catholicity must mutually inform one another for "uniformity suffocates *communion*, whereas certain differences on fundamental points make it nonviable."[53]

A Free Church observer might even say that Anglicanism has gotten no further in its justification of episcopacy and its understanding of its relation to unity and catholicity than the account given by Cyprian in his *On the Unity of the Catholic Church*. There, writing of Peter as understood from a Roman interpretation of Matthew 16, he says,

> It is [through] one man that He builds the Church, and although He assigns a like power to all the Apostles after His resurrection . . . yet, in order that the oneness might be unmistakable, He established by His own authority a course for that oneness having its origin in one man alone. No doubt the other Apostles were all that Peter was, endowed with equal dignity and power, but the start comes from him alone, in order to show that the Church of Christ is [one].[54]

The emphasis on oneness is dominant, while the note of diversity is absent. This emphasis continues as Cyprian moves from speaking about the apostles to speaking about bishops around the world:

> Now this oneness we must hold to firmly and insist on—especially we who are bishops and exercise authority in the Church—so as to demonstrate that the episcopal power is one and undivided too. . . . The authority of the bishops forms a unity, of which each holds his part in its totality. And the Church forms a unity, however far she spreads and multiplies by the progeny of her

---

Catholicity—Concept and History," in *The Church: Readings in Theology*, ed. Gustave Wegel (New York: P. J. Kenedy & Sons, 1963), 67.

[52] Lukas Vischer, "Introduction," in *Unity of the Church in the New Testament and Today*, by Lukas Vischer, Ulrich Luz, and Christian Link, trans. James E. Crouch (Grand Rapids, MI: Eerdmans, 2010), 5.

[53] Jean Marie Tillard, *Church of Churches: The Ecclesiology of Communion*, trans. R. C. De Peaux (Collegeville, MN: Liturgical Press, 1992), 320.

[54] Quoted in Jonathan Leeman, "A Congregational Approach to Unity, Holiness, and Apostolicity: Faith and Order," in *Baptist Foundations: Church Government for an Anti-Institutional Age*, ed. Mark Dever and Jonathan Leeman (Nashville: B&H Academic, 2015), 338.

fecundity; just as the sun's rays are many, yet the light is one, and a tree's branches are many, yet the strength deriving its sturdy root is one.[55]

For Cyprian, in the words of Evans, "the Church's bishops are the essential organs of her unity and the essential bearers of her holiness."[56] Despite the spreading of the tree's branches to the ends of the earth, drawing in all peoples and manifesting in all places, there is no mention of how catholicity ought to relate to and inform this bishop-centric vision of the church and her unity, one always in danger of exchanging the gift of catholic unity for the gall of rigid uniformity.

To Free Church ears, Cyprian's privileging of unity upstream still very much manifests in Anglican discussions of catholicity downstream. Even though the discussions might begin with the church's catholicity, they often end up drifting into how bishops best guard or serve or symbolize or exhibit the *unity* of the church. The neglect of full-orbed catholicity due to this conflation has led to a blind spot in the Episcopal tradition: that catholicity has a local orientation because Christ rules in every place two or three gather ecclesialy in his name. Here Yoder expresses the Free Church objection well: "A definition [of catholicity] centered on the adequacy of a particular past historical instantiation (e.g., episcopal succession) is structurally contradictory to . . . 'catholicity' not only in the formal sense of rejecting other sees but even more by virtue of the criterion's inaccessibility to others."[57] In other words, defining catholicity in a way that rules out any true churches privileges a uniform universal church rather than valuing the diverse local manifestations of the catholic church. Brown recognizes this: "When an overemphasis is placed on the universal church, the church's catholicity is too easily identified with the spread of ecclesial uniformity."[58] This same point is made in Murray's description of Catholicism, one equally fitting of Anglicanism: "*The* core dysfunction of contemporary Catholicism relates to an imbalance between its centralising pole on the one hand and

---

[55]Quoted in Leeman, "Congregational Approach to Unity," 338-39.
[56]Quoted in Leeman, "Congregational Approach to Unity," 340.
[57]John Howard Yoder, *The Royal Priesthood: Essays Ecclesiastical and Ecumenical*, ed. Michael G. Cartwright (Scottdale, PA: Herald Press, 1998), 305.
[58]R. Kevin Brown, "The Local and Universal Churches: Expressing Catholicity Through Their Reciprocity," in *Visions of Hope: Emerging Theologians and the Future of the Church*, ed. Kevin Ahern (Maryknoll, NY: Orbis Books, 2013), 208.

the far flung particular local churches on the other. This imbalance has secured the visible unity of Catholicism at the cost of a significant diminishing and disempowering of its legitimate local diversity."[59]

So, where do we go from here? Volf observes that the debate between the Episcopal and Free Church traditions continually sets forth the contested nature of catholicity and forces the question "of whether ecclesiology is to begin in the tradition of universalization with the priority of the one, or in the tradition of pluralization with the priority of the many." He then adds a third option: "Or is it perhaps possible to escape this alternative altogether?"[60] Escaping the fate of continually talking past each other will require listening to the insights into the nature of the church that our Lord has graciously given to each tradition. Vatican II's "Decree on Ecumenism" pointed in much the same direction: "It is hardly surprising . . . if sometimes one tradition has come nearer to a full appreciation of some aspects of a mystery of revelation than the other, or has experienced them better. In such cases, these various theological formulations . . . [are] complementary rather than conflicting."[61] In this case we propose, as counterintuitive as it may at first seem, that while the Episcopal tradition might rightly be said to better guard, spotlight, and maximize the *unity* of the church, it is actually the Free Church tradition that better guards, spotlights, and maximizes the *catholicity* of the church, rightly understood. Acknowledging this possibility is vitally important for *both* traditions to be able to offer the gifts they have been given to the catholic whole. Without a proper recognition of catholicity, the unity offered by the Episcopal tradition deforms into uniformity and produces the judgment "bishops divide." Without a proper appreciation of unity, Free Church catholicity spoils into pluralism and issues in endless sectarianism. This is because, as Tillard so vividly portrayed it, "Unity without diversity makes the Church a dead body: pluralism without unity makes it a body which is dismembered."[62]

---

[59]Paul D. Murray, "Redeeming Catholicity for a Globalising Age: The Sacramentality of the Church," in *Believing in Community: Ecumenical Reflections on the Church*, ed. Peter De Mey, Pieter De Witte, and Gerard Mannion (Leuven: Uitgeverij Peeters, 2013), 236.
[60]Volf, *After Our Likeness*, 263.
[61]Quoted in Yves Congar, *Diversity and Communion*, trans. John Bowden (London: SCM Press, 1984), 76.
[62]Tillard, *Church of Churches*, 320.

A Free Church Account of Local Catholicity

The audacious possibility just proposed will only be compelling if we can show that the Free Church tradition is capable of articulating a particularly robust notion of the church's catholicity. This possibility should not be dismissed from the start, for we have insisted that catholicity is not the exclusive domain of the Episcopal tradition, any more than locality is the exclusive domain of the Free Church tradition. But it is also true, as we have acknowledged, that catholicity has not been a strong suit of the Free Church tradition, in large part because so much emphasis has been placed on the local dimension of the church over the universal dimension.[63] But could this localist orientation actually serve to further elucidate the true nature of the church's catholicity? If so, what does it actually mean to say that genuine catholicity is *local* catholicity, that the catholicity of the church is *located* not in the aggregate of the invisible church, nor in a visible translocal institution (including its ministers), nor even in the assembly of God's people in the eschaton, but in the assembly of even just two or three today? And in what ways does the universal church stand to benefit from such reflection? It is to these questions that we now turn in articulating Free Church catholicity as local catholicity.

Quantitative local catholicity: Connecting all times, peoples, places. We begin with the claim that catholicity is best understood, according to its quantitative dimension, as the scope of the gospel's reception as it manifests in the assembly of God's people. This catholic scope must not be limited because the gospel message is that "God was reconciling *the world* to himself in Christ" (2 Cor 5:19). The gospel's reception is what makes the church, a fact we affirm with Avis when he says with the Reformers that "where the gospel is, Christ is; and where Christ is, there is the Church. All that is necessary to authentic 'Churchhood' is the possession of the gospel."[64] In fact, Avis himself makes connections between this truth and the catholicity of the

---

[63]Indeed, to amend Richard Mouw's observation about evangelical ecclesiology, we can say that the Free Church tradition exhibits a "*localist* impulse" and ecclesiological instincts "grounded in a deep commitment to the local." Richard J. Mouw, "The Problem of Authority in Evangelical Christianity," in *Church Unity and the Papal Office: An Ecumenical Dialogue on John Paul II's Encyclical Ut Unum Sint*, ed. Carl E. Braaten and Robert W. Jenson (Grand Rapids, MI: Eerdmans, 2001), 135.

[64]Paul Avis, *The Church in the Theology of the Reformers* (Atlanta: John Knox Press, 1980), 221.

church: because "only the gospel [is] of the *esse* [of the church]" this has "profound implications for the doctrine of [apostolic] succession and with it the key concept of catholicity. . . . [For] the gospel of truth was held to be sufficient to secure the catholicity of the Church. The Reformers believed . . . that the Church was one, holy, catholic and apostolic, but . . . [with] the gospel itself [as] the decisive and dominant criterion."[65] Where the gospel is truly received, the church necessarily manifests. And here we are highlighting that the Free Church tradition joins the consensus regarding the quantitative dimension of catholicity: as the biblical witness makes clear, it is God's covenantal intention to gather a people to himself from all times, all peoples, and all places, a people who gather in more and more local churches as redemptive history moves from Pentecost to parousia. In this, the geographical, missional, and chronological aspects of catholicity are on full display.

We thus affirm that the church is catholic because it manifests *at all times*. This is, as we acknowledged in chapter three, a particular strength of Anglicanism, appropriately calling the church of today to learn from and keep with the church of yesterday. The primary means by which this occurs is attending to church tradition, the "handing down" what has been "handed on" going all the way back to the apostolic "handoff" (1 Cor 15:1-5). Here we follow Pelikan in recognizing that "the Christian tradition [is] what the church of Jesus Christ believes, teaches, and confesses on the basis of the Word of God."[66] Elizabeth Newman highlights how tradition is a way to understand what the church of previous times has given to us: "Tradition . . . is another way of naming what the communion of saints has given to the church."[67] Melanchthon made the connection between tradition and catholicity explicit when he noted that the church is catholic because "its members, wherever they are, and however separated in place, embrace and externally profess one and the same utterance of true doctrine in all ages from the beginning until the very end. . . . [It is a doctrine] supported by the witness

---

[65] Avis, *Church in the Theology of the Reformers*, 128.
[66] Jaroslav Pelikan, *The Christian Tradition: A History of the Development of Doctrine*, 5 vols. (Chicago: University of Chicago Press, 1971–1989), 1:1.
[67] Elizabeth Newman, "Remembering How to Remember: Harmon's Subversive Orthodoxy," *Pro Ecclesia* 18, no. 4 (Fall 2009): 376.

of *all time, of all ages*, which believes what the prophets and apostles taught."[68] From a Free Church vantage point, Williams can commend tradition to "suspicious Protestants" because "the Tradition of the church is . . . the outcome of a testing and sharpening process by which the Spirit moved through the worshipping, praying, baptizing and confessing community . . . or what can be called a consensus of faith through time."[69] This is the pneumatically effective history of interpreting the Word.

Williams particularly commends *the early church* to a Free Church tradition that has often been skeptical or ignorant regarding what can be learned from the fathers. Indeed, Williams applauds the work of Tom Oden and others who have brought attention to the significance of the "Great Tradition," calling it "the core teaching and preaching of the early church which has bequeathed to us the fundamentals of what it is to think and believe Christianly."[70] The early church played a particularly vital role in developing what we call the "rule of faith" as a concrete expression of gospel tradition.[71] The rule of faith attempted to guard the integrity of the gospel to be handed down to the next generation by distinguishing true versus heretical interpretations of the gospel story (biblical narrative) and the gospel statement (biblical doctrine). Eventually the locally developed expressions of the rule of faith came to be summarized in the ecumenical creeds as a more consistent and dependable way to faithfully hand down the gospel and its doctrinal entailments from one generation to another. It is important to recognize that though there are strands of the Free Church tradition that have manifested an anticreedal or even an antitradition mentality, there is nothing inherent in the DNA of the tradition to make that necessarily the case.[72] Matt Emerson and Luke Stamps are exemplary in their commending the ecumenical creeds to the broader Free Church, arguing that they belong "to the worldwide church in all its manifold expressions. . . . The Trinitarian and christological formulae expressed in the

---

[68]Quoted in Dulles, *Catholicity*, 182.

[69]D. H. Williams, *Retrieving the Tradition and Renewing Evangelicalism: A Primer for Suspicious Protestants* (Grand Rapids, MI: Eerdmans, 1999), 207.

[70]Williams, *Retrieving the Tradition*, 6.

[71]Here see Everett Ferguson, *The Rule of Faith: A Guide* (Eugene, OR: Cascade Books, 2015).

[72]In fact, chapters 4 and 5 have demonstrated the capacity of the Free Church to make much of tradition and to be able to stand in continuity with church tradition as a vital manifestation of its catholicity.

ecumenical creeds have served and continue to serve as the touchstone for Christian orthodoxy."[73] Free Church catholicity recognizes tradition as a key element of our connection to the church as it has manifested in earlier times.

But it equally confesses that the church is catholic because it manifests among *all peoples*. Indeed, this is perhaps the strongest emphasis of the biblical theology of catholicity we developed in chapter one: as we move from Genesis to Revelation, the plan and purpose of God to bless the nations by calling a people to himself from among all the peoples of the world through the Jewish Messiah is increasingly on stunning display. We celebrate that this "missional aspect" of catholicity is emphasized across ecclesial traditions, even while it tends to be particularly emphasized among evangelicals. Emerson and Stamps rightly note that "Roman Catholics have explicitly grounded missionary work in their notion of the church's catholicity" and go on to argue that folks in the Free Church tradition "would have [just as] good [a] warrant for doing so, leveraging belief in the catholicity of the church in the service of Christian mission, which has always been at the heart of the [Free Church] vision."[74] In fact, Peter Tie, reflecting on the work of James Leo Garret, makes an explicit connection between the doctrine of the priesthood of all believers (which has been a strong Free Church emphasis) and the missional aspect of catholicity, saying "the mission of the church reflects the universal nature of the Christian priesthood. Church mission is universal because of the 'purposive movement' of the eternally triune God who called, consecrated, and commanded a distinct and distinctive people, a kingdom of priests, for the purpose of saving and blessing other peoples."[75] He draws the conclusion: "The result of the universal mission of the church is a universal priesthood made up of various peoples worthy of serving the living God (Rev 4:11; 5:8-9; 20:6)."[76] Indeed, Garrett himself makes the connection between mission and catholicity explicit: "The unfulfilled mission of the

---

[73]Matthew Y. Emerson and R. Lucas Stamps, "Baptists and the Catholicity of the Church: Toward an Evangelical Baptist Catholicity," *Journal of Baptist Studies* 7 (2015): 51-52.
[74]Emerson and Stamps, "Baptists and the Catholicity of the Church," 49.
[75]Peter L. Tie, *Restore Unity, Recover Identity, Refine Orthopraxy: The Believers' Priesthood in the Ecclesiology of James Leo Garrett Jr.* (Eugene, OR: Wipf & Stock, 2012), 31.
[76]Tie, *Restore Unity, Recover Identity*, 114-15.

church to the nations (Mt 24:14) can lead to a teleological or eschatological understanding of catholicity."[77] Schnackenburg observes from another angle that the church's "universality imperatively demands the mission. The Church does not become universal (or 'Catholic') because it engages in missionary activity but engages in missionary activity because by nature the Church is universal."[78] Here the Free Church tradition offers nothing truly distinctive but simply joins with other ecclesial traditions in recognizing the importance of missional catholicity to a full-orbed account of the church's catholicity.

But, it could be argued, where the Free Church tradition *does* offer a distinctive perspective and an evident strength when it comes to the quantitative dimension of catholicity is in emphasizing, based on its privileging of the local dimension of the church, that the church is also catholic because it manifests in *all places*. Indeed, geographical catholicity is something that the Free Church tradition intuitively maximizes, emphasizing as it does that properly working out the scope of the gospel's reception involves recognizing that the church manifests in *every locale* where the gospel-shaped people assemble. The Free Church localist impulse appeals to verses like 1 Corinthians 1:2: "To the church of God that is in Corinth . . . called to be saints together with all those who *in every place* call upon the name of our Lord Jesus Christ, both their Lord and ours" (ESV). Every local church is connected to every other local church in every single locale, for there are (many!) others who have been called to be saints in the places where they, too, have received the gospel. Armstrong expresses this profound reality: "Every single church is a true church in its own place, and at the same time every church is the church catholic."[79] Indeed, Armstrong is right that the local church acts as an ambassador of the catholic church because "the catholic church can only be visible at one moment and place. We who are alive in Christ represent in one place and time that whole which God alone sees in its completeness."[80] The big issue, and the lacuna of the Episcopal tradition from the Free Church vantage point, concerns exactly this "all

---

[77]James Leo Garrett Jr., *Systematic Theology*, vol. 2, 2nd ed. (Eugene, OR: Wipf & Stock, 2014), 532.
[78]Rudolf Schnackenburg, *The Church in the New Testament* (New York: Herder & Herder, 1965), 139.
[79]John H. Armstrong, *Your Church Is Too Small* (Grand Rapids, MI: Zondervan, 2010), 111.
[80]Armstrong, *Your Church Is Too Small*, 112.

places" dimension; by failing to emphasize that the catholic church manifests in *every* local gathering of just two or three believers, the geographical dimension is curtailed in a way that hinders the fullness of the church's catholic scope from being witnessed. But this raises the vital question: What is it *qualitatively* that enables every local church to be connected to every other local church within the catholic whole? In other words, what is it in the church's *nature* that enables us to locate catholicity at the local level? Here we move into the heart of the debate between the Episcopal and Free Church traditions regarding the church's catholicity.

Qualitative local catholicity: Unified diversity in Christ by the Spirit. Catholicity, as we have argued, concerns the nature of God's people as a unified diversity, one that manifests in greater and greater degrees as the church works through the whole of all times, peoples, and places. This understanding builds on what Volf considers to be an "ecumenical consensus . . . that both unity and multiplicity are constitutive for the catholicity of the church."[81] But, we might ask, what *grounds* the catholic nature of the church as a unified diversity? In some sense the answer to the question is clear and shared across ecclesial traditions: following Ignatius's dictum that "wherever Jesus Christ is, there is the Catholic Church," catholicity has been understood as stemming from a common connection to Christ through the Holy Spirit. For instance, *The Catechism of the Catholic Church* defines catholicity as "keeping with the whole" while holding that the Church is catholic in two senses: (1) having the presence of Christ in her (quoting Ignatius, qualitative) and (2) being sent out on a mission to all of humanity (quoting *LG*, quantitative).[82] Hallig notes the same in saying, "The word

---

[81]Volf, *After Our Likeness,* 262. Ruddy provides evidence of Volf's claim by pointing to Vatican II, for he says that in the mind of the council "the opposite of catholicity is not locality or diversity, but uniformity. 'Redemptively integrated' diversity builds up the catholicity and communion of the church of Christ." Ruddy, *Local Church,* 47, 49. Walter Kasper can even say that Vatican II saw "a radical reconsideration of the essential nature of catholicity . . . [understanding it] as the involvement of all individuals, the various ministries and offices, all church bodies and peoples, collectively contributing their gifts under the one head, Christ. Accordingly, catholicity is understood as *a dynamic unity in diversity*." Walter Kasper, "'Credo Unam Sanctam Ecclesiam'—the Relationship Between the Catholic and the Protestant Principles in Fundamental Ecclesiology," in *Receptive Ecumenism and the Call to Catholic Learning: Exploring a Way for Contemporary Ecumenism,* ed. Paul D. Murray (Oxford: Oxford University Press, 2008), 79-80, emphasis added.

[82]*The Catechism of the Catholic Church,* 2nd ed. (Vatican: Libreria Editrice Vaticana, 2000), 220.

'catholic' may indeed embody the universal connection and unity of the churches of Jesus Christ around the world, but the connection and the unity of the church [are] primarily anchored in the church's relationship with Jesus Christ.... The church is catholic first and foremost because of Christ."[83]

The challenge and the point of contention is going on to say *more* than that, namely *how* the church's catholicity is connected to Christ. The Episcopal tradition has emphasized the broader context of Ignatius's statement to make sense of his rule, particularly noting that his "wherever the bishop appears, there let the people be" is parallel to his *ubi Christus, ibi ecclesia* (where Christ is, there is the church) dictum and holding that the church's catholicity derives from its connection to Christ *through* a bishop in apostolic succession. For example, *The Catechism of the Catholic Church* defines particular churches as communities "of the Christian faithful in communion of faith and sacraments with their bishop ordained in apostolic succession" and goes on to indicate that these churches "are fully catholic through their communion with one of them, the Church of Rome."[84]

Free Church theologians agree with the second part of Ignatius's statement and argue that it is critical for properly understanding the nature of the church's catholicity. For example, Harmon can say that "[Ignatius's] emphasis on the Christological basis of the church's universality is what seventeenth-century Baptist confessions that affirmed the catholicity of the church had in mind."[85] But Free Church theologians refuse to concede the *essentiality* of the first part of Ignatius's statement and the way it is understood later in the tradition as asserting that bishops are *required* for the church. From a Free Church vantage point, if bishops are viewed through the lens of the *bene esse* (well-being) or even the *plene esse* (fullness of being) of the church, then there is room for dialogue; but if they are viewed as part of the *esse* (essence) of the church, there is no room for debate. A Free Church vantage point insists that the rule of "no bishop, no church," though it may be found in church tradition and have a long pedigree, does not stand biblical scrutiny.

---

[83]Jason Valeriano Hallig, *We Are Catholic: Catholic, Catholicity, and Catholicization* (Eugene, OR: Wipf & Stock, 2016), 15.
[84]*Catechism of the Catholic Church*, 221.
[85]Steven R. Harmon, "Qualitative Catholicity in the Ignatian Correspondence—and the New Testament: The Fallacies of a Restorationist Hermeneutic," *Perspectives in Religious Studies* 38, no. 1 (Spring 2011): 36-37.

Particularly, the Free Church tradition insists that the biblical testimony of verses like Matthew 18:20 show us what is, in fact, constitutive for the church and provide us with a more biblically normed way of understanding the church's connection to Christ as the ground of its catholicity: namely, the assembly of even just two or three believers in Christ's name. Specifically *Christ's presence by the Spirit* is found in every faith-filled community of even just two or three gathered in Christ's name as evidenced by its being under the Word (gospel message), around the sacraments (gospel practices), and amid oversight (gospel order). This is what makes a church a church, and thus what makes a local church catholic, that is, connected to the unified-yet-diverse whole of all other local churches through all times, among all peoples, and in all places.

To establish this, appeal is consistently made to Matthew 18:20 as constitutive for the church, a verse that has "shaped the entire Free Church tradition."[86] Although Volf acknowledges that "it was the Free Church theologians who accorded Mt 18:20 a key systematic role in ecclesiology . . . taking [it] as the foundation not only for determining what the church is, but also for how it manifests itself externally as a church," he also makes the claim that "this particular passage acquired preeminent importance quite early in church history."[87] He cites as evidence that "Ignatius obviously bases his own ecclesiological principle" on the verse, that Tertullian likely had it in mind when he offered his rule "where three are, the church is," and that Cyprian "seems to presuppose that [it] is of significance for ecclesiology rather than only for spirituality."[88] Volf supports the statement made by Rudolph Sohm that "this passage traverses the entirety of church history" by citing the passage's use by Huss, Calvin, Smyth, the later Reformed tradition exhibited by Barth and Brunner, and even Roman Catholics such as Schillebeeckx and Pope Paul VI.[89] Haight makes the connection between this passage and

---

[86]Volf, *After Our Likeness*, 135. As evidence of this claim Volf demonstrates that John Smyth's understanding of the church at the fountainhead of the Free Church tradition is clearly indebted to Mt 18:20 when he says, "A visible communion of Saints is two, three, or more Saints joined together by covenant with God & themselves, freely to use all the holy things of God, according to the word, for their mutual edification, & God's glory. . . . This visible communion of Saints is a visible Church." Volf, *After Our Likeness*, 135, language updated.
[87]Volf, *After Our Likeness*, 135-36.
[88]Volf, *After Our Likeness*, 135-36.
[89]Volf, *After Our Likeness*, 135-36.

Luther's early ecclesiology with its emphasis that "the essence of the church lies not in organizational structures but in a community constituted by Christ in the faith of the community members."[90] Clearly the Free Church tradition interprets Matthew 18:20 in a manner very different from the Episcopal tradition does, but both traditions recognize the vital role this verse plays (along with other central verses such as Mt 16:18 and 1 Pet 2:4-10) in locating the church.

Perhaps no contemporary Free Church theologian has provided a more substantial and compelling account of why Matthew 18:20 is constitutive for the church (and thus for its catholicity) than Jonathan Leeman. Leeman reflects on the broader passage, Matthew 18:15-20, which states,

> If your brother or sister sins, go and point out their fault, just between the two of you. If they listen to you, you have won them over. But if they will not listen, take one or two others along, so that "every matter may be established by the testimony of two or three witnesses." If they still refuse to listen, tell it to the church; and if they refuse to listen even to the church, treat them as you would a pagan or a tax collector. Truly I tell you, whatever you bind on earth will be bound in heaven, and whatever you loose on earth will be loosed in heaven. Again, truly I tell you that if two of you on earth agree about anything they ask for, it will be done for them by my Father in heaven. For where two or three gather in my name, there am I with them.

Leeman argues from this passage that the gathered church is the basic unit of kingdom authority, as evidenced by the fact that in Matthew 18:17-18 "Jesus authorizes the entire assembly to wield the keys of the kingdom" and that Matthew 18:19-20 "strengthen the case and locate the existence of the authoritative congregation . . . in the gathering" particularly by equating "the 'two or three' gathered together in verse 20 . . . with the 'church' of verse 17" and showing that "Jesus' presence there is what gives intrinsic authority and 'church-ness' to that gathering."[91] He notes that the mention of the keys in this passage makes explicit connection to Matthew 16:13-19 and implicit connection to Matthew 28:18-20. In fact, Leeman acknowledges that if Matthew 16 "were the only biblical text we had, we might be hard

---

[90]Haight, *Christian Community*, 2:29.
[91]Jonathan Leeman, *Don't Fire Your Church Members: The Case for Congregationalism* (Nashville: B&H Academic, 2016), 100-101.

pressed to disagree with the Roman Catholic position," but by interpreting Matthew 16, 18 and 28 as mutually informing one another Leeman concludes that "Christ's kingly authority is regnant in the universal church, but it is given concrete expression in the local church."[92] Leeman holds that the testimony of Matthew 18 makes it clear that "the local church exists wherever Christians regularly gather in Christ's name to proclaim the gospel and to affirm one another as his disciples through the authority of the keys in the ordinances."[93] Specifically, he notes how "verse 20 . . . provides the 'theological basis' for verse 19. Two or three can gather in Jesus' name to bind and loose and to pray, expecting the Father will hear them *because* Christ is present and has given them authority."[94] Leeman's theological interpretation of Matthew 18:20, derived from putting it in dialogue particularly with Matthew 28:20 and 1 Corinthians 5:4, paraphrases Jesus as saying, "For where two or three witnesses gather to testify to my name and their shared union under my rule through exercising the keys together, that is, in any such church, my presence and authority are with them such that this church speaks on my behalf."[95] In sum, Leeman holds that "when two or three come together . . . [Jesus says:] 'You are a church (vs. 17), speaking on behalf of heaven (vs. 18), knowing the Father hears you (vs. 19), and all of this is true because my name, authority, and Spirit are present with you (vs. 20)."[96] Here is the seed of Free Church ecclesiology.

Volf similarly concludes from a reading of this passage that the only condition for ecclesiality is Christ's presence by the Spirit amid the believing community. Volf reflects on the rule of both Ignatius (*ubi Christus, ibi ecclesia*) and Irenaeus (*ubi Spiritus, ibi ecclesia*) to arrive at the more specific conclusion that the presence of Christ among the gathered two or three is mediated by the Spirit through the confessing congregation (rather than, as the Episcopal tradition would insist, the bishop in apostolic succession).[97] Volf specifically claims that

---

[92]Leeman, *Don't Fire Your Church Members*, 97, 72.
[93]Jonathan Leeman, *Political Church: The Local Assembly as Embassy of Christ's Rule* (Downers Grove, IL: IVP Academic, 2016), 364.
[94]Leeman, *Don't Fire Your Church Members*, 101.
[95]Leeman, *Don't Fire Your Church Members*, 103.
[96]Leeman, *Don't Fire Your Church Members*, 102.
[97]Volf says, "Wherever the Spirit of Christ . . . is present in its *ecclesially constitutive* activity, there is the church. The Spirit unites the gathered congregation with the triune God and integrates it

Christ does not enter the church through the "narrow portals" of *ordained office*, but rather *through the dynamic life of the entire church*. The presence of Christ is not attested merely by the institution of office, but rather through the multidimensional confession of the entire assembly. In whatever way "office" may indeed be desirable for church life, either in apostolic succession or not, it is *not necessary for ecclesiality*. Ordained office [thus] belongs not to the *esse*, but rather to the *bene esse* of the church.[98]

Freeman nicely summarizes how Leeman and Volf's Free Church reading of Matthew 18:20 leads to certain conclusions regarding the nature of the church and its catholicity, saying "this gathered-church understanding of ecclesial identity has important implications: (1) Christ is present through his Spirit in every gathered community that assembles in his name and professes faith in him; (2) Each congregation is simultaneously independent of *and interconnected with* other churches through the Spirit which makes Christ present."[99] Here we particularly highlight the way that the church's catholicity is understood by the Free Church tradition as grounded christologically (agreeing that where Jesus Christ is, there is the catholic church), mediated pneumatologically (recognizing that Christ's presence is through the Spirit), and expressed locally (arguing that this christological connection through the Spirit occurs when two or three believers gather in Christ's name). This is why we insist that genuine catholicity is local catholicity, for the diversity of ten thousand (and more) local churches gathering through the whole of all times, peoples, and places is united by a common connection to Christ. God's people are those in communion with Christ and one another through faith by the Spirit, and that communion is fully expressed whenever even two or three are gathered in Christ's name. Here is the church, and so here, there can be no doubt, its catholicity, its connection to the whole, is to be found.

Confirmed local catholicity: Need for Word, sacrament, oversight. Or, *can* there be doubt? We have insisted throughout the project that catholicity

---

into a history extending from Christ, indeed, from the Old Testament saints, to the eschatological new creation. This Spirit-mediated relationship with the triune God and with the entire history of God's people . . . constitutes an assembly into a church." Volf, *After Our Likeness*, 129.

[98]Volf, *After Our Likeness*, 152.

[99]Curtis W. Freeman, "Where Two or Three Are Gathered: Communion Ecclesiology in the Free Church," *Perspectives in Religious Studies* 31, no. 3 (Fall 2004): 267, emphasis added.

is contested. Related to this is the fact that ecclesiality itself is contested, for as we have seen, catholicity and ecclesiality are integrally related. The crisis of the Reformation made this abundantly clear: any "church," from Roman to Anglican to Anabaptist to Socinian, could *claim* to be a true church exhibiting the creedal attributes. But how was this claim to be verified? In other words: Where was the catholic church *actually* to be found? The answer was consistently delineated in either two or three marks of the true church. Calvin classically said, "Whenever we see the Word of God purely preached and listened to, and the sacraments administered according to the institution of Christ, we must not doubt that there is a Church."[100] The Lutheran Augsburg Confession said much the same: "The one holy Christian church ... is the assembly of all believers among whom the Gospel is preached in its purity and the holy sacraments are administered according to the Gospel ... [that is,] in accordance with the divine Word."[101] The *Thirty-Nine Articles* similarly attested that "the visible Church of Christ is a congregation of faithful men, in which the pure Word of God is preached, and the Sacraments be duly administered according to Christ's ordinance."[102] While other confessions (such as the Scots Confession) explicitly added the third mark of church discipline implying ministerial oversight, it is clear that all of the Protestant confessions seem to *imply* some degree of oversight in their use of qualifiers (such as "true," "pure," and "duly") to describe how the preaching of the Word and administration of the sacraments are ensured as *proper*.[103] Thus Avis can summarize that in the Protestant conception, Free Church ecclesiology included, "the catholic Church consists of all Christians united to Christ in the Holy Spirit through faith and baptism and ordered in their various communities under the ministry of word, sacrament and pastoral oversight."[104]

---

[100]John Calvin, *Institutes of the Christian Religion*, trans. Ford Lewis Battles, ed. John T. McNeill (Louisville, KY: Westminster John Knox, 2001), 1023.
[101]John H. Leith, ed., *The Creeds of the Church*, rev. ed. (Richmond, VA: John Knox Press, 1973), 70.
[102]Leith, *Creeds of the Church*, 273. George makes clear that "the early Baptists follow Luther and Calvin in regarding the Word purely preached and the sacraments duly administered as the two irreducible marks of the visible church, although they ... expanded and formalized the *notae* concept to include discipline as an indicator of a true visible church." George, "Sacramentality of the Church," 314.
[103]Indeed, this was Martin Bucer's motivation for adding discipline as a third mark, understanding it as an essential means of preserving the integrity of the first two marks.
[104]Avis, *Anglican Understanding*, 81-82.

As we noted earlier, these Reformational marks do not compete with the creedal attributes but rather help us recognize where the church of those attributes can be found. In this sense the marks become ways we can *confirm* local catholicity amid contested claims. This is what George means:

> The Reformers . . . sought to reconstruct a purified form of catholic Christianity, a real life and blood community of faith that would bear the "marks of the true church" (*notae verae ecclesiae*). The *notae* do not replace the traditional Nicene attributes (*una, catholica, apostolica, sancta*), but they rather call into question the unity, catholicity, apostolicity, and holiness of every congregation which claims to be a church, thus subjecting it to an outward, empirical examination.[105]

Volf also notes the importance of the marks for local catholicity because "even if the presence of these marks cannot *prove* catholicity, their absence can falsify or at least damage the credibility of a community's claim to catholicity."[106] This takes us to the heart of an (understandable) Episcopal concern: If every group of two or three claim to be assembling in Jesus' name, how can that claim be verified? The Episcopal answer has ultimately proved to be something like this: if the gathering is connected to a bishop in apostolic succession, then the claim is guaranteed. Free Church catholicity, as a particular manifestation of Protestant catholicity, holds that there is a better way: looking for what we have called orthodox catholicity (Word), liturgical catholicity (sacrament), and institutional catholicity (oversight). This way is particularly to be commended because it provides a connection to the other creedal attributes. Though a bit simplistic, Dever draws this out nicely when he says that the church's catholicity "is simply its other attributes—unity, holiness, apostolicity—appearing everywhere and anytime there has been a true church."[107] If that's true, we can affirm an assembly is actually a church connected to the catholic whole by seeing its *apostolicity* verified in its gathering under the Word, its *holiness* verified in its gathering around the sacraments, and its *unity* verified in its gathering under oversight.

---

[105]George, "Sacramentality of the Church," 314.
[106]Volf, *After Our Likeness*, 274, emphasis added.
[107]Mark E. Dever, "A Catholic Church," in *The Church: One, Holy, Catholic, and Apostolic*, by Richard D. Phillips, Philip G. Ryken, and Mark E. Dever (Phillipsburg, NJ: P&R, 2004), 70.

Before we look at each of these in turn, we recognize here that confirming catholicity addresses the (legitimate) concern that catholicity not emphasize diversity to the exclusion of unity. Or, to say it another way, confirming catholicity in this manner ensures that catholicity is distinct from a boundless pluralism. We saw in chapter one how the biblical testimony regarding the church's catholic character insisted that even the diversity of ten thousand local churches is unified. There are proper constraints to catholicity, constraints that, as Williams recognizes, particularly have a "doctrinal character" because "a catholic Christian [is] an *orthodox* Christian. . . . [And] this means . . . that there is a certain quality of exclusivity within catholicity. To stress catholicity as a principle of universality and wholeness which breaks down walls of division is useful only to the degree that we understand that it contains inherent limitations."[108] Williams goes on rightly to insist that

> the inclusive character of catholicity is based, not on a kind of all-incorporation of diversity that invites theological syncretism or dilution, but on the reception from God of a unique message and gift that transcends any one history or location. . . . To have a substantive vitality . . . catholicity operates on the understanding that there exist true doctrines and practices, an understanding which is meant to distinguish the Christian church from theological or moral corruption.[109]

Hopefully this is a great reassurance to Episcopal interlocutors particularly concerned with the church's unity, for we fully realize that boundless diversity without unity is actually no catholicity at all.

This is why we insist, first, that an assembly's catholicity is confirmed when we see its apostolicity verified in their gathering under the Word. For an assembly to properly gather in Christ's name, Christ's Word (Holy Scripture) centered on the gospel has to be proclaimed and received. Volf recognizes this when he says that even though "*openness* of each church to all other churches" is a "minimal requirement for catholicity" because "the catholicity of the local church presupposes that the channels for synchronic and diachronic communication between churches remain open," this is not enough to verify that assembly as catholic.[110] Why not? Because this criterion

---

[108]Williams, *Retrieving the Tradition*, 226.
[109]Williams, *Retrieving the Tradition*, 226.
[110]Volf, *After Our Likeness*, 275.

"is unable to identify those Christian groups to whom a church must be open if it is to be catholic."[111] And so Volf says that the material mark of a catholic church is *"loyalty to the apostolic tradition,"* because "only from the perspective of the apostolic tradition can the catholicity of the church be determined in the first place."[112] In short, catholicity depends first on apostolicity. Of course, various ecclesial traditions mean very different things in speaking of the church's apostolicity. While recognizing this, Volf says, "According to the Free Church model, [as] catholicity is . . . constituted . . . by way of the presence of the Spirit . . . so also the connection with apostolic tradition, a connection demonstrating and guaranteeing catholicity . . . comes about through direct access to the historically mediated apostolic *scriptures.*"[113] Volf is right to highlight that Free Church apostolicity is thus Protestant apostolicity because "the church is the church only if it is built on the Jesus Christ attested by the apostolic writings."[114] Volf is clear that this Word-oriented apostolicity does not negate the need to consult with other churches; on the contrary, Volf says, "even in such dealings with the apostolic scriptures, however, the catholic demand for openness to all churches remains in effect. An adequate interpretation of the apostolic scriptures, and thus also the identification of the apostolic tradition, can take place only through synchronic and diachronic ecclesial communication."[115] This accords with Williams's statement that

> to be "catholic" is indeed a confession of faith; it is a confession of our *wholeness* as believers scattered throughout the world, placed upon the bedrock of the consensual truth as expressed in the New Testament. . . . The emphasis on the church's catholicity is [thus] not merely on its universality and encompassing character, but on its authenticity, that is, its continuity with apostolic truth which throws into relief what is right and wrong Christian teaching.[116]

The Free Church tradition holds, with the Reformers, that the church is indeed a *creatura verba* (creature of the Word), for it is ultimately the

---

[111] Volf, *After Our Likeness,* 275.
[112] Volf, *After Our Likeness,* 275.
[113] Volf, *After Our Likeness,* 275-76, emphasis added.
[114] Volf, *After Our Likeness,* 276.
[115] Volf, *After Our Likeness,* 276.
[116] Williams, *Retrieving the Tradition,* 218.

apostolic Word of God that gives birth to the one catholic church manifest in many churches.

Here it is important to recognize the need for some sort of dogmatic rank to determine what rises to the level of doctrinal adherence to (or departure from) apostolic doctrine. Roger Olson, for instance, distinguishes between dogma, doctrine, and opinion. He argues that dogmas are at the heart of the Christian faith, where to deny a dogma "would constitute rank heresy if not outright apostasy."[117] Doctrines "are important to a particular tradition-community of Christians (e.g., a denomination in the broad or narrow sense) but are not essential to Christianity itself."[118] Opinions "are beliefs which enjoy no consensus, are not clearly taught in Scripture, and do not impinge upon the gospel itself."[119] There will continue to be debate between ecclesial traditions regarding where various doctrines belong in what has also been called the "hierarchy of truths." But, Williams reassures us, just because "there is not perfect agreement on these essentials does not entail the opposite is true, namely, that there are no essentials and all is left to the standards of each generation or cultural context. In effect, a mark of catholicity always entails the reality of heresy."[120] Williams, for his part, commends the fifth-century Athanasian Creed for establishing the doctrinal essentials as centering on the Trinity, Christology, and the coming judgment.[121] Calvin offered a dogmatic rank of sorts when he proposed that catholic churches affirm that "God is one; Christ is God and the Son of God; our salvation rests in God's mercy, and the like" while insisting that "among the churches there are other articles of doctrine disputed which . . . do not break the unity of faith."[122] Thus when Avis insists that the "the catholic character of Anglicanism is revealed in its adherence to the Scriptures, the creeds and the councils of the undivided Church (canonically, the first four), which gave the Church its Christological and trinitarian dogmas," there is no reason why such a means of confirming catholicity could not be used by the Free Church tradition.[123]

---

[117]Roger Olson, *The Mosaic of Christian Belief: Twenty Centuries of Unity and Diversity* (Downers Grove, IL: IVP Academic, 2002), 45.
[118]Olson, *Mosaic of Christian Belief*, 45.
[119]Olson, *Mosaic of Christian Belief*, 45.
[120]Williams, *Retrieving the Tradition*, 227.
[121]Williams, *Retrieving the Tradition*, 227.
[122]Calvin, *Institutes*, 1026.
[123]Avis, "What Is 'Anglicanism'?" 472.

Next, we insist that an assembly's catholicity is confirmed when we see its holiness verified in its gathering around the sacraments. It has been said that "the Eucharist makes the church" and it might just as easily be said that "baptism makes the church." From a Free Church vantage point, these statements overreach, for it is the gospel's reception by faith that ultimately makes the church. But, properly understood, the sacraments are necessary for the church because they are the *enactment* of the gospel that inevitably accompanies its true reception by a community of believers. In other words, if two or three people are gathering ecclesially in Christ's name, they are going to enact the gospel practices of baptism and the Lord's Supper. Volf argues that "the sacraments—baptism and the Lord's Supper—belong to the *esse* of the church . . . [for unlike diocesan bishops] there does not seem to have been any initial period in church history without [these]. . . . Without baptism and the Lord's Supper, there is no church."[124] This is the case because they are part of what Volf calls the "pluriform confession of faith in Christ" and even "a public representation of such a confession" which is necessary for confirming that these two or three are truly gathering in Christ's name.[125] Specifically, their catholic connection is confirmed by their bond of holiness with other local churches, similarly "set apart" as holy before a watching world by these gospel practices. Enacting the sacraments validated by the authority of Christ's presence among even two or three believers gathered in his name is yet another way that the ecclesial nature of that assembly is affirmed, for it is part and parcel of what it means to be a catholic church.

Last, we insist that an assembly's catholicity is confirmed when we see its unity verified in its gathering under oversight (*episcope*). As we observed, certain Reformational movements, such as the Baptist movement, added discipline as a formal mark of a true church. Discipline inherently requires some degree of oversight, some regulation of the church's confession of faith expressed in Word and sacrament and some determination regarding who is a proper confessor. Here Webster's observation is apt: "Oversight is a necessary implication of the gospel through which the church is brought into being and which it is commissioned to proclaim."[126] Volf insists that ordained

---

[124] Volf, *After Our Likeness*, 152-53.
[125] Volf, *After Our Likeness*, 153-54.
[126] Webster, "Self-Organizing Power," 81.

ministry is not of the *esse* of the church, and he (along with the entire Free Church tradition) is particularly adverse to saying that bishops are *required* for the church. But if we keep in mind Webster's insistence on the key distinction "between *episcope*, a ministry of oversight" and "particular, contingent orderings of the episcopal office in a given context" then we are led to recognize the possibility of a "congregational episcopate" as in keeping with the Free Church ecclesial vision.[127] Volf inherently recognizes this requirement when he says, "The presence of Christ, which constitutes the church, is mediated not simply through the ordained ministers but through the whole congregation."[128] In fact, the broader context of Matthew 18:15-20 points in exactly this direction: the gathered congregation is involved in *episcope* in the sense that all seem to be involved in the judgments related to binding and loosing. Webster is right that the church and its catholicity requires "an evangelical dogmatics of order," and we hold that that this order is one of the ways that unity is shown within the church and kept between other local churches in the *catholica*.[129] Because *episcope* has the task "of overseeing the unity and authenticity of the testimony of the church . . . *episcope*, oversight, is the basic ministry of the church."[130] Recognizing this is one of the key ways that each local church can be confirmed as catholic, for each regulates its own congregational life.

When we survey these means of confirming the catholicity of local churches connected to Christ and assembling through the whole of all times, people, and places, we trust that Free Church catholicity will be better received by our Episcopal brothers and sisters. Avis has said that

> Anglicans acknowledge a genuine *koinonia*, or fellowship with God the Holy Trinity and with one's fellows Christians, in Churches that do not have bishops in historical succession. . . . Manifestly they share the faith of the Church; they have baptism and the Eucharist; ministers who are commissioned by the Church and given authority to minister word and sacrament; structures of conciliarity that enable the Churches to govern themselves under the guidance of the Holy Spirit; and forms of *episcope* or pastoral

---

[127]Webster, "Self-Organizing Power," 71, 81.
[128]Volf, *After Our Likeness*, 2.
[129]Webster, "Self-Organizing Power," 71.
[130]Webster, "Self-Organizing Power," 77.

oversight that involve the essential biblical principle of orderly transmitted authority from person to person.[131]

If this is the case, Free Church theologians simply ask that the catholicity of local churches, churches where Christ rules by his Word proclaimed from Scripture and the gospel is enacted in the sacraments as overseen by the faith-filled congregation and those it chooses to ordain, would not be denied, for these are congregations, even of just two or three gathered in Christ's name, speaking gospel words, enacting gospel actions, and exhibiting gospel order in faith. There, no doubt, Christ is present with his people by the Spirit, enabling them to be a catholic local church.

Episcopal Objections to Local Catholicity

But despite the apologetic that has been offered for Free Church catholicity over the years, it is still contested by the Episcopal tradition in certain ways. Volf acutely observes that the tradition's objections, while many, can be boiled down to the same two primary criticisms that Cyprian offered of separatist groups in his day. In his *De Unitate*, Cyprian saw himself as defending "the unity, undividedness, and indivisibility of the church's salvific authority" against those he perceived as misconstruing Scripture (particularly the teaching of Mt 18:20) by "cut[ting] up the sense of [this] single passage" as they have "cut themselves off from the church."[132] Volf summarizes that the first objection was that these groups were breaking with the unity of the church, especially as that unity was embodied in the bishops throughout the whole world. The second objection was that these groups had no proper ecclesial authority, particularly because they have "cut themselves off from Christ and his gospel" by "cutting themselves off" from the one church "as the source and origin of truth."[133] Here we take up these two Episcopal objections concerning catholic unity (via bishops) and catholic authority (via magisterium).

The question of catholic unity: Free Church bishops? The objection regarding catholic unity might best be introduced by returning to the question Ramsey posed to all Protestantism as to whether "the historic Church order

---

[131] Avis, *Anglican Understanding*, 86.
[132] Volf, *After Our Likeness*, 136.
[133] Quoted in Volf, *After Our Likeness*, 136.

has not something to do with the Gospel of God. [A non-Episcopal church] need not deny its own experience nor the power of its own ministries; it needs to own, in common with all Christendom, the need for the one Apostolate, as the organ of unity and continuity, to be made universal for all Christians."[134] That one apostolate, to the Episcopal mind, is expressed through bishops in apostolic succession, and as we have observed, the Episcopal tradition understands that the unity (and thus the catholicity) of the church is very much at stake in whether that succession is embraced.

This is expressed, in seed form, in Ignatius's own correspondence, as Harmon notes: "Regardless of how one reads the role of the bishop in [Ignatius's] letters, it is indisputable that we have here a threefold ministry—bishop, elder, deacon—in which the office of bishop is distinguished from the office of elder and in which the episcopate serves to guard the church against various threats to catholic unity."[135] Indeed, in the larger context of Ignatius's *ubi Christus, ibi ecclesia* statement we find some lofty assessments of the bishop, including the following:

> All of you should follow the bishop as Jesus Christ follows the Father.... Let no one do anything involving the church without the bishop. Let that eucharist be considered valid that occurs under the bishop or the one to whom he entrusts it.... It is not permitted either to baptize or to hold a love feast without the bishop. But whatever he approves is acceptable to God, so that everything you do should be secure and valid.[136]

In fact, in another place Ignatius makes explicit that "without these [deacons, presbyters, bishops] no [group] can be called a church."[137] DeGroot summarizes that Ignatius's understanding is "that the presence of Christ is the essence of the church universal" and "that the bishop is the essence of the church local and is its tie to the church universal."[138] Thus going back to Ignatius, the Episcopal tradition has called into question the unity (and thus catholicity) of churches without bishops. In the Anglican tradition these

---

[134] Ramsey, *Gospel and the Catholic Church*, 201.
[135] Harmon, "Qualitative Catholicity," 38.
[136] Quoted in Harmon, "Qualitative Catholicity," 38.
[137] Quoted in Volf, *After Our Likeness*, 152.
[138] Alfred T. DeGroot, "A People Under the Word: Historical Background," in *Concept of the Believers' Church*, ed. Garrett, 188.

questions are pressing because Lambeth's requirements for visible unity and full communion with other churches are often the basis of ecumenical dialogue. The fourth article (following Scriptures, sacraments, and creeds) requires "the Historic Episcopate, locally adapted in the methods of its administration to the varying needs of the nations and peoples called of God into the Unity of His Church." The challenge from a Free Church vantage point involves what is meant by "historic," especially where this is interpreted as a diocesan bishop in apostolic succession; however, the opportunity from a Free Church vantage point is that provision is made within the article for its "*local* adaption."

In responding to this objection, we have already insisted on the crucial distinction between *episcope* (oversight) and *episcopos* (bishop); the Free Church tradition is compatible with the former (and, in some sense, requires it) but is incompatible with the latter if it is defined narrowly as a diocesan bishop: such an understanding of proper oversight violates the Free Church principle of being corporately local and understanding the flow of ecclesial authority as "from below." But this leaves us with an interesting question: Could Free Church ecclesiology, in some sense, countenance *bishops*? If so, this may go a long way in assuaging (some) Episcopal concerns and giving local churches a way to better demonstrate their unity with the catholic whole.

John Howard Yoder gave much thought to this exact question. His general answer is that "the free church tradition would find nothing wrong with the notion of 'bishops,' since the word is biblical, if it were not given an anti-biblical definition on post-biblical grounds."[139] Specifically, Yoder takes issue with the fact that "because [Episcopal churches have] a network of bishops linked by mutual recognition around the globe" they assume that ecclesial unity "would be having all other Christians likewise in the same network of the mutual recognition of bishops."[140] But Yoder then wonders whether, for the sake of pursuing the unity Jesus prayed for in John 17, Free Church folk could embrace not just *episcope*, but also *episcopos*. In other words: Could there be a "Baptist bishop"? Yoder believes that the legitimacy

---

[139]Yoder, *Royal Priesthood*, 315-16.
[140]John Howard Yoder, "Could There Be a Baptist Bishop?," *Ecumenical Trends* 9, no. 7 (July/August 1980): 104.

of taking this step would come down to whether there is, from the start, a mutual recognition of true ecclesiality on both sides. To start with the assumption "that other churches, with which we are not united according to our particular connectional definitions, are, nonetheless, Christian congregations or parishes" would mean that "mutual recognition as Christian ecclesial fellowships need not be identified with or boiled down to the narrower questions of the recognition of specific ordained ministries or of other sacramental practices."[141] For Yoder it is vital that "the ongoing debate about specific orders and sacraments is, then, subsequent to, rather than prior to, the affirmation of parish-to-parish commitment."[142] In this vision, "Congregations recognize one another as locally gathered around the Scriptures, in Christ's name . . . and then discuss . . . the many questions on which they may very well continue, for a long time, to differ."[143]

Yoder believes that this vision is more likely to come to pass if each communion is given an opportunity to show the others how what they deem essential to being a church is actually present in itself, just in other terms or expressed in different ways. He points to the specific example of communions that argue for the necessity of episcopacy and sees an open door for greater unity between Episcopal churches and those "congregationalistic traditions which have insisted strongly on the dignity of the local gathering" in the fact that "there is nothing in [Episcopal theology] which prescribes the size of the diocese."[144] Yoder then opines,

> Certainly, there is nothing in the argument from Scripture, or from the example of the earliest churches, to give anyone the notion that episcopacy can be properly exercised by one man for a whole political province. Even less are there any (theological) grounds for demanding that the diocese be large, with the effect that most parishes do not have a resident bishop. . . . The [Episcopal] argument says, rather, that for a given gathering of people to be fully a church they need to have a bishop. The more seriously the argument is taken theologically, the less easily it can be explained why that bishop must be an absentee, not residing in the parish, and seldom appearing in the meetings.[145]

---

[141]Yoder, "Could There Be a Baptist Bishop?," 105.
[142]Yoder, "Could There Be a Baptist Bishop?," 105.
[143]Yoder, "Could There Be a Baptist Bishop?," 106.
[144]Yoder, "Could There Be a Baptist Bishop?," 106
[145]Yoder, "Could There Be a Baptist Bishop?," 106.

If this be permitted, he contends, there is "nothing *theologically* preventing the flowing together of the Episcopalian . . . and the [Free Church] extremes of church structure . . . [because] the claim that churches need bishops is biblical . . . [while] the claim that the diocese must be large is not."[146]

Yoder pressed this claim in another place by reflecting on the New Delhi WCC assembly statement that church unity should be sought between "all *in each place* who are baptized into Jesus Christ and confess him as Lord and Savior and are brought by the Holy Spirit into one fully committed fellowship, breaking the one bread, joining in common prayer, and having a corporate life reaching out in witness and service to all."[147] Yoder asks, "Can a 'place' really be larger than a parish and do the things the statement describes? Might it have to be smaller than a parish?"[148] Yoder expresses a characteristic Free Church concern when in response to his questions he states,

> "Each place" must be functionally so defined that the people who meet together can do so repeatedly, if not daily or weekly, so as responsibly to support and govern the ministries exercised in their name. The normal designation used by historians for that position since the late sixteenth century is "congregationalism." It is, however, not incompatible with the theological case that can be made for episcopacy or for presbyterianism, as long as the geographical or numerical size of the diocese or synod is not unmanageably large.[149]

For Yoder, then, the Free Church tradition can absolutely continence bishops, provided their see doesn't violate the local orientation and their installment doesn't require a "top down" flow of ecclesial authority. Yoder maintains, consistent with Free Church principles, that "the claim that episcopacy is normatively constitutive of valid ecclesiastical practice—at least as this claim can be based on the 'primitive unity' of the first centuries—is singularly weakened if the diocese is permitted to be so large that fewer than one percent of the faithful can regularly worship with the bishop present."[150]

---

[146]Yoder, "Could There Be a Baptist Bishop?," 106-7.
[147]Quoted in Yoder, *Royal Priesthood*, 315.
[148]Yoder, *Royal Priesthood*, 315-16.
[149]Yoder, *Royal Priesthood*, 316.
[150]Yoder, *Royal Priesthood*, 316.

If Episcopal churches want Free Churches to consider how bishops help better express the (catholic) unity of the church, they do well to consider a more adequate conception of the local church and to recognize the full ecclesiality of the same.

Another, related, line of Free Church response to this Episcopal objection is to call for a retrieval of an even more ancient form of *episcopos*. Paul Fiddes makes the case, drawing on the argumentation of Walter Kasper, that "the New Testament portrays an ecclesiology that starts from the local church, led by a single bishop, in which local community the one, universal church of God is represented and is present."[151] Recent work on bishops in the first two centuries goes a long way in establishing that the original bishops gave oversight to a particular local church rather than a broader diocese (a later development).[152] Fiddes makes the case that, in some sense, the difference between the Episcopal understanding of the local church as diocese and the Free Church understanding of the local church as an assembling congregation is not as great as it might first appear if we consider that in certain segments of the Free Church tradition, "the local minister of word and sacrament may be called 'bishop' (*episkopos*), [with] no distinction being drawn between bishop and presbyter (elder) in a basically two-fold order of ministry, *episcope* and *diakonia*."[153] Fiddes notes that "Baptists have, moreover, usually understood that the local pastor *represents* the wider church on the local scene, opening up the vision of a single congregation to the wider [church]."[154] He even goes so far to say that Baptists have "an office of inter-church *episcope* ('oversight') in an area like a diocese, a pastor who may go by the name of 'regional minister,' 'executive minister,' 'superintendent,' or even 'bishop,' but this ministry is generally seen as an extension of congregational *episcope* rather than a third office, and he or she has pastoral influence but no executive authority

---

[151]Paul S. Fiddes, "The Church Local and Universal: Catholic and Baptist Perspectives on *Koinonia* Ecclesiology," in *Revisioning, Renewing, Rediscovering the Triune Center*, ed. Derek J. Tidball, Brian S. Harris, and Jason S. Sexton (Eugene, OR: Cascade Books, 2014), 112.

[152]See here Alistair C. Steward, *The Original Bishops: Office and Order in the First Christian Communities* (Grand Rapids, MI: Baker Academic, 2014).

[153]Fiddes, "Church Local and Universal," 101. He cites the Second London Confession for proof here.

[154]Fiddes, "Church Local and Universal," 101.

in a local congregation."[155] This is no diocesan bishop, and certainly not one conceived as enthroned and enjoying apostolic succession. But there is an argument to be made that there is "a broad [Free Church] continuity . . . [with] early catholic Christianity. [Free Church folk] do typically grant that the teaching office has a responsibility to see to the unity of the church, and inasmuch as they have historically equated the office and function of the pastor with that of the bishop on the basis of New Testament texts, [they] have understood this to be an exercise of episcopacy."[156]

Yoder and Fiddes can be understood as Free Church theologians with great respect for the Episcopal tradition taking up the offer of the Anglo-Catholic authors of *Catholicity*: "It is for those who at present possess these elements of Catholic faith and order, to let their use of them be criticized and corrected in light of primitive standards, and in light of truths to which . . . other traditions have borne witness in separation."[157] That correction might come in reflecting on the statements of Turnbull (an Anglican) when he says that while bishops are a "sign of continuity and catholicity . . . [which provide] for the well-being of the Church" we must not forget that "the real *locus* of apostolicity lies not in the succession of bishops but in the faithful handing on of the deposit of the faith. Bishops are a useful way of ensuring and providing for this continuity but do not guarantee it."[158] This is true; and congregations of just two or three communing in Christ are useful for this purpose too.

In fact, given the Free Church argument that the Episcopal tradition tends to privilege unity over genuine catholicity and the Episcopal argument that the Free Church tradition tends to neglect the catholic unity of the church that can be (uniquely?) displayed by bishops, we might conclude that we need *both* these traditions to properly exhibit the catholic unity and the unified diversity that mark the church. If it is true, as Avis has said, that "*nothing* but the reception of the gospel is required to constitute a given

---

[155] Fiddes, "Church Local and Universal," 101. Fiddes notes two Baptist examples of a threefold ministry that are the exceptions proving the rule: seventeeth-century General Baptists (as attested in their Orthodox Creed and seen in the example of Thomas Grantham) and the Evangelical Baptist Church of Georgia today.
[156] Harmon, "Qualitative Catholicity," 43.
[157] Gregory Dix, ed., *Catholicity: A Study in the Conflict of Christian Traditions in the West* (London: Dacre, 1947), 55.
[158] Richard Turnbull, *Anglican and Evangelical?* (London: Continuum, 2007), 45.

ministry as [a] ministry of the Christian Church" then it seems that both of these traditions are valid.[159] Avis acknowledges that "other considerations may have to be introduced to define a *regular* ministry and to safeguard good order in the Christian community, but that is a separate question over and above the primary question of the *validity* of a ministry. That can only be determined by the gospel that is being preached."[160] Avis says that this was the great insight of the Reformation, which brought "a judgment to bear on all attempts to invalidate or withhold recognition from the ministries of Churches that lack the historic episcopate. To import an exclusive theory of apostolic succession to the central *place* in the doctrine of the ministry is to overthrow the Christological foundation and to attempt to over-define the circumference at the expense of the center."[161] This is a way of expressing the very concern Free Church theologians have with Episcopal forms of ministry: neglecting the christological grounding of catholicity that ensures that the gathering of even just two or three is fully a catholic church. In light of this truth, Free Church theologians insist that congregational episcopates not be immediately ruled out of bounds as gospel-testifying, unity-serving, and catholic-oriented developments alongside Episcopal ones. If this is permitted, it would go a long way toward acknowledging the possibility that the Episcopal tradition might best serve the church's unity while the Free Church tradition might best serve its catholicity. This would point to the fact that we need both traditions (along with others) to capture and express the full-orbed nature of the church as one, holy, catholic, and apostolic, locally expressed and universal in scope.

The question of catholic authority: A Free Church magisterium? The problem of catholic unity and "Baptist bishops" is interrelated to the second objection originally voiced by Cyprian and noted today by Avis in his engagement with Harmon's Baptist catholicity, namely, *By what authority* could a catholic pattern of Free Church faith and practice be established and commended? Harmon himself recognized how crucial this question was, acknowledging that "without greater specificity in its location of ecclesial authority" the Free Church tradition largely

---

[159] Avis, *Church in the Theology of the Reformers*, 221, emphasis added.
[160] Avis, *Church in the Theology of the Reformers*, 221-22, emphasis added.
[161] Avis, *Church in the Theology of the Reformers*, 222.

lacks adequate safeguards against the very thing it seeks to avoid: self-chosen patterns of faith and practice by independent individuals and autonomous congregations in the configuration of a "selective catholicity" . . . that . . . embraces certain ancient marks of catholicity but ignores the episcopal office and its historical role as the ecclesial location of teaching authority that authorizes the other marks of catholicity.[162]

It is the last part of this concern that we seek to address here: In an account of local catholicity, who or what can serve as a teaching authority, or "where is the magisterium that could reliably guide [the Free Church] toward [greater] catholicity?"[163] The Episcopal tradition has consistently underscored the importance of the episcopate as the embodiment of ecclesial authority, specifically *magisterial* authority (the authority to teach doctrine). Where does that authority reside in a Free Church account, and how does that relate to the catholicity of the local church? If, as Avis has claimed, "the catholicity of Anglican faith is further evinced by the fact that it acknowledges the authority of the Church gathered in council," is this a possibility for the Free Church tradition as well?[164]

Harmon notes certain similarities between the traditions "despite the real differences . . . in the way they configure teaching authority in the church," namely that "magisterium is subservient to the Word of God; second, it is a communal practice that in various ways involves the whole Body of Christ; and third, those who exercise *episcope* in the church play a key role in helping the community discern the mind of Christ."[165] Timothy George has also pointed toward similitude in making the intriguing observation that "Baptists and Catholics differ on the scope and locale of the *magisterium* but

---

[162]Steven R. Harmon, "Why Baptist Catholicity, and by What Authority?," *Pro Ecclesia* 18, no. 4 (Fall 2009): 388-89.
[163]Harmon, "Why Baptist Catholicity," 388.
[164]Avis, "What Is 'Anglicanism'?," 472.
[165]Steven R. Harmon, "The Nicene Faith and the Catholicity of the Church: Evangelical Retrieval and the Problem of Magisterium," in *Evangelicals and Nicene Faith: Reclaiming the Apostolic Witness*, ed. Timothy George (Grand Rapids, MI: Baker Academic, 2011), 91. Harmon describes both the strengths and weaknesses of Roman Catholic and magisterial Protestant conceptions of the magisterium, especially noting their common drift into "an overly realized eschatology of the church," backed by the chilling observation that "this susceptibility is exemplified by the most significant ecumenical agreement reached between Roman Catholic and magisterial Protestants during the sixteenth century, namely, that it was okay to kill Anabaptists." Harmon, "Nicene Faith and the Catholicity of the Church," 86.

not on whether it exists as a necessary component in the ongoing life of the Church."¹⁶⁶ Initially it seems like such a Free Church magisterium would be limited in scope to the ministerial authorities of the local church, at most a bishop of a local church. Such teaching authority is understood as deriving from Christ himself but through the gathered congregation because, as Harmon notes, the "functional" Free Church conception of the magisterium emphasizes "the authority of the congregation of baptized believers gathered in a covenanted community under the lordship of Christ."¹⁶⁷ Fiddes says much the same when he argues that "the liberating rule of Christ is what ... allows for spiritual oversight (*episcope*) both by the *whole* congregation gathered together ... and by the minister(s) called to lead the congregation."¹⁶⁸ Harmon goes on to clarify that in a Baptist context pastors are particularly charged with the responsibility of *episcope*, "which carries with it the catechetical task of equipping the members of the congregation with the resources they need *from beyond the congregation* for seeking the mind of Christ—resources including the doctrine, worship, and practice of other congregations, other Christian traditions, and indeed the whole Christian tradition."¹⁶⁹ So far, the extent of the magisterium in view remains local, embodied in the *episcope* of each church, but one that wisely consults resources from outside that church.

But there is a line of thinking that could potentially expand that scope, something that Harmon calls "a magisterium of the whole." He develops this construct by arguing that Scripture and the creed implicitly argue for "'the authority of the communion of all the saints,' including not only modern ... saints but also those saints long since deceased but now alive in Christ."¹⁷⁰ This communion constitutes "a real community under the lordship of Christ that transcends space and time," and drawing on a MacIntyrian account of tradition, Harmon argues that the church's teaching authority can be located in this communion of saints, where as "[every voice is] heard and weighed along with other ecclesial voices" there is greater clarity regarding "the goods that constitute the [Christian]

---

¹⁶⁶Quoted in Harmon, "Nicene Faith and the Catholicity of the Church," 81.
¹⁶⁷Harmon, "Nicene Faith and the Catholicity of the Church," 86.
¹⁶⁸Quoted in Harmon, "Nicene Faith and the Catholicity of the Church," 88.
¹⁶⁹Harmon, "Nicene Faith and the Catholicity of the Church," 89, emphasis added.
¹⁷⁰Newman, "Remembering How to Remember," 376.

tradition."[171] Harmon knows there are important questions to answer here: "If all members of the communion of saints are participants in this ongoing argument, do they all participate in the same way? Do the voices of all the participants carry the same weight, so that the argument is decided by majority?"[172] These questions lead Harmon to acknowledge that we need to "[more] clearly locate socially embodied ecclesial authority" and that our best option is to follow the Free Church instinct to locate it "in the gathered congregation."[173] He names this the "magisterium-hood of all believers," but that doesn't seem to produce a magisterium that gets beyond the local church or transcend the individual saints that make up that church, still leaving us with the problem of a more "selective catholicity." Instead, I'd like to suggest that a Free Church magisterium, while it must honor the consciences and contributions of each saint and maintain the primacy of the local church, can move beyond a local scale by being envisioned as the "magisterium-hood of all *local churches*."

Clearly one of the doctrinal resources that could fund such a conception is the doctrine of the priesthood of all believers, a Free Church signature emphasis but also one that is shared across ecclesial traditions. Briggs traces out how underlying the historic Free Church understanding of "defined covenant membership of regenerate believers gathered out of the world" and its "powers through church meeting . . . to discern the mind of Christ . . . and therefore to appoint its own officers" is "the theology of the priesthood of all believers, [which] without deprecating the importance of ordination, underlines the participatory nature of the church with high responsibilities assigned to the laity."[174] Tie notes how "the doctrine of the universal priesthood is particularly and pastorally applied to congregational polity. . . . [For] the priesthood doctrine . . . necessarily implies the participation of the whole local Christian congregation in discerning and determining God's will for the church under the lordship of Christ and leadership of the Spirit."[175]

---

[171]Harmon, "Why Baptist Catholicity?," 388-89; Harmon, "Nicene Faith and the Catholicity of the Church," 87.
[172]Harmon, "Nicene Faith and the Catholicity of the Church," 87.
[173]Harmon, "Nicene Faith and the Catholicity of the Church," 87.
[174]John H. Y. Briggs, "The Changing Shape of Nonconformity, 1662–2000," in *T&T Clark Companion to Nonconformity*, ed. Stephen J. Pope (London: Bloomsbury, 2013), 4. He cites John Owen as exhibit A of this perspective.
[175]Tie, *Restore Unity, Recover Identity*, 19.

Here again we see the potential for a Free Church magisterium, but still constrained to the local level. When we consider the possibility of local catholicity, a *local church's* connectedness to the whole *as a church*, we see that there are still further implications to draw from this doctrine, namely that *each local church ought to acknowledge that there are other congregations of equally authoritative priests that, wisdom says, ought to be heeded.*

This follows from the insight of John Smyth that "every true visible Church is of *equal power* with all other visible Churches."[176] Armstrong expressed the same principle when he says that "one local congregation is as much the church as any other. But the church is also the whole of all such congregations throughout the whole earth."[177] Birch can say, consistent with Free Church principles, that "while the local congregation is not deficient in anything that is required for it to be a local manifestation of Christ's body" it is simultaneously true that "the single congregation cannot function in isolation from . . . the universal body of Christ to which it is essentially joined."[178] But how does this universal body find expression to the Free Church mind? In other *equally authoritative* local churches. The British Congregationalists understood this well when they expressed in article twenty-six of the Savoy Declaration that local church sufficiency never implies abandoning mutual cooperation and interdependence with other local churches, noting that "in case of Difficulties or Differences, either in point of Doctrine or Administrations . . . it is according to the mind of Christ that many Churches holding communion together, do by their messengers meet in a Synod or Council, to consider and give their advice. . . . Howbeit these Synods . . . are not entrusted with any Church-Power, or with any jurisdiction over the Churches themselves."[179] Notice that churches are called to heed one another not just regarding administrative matters or missional endeavors, but also regarding *proper doctrine*. This points to the potential of a magisteriumhood of all local churches.

---

[176] Quoted in Volf, *After Our Likeness*, 154, emphasis added.
[177] Armstrong, *Your Church Is Too Small*, 108.
[178] Ian Birch, "'The Counsel and Help of One Another': The Origins and Concerns of Early Particular Baptist Churches in Association," *The Baptist Quarterly* 45, no. 1 (January 2013): 17.
[179] Henry Bettenson and Chris Maunder, eds., *The Documents of the Christian Church*, 3rd ed. (Oxford: Oxford University Press, 1999), 331, language updated.

But, we ask, what *authority* could such a Free Church magisterium exercise if in fact each local church is free to govern its own affairs (including doctrinal affairs) under the lordship of Christ? Based on the logic of the priesthood of all believers, every member of the universal church is a priest-king, and thus exercises equal authority in a way that congregationalism attempts to acknowledge in congregationally discerning the mind of Christ together. But if, on Free Church principles, these priest-kings are assembled in *many* local churches across the whole of all times, all peoples, and all places, it would seem that each local congregation would be obliged to heed the input of other congregations of priest-kings to whatever extent reasonable.

Here the insights of Leeman will once again prove helpful, for Leeman makes an important distinction between "authority of command" and "authority of counsel."[180] The former possesses the power of enforcement while the latter does not; the authority of the latter involves an appeal to truth and wisdom. Leeman is consistent with Free Church ecclesiology in saying that only the gathered congregation possesses the authority of command, ecclesially speaking, for the assembly is where the keys are properly exercised. But interestingly, Leeman points to elders/pastors as an example of ecclesial authority of counsel being exercised in the local church, saying things like pastors "teach Scripture and give oversight to the congregation on how to use the keys"[181] and elders "have a morally binding authority to lead or instruct a church in its use of the keys through their Spirit-given and congregationally affirmed authority to teach."[182] This pastoral authority "is an authority of truth" that "is characterized by teaching, persuading, counseling, exhorting, recommending. Its tenor and presentation is pastoral, fatherly, and patient," and it is significant that Leeman notes that "their instruction and recommendations do impose a relative . . . obligation on the congregation since the Lord has installed the elders in this teaching office."[183] While noting that there are times when the congregation shouldn't follow

---

[180]Leeman derives these categories from Oliver O'Donovan, *Resurrection and Moral Order: An Outline for Evangelical Ethics* (Grand Rapids, MI: Eerdmans, 1986).
[181]Jonathan Leeman, *The Rule of Love: How the Local Church Should Reflect God's Love and Authority* (Wheaton, IL: Crossway, 2018), 154-55.
[182]Leeman, *Don't Fire Your Church Members*, 67.
[183]Leeman, *Don't Fire Your Church Members*, 68.

the recommendation of the elders, such as when they "recommend a course of action that jeopardies the integrity, nature, or mission of the church and its doctrine," it is clear that the congregation is called to give the elders the benefit of the doubt and generally submit to their authority, even though theirs is always the authority of counsel rather than of command.[184]

It seems that, based on the doctrine of the priesthood of all believers and the recognition that those believers have gathered in many local churches through the whole of redemptive history, there is reason to understand these other local churches as also exercising an authority of counsel that each local church is wise to generally heed. The local church still exercises ecclesial authority of command in the exercise of the keys; it simply expands the pattern of ecclesial authority of council based on the conviction that it is wise to consult with equally authoritative local churches made up of equally authorized priest-kings. Local catholicity cultivates the instinct for the local church to press into the whole of other local churches and determine the extent to which there is a consensus that has emerged from their decisions, recognizing that it is wise to largely stay with the whole as expressed in a magisterium of all churches. Local churches do well to recognize that consulting other local churches that have given careful attention to particular doctrinal and ethical questions (perhaps more attention than that local church is able to give to the matter) is both wise and good.

Vanhoozer is right to note in this regard that in an era marked by a conflict of interpretations, there is good reason *provisionally* to acknowledge the superiority of an interpretation that has catholic consensus.[185] Because each local church recognizes it is not the only church that has received illumination into the proper sense of Scripture's teaching, there should be an openness to how the Spirit might use the catholic whole of other churches to guide and even correct any particular local church. And to the question of how local churches know *which* other churches to heed and learn from, the answer might be the same way the congregation discerns which of its members to install as elders: by watching to see which ones are most conducive for faithful Christian life and doctrine. Yet, based on the implications of the priesthood of all believers, every local church with confirmed

---

[184]Leeman, *Rule of Love*, 154-55.
[185]See Vanhoozer, *Biblical Authority After Babel*, 146, 195, 208.

catholicity should be respected to the extent that it represents another assembly of priest-kings. Just as, from a congregational standpoint, pastoral leadership is not pastoral rule, so here the magisterium of all local churches is an authority that supports, rather than trumps, the authority of the assembled congregation. Such an understanding allows us to expand the sense of a magisterium beyond the local church (and thus begin to address the Episcopal concerns about catholic authority and the place for a magisterium) while still being consistent with a proper Free Church position that while "a local congregation is self-governing. . . . every congregation should be wholly submitted to King Jesus and generally submissive to the wisdom, counsel, and instruction of other churches."[186]

Here we should briefly draw attention to how such a construct might lead to a more formal role for creeds to play in a Free Church pattern of ecclesial authority. The ecumenical creeds offer the best candidates for representing a catholic consensus, even though isolated aspects of their content are still contested in the catholic church.[187] In a Free Church pattern the creeds do not exercise any intrinsic authority to bind consciences. But through the lens of a "magisterium of all churches" undergirded by an inference from the doctrine of the priesthood of all believers, they can be embraced by local churches as perhaps the greatest expression of an authority of counsel because they represent the judgment of the vast majority of local churches through all times, peoples, and places. In this sense creedal judgments can be understood *provisionally* as judgments that the whole church ought to affirm in order to display catholic unity and ensure that the logic of the gospel is secure. In other words, while the Bible alone has magisterial authority, the catholic consensus has ministerial authority insofar as it displays biblical judgments. Because the creeds have stood the test of church-historical time and have been embraced by every people in every place as rightly summarizing biblical judgments, we should recognize that departing from them means going against a huge swath of the catholic church on doctrinal matters of the first order. Thus they are particularly to be consulted as local churches exercise the ecclesial authority that is rightfully theirs under Christ.

---

[186]Leeman, *Don't Fire Your Church Members*, 9.

[187]Here I am thinking particularly of Christ's descent in the Apostles' Creed and the addition of the *filioque* clause to the Nicene Creed.

Such an understanding of a Free Church magisterium is still miles away from an Episcopal understanding of the magisterium. But by understanding magisterium as the teaching authority found in the council of all local churches, it opens up opportunities for greater dialogue about the ways that Free Churches might engage in ecclesial consultation at every scale of the church's life. It might even contribute to the possibility of Harmon's hoped-for ecumenical future, one where there might be "some form of shared magisterium, or at least the mutual recognition of one another's teaching authorities as they converge toward a genuine unity in the truth in the teaching of the catholic faith."[188] Again, each tradition would have something to bring to the other. Kärkkäinen notes that the Free Church contribution would likely be to "challenge . . . other churches . . . to flesh out the implications of the priesthood of all [believers]."[189] But the challenge presented to the Free Church would be to recognize that Augustine was right when he insisted that "the judgment of the whole world is reliable."[190] This insight can be applied by Free Churches if they grasp, as Harmon puts it, that "the rule of Christ in the plurality of local congregations . . . has implications for the efforts of every single local congregation to discern the mind of Christ. . . . Together in their mutual relations they [can] seek to walk under the government of Christ, seeking from him a fuller grasp of the truth, as one ecclesial communion—a communion that it is hoped, might extend beyond [Free] churches in association to include all the saints [and all their churches]."[191]

Conclusion: The Catholicity of Ten Thousand Local Churches

We have argued here that Free Church catholicity makes an important contribution to *guarding, spotlighting, and maximizing* the church's catholicity because it locates catholicity where even just two or three gather in Christ's name: the local church. Free Church catholicity as local catholicity *guards* catholicity by drawing attention to its local locus and ensuring that it is not

---

[188]Harmon, "Nicene Faith and the Catholicity of the Church," 91.
[189]Veli-Matti Kärkkäinen, *An Introduction to Ecclesiology: Ecumenical, Historical & Global Perspectives* (Downers Grove, IL: IVP Academic, 2002), 140.
[190]Quoted in Pelikan, *Christian Tradition*, 1:334.
[191]Harmon, "Nicene Faith and the Catholicity of the Church," 88.

conflated with unity (thus resulting in ecclesial uniformity). It *spotlights* catholicity because the church's unified diversity grounded in Christ is on fuller display amid ten thousand local churches than amid one thousand dioceses, one hundred provinces, ten national churches, or one monoepiscopate. And it *maximizes* catholicity because it ensures that when we confess the church as catholic, we mean the church as it has manifested at all times, among all peoples, and *particularly in all places* by insisting there is no fulsome catholicity without sufficient locality. The nature of this local catholicity reminds the whole church that we still await the fullness of consummative catholicity and encourages each local church to further embrace its inaugurated catholicity.

Local catholicity, we have argued, thus brings an important complement to the Episcopal tradition and course corrects against its tendency to inadequately define the local and to privilege unity over catholicity. Episcopal traditions have emphasized the *united* aspect of catholicity's nature as "unified diversity" and the "all times" part of its scope; these emphases are vital to a full-orbed account of catholicity. But they need the Free Church tradition's complementary emphasis on the *diversity* side of catholicity's nature and the "all places" part of its scope. This emphasis comes from a consistent attempt to parse out the implications that the church is present in every locale where even just two or three believers gather in Christ's name. It is from this foundational ecclesial conviction that Essick and Medley argue that "locality and catholicity incorporate one another and must account for one another.... A locally catholic vision of the church emphasizes the visible, gathered church as a 'placed people,' which holds in appropriate tension the local and the catholic without retreating to isolated places or escaping to a disembodied universal conception of the church."[192] Indeed, placing the locus of the church's catholicity in either the believing individual (the tendency of anticatholic traditions) or the episcopate of a translocal institution (the tendency of the Episcopal tradition) fails to maximize genuine catholicity, the former because its diversity fails to be truly ecclesial, the latter because its unity fails to be sufficiently diversified. We also can't be content to ascribe catholicity merely to the invisible church; catholicity has

---

[192]John Inscore Essick and Mark S. Medley, "Local Catholicity: The Bodies and Places Where Jesus Is (Found)," *Review & Expositor* 112, no. 1 (February 2015): 47.

to "touch down" somewhere, be worked out among a community, and this, to the Free Church mind, is primarily the local church.

That said, we close by expressing a hope that the Free Church and Episcopal traditions will continue to collaborate on the nature of the church's catholicity, recognizing the distinctive insights that each brings to the table. Indeed, it is fitting that the doctrine of the church's catholicity, a doctrine concerned with the wholeness of the body of Christ, cannot be fully parsed out without the contribution of every ecclesial tradition and even every local church. This collaboration will surely advance the more that each tradition embraces and affirms the full ecclesiality of the other, even if this is done by employing the framework of viewing the churches in the other tradition as valid but irregular. This can be done the more we aspire to embrace the attitude of John Owen toward ecclesial communities not his own, whose fundamental attitude van Vlastuin summarizes as being "open and positive towards every assembly of two or three people who are gathered in the name of Christ."[193] For the Episcopal tradition this would mean continuing to work out the implications of the position summarized by Avis that "the Anglican Church's adherence to episcopacy is in the interests of her own catholicity of order . . . but it does not imply any adverse judgment on the ministries of other communions."[194] This would involve, in Harmon's words, an Episcopal recognition "that the catholic church subsists 'where two or three are gathered in [Christ's] name' . . . [and thus in] churches that exercise congregational oversight as they gather in the name of Christ."[195] But it would also have to involve, from the Free Church side, the recognition that the catholic church simultaneously subsists "'wherever the bishop is' . . . [and thus in churches] overseen by the historic episcopate."[196] This is simply to work out the logic of Avis's statement that the doctrine of catholicity itself suggests "that the Church has the capacity to embrace diverse ways of believing and worshipping and

---

[193]Willem van Vlastuin, "John Owen as a Modern Theologian: A Comparison of Catholicity in Cyprian and Owen," in *John Owen Between Orthodoxy and Modernity*, ed. Willem van Vlastuin and Kelly M. Kapic (Leiden: Brill, 2019), 173.

[194]Paul Avis, *Anglicanism and the Christian Church: Theological Resources in Historical Perspective* (Minneapolis: Fortress, 1989), 308.

[195]Harmon, "Why Baptist Catholicity?," 391-92.

[196]Harmon, "Why Baptist Catholicity?," 391-92.

that this diversity comes about through the 'incarnation' of Christian truth in many different . . . forms, which it both critiques and affirms," and provides "a mandate for [ecclesial] hospitality," by standing against "authoritarianism, uniformity, and the crushing of local traditions by central authority."[197] This is, in other words, to embrace the catholicity of ten thousand churches, or what we are calling local catholicity.

---

[197] Avis, *Anglican Understanding of the Church*, 65.

Conclusion
Local Catholicity and Catholic Locality

W E HAVE FOUND THAT THE FREE CHURCH TRADITION can not only account for and appreciate the church's catholicity more than it has often done in the past, but that it also has an important contribution to make to a faithful, fuller-orbed doctrine of that catholicity. That contribution, grounded in the witness of Scripture, integrating aspects of the doctrine that have emerged in church history, and providing complementary and corrective insights to the Episcopal tradition, is that catholicity is located where even just two or three are ecclesially gathered in Christ's name. Local catholicity best spotlights the church's catholic nature as a unified diversity manifesting through the whole of all times, peoples, and *places*. We thus insist, based on Free Church ecclesial convictions, that there is no fulsome catholicity without sufficient locality, because it is the localized diversity of ten thousand (and many more!) local churches united in Christ by the Spirit that maximizes the creedal confession that the one church is catholic, that the universal church is marked by a variegated wholeness that is beheld in greater and greater degrees as the multifarious nature of its parts is seen more clearly. When Christ rules in ten thousand places and the unity of "one Lord, one faith, one baptism" (Eph 4:5) manifests through the diversified whole, we recognize that "catholic diversity is the opposite of sectarianism."[1]

---

[1] John H. Armstrong, *Your Church Is Too Small* (Grand Rapids, MI: Zondervan, 2010), 93.

The catholic church thus needs the witness of the Free Church regarding the nature of catholicity. Varying ecclesial traditions have distinctive understandings of catholicity, and we recognize that these different traditions bring complementary insights; indeed, it is fitting that a doctrine concerned with the church's diversified wholeness would require all of the ecclesial traditions for its fullest expression. Richard Hooker counsels us to consider the glories of God in this reality when he says "a more dutiful and religious way for us were to admire the wisdom of God, which shineth in the beautiful variety of all things, but most in the manifold and yet harmonious dissimilitude of those ways, whereby his Church upon earth is guided from age to age, throughout all generations of men."[2] To overcome Episcopal oversights and arrive at a fuller-orbed doctrine of catholicity, "the catholicity of two or three" needs to be recognized. At the same time, the Free Church requires the insights of the Episcopal tradition (along with others) to overcome its own blindspots. For instance, while the problem of Free Church *catholicity* has been examined and found quite solvable, the problem of Free Church *unity* may well prove more difficult, likely requiring Episcopal voices that have rightly emphasized the significance of the visible unity of Christ's body. This is another project for another day. But for now, we briefly reflect on three implications of *this* project.

A Truly Free Church: Free to Embrace Catholicity

First, we consider what the *free* in the Free Church tradition ought to indicate in light of our study. A longstanding ecclesiological conviction of the Free Church is that the nature of God's people, gathered and scattered, is marked by *freedom*. Indeed, perhaps the most programmatic verse for the entire tradition (apart from Mt 18:20) is 2 Corinthians 3:17: "Now the Lord is the Spirit, and where the Spirit of the Lord is, there is freedom." Christ's rule over the church through his Spirit enables God's people to be free in the fullest sense. To restrict this freedom to a mere independence from state interference, or a passionate salvo against Episcopal polity, or a shallow insistence on the "autonomy of the local church," is to shortchange the depths of the freedom God has won for the church in Christ by the Spirit according

---

[2]Quoted in Stephen Sykes, *Unashamed Anglicanism* (Nashville: Abington Press, 1995), 81, language updated.

to the gospel. This freedom is ultimately a freedom from spiritual bondage to live lives of worship unto God and to do so as a gathered people. It is ultimately a freedom *for* rather than just a freedom *from*.

So here we insist that the Free Church tradition consider more carefully the implications of the freedom that Christ has won for us, specifically by enacting our freedom to *embrace catholicity*, to embrace the catholic church with the riches of its tradition and the insights that can come from the myriad of other congregations of priest-kings at all times, among all peoples, and in all places. The local church, under the authority of Christ and his Word, is *free* to embrace the Great Tradition and the insights of other ecclesial traditions. It is *free* to emphasize our interdependence with other local churches rather than our independence from them. It is *free* to recognize its responsibility to the broader church and the need to think in terms of gospel partnership rather than suspicious competition. It is *free* to recognize the wisdom of Bavinck when he said "the Christian life is too rich to unfold its full glory in only one form or within the walls of one church."[3] It is *free*, in short, to be catholic in the fullest sense of the term.

Indeed, we would say that ultimately for the Free Church account of catholicity presented here to be persuasive to the catholic church, Free Churches must demonstrate, in the words of Williams, that "the liberty of the Spirit in a believer's life [can] be balanced by continuity of the church in history" and that "the Protestant Reformation [can] be integrated with the larger and older picture of what it means to be catholic."[4] This was indeed what Congregationalist theologian P. T. Forsyth called for a century ago when he emphasized the need for "the Free Churches . . . to cultivate a sense of the great Church, if their freedom is not to lose all its greatness."[5] Forsyth, in recognizing the tendency in Free Churches for independence to crowd out catholicity, appealed to the freedom it trumpeted by insisting that "in so far as Independency claims to be a branch of the true Church, its principle is not rational liberty, nor spiritual liberty, but evangelical liberty, which is

---

[3] Quoted in James Eglington, *Trinity and Organism: Towards a New Reading of Herman Bavinck's Organic Motif* (London: T&T Clark, 2012), 92.
[4] D. H. Williams, *Evangelicals and Tradition: The Formative Influence of the Early Church* (Grand Rapids, MI: Baker Academic, 2005), 10.
[5] David M. Thompson, J. H. Y. Briggs, and John Munsey Turner, eds., *Protestant Nonconformist Texts*, vol. 4: *The Twentieth Century* (Aldershot, UK: Ashgate, 2007), 181.

the true Catholic tradition."[6] Forsyth held that "evangelical" and "catholic" weren't enemies but good friends, and we might say that an implication of this project is that the same can be said of "Free Church" and "catholic." But ultimately Free Churches must prove that this is true not just in word but also in deed.

Catholic Locality: Inaugurated Local Catholicity

This leads to a second implication of our study, which comes by revisiting the doctrinal rule we have insisted on: no fulsome catholicity without sufficient locality. We mentioned that the rule has an important corollary: no fulsome locality without sufficient catholicity. This derives from our analysis of the dimensions of catholicity earlier, where we said that in addition to quantitative, qualitative, and consummative catholicity there was also *inaugurated* catholicity. Gibaut speaks about this dimension when he notes that "catholicity is a gift, not an achievement; the gift, however, carries with it demands that catholicity is to be made visible and manifest in history."[7] The gift of catholicity should increasingly manifest in the life of the local church. In fact, such catholic manifestations are required for the church to be the body of Christ locally because "a *truly* local church is catholic. Local catholicity calls [us] to reimagine the local, gathered community of believers as one embodiment of the church's catholicity—one of the places where Jesus can be found."[8] Brown expresses this well: "Inculturation allows a church to express the catholicity of the whole church by its very practice being local. Such an expression of the church's universality, however, *is only possible if the local church also maintains strong bonds of communion with the universal church.*"[9]

That is, each local church only fully embodies the presence of Christ locally by being connected to the whole, by recognizing that what is locally manifested in that particular church only has substance because it is an

---

[6]Thompson, Briggs, and Turner, *Protestant Nonconformist Texts*, 4:186.
[7]John St-Helier Gibaut, "Catholicity, Faith and Order, and the Unity of the Church," *Ecumenical Review* 63, no. 2 (July 2011): 181.
[8]John Inscore Essick and Mark S. Medley, "Local Catholicity: The Bodies and Places Where Jesus Is (Found)," *Review & Expositor* 112, no. 1 (February 2015): 48, emphasis added.
[9]R. Kevin Brown, "The Local and Universal Churches: Expressing Catholicity Through Their Reciprocity," in *Visions of Hope: Emerging Theologians and the Future of the Church*, ed. Kevin Ahern (Maryknoll, NY: Orbis Books, 2013), 204, emphasis added.

expression of the one body of Christ. Without this fulsome wholeness, a local church is merely a voluntary organization requiring no theological account. A catholic sensibility must therefore not only increasingly define the Free Church tradition, but it must also impact praxis at the local church level and in the myriad of contexts in which we have been called to be witnesses of Christ. Churches that focus merely on their own life and remain self-sufficient islands to themselves will fail to live out the implications of their confession in that locale. But churches that grow in their *enactment* of their catholic nature offer a greater witness to Christ where the Lord has placed them.

Harmon speaks to the importance of Free Churches pressing into the implications of their catholic nature: "I hope that the journey to the ecumenical future includes Catholic recognition of the Baptist instances of catholicity that exist outside the Catholic Church. In the meantime, Baptists must see to it *that there is catholicity existing among them to be recognized.*"[10] If Free Churches' desire for their local catholicity to be recognized, they have an obligation to grow in manifesting an inaugurated catholicity where it is currently lacking. There is much work to be done here. But we must press into that work out of a conviction that a robust doctrine of catholicity should result in local churches exhibiting a greater catholicity of doctrine and of practice, laboring with other churches for the good of the whole church, the life of the whole world, and the glory of the triune God.

The Future of the (Free) Church: Consummative Local Catholicity

A third implication of our study concerns the future of the church. As was discussed in the introduction, the Free Church tradition is recognized in many ways as "the church of the future." Consider as only one example that Pentecostalism in the Global South is the fastest growing segment of Christianity; it leads Kärkkäinen to say without hesitation that the "Free Church congregational model will be the major paradigm in the third millennium."[11]

---

[10] Steven R. Harmon, "Why Baptist Catholicity, and by What Authority?" *Pro Ecclesia* 18, no. 4 (Fall 2009): 392, emphasis added.
[11] Veli-Matti Kärkkäinen, *An Introduction to Ecclesiology: Ecumenical, Historical & Global Perspectives* (Downers Grove, IL: IVP Academic, 2002), 8.

We can return to Bavinck's comment that "the free churches undoubtedly have the promise of the future" but we remember with greater urgency his proviso: "*if* they preserve the catholicity of the Christian faith and the Christian church."[12] Given the rise of Free Church Christianity globally, there is all the more reason for other ecclesial traditions to help the Free Church tradition to embody a greater catholic spirit, learn more catholic doctrine, and enact more catholic practices.[13]

But regardless of whether these global predictions come to pass or flounder, there is a greater future of which we can be assured: the consummative catholicity of the church *will* manifest one day. Williams speaks about this dimension: "The catholic principle is both a present reality and *an eschatological hope*. Its full realization will be on that day when we will drink anew with Christ the cup of communion in the Father's kingdom (Mt 26:29)."[14] That eschatological future informs our work today, for as Kuiper has said, "The most important positive implication of the church's catholicity is its solemn duty to proclaim the gospel of Jesus Christ to all nations and tribes on the face of the globe, and to receive all who believe, of whatever race or color, into the church by holy baptism."[15] This is because we know it is God's missional intention to gather one priestly people into triune communion, a diverse people who assemble in a myriad of local churches found in increasingly manifold places to extol God as they are united by the presence of Christ through his Spirit. Indeed, this is the promised future we behold in Revelation 7:9-10 (ESV): "After this I looked, and behold, a great multitude that no one could number, from every nation, from all tribes and peoples and languages, standing before the throne and before the Lamb, clothed in white robes, with palm branches in their hands, and crying out with a loud voice, 'Salvation belongs to our God who sits on the throne, and to the Lamb!'"

---

[12] Herman Bavinck, "The Catholicity of Christianity and the Church," trans. John Bolt, *Calvin Theological Journal* 27, no. 2 (November 1992): 250.

[13] In fact, I aspire to assist in this important work by providing two follow-up volumes to this one. After this first volume focused on "locating catholicity," which seeks to develop a Free Church doctrine of catholicity, I hope to provide a second volume developing a Free Church catholicity of doctrine ("Learning Catholicity: Doing Free Church Theology with the Catholic Church") and a third volume developing a Free Church catholicity of practice ("Living Catholicity: Doing Free Church Ministry as a Catholic Church").

[14] D. H. Williams, *Retrieving the Tradition and Renewing Evangelicalism: A Primer for Suspicious Protestants* (Grand Rapids, MI: Eerdmans, 1999), 228, emphasis added.

[15] R. B. Kuiper, *The Glorious Body of Christ* (Edinburgh: Banner of Truth, 1966), 65.

In light of this assured catholic future, we close with three words: a confession, a reminder, and a prayer. The confession comes from the 1644 First London Confession and is to be commended as an example of the catholic spirit mixed with evangelical conviction that the Free Church tradition is wonderfully capable of:

> We confess that we know but in part, and that we are ignorant of many things which we desire and seek to know: and if any shall do us that friendly part to show us from the word of God that we see not, we shall have cause to be thankful to God and them. But if any man shall impose upon us anything that we see not to be commanded by our Lord Jesus Christ, we should in his strength, rather embrace all reproaches and tortures of men, to be stripped of all outward comforts, and if it were possible, to die a thousand deaths, rather than to do anything against the least tittle of the truth of God, or against the light of our own consciences.[16]

The reminder comes from Bavinck, who not only felt so acutely the need for the Free Church tradition to preserve the catholicity of the Christian faith and the Christian church but also recognized the attractive and edifying force ecclesial catholicity can be:

> This catholicity of the church, as the Scriptures portray it for us and the early churches exemplify it for us, is breathtaking in its beauty. Whoever becomes enclosed in the narrow circle of a small church or conventicle, does not know it and has never experienced its power and comfort. Such a person shortchanges the love of the Father, the grace of the Son, and the fellowship of the Spirit and incurs a loss of spiritual treasures that cannot be made good by meditation and devotion. . . . By contrast, whoever is able to see beyond this to the countless multitudes who have been purchased by the blood of Christ from every nation and people and age, whoever experiences the powerful strengthening of faith, the wondrous comfort in times of suffering to know that unity with the whole church militant that has been gathered out of the whole human race from the beginning to the end of the world, such a person can never be narrow-minded and narrow-hearted.[17]

---

[16]Quoted in Paul S. Fiddes, "The Church Local and Universal: Catholic and Baptist Perspectives on *Koinonia* Ecclesiology," in *Revisioning, Renewing, Rediscovering the Triune Center*, ed. Derek J. Tidball, Brian S. Harris, and Jason S. Sexton (Eugene, OR: Cascade Books, 2014), 105, language updated.

[17]Bavinck, "Catholicity of Christianity and the Church," 227.

And the prayer comes from Anglican Archbishop William Laud, in hopes that all those who inhabit the Episcopal and Free Church traditions (indeed, all ecclesial traditions found in the one, holy, catholic and apostolic church) would call on our great God and Savior, Jesus Christ, to guide us into all truth, sanctify us by his Spirit, and unify us in the gospel of grace:

> Gracious Father, I humbly pray thee for thy Holy Catholic Church; fill it with all truth, in all truth with all peace; where it is corrupt, purge it; where it is in error, direct it; where it is superstitious, rectify it; where anything is amiss, reform it; where it is right, strengthen and confirm it; where it is in want, furnish it; where it is divided and rent asunder, make up the breaches of it; O Thou Holy One of Israel. Amen.[18]

---

[18]Quoted in Christopher Green, *The Message of the Church: Assemble the People Before Me* (Downers Grove, IL: InterVarsity Press, 2013), 5.

Bibliography

Adams, Edward. "The Shape of the Pauline Churches." In *The Oxford Handbook of Ecclesiology*, edited by Paul Avis, 119-46. Oxford: Oxford University Press, 2018.

Alexander, Loveday C. A. "The Church in the Synoptic Gospels and Acts." In *The Oxford Handbook of Ecclesiology*, edited by Paul Avis, 55-98. Oxford: Oxford University Press, 2018.

Allison, Gregg. *Historical Theology: An Introduction to Christian Doctrine*. Grand Rapids, MI: Zondervan, 2011.

———. "Holy God and Holy People: Pneumatology and Ecclesiology in Intersection." In *Building on the Foundations of Evangelical Theology*, edited by Gregg R. Allison and Stephen J. Wellum, 235-62. Wheaton, IL: Crossway, 2015.

———. *Sojourners and Strangers: The Doctrine of the Church*. Wheaton, IL: Crossway, 2012.

Allison, S. F., ed. *The Fullness of Christ: The Church's Growth into Catholicity*. London: SPCK, 1950.

Armstrong, John H. *Your Church Is Too Small*. Grand Rapids, MI: Zondervan, 2010.

Arnold, Bill T. *Genesis*. Cambridge: Cambridge University Press, 2009.

Ashmall, Donald H. "Spiritual Development and the Free Church Tradition: The Inner Pilgrimage." *Andover Newton Quarterly* 20, no. 3 (January 1980): 141-52.

Auer, Johann. *The Church: The Universal Sacrament of Salvation*. Washington, DC: The Catholic University of America Press, 1993.

Aulén, Gustaf. *Reformation and Catholicity*. Translated by Eric H. Wahlstrom. Philadelphia: Muhlenberg Press, 1961.

Avis, Paul. "Anglican Ecclesiology." In *The Oxford Handbook of Ecclesiology*, edited by Paul Avis, 239-61. Oxford: Oxford University Press, 2018.

———. *Anglicanism and the Christian Church: Theological Resources in Historical Perspective*. Minneapolis: Fortress, 1989.

———. *The Anglican Understanding of the Church*. 2nd ed. London: SPCK, 2013.

———. "Catholic and Reformed?" *Ecclesiology* 12, no. 2 (2016): 139-45.

———. *The Church in the Theology of the Reformers*. Atlanta: John Knox Press, 1980.

———. *The Vocation of Anglicanism*. London: Bloomsbury T&T Clark, 2016.

———. "What Is 'Anglicanism'?" In *The Study of Anglicanism*, edited by Stephen Sykes, John Booty, and Jonathan Knight, 459-76. Rev. ed. Minneapolis: Fortress Press, 1998.

Badcock, Gary D. *The House Where God Lives: Renewing the Doctrine of the Church for Today*. Grand Rapids, MI: Eerdmans, 2009.

Barth, Karl. *Church Dogmatics*. III/1. Translated by G. W. Bromiley, edited by T. F. Torrance. Edinburgh: T&T Clark, 1975.

Bavinck, Herman. "The Catholicity of Christianity and the Church." Translated by John Bolt. *Calvin Theological Journal* 27, no. 2 (November 1992): 220-51.

———. *Reformed Dogmatics: Holy Spirit, Church, and New Creation*. Edited and translated by John Bolt. Grand Rapids, MI: Baker, 2008.

Bebbington, David, Kenneth Dix, and Alan Ruston, eds. *Protestant Nonconformist Texts*. Vol. 3, *The Nineteenth Century*. Aldershot, UK: Ashgate, 2006.

Berkhof, Louis. *Systematic Theology*. New ed. Grand Rapids, MI: Eerdmans, 1996.

Berkouwer, G. C. *The Church*. Grand Rapids, MI: Eerdmans, 1976.

Bettenson, Henry, and Chris Maunder, eds. *The Documents of the Christian Church*. 3rd ed. Oxford: Oxford University Press, 1999.

Bidwell, Kevin J. *"The Church as the Image of the Trinity": A Critical Evaluation of Miroslav Volf's Ecclesial Model*. Eugene, OR: Wipf & Stock, 2011.

Bingham, Matthew C. *Orthodox Radicals: Baptist Identity in the English Revolution*. Oxford: Oxford University Press, 2019.

Birch, Ian. "'The Counsel and Help of One Another': The Origins and Concerns of Early Particular Baptist Churches in Association." *The Baptist Quarterly* 45, no. 1 (January 2013): 4-29.

Bird, Michael F. *Evangelical Theology*. Grand Rapids, MI: Zondervan, 2013.

———. *What Christians Ought to Believe: An Introduction to Christian Doctrine Through the Apostles' Creed*. Grand Rapids, MI: Zondervan, 2016.

Braaten, Carl E. *Mother Church: Ecclesiology and Ecumenism*. Minneapolis: Fortress, 1998.

Braaten, Carl E., and Robert W. Jenson, eds. *The Catholicity of the Reformation*. Grand Rapids, MI: Eerdmans, 1996.

———. *In One Body Through the Cross: The Princeton Proposal for Christian Unity*. Grand Rapids, MI: Eerdmans, 2003.

Bradshaw, Tim. *The Olive Branch: An Evangelical Anglican Doctrine of the Church*. Carlisle, UK: Paternoster Press, 1992.

Brand, Chad Owen, and R. Stanton Norman. "Introduction: Is Polity That Important?" In *Perspectives on Church Government: Five Views of Church Polity*, edited by Chad Owen Brand and R. Stanton Norman, 1-23. Nashville: Broadman & Holman, 2004.

Bray, Gerald L., ed. *Documents of the English Reformation 1526–1701*. Cambridge: James Clarke, 2004.

———. "Why I Am an Anglican and an Evangelical." In *Why We Belong: Evangelical Unity and Denominational Diversity*, edited by Anthony L. Chute, Christopher W. Morgan, and Robert A. Peterson, 65-92. Wheaton, IL: Crossway, 2013.

Briggs, John H. Y. "The Changing Shape of Nonconformity, 1662–2000." In *T&T Clark Companion to Nonconformity*, edited by Stephen J. Pope, 3-26. London: Bloomsbury, 2013.

———. "The Influence of Calvinism on Seventeenth-Century English Baptists." *Baptist History and Heritage* 39, no. 2 (Spring 2004): 8-25.

Brown, R. Kevin. "The Local and Universal Churches: Expressing Catholicity Through Their Reciprocity." In *Visions of Hope: Emerging Theologians and the Future of the Church*, edited by Kevin Ahern, 191-212. Maryknoll, NY: Orbis Books, 2013.

Bruce, F. F. *God's Kingdom and Church*. London: Scripture Union, 1978.

Buschart, W. David. *Exploring Protestant Traditions: An Invitation to Theological Hospitality*. Downers Grove, IL: IVP Academic, 2006.

Calvin, John. *Institutes of the Christian Religion*. Translated by Ford Lewis Battles, edited by John T. McNeill. Louisville, KY: Westminster John Knox, 2001.

———. *Theological Treatises*. Edited and translated by J. K. S. Reid. Louisville, KY: Westminster John Knox, 2001.

Calvin, John, Jacopo Sadoleto, and John C. Olin. *A Reformation Debate: Sadoleto's Letter to the Genevans and Calvin's Reply*. Edited by John C. Olin. Grand Rapids, MI: Baker Book House, 1976.

Cartwright, Michael G. "Radical Reform, Radical Catholicity: John Howard Yoder's Vision of the Faithful Church." In John Howard Yoder. *The Royal Priesthood: Essays Ecclesiastical and Ecumenical*, edited by Michael G. Cartwright. Scottdale, PA: Herald Press, 1998.

Cary, Jeffrey W. *Free Churches and the Body of Christ: Authority, Unity, and Truthfulness*. Eugene, OR: Cascade, 2012.

The Catechism of the Catholic Church. 2nd ed. Vatican: Libreria Editrice Vaticana, 2000.

Chadwick, Henry. "Local and Universal: An Anglican Perspective." *The Jurist* 52, no. 1 (1992): 509-17.

Chapman, Mark D. *Anglicanism: A Very Short Introduction*. Oxford: Oxford University Press, 2006.

———. "Catholicity and the Future of Anglicanism." In *The Hope of Things to Come: Anglicanism and the Future*, edited by Mark Chapman, 102-24. London: Mowbray, 2010.

———. "William Reed Huntington, American Catholicity, and the Chicago-Lambeth Quadrilateral." In *The Lambeth Conference: Theology, History, Polity and Purpose*, edited by Paul Avis and Benjamin M. Guyer, 84-106. London: Bloomsbury, 2017.

Chapman, Mark D., Sathianathan Clarke, and Martyn Percy. "Introduction." In *The Oxford Handbook of Anglican Studies*, edited by Mark D. Chapman, Sathianathan Clarke, and Martyn Percy, 1-18. Oxford: Oxford University Press, 2015.

The Church: Toward a Common Vision. Faith and Order Paper 214. Geneva: WCC Publishing, 2013.

Chute, Anthony L., Nathan A. Finn, and Michael A. G. Haykin. *The Baptist Story: From English Sect to Global Movement*. Nashville: B&H Academic, 2015.

Clary, Ian Hugh. "Hot Protestants: A Taxonomy of English Puritanism." *Puritan Reformed Journal* 2, no. 1 (January 2010): 41-66.

Clines, D. J. A. "Theme in Genesis 1-11." In *I Studied Inscriptions from Before the Flood: Ancient Near Eastern, Literary, and Linguistic Approaches to Genesis 1-11*, edited by Richard S. Hess and David Toshio Tsumura, 285-309. Winona Lake, IN: Eisenbrauns, 1994.

Clowney, Edmund P. "The Biblical Theology of the Church." In *The Church in the Bible and the World*, edited by D. A. Carson, 13-87. Grand Rapids, MI: Baker, 1987.

———. *The Church*. Downers Grove, IL: InterVarsity Press, 1995.

———. *The Doctrine of the Church*. Philadelphia: Presbyterian and Reformed, 1974.

Coffey, John. "Church and State, 1550–1750: The Emergence of Dissent." In *T&T Clark Companion to Nonconformity*, edited by Stephen J. Pope, 47-74. London: Bloomsbury, 2013.

Coffey, John, and Paul C. H. Lim. "Introduction." In *The Cambridge Companion to Puritanism*, edited by John Coffey and Paul C. H. Lim, 1-17. Cambridge: Cambridge University Press, 2008.

Cole, Graham. "The Doctrine of the Church: Towards Conceptual Clarification." In *Church, Worship and the Local Congregation*, edited by B. G. Webb, 3-17. Homebush West, New South Wales: Lancer, 1987.

———. *He Who Gives Life: The Doctrine of the Holy Spirit*. Wheaton, IL: Crossway, 2007.

Confessing the One Faith, Faith and Order Paper 153. Geneva: WCC Publications, 1991.

Congar, Yves. *Diversity and Communion*. Translated by John Bowden. London: SCM Press, 1984.

———. *Divided Christendom: A Catholic Study of the Problem of Reunion*. Translated by M. A. Bousfield. London: Centenary Press, 1939.

———. *The Mystery of the Church*. Translated by A. V. Littledale. Baltimore: Helicon Press, 1960.

Cowan, Steven B. "Introduction." In *Who Runs the Church? Four Views on Church Government*, edited by Steven B. Cowan, 7-18. Grand Rapids, MI: Zondervan, 2004.

Cullman, Oscar. *Unity Through Diversity*. Translated by M. Eugene Boring. Philadelphia: Fortress, 1988.

Daley, Brian E. "The Ministry of Primacy and the Communion of Churches." In *Church Unity and the Papal Office: An Ecumenical Dialogue on John Paul II's Encyclical Ut Unum Sint*, edited by Carl E. Braaten and Robert W. Jenson, 27-58. Grand Rapids, MI: Eerdmans, 2001.

Davies, John G. "Pentecost and Glossolalia." *The Journal of Theological Studies* 3, no. 2 (October 1952): 228-31.

DeGroot, Alfred T. "A People Under the Word: Historical Background." In *The Concept of the Believers' Church: Addresses from the 1968 Louisville Conference*, edited by James Leo Garrett Jr., 185-206. Scottdale, PA: Herald Press, 1969.

Dever, Mark E. "A Catholic Church." In *The Church: One, Holy, Catholic, and Apostolic*, by Richard D. Phillips, Philip G. Ryken, and Mark E. Dever. Phillipsburg, NJ: P&R, 2004.

Dever, Mark, and Jonathan Leeman, "Preface." In *Baptist Foundations: Church Government for an Anti-Institutional Age*, edited by Mark Dever and Jonathan Leeman, xv-xxii. Nashville: B&H Academic, 2015.

Di Berardino, Angelo, ed. *We Believe in One Holy Catholic and Apostolic Church*. Downers Grove, IL: IVP Academic, 2010.

Dix, Gregory, ed. *Catholicity: A Study in the Conflict of Christian Traditions in the West*. London: Dacre, 1947.

D'Onofrio, Giulio. *History of Theology*. Vol. 2, *The Middle Ages*. Translated by Matthew J. O'Connell. Collegeville, MN: Liturgical Press, 2008.

Dulles, Avery. *The Catholicity of the Church*. Oxford: Oxford University Press, 1985.

Durnbaugh, Donald F. *The Believers' Church: The History and Character of Radical Protestantism*. Scottdale, PA: Herald Press, 1985.

———, ed. *Every Need Supplied: Mutual Aid and Christian Community in the Free Churches, 1525–1675*. Philadelphia: Temple University Press, 1974.

———. "Free Churches, Baptists, and Ecumenism: Origins and Implications." In *Baptists and Ecumenism*, edited by William Jerry Boney and Glenn A. Igleheart, 3-20. Valley Forge, PA: Judson Press, 1980.

Early, Joseph, Jr. *Readings in Baptist History: Four Centuries of Selected Documents*. Nashville: B&H, 2008.

Easley, Kendell H. "The Church in Acts and Revelation: New Testament Bookends." In *The Community of Jesus: A Theology of the Church*, edited by Kendell H. Easley and Christopher W. Morgan, 65-102. Nashville: B&H Academic, 2013.

Eglinton, James. *Trinity and Organism: Towards a New Reading of Herman Bavinck's Organic Motif*. London: T&T Clark, 2012.

Emerson, Matthew Y., and R. Lucas Stamps. "Baptists and the Catholicity of the Church: Toward an Evangelical Baptist Catholicity." *Journal of Baptist Studies* 7 (2015): 42-66.

———. "Toward an Evangelical Baptist Catholicity." In *Baptists and the Christian Tradition: Toward an Evangelical Baptist Catholicity*, edited by Matthew Y. Emerson, Christopher W. Morgan, and R. Lucas Stamps, 351-56. Nashville: B&H Academic, 2020.

Emerson, Matthew Y., Christopher W. Morgan, and R. Lucas Stamps. "Baptists and the Christian Tradition: What Hath Nicaea to Do with Nashville?"

In *Baptists and the Christian Tradition: Toward an Evangelical Baptist Catholicity*, edited by Matthew Y. Emerson, Christopher W. Morgan, and R. Lucas Stamps, 1-4. Nashville: B&H Academic, 2020.

Essick, John Inscore, and Mark S. Medley. "Local Catholicity: The Bodies and Places Where Jesus Is (Found)." *Review & Expositor* 112, no. 1 (February 2015): 47-59.

Estep, W. R. "Balthasar Hubmaier: Martyr Without Honor." *Baptist History and Heritage* 13, no. 2 (April 1978): 5-10.

Evangelical Convictions: A Theological Exposition of the Statement of Faith of the Evangelical Free Church of America. Minneapolis: Free Church Publications, 2011.

Evans, G. R., and J. Robert Wright, eds. *The Anglican Tradition: A Handbook of Sources*. Minneapolis: Fortress, 1991.

Fahey, Michael A. "The Catholicity of the Church in the New Testament and in the Early Patristic Period." *The Jurist* 52, no. 1 (1992): 44-70.

Ferguson, Everett. *The Church of Christ: A Biblical Ecclesiology for Today*. Grand Rapids, MI: Eerdmans, 1996.

———. *The Rule of Faith: A Guide*. Eugene, OR: Cascade Books, 2015.

Feurth, Patrick W. *The Concept of Catholicity in the Documents of the World Council of Churches 1948–1968*. Rome: Editrace Anselmiana, 1973.

Fiddes, Paul. "The Church Local and Universal: Catholic and Baptist Perspectives on *Koinonia* Ecclesiology." In *Revisioning, Renewing, Rediscovering the Triune Center*, edited by Derek J. Tidball, Brian S. Harris, and Jason S. Sexton. Eugene, OR: Cascade Books, 2014.

———. "A Fourth Strand of the Reformation." *Ecclesiology* 13, no. 2 (2017): 153-59.

Finger, Thomas N. *A Contemporary Anabaptist Theology: Biblical, Historical, Constructive*. Downers Grove, IL: InterVarsity Press, 2004.

Finn, Nathan A. "Contesting *Catholicity*: Some Conservative Reflections on Curtis Freeman's Theology for 'Other Baptists.'" *Southeastern Theological Review* 6, no. 2 (2015): 151-70.

FitzGerald, Thomas E. *The Ecumenical Movement: An Introductory History*. Westport, CT: Praeger, 2004.

Flew, R. Newton and Rupert E. Davies, eds. *The Catholicity of Protestantism: Being a Report Presented to His Grace the Archbishop of Canterbury by a Group of Free Churchmen*. London: Lutterworth Press, 1950.

Freeman, Curtis W. "A Confession for Catholic Baptists." In *Ties That Bind: Life Together in the Baptist Vision*, edited by Gary Furr and Curtis W. Freeman, 83-97. Macon, GA: Smyth & Helwys, 1994.

———. *Contesting Catholicity: Theology for Other Baptists*. Waco, TX: Baylor University Press, 2014.

———. "Where Two or Three Are Gathered: Communion Ecclesiology in the Free Church." *Perspectives in Religious Studies* 31, no. 3 (Fall 2004): 259-72.

Freeman, Curtis W., James Wm. McClendon Jr., and C. Rosalee Velloso da Silva, eds. *Baptist Roots: A Reader in the Theology of a Christian People*. Valley Forge, PA: Judson Press, 1999.

Friesen, John. J., ed. *Peter Riedemann's Hutterite Confession of Faith*. Scottdale, PA: Herald Press, 1999.

Garrett, James Leo, Jr. "Preface." In *The Concept of the Believers' Church: Addresses from the 1968 Louisville Conference*, edited by James Leo Garrett Jr., 5-9. Scottdale, PA: Herald Press, 1969.

———. "Restitution and Dissent Among Early English Baptists: Part I." *Baptist History and Heritage* 12, no. 4 (October 1977): 198-210.

———. *Systematic Theology*. Vol. 2. 2nd ed. Eugene, OR: Wipf & Stock, 2014.

Gassmann, Günther. "The Church—Local and Catholic: A Lutheran Perspective." *The Jurist* 52, no. 1 (1992): 518-24.

Gatiss, Lee. "Anglicanism and John Owen." *Crux* 52, no. 7 (Spring 2016): 44-53.

Gazal, Andre. "Reforming Catholicity in Tudor England: John Jewel's Doctrine of the Universal Church." In *Reforming the Catholic Tradition: The Whole Word for the Whole Church*, edited by Joseph Minich, 33-46. Leesburg, VA: Davenant Institute, 2019.

George, Timothy. "Evangelicals and Others." *First Things* 160 (February 2006): 15-23.

———. "Foreword." In *Baptists and the Christian Tradition: Toward an Evangelical Baptist Catholicity*, edited by Matthew Y. Emerson, Christopher W. Morgan, and R. Lucas Stamps, xv-xviii. Nashville: B&H Academic, 2020.

———. "Introduction." In *John Calvin and the Church: A Prism of Reform*, edited by Timothy George. Louisville, KY: Westminster John Knox, 1990.

———. "Is Jesus a Baptist?" *First Things*. August 12, 2013. www.firstthings.com/web-exclusives/2013/08/is-jesus-a-baptist.

———. "The Priesthood of All Believers." In *The People of God: Essays on the Believers' Church*, edited by Paul Basden and David S. Dockery, 85-95. Nashville: Broadman Press, 1991.

———. "The Reformation Roots of the Baptist Tradition." *Review & Expositor* 86, no. 1 (Winter 1989): 9-22.

———. "Retrieval for the Sake of Renewal." *Reformed Faith & Practice* 2, no. 2 (September 2017): 72-73.

———. "The Sacramentality of the Church: An Evangelical Baptist Perspective." *Pro Ecclesia* 12, no. 3 (Summer 2003): 309-23.

———. "Toward an Evangelical Ecclesiology." *Evangelical Review of Theology* 41, no. 2 (April 2017): 100-118.

———. "Why I Am an Evangelical and a Baptist." In *Why We Belong: Evangelical Unity and Denominational Diversity*, edited by Anthony L. Chute, Christopher W. Morgan, and Robert A. Peterson, 93-109. Wheaton, IL: Crossway, 2013.

George, Timothy, and Denise George, eds. *Baptist Confessions, Covenants, and Catechisms*. Nashville: Broadman & Holman, 1999.

Gibaut, John St-Helier. "Catholicity, Faith and Order, and the Unity of the Church." *Ecumenical Review* 63, no. 2 (July 2011): 177-85.

Gilchrist, Paul R. *Distinctives of Biblical Presbyterianism*. Atlanta: World Reformed Fellowship, 2002.

Goldsworthy, Graeme. *According to Plan: The Unfolding Revelation of God in the Bible*. Downers Grove, IL: IVP Academic, 1991.

Gombis, Timothy G. *The Drama of Ephesians: Participating in the Triumph of God*. Downers Grove, IL: IVP Academic, 2010.

González, Justo L. *The Story of Christianity: The Early Church to the Present Day*. Peabody, MA: Prince Press, 2007.

Green, Christopher. *The Message of the Church: Assemble the People Before Me*. Downers Grove, IL: InterVarsity Press, 2013.

Greggs, Tom. *Dogmatic Ecclesiology: The Priestly Catholicity of the Church*. Grand Rapids, MI: Baker Academic, 2019.

Guarino, Thomas G. *Vincent of Lerins and the Development of Christian Doctrine*. Grand Rapids, MI: Baker Academic, 2013.

Haar, Miriam. "The Struggle for an Organic, Conciliar and Diverse Church: Models of Church Unity in Earlier Stages of the Ecumenical Dialogue." In *Ecumenical Ecclesiology: Unity, Diversity, and Otherness in a Fragmented World*, edited by Gesa Elsbeth Thiessen, 49-61. London: T&T Clark, 2009.

Haight, Roger. *Christian Community in History*. Vol. 2. New York: Continuum, 2005.

Hallig, Jason Valeriano. *We Are Catholic: Catholic, Catholicity, and Catholicization*. Eugene, OR: Wipf & Stock, 2016.

Harmon, Steven R. *Baptist Identity and the Ecumenical Future*. Waco, TX: Baylor University Press, 2016.

———. "Baptists, Bapto-Catholic Baptists, and the Christian Tradition." In *Baptists and the Christian Tradition: Toward an Evangelical Baptist Catholicity*, edited by Matthew Y. Emerson, Christopher W. Morgan, and R. Lucas Stamps, 357-72. Nashville: B&H Academic, 2020.

———. "The Nicene Faith and the Catholicity of the Church: Evangelical Retrieval and the Problem of Magisterium." In *Evangelicals and Nicene Faith: Reclaiming the Apostolic Witness*, edited by Timothy George, 74-92. Grand Rapids, MI: Baker Academic, 2011.

———. "Qualitative Catholicity in the Ignatian Correspondence—and the New Testament: The Fallacies of a Restorationist Hermeneutic." *Perspectives in Religious Studies* 38, no. 1 (Spring 2011): 33-45.

———. *Towards Baptist Catholicity: Essays on Tradition and the Baptist Vision*. Eugene, OR: Wipf & Stock, 2006.

———. "Why Baptist Catholicity, and by What Authority?" *Pro Ecclesia* 18, no. 4 (Fall 2009): 386-92.

Harrison, Paul H. *Authority and Power in the Free Church Tradition*. Carbondale, IL: Southern Illinois University Press, 1959.

Hatch, Derek C. *Thinking with the Church: Toward a Renewal of Baptist Theology*. Eugene, OR: Cascade Books, 2018.

Hays, J. Daniel. *From Every People and Nation: A Biblical Theology of Race*. Downers Grove, IL: InterVarsity Press, 2003.

Hegeman, David Bruce. *Plowing in Hope: Toward a Biblical Theology of Culture*. 2nd ed. Moscow, ID: Canon Press, 2007.

Hesselink, I. John. "Calvin's Theology." In *The Cambridge Companion to John Calvin*, edited by Donald K. McKim, 74-92. Cambridge: Cambridge University Press, 2004.

Hiebert, Theodore. "Babel: Babble or Blueprint? Calvin, Cultural Diversity, and the Interpretation of Genesis 11:1-9." In *Reformed Theology: Identity and Ecumenicity II: Biblical Interpretation in the Reformed Tradition*, edited by Wallace M. Alston Jr. and Michael Welker, 127-49. Grand Rapids, MI: Eerdmans, 2007.

———. "Cultural Diversity: Punishment or Plan? Two Interpretations of the Story of the Tower of Babel." In *Toppling the Tower: Essays on Babel and Diversity*, edited by Theodore Hiebert, 1-10. Chicago: McCormick Theological Seminary, 2004.

———. "The Tower of Babel and the Origin of the World's Cultures." *Journal of Biblical Literature* 126, no. 1 (Spring 2007): 29-58.

Hilburn, Glenn O. "Medieval Views of the Church." In *The People of God: Essays on the Believers' Church*, edited by Paul Basden and David S. Dockery, 193-208. Nashville: Broadman Press, 1991.

Hinchliff, Peter. "Church-State Relations." In *The Study of Anglicanism*, edited by Stephen Sykes, John Booty, and Jonathan Knight, 392-404. Rev. ed. Minneapolis: Fortress, 1998.

Hinson, E. Glenn. "The Authority of Tradition: A Baptist View." In *The Free Church and the Early Church: Bridging the Historical and Theological Divide*, edited by D. H. Williams, 141-62. Grand Rapids, MI: Eerdmans, 2002.

Hodgson, Leonard. *The Doctrine of the Church as Held and Taught in the Church of England*. Oxford: Blackwell, 1946.

Holmes, Stephen R. *Baptist Theology*. London: T&T Clark, 2012.

Horst, Irvin Buckwalter. *The Radical Brethren: Anabaptism and the English Reformation to 1558*. Nieuwkoop, Netherlands: B. De Graaf, 1972.

Hütter, Reinhard. *Bound to Be Free: Evangelical Catholic Engagements in Ecclesiology, Ethics, and Ecumenism*. Grand Rapids, MI: Eerdmans, 2004.

Jonker, W. B. "Catholicity, Unity and Truth." In *Catholicity and Secession: A Dilemma?*, edited by Paul G. Schrotenboer, 16-27. Kampen, Netherlands: J. H. Kok, 1992.

Jorgenson, Cameron H. "Bapto-Catholicism: Recovering Tradition and Reconsidering the Baptist Identity." PhD diss., Baylor University, 2008.

Kärkkäinen, Veli-Matti. *An Introduction to Ecclesiology: Ecumenical, Historical & Global Perspectives*. Downers Grove, IL: IVP Academic, 2002.

Kasper, Walter. "'Credo Unam Sanctam Ecclesiam'—the Relationship Between the Catholic and the Protestant Principles in Fundamental Ecclesiology." In *Receptive Ecumenism and the Call to Catholic Learning: Exploring a Way for Contemporary Ecumenism*, edited by Paul. D. Murray, 78-88. Oxford: Oxford University Press, 2008.

Kater, John L., Jr. "Whose Church Is It Anyway? Anglican 'Catholicity' Re-examined." *Anglican Theological Review* 76, no. 1 (Winter 1994): 44-60.

Kaye, Bruce. "Reality and Form in Catholicity." *Journal of Anglican Studies* 10, no. 1 (June 2012): 3-12.

Kelley, Douglas. "The Catholicity of Calvin's Theology." In *Tributes to John Calvin: A Celebration of His Quincentenary*, edited by David W. Hall, 189-216. Phillipsburg, NJ: P&R, 2010.

Kelley, J. N. D. *Early Christian Creeds*. 3rd ed. London: Longman, 1972.

Kiwiet, John J. "Anabaptist Views of the Church." In *The People of God: Essays on the Believers' Church*, edited by Paul Basden and David S. Dockery, 225-34. Nashville: Broadman Press, 1991.

Klaasen, Walter. "A Fire That Spread: Anabaptist Beginnings." *Christian History Magazine* 4, no. 1 (1985): 7-9.

Klager, Andrew P. "Balthasar Hubmaier's Use of the Church Fathers: Availability, Access and Interaction." *Mennonite Quarterly Review* 84, no. 1 (January 2010): 5-65.

Knapp, Henry M. "John Owen, on Schism and the Nature of the Church." *The Westminster Theological Journal* 72, no. 2 (Fall 2010): 333-58.

Koskela, Douglas M. "Holiness and Catholicity: A Fruitful Tension for the Wesleyan Tradition." *Wesleyan Theological Journal* 49, no. 1 (Spring 2014): 67-77.

Köstenberger, Andreas. "The Church According to the Gospels." In *The Community of Jesus: A Theology of the Church*, edited by Kendell H. Easley and Christopher W. Morgan, 35-63. Nashville: B&H Academic, 2013.

Köstenberger, Andreas J., and Peter T. O'Brien, *Salvation to the Ends of the Earth: A Biblical Theology of Mission*. Downers Grove, IL: InterVarsity Press, 2001.

Kuiper, R. B. *The Glorious Body of Christ*. Edinburgh: Banner of Truth, 1966.

La Due, William J. *The Trinity Guide to the Christian Church*. New York: Continuum, 2006.

Larsen, Timothy. "Defining and Locating Evangelicalism." In *The Cambridge Companion to Evangelical Theology*, edited by Timothy Larsen and Daniel J. Treier, 1-14. Cambridge: Cambridge University Press, 2007.

Lash, Nicholas. *Believing Three Ways in One God: A Reading of the Apostles' Creed*. Notre Dame, IN: University of Notre Dame Press, 1993.

Latourette, Kenneth Scott. "A People in the World: Historical Background." In *The Concept of the Believers' Church: Addresses from the 1968 Louisville Conference*, edited by James Leo Garrett Jr., 241-49. Scottdale, PA: Herald Press, 1969.

Laurense, Leo. "The Catholicity of the Anabaptists." *Mennonite Quarterly Review* 38, no. 3 (July 1964): 266-79.

Leeman, Jonathan. "Are You a Universal Church-er or a Local Church-er?" The Gospel Coalition. July 27, 2016. www.thegospelcoalition.org/reviews/the-church/.

———. "A Baptist View of the Royal Priesthood of All Believers." *The Southern Baptist Journal of Theology* 23, no. 1 (Spring 2019): 113-35.

———. "The Church: Universal and Local." The Gospel Coalition. www.thegospelcoalition.org/essay/the-church-universal-and-local/.

———. "A Congregational Approach to Catholicity: Independence and Interdependence." In *Baptist Foundations: Church Government for an Anti-Institutional Age*, edited by Mark Dever and Jonathan Leeman, 367-80. Nashville: B&H Academic, 2015.

———. "A Congregational Approach to Unity, Holiness, and Apostolicity: Faith and Order." In *Baptist Foundations: Church Government for an Anti-Institutional Age*, edited by Mark Dever and Jonathan Leeman, 333-66. Nashville: B&H Academic, 2015.

———. *Don't Fire Your Church Members: The Case for Congregationalism*. Nashville: B&H Academic, 2016.

———. *One Assembly: Rethinking the Multisite and Multiservice Church Models*. Wheaton, IL: Crossway, 2020.

———. *Political Church: The Local Assembly as Embassy of Christ's Rule*. Downers Grove, IL: IVP Academic, 2016.

———. *The Rule of Love: How the Local Church Should Reflect God's Love and Authority*. Wheaton, IL: Crossway, 2018.

Leer, Teun van der. "Which Future Church (Form)? A Plea for a 'Believers Church' Ecclesiology." *Journal of European Baptist Studies* 9, no. 3 (May 2009): 40-51.

Leith, John H., ed. *The Creeds of the Church*. Rev. ed. Richmond, VA: John Knox Press, 1973.

Littell, Franklin H. "The Claims of the Free Churches." *The Christian Century* 78, no. 14 (April 5, 1961): 417-19.

———. "The Concept of the Believers' Church." In *The Concept of the Believers' Church: Addresses from the 1968 Louisville Conference*, edited by James Leo Garrett Jr., 15-34. Scottdale, PA: Herald Press, 1969.

———. *The Free Church*. Boston: Starr King Press, 1957.

———. "The Historical Free Church Defined." *Brethren Life and Thought* 50, nos. 3–4 (Summer–Fall 2005): 51-65.

———. *The Origins of Sectarian Protestantism: A Study of the Anabaptist View of the Church*. New York: Macmillan Company, 1964.

Littlejohn, W. Bradford. *The Mercersburg Theology and the Quest for Reformed Catholicity*. Eugene, OR: Pickwick, 2009.

Louth, Andrew. "Unity and Diversity in the Church of the Fourth Century." In *Doctrinal Diversity: Varieties of Early Christianity*, edited by Everett Ferguson, 1-17. New York: Garland, 1999.

Lumpkin, William L. and Bill J. Leonard, eds. *Baptist Confessions of Faith*. 2nd rev. ed. Valley Forge, PA: Judson Press, 2011.

Mabry, Eddie. *Balthasar Hubmaier's Doctrine of the Church*. Lanham, MD: University Press of America, 1994.

Maclear, James Fulton. "The Birth of the Free Church Tradition." *Church History* 26, no. 2 (June 1957): 99-131.

Macoskey, Robert A. "The Contemporary Relevance of Balthasar Hubmaier's Concept of the Church." *Foundations* 6, no. 2 (April 1963): 99-122.

Marthaler, Berard L. *The Creed*. Mystic, CT: Twenty-Third Publications, 1987.

McClendon, James William, Jr. "Balthasar Hubmaier, Catholic Anabaptist." *The Mennonite Quarterly Review* 65, no. 1 (January 1991): 20-33.

Meyendorff, John. *Catholicity and the Church*. Crestwood, NY: St. Vladimir's Seminary Press, 1983.

Michener, Ronald T. *Postliberal Theology: A Guide for the Perplexed*. London: Bloomsbury T&T Clark, 2013.

Middelmann, Udo W. *The Innocence of God*. Colorado Springs, CO: Paternoster, 2007.

Milne, Bruce. *Dynamic Diversity: Bridging Class, Age, Race and Gender in the Church*. Downers Grove, IL: IVP Academic, 2007.

Milner, Benjamin Charles. *Calvin's Doctrine of the Church*. Leiden: Brill, 1970.

Minear, Paul S. *Images of the Church in the New Testament*. Philadelphia: Westminster Press, 1960.

Morris, Jeremy. "The Unity We Seek: Prospects for the Local Church." In *The Unity We Have and the Unity We Seek*, edited by Jeremy Morris and Morris Sagovsky, 91-117. London: T&T Clark, 2003.

Mouw, Richard J. "The Problem of Authority in Evangelical Christianity." In *Church Unity and the Papal Office: An Ecumenical Dialogue on John Paul II's Encyclical Ut Unum Sint*, edited by Carl E. Braaten and Robert W. Jenson, 124-41. Grand Rapids, MI: Eerdmans, 2001.

Murray, Paul D. "Redeeming Catholicity for a Globalising Age: The Sacramentality of the Church." In *Believing in Community: Ecumenical Reflections on the Church*, edited by Peter De Mey, Pieter De Witte, and Gerard Mannion, 229-40. Leuven: Uitgeverij Peeters, 2013.

Nataf, Francis. *Redeeming Relevance in the Book of Numbers: Explorations in Text and Meaning*. New York: Urim Publications, 2014.

The Nature and Purpose of the Church: A Stage on the Way to a Common Statement. Faith and Order Paper 181. Bialystok, Poland: Orthdruk, 1998.

Neuner, Josef. "The Idea of Catholicity—Concept and History." In *The Church: Readings in Theology*, edited by Gustave Wegel, 61-91. New York: P. J. Kenedy & Sons, 1963.

Newman, Elizabeth. *Attending to the Wounds on Christ's Body: Teresa's Scriptural Vision*. Eugene, OR: Cascade Books, 2012.

———. "Remembering How to Remember: Harmon's Subversive Orthodoxy." *Pro Ecclesia* 18, no. 4 (Fall 2009): 375-80.

Newman, John Henry. *An Essay on the Development of Christian Doctrine*. New York: Cosimo Classics, 2007.

Norris, Richard A. "Episcopacy." In *The Study of Anglicanism*, edited by Stephen Sykes, John Booty, and Jonathan Knight, 333-50. Rev. ed. Minneapolis: Fortress, 1998.

Oberman, Heiko A. *The Dawn of the Reformation: Essays in Late Medieval and Early Reformation Thought*. Edinburgh: T&T Clark, 1992.

O'Brien, P. T. "The Church as Heavenly and Eschatological Entity." In *The Church in the Bible and the World*, edited by D. A. Carson, 88-119. Grand Rapids, MI: Baker, 1987.

Oded, B. "The Table of Nations (Genesis 10): A Socio-cultural Approach." *Zeitschrift Für Die Alttestamentliche Wissenschaft* 98, no. 1 (1986): 14-31.

O'Donovan, Oliver. *Resurrection and Moral Order: An Outline for Evangelical Ethics*. Grand Rapids, MI: Eerdmans, 1986.

O'Grady, Colm. *The Church in Catholic Theology: Dialogue with Karl Barth*. London: Geoffrey Chapman, 1969.

Olson, Roger. *The Mosaic of Christian Belief: Twenty Centuries of Unity and Diversity*. Downers Grove, IL: IVP Academic, 2002.

Ortlund, Gavin. *Finding the Right Hills to Die On: The Case for Theological Triage*. Wheaton, IL: Crossway, 2020.

Owen, John. *The True Nature of a Gospel Church and Its Government*. Edited by John Huxtable. London: James Clarke, 1947.

———. *The Works of John Owen*. Vol. 15, edited by William H. Gould. Edinburgh: T&T Clark, 1862.

Paget, James Carleton. "The Vison of the Church in the Apostolic Fathers." In *A Vision for the Church: Studies in Early Christian Ecclesiology in Honour of J. P. M. Sweet*, edited by Markus Bockmuehl and Michael B. Thompson, 193-206. Edinburgh: T&T Clark, 1997.

Pelikan, Jaroslav. *The Christian Tradition: A History of the Development of Doctrine*. 5 vols. Chicago: University of Chicago Press, 1971–89.

Peters, Greg. "Confessions, Creeds, and Reformed Catholicity—an Anglican Perspective." Paper presented at the Evangelical Theological Society. Denver, November 13–15, 2018.

Pickering, W. S. F. "Sociology of Anglicanism." In *The Study of Anglicanism*, edited by Stephen Sykes, John Booty, and Jonathan Knight, 405-26. Rev. ed. Minneapolis: Fortress, 1998.

Plantinga, Cornelius. *Not the Way It's Supposed to Be: A Breviary of Sin*. Grand Rapids, MI: Eerdmans, 1995.

Pobee, John S. "Non-Anglo Saxon Anglicanism." In *The Study of Anglicanism*, edited by Stephen Sykes, John Booty, and Jonathan Knight, 446-58. Rev. ed. Minneapolis: Fortress, 1998.

Priestly, David T. "Believers' Assembly or Believers Church: A Seventeenth-Century Rationale for Congregational Polity." In *The Believers Church: A Voluntary Church*, edited by William H. Brackney, 9-24. Kitchener, Ontario: Pandora Press, 1998.

Putman, Rhyne R. *In Defense of Doctrine: Evangelicalism, Theology, and Scripture*. Minneapolis: Fortress, 2015.

Radmacher, Earl D. *The Nature of the Church*. Portland, OR: Western Baptist Press, 1972.

Ramm, Bernard. *The Pattern of Religious Authority*. Grand Rapids, MI: Eerdmans, 1959.

Ramsey, Michael. *The Gospel and the Catholic Church*. Cambridge, MA: Cowley Publications, 1990.

Rausch, Thomas P. *Towards a Truly Catholic Church: An Ecclesiology for the Third Millennium*. Collegeville, MN: Liturgical Press, 2005.

Regier, P. K., ed. *Proceedings of the Study Conference on the Believers' Church*. Newton, KS: Mennonite Press, 1955.

Reymond, Robert. "The Presbytery-Led Church." In *Perspectives on Church Government: Five Views of Church Polity*, edited by Chad Owen Brand and R. Stanton Norman, 87-156. Nashville: Broadman & Holman, 2004.

Ruddy, Christopher. *The Local Church: Tillard and the Future of Catholic Ecclesiology*. New York: Crossroad, 2006.

Runia, Klaas. "Catholicity in the Reformed Confessions and in Reformed Theology." In *Catholicity and Secession: A Dilemma?*, edited by Paul G. Schrotenboer, 58-75. Kampen, Netherlands: J. H. Kok, 1992.

Rupp, Gordon. *Protestant Catholicity: Two Lectures*. London: Epworth Press, 1960.

Schnackenburg, Rudolf. *The Church in the New Testament*. New York: Herder & Herder, 1965.

Schwöbel, Christoph. "The Creature of the Word: Recovering the Ecclesiology of the Reformers." In *On Being the Church: Essays on the Christian Community*, edited by Colin E Gunton and Daniel W. Hardy, 110-55. Edinburgh: T &T Clark, 1989.

Scott, James M. *Paul and the Nations: The Old Testament and Jewish Background of Paul's Mission to the Nations with Special Reference to the Destination of Galatians*. Tübingen: Mohr Siebeck, 1995.

Smith, David. "What Hope After Babel? Diversity and Community in Gen 11:1-9; Exod 1:1-14; Zeph 3:1-13 and Acts 2:1-3." *Horizons in Biblical Theology* 18, no. 2 (December 1996): 169-91.

St. Amat, C. Penrose. "Reformation Views of the Church." In *The People of God: Essays on the Believers' Church*, edited by Paul Basden and David S. Dockery, 209-24. Nashville: Broadman Press, 1991.

Steward, Alistair C. *The Original Bishops: Office and Order in the First Christian Communities*. Grand Rapids, MI: Baker Academic, 2014.

Strong, Augustus Hopkins. *Systematic Theology*. Philadelphia: The Judson Press, 1907.

Sung, Elizabeth Yao-Hwa. "'Race' and Ethnicity Discourse and the Christian Doctrine of Humanity: A Systematic Sociological and Theological Appraisal." PhD diss., Trinity Evangelical Divinity School, 2011.

Sweeney, Douglas A. "Why I Am an Evangelical and a Lutheran." In *Why We Belong: Evangelical Unity and Denominational Diversity*, edited by Anthony L. Chute, Christopher W. Morgan, and Robert A. Peterson, 111-32. Wheaton, IL: Crossway, 2013.

Sykes, Stephen. "The Papacy and Power: An Anglican Perspective." In *Church Unity and the Papal Office: An Ecumenical Dialogue on John Paul II's Encyclical Ut Unum Sint*, edited by Carl E. Braaten and Robert W. Jenson, 59-75. Grand Rapids, MI: Eerdmans, 2001.

———. *Unashamed Anglicanism*. Nashville: Abingdon Press, 1995.

Tabb, Brian J. *All Things New: Revelation as Canonical Capstone*. Downers Grove, IL: IVP Academic, 2019.

Tanner, Mary "The Ecumenical Dimension of the Lambeth Conference." In *The Lambeth Conference: Theology, History, Polity and Purpose*, edited by Paul Avis and Benjamin M. Guyer, 358-87. London: Bloomsbury, 2017.

Taylor, L. Roy. "Presbyterianism." In *Who Runs the Church? Four Views on Church Government*, edited by Steven B. Cowan, 73-98. Grand Rapids, MI: Zondervan, 2004.

———. "A Presbyterian's Response." In *Who Runs the Church? Four Views on Church Government*, edited by Steven B. Cowan, 42-48, 160-67, 229-36. Grand Rapids, MI: Zondervan, 2004.

Thomas, Philip H. E. "Doctrine of the Church." In *The Study of Anglicanism*, edited by Stephen Sykes, John Booty, and Jonathan Knight, 249-61. Rev. ed. Minneapolis: Fortress, 1998.

Thompson, David M., J. H. Y. Briggs, and John Munsey Turner, eds. *Protestant Nonconformist Texts*. Vol. 4, *The Twentieth Century*. Aldershot, UK: Ashgate, 2007.

Tie, Peter L. *Restore Unity, Recover Identity, Refine Orthopraxy: The Believers' Priesthood in the Ecclesiology of James Leo Garrett Jr.* Eugene, OR: Wipf & Stock, 2012.

Tillard, Jean Marie. *Church of Churches: The Ecclesiology of Communion*. Translated by R. C. De Peaux. Collegeville, MN: Liturgical Press, 1992.

———. *L'Église locale: Ecclésiologie de communion et catholicité*. Paris: Cerf, 1995.

Toon, Peter. "Episcopalianism." In *Who Runs the Church? Four Views on Church Government*, edited by Steven B. Cowan, 21-41. Grand Rapids, MI: Zondervan, 2004.

Torrance, J. B. "Authority, Scripture and Tradition." *Evangelical Quarterly* 59, no. 3 (July 1987): 245-51.

Townsend, Henry. *The Claims of the Free Churches*. London: Hodder and Stoughton, 1949.

Treat, Jeremy R. *The Crucified King: Atonement and Kingdom in Biblical and Systematic Theology*. Grand Rapids, MI: Zondervan, 2014.

Trueman, Carl R. *The Creedal Imperative*. Wheaton, IL: Crossway, 2012.

———. *John Owen: Reformed Catholic, Renaissance Man*. Aldershot, UK: Ashgate, 2007.

Turnbull, Richard. *Anglican and Evangelical?* London: Continuum, 2007.

Turner, Philip. "Episcopal Authority in a Divided Church: On the Crisis of Anglican Identity." *Pro Ecclesia* 8, no. 1 (Winter 1999): 23-50.

Van der Borght, Eddy. "Evangelical Ecclesiology as an Answer to Ethnic Impaired Christian Community? An Inquiry into the Theology of Miroslav Volf." In *Ecumenical Ecclesiology: Unity, Diversity and Otherness in a Fragmented World*, ed. Gesa Elsbeth Thiessen, 161-74. London: T&T Clark, 2009.

Van Gelder, Craig. *The Essence of the Church: A Community Created by the Spirit*. Grand Rapids, MI: Baker Books, 2000.

van Vlastuin, Willem. "John Owen as a Modern Theologian: A Comparison of Catholicity in Cyprian and Owen." In *John Owen Between Orthodoxy and Modernity*, edited by Willem van Vlastuin and Kelly M. Kapic, 164-85. Leiden: Brill, 2019.

van Vlastuin, Willem, and Kelly M. Kapic. "Introduction, Overview and Epilogue." In *John Owen Between Orthodoxy and Modernity*, edited by Willem van Vlastuin and Kelly M. Kapic, 3-34. Leiden: Brill, 2019.

Vanhoozer, Kevin J. *Biblical Authority After Babel: Retrieving the Solas in the Spirit of Mere Protestant Christianity*. Grand Rapids, MI: Brazos Press, 2016.

——. *The Drama of Doctrine: A Canonical-Linguistic Approach to Christian Theology*. Louisville, KY: Westminster John Knox, 2005.

——. "Hocus Totus: The Elusive Wholeness of Christ." *Pro Ecclesia* 29, no. 1 (2020): 31-42.

——. "Imprisoned or Free: Text, Status, and Theological Interpretation in the Master/Slave Discourse of Philemon." In *Reading Scripture with the Church: Toward a Hermeneutic for Theological Interpretation*, by A. K. M. Adam, Stephen E. Fowl, Kevin J. Vanhoozer, and Francis Watson. Grand Rapids, MI: Baker Academic, 2006.

——. "Improvising Theology According to the Scriptures." In *Building on the Foundations of Evangelical Theology*, edited by Gregg R. Allison and Stephen J. Wellum, 15-50. Wheaton, IL: Crossway, 2015.

——. "May We Go Beyond What Is Written After All? The Pattern of Theological Authority and the Problem of Doctrinal Development." In *The Enduring Authority of the Christian Scriptures*, edited by D. A. Carson, 747-92. Grand Rapids, MI: Eerdmans, 2016.

——. "A Mere Protestant Response." In *Was the Reformation a Mistake? Why Catholic Doctrine Is Not Unbiblical*, by Matthew Levering, 191-231. Grand Rapids, MI: Zondervan, 2017.

Vischer, Lukas. "Introduction." In *Unity of the Church in the New Testament and Today*, by Lukas Vischer, Ulrich Luz, and Christian Link, 1-6. Translated by James E. Crouch. Grand Rapids, MI: Eerdmans, 2010.

Volf, Miroslav. *After Our Likeness: The Church as the Image of the Trinity*. Grand Rapids, MI: Eerdmans, 1998.

——. "Catholicity of 'Two or Three': Free Church Reflections on the Catholicity of the Local Church." *The Jurist* 52, no. 1 (1992): 525-46.

———. "The Nature of the Church." *Evangelical Review of Theology* 26, no. 1 (January 2002): 68-75.
Waldron, Samuel E. *A Modern Exposition of the 1689 Baptist Confession of Faith.* Durham, UK: Evangelical Press, 1989.
Wallace, Dewy D., Jr. "Puritan Polemical Divinity and Doctrinal Controversy." In *The Cambridge Companion to Puritanism*, edited by John Coffey and Paul C. H. Lim, 206-23. Cambridge: Cambridge University Press, 2008.
Walton, Robert C. *The Gathered Community.* Greenwood, SC: The Attic Press, 1946.
Watson, David. *I Believe in the Church.* Grand Rapids, MI: Eerdmans, 1978.
Weaver, G. Stephen, Jr. *Orthodox, Puritan, Baptist: Hercules Collins (1647–1702) and Particular Baptist Identity in Early Modern England.* Bristol, CT: Vandenhoeck & Ruprecht, 2015.
Weber, Max. *The Protestant Ethic and the Spirit of Capitalism.* New York: Charles Scribner's Sons, 1958.
Webster, John. "Biblical Reasoning." *Anglican Theological Review* 90, no. 4 (Fall 2008): 733-51.
———. "Ministry and Priesthood." In *The Study of Anglicanism*, edited by Stephen Sykes, John Booty, and Jonathan Knight, 285-96. Rev. ed. Minneapolis: Fortress, 1998.
———. "The Self-Organizing Power of the Gospel of Christ: Episcopacy and Community Formation." *International Journal of Systematic Theology* 3, no. 1 (March 2001): 69-82.
Wellum, Stephen J., and Kirk Wellum. "The Biblical and Theological Case for Congregationalism." In *Baptist Foundations: Church Government for an Anti-Institutional Age*, edited by Mark Dever and Jonathan Leeman, 47-78. Nashville: B&H Academic, 2015.
Westin, Gunnar. *The Free Church Through the Ages.* Nashville: Broadman, 1958.
White, B. R. *The English Separatist Tradition from the Marian Martyrs to the Pilgrim Fathers.* London: Oxford University Press, 1971.
Wilhite, David E. "The Baptists 'and the Son': The Filioque Clause in Noncreedal Theology." *Journal of Ecumenical Studies* 44, no. 2 (Spring 2009): 285-302.
Williams, D. H. "The Disintegration of Catholicism into Diffuse Inclusivism." *Pro Ecclesia* 12, no. 4 (Fall 2003): 389-93.
———. *Evangelicals and Tradition: The Formative Influence of the Early Church.* Grand Rapids, MI: Baker Academic, 2005.

———. "Preface." In *The Free Church & the Early Church: Bridging the Historical & Theological Divide*, edited by D. H. Williams, vii-xiii. Grand Rapids, MI: Eerdmans, 2002.

———. *Retrieving the Tradition and Renewing Evangelicalism: A Primer for Suspicious Protestants*. Grand Rapids, MI: Eerdmans, 1999.

———, ed. *Tradition, Scripture, and Interpretation: A Sourcebook of the Ancient Church*. Grand Rapids, MI: Baker Academic, 2006.

Williams, George Huntston. "A People in Community: Historical Background." In *The Concept of the Believers' Church: Addresses from the 1968 Louisville Conference*, edited by James Leo Garrett Jr., 97-142. Scottdale, PA: Herald Press, 1969.

———. "Sectarian Ecumenicity: Reflections on a Little Noticed Aspect of the Radical Reformation." *Review and Expositor* 64, no. 2 (Spring 1967): 141-60.

Willis, John R., ed. *The Teachings of the Church Fathers*. San Francisco: Ignatius Press, 2002.

Wright, Christopher J. H. *The Mission of God: Unlocking the Bible's Grand Narrative*. Downers Grove, IL: IVP Academic, 2006.

Yeago, David. "The New Testament and the Nicene Dogma: A Contribution to the Recovery of Theological Exegesis." *Pro Ecclesia* 3, no. 2 (Spring 1994): 152-64.

Yoder, John Howard. "The Believers' Church Conferences in Historical Perspective." *The Mennonite Quarterly Review* 65, no. 1 (January 1991): 5-19.

———. "Could There Be a Baptist Bishop?" *Ecumenical Trends* 9, no. 7 (July/August 1980): 104-7.

———. *The Royal Priesthood: Essays Ecclesiastical and Ecumenical*. Edited by Michael G. Cartwright. Scottdale, PA: Herald Press, 1998.

Zahl, Paul. "The Bishop-Led Church." In *Perspectives on Church Government: Five Views of Church Polity*, edited by Chad Owen Brand and R. Stanton Norman, 209-54. Nashville: Broadman & Holman, 2004.

General Index

Anabaptist tradition, 5, 15, 17, 137-43, 158-60, 181-83
Anglican tradition, 3, 5, 14, 16, 18, 98-130, 134, 145, 193, 197, 203-10, 213, 231, 238, 247
Apostolicity, 7-9, 11-12, 22, 71-72, 86, 97, 107, 114-15, 119-21, 123-24, 127, 130, 158-60, 164-67, 187, 193, 198-99, 224-27, 236-37
Aquinas, 77-78, 96
Augustine, 73-74, 83, 87, 96, 245
Avis, Paul, 105-7, 109-11, 118-21, 125, 129-32, 161, 174-75, 206-7, 223, 227, 236-37
Baptist tradition, 1, 5, 17, 145-51, 171-84, 235-39
Bavinck, Herman, 1-2, 50, 60, 251, 254-55
Believers' Church tradition, 15-17, 145
Bellarmine, Robert, 84, 86, 96
Calvin, 80-83, 85-86, 93, 96, 110, 139, 196, 219, 223, 227
Catholicity, 114-15
Catholicity
    Christological, 67, 69, 74-75, 87, 91, 93, 96-97, 126, 170, 188, 191, 218, 222, 237
    Chronological, 74-75, 95, 97, 112, 126, 142, 181, 187, 199, 206, 213, 242, 244, 246, 249
    Consummative, 56, 200-202, 246, 252-54
    Differentiated, 13, 69-70, 74-75, 79, 86, 93, 97, 125, 167, 187, 191, 199
    Definition, 7-13
    Holistic, 69, 75, 87, 96-97, 125, 187, 202
    Geographical, 45, 64, 69, 73-75, 86, 91, 95-97, 112, 125, 142, 181, 187, 199, 213, 216-17
    Inaugurated, 201-2, 246, 252-53
    Institutional, 65, 69-70, 75, 79, 85-87, 92, 93, 97, 126, 184, 187-88, 201, 224
    Liturgical, 87, 92-93, 96-97, 125, 187, 191, 201, 224
    Missional, 12, 59, 74-75, 95, 97, 112, 125, 142, 181, 186-87, 199, 213, 215-16, 254
    Numerical, 87, 94-95
    Orthodox, 65, 70-75, 79, 86-87, 92, 96-97, 116, 126, 187, 191, 201, 224
    Qualitative, 12, 96, 118, 172, 174-75, 187, 191, 198-203, 217-22, 252
    Quantitative, 12, 96, 174, 187, 191, 198-203, 212-17
    Taxonomy, 64-65
The Catholicity of Protestantism, 101, 163-66, 183
Clowney, Edmund, 22-23, 35, 48, 67, 73, 86-87, 195
Cole, Graham, 23, 197
Congregational tradition, 5, 151-58, 182-83
Congregationalism, 13, 18-19, 131, 242
Council of Trent, 84-85, 87
Council of Vatican II, 87-89, 93, 96, 211
Creeds, 7, 11, 24, 58, 71-77, 97, 111, 113, 139-41, 149, 198-99, 224, 244
Cyprian, 68, 83, 209-10, 219, 230, 237
Cyril of Jerusalem, 72-74, 96, 224
Dever, Mark, 50-53, 59, 176
Doctrinal Development, 3 62-63, 94, 129
Dulles, Avery, 12, 64-65, 69, 73, 75, 79, 89, 94, 199
Eastern Orthodox tradition, 3, 14, 16, 18, 102-3
Ecumenical movement, 22, 90-94, 121
Episcopal tradition
    Characteristics, 17-18, 99-100, 202-11
    Definition, 100-102
Evangelical tradition, 4, 12, 22, 99, 171, 252
Free Church tradition
    Characteristics, 13-14, 19-20
    Definition, 13-20

Freeman, Curtis, 1, 171, 222
The Fullness of Christ, 115-16
Garrett, James Leo, 16, 215
George, Timothy, 22, 51, 143, 146, 160, 195, 198, 224, 238-39
Gospel, 7-9, 11-12, 20, 26, 39, 42, 50-52, 56, 66, 71, 73, 86, 94-95, 117, 120-24, 128-31, 160-61, 164-65, 177-78, 188-89, 208, 212-14, 228, 251
Harmon, Steven, 171-75, 183-84, 218, 231, 237-40, 245, 247, 253
Hiebert, Theodore, 29-30
Holiness, 7-8, 12, 22
Holy Spirit, 11-12, 15, 19-20, 26-27, 50, 91-92, 130, 181, 223
Ignatius of Antioch, 9, 66-69, 96, 164, 217-19, 221, 231
Israel, 8-9, 33-39, 41-42
Jewel, John, 112, 125
Lambeth Quadrilateral, 113-14, 125-26, 232
Laurense, Leo, 139-43
Leeman, Jonathan, 171, 175-81, 194, 220-22, 242-44
Littell, Franklin, 15-17, 133, 137, 139, 151
Lumen Gentium, 88-89, 93, 217
Lutheran tradition, 3, 18, 102, 110, 136, 223
Owen, John, 19, 154-58, 189, 247
Oxford Movement, 106, 114, 116
Pelikan, Jaroslav, 74, 78-79, 213
Pentecost, 12, 32, 39, 44-47, 190, 194, 200, 213
Polity, 13, 18-19, 100-101, 134-35, 153, 156, 205, 240, 250
Presbyterian tradition, 14, 103, 135-36, 147, 234

Protestant tradition, 16-17, 21, 64, 79-80, 84-85, 87, 89, 93, 103, 132, 145, 161, 164-65, 183, 185, 223-24, 251
Ramsey, Michael, 116-18, 120-22, 128-29, 131, 205-6, 230-31
Reformation, 5, 63, 75, 78-80, 86, 95, 98, 116, 132-33, 136, 160-61, 183, 198, 201, 237
Roman Catholic tradition, 3-4, 14, 16, 79-80, 82-90, 93, 101-3, 197, 221
Sadoleto, Jacopo, 82-83
Savoy Declaration, 152-53, 241
Sola Scriptura, 4, 21, 140, 144
Sykes, Stephen, 103-7
Table of Nations, 29-33, 37, 45
Thirty-Nine Articles, 111, 126, 157, 223
Tower of Babel, 29-33, 44-45
Unity, 6-8, 10, 12-13, 22, 26-28, 40-42, 46-51, 53-56, 68-72, 89-93, 110, 113-15, 118, 123-24, 127-28, 156-57, 167, 178, 187, 205-12, 224-25, 229-40, 246, 249-50
Webster, John, 121-24, 127-28, 207-8, 228-29
Williams, D. H., 61-64, 67-68, 72-74, 99-100, 131, 133, 137, 214, 225-27, 251, 254
Williams, George, 136-37, 143, 145
Williams, Rowan, 205-7
World Council of Churches, 90-92, 234
Vanhoozer, Kevin, 12-13, 62-63, 99, 160, 194, 243
Volf, Miroslav, 1-3, 10, 13-14, 18, 44, 69, 99-100, 166-70, 184-85, 197, 200-201, 211, 217, 219, 221-22, 224-26, 228-30
Yoder, John Howard, 14-17, 32, 188-89, 210, 232-34, 236

Scripture Index

OLD TESTAMENT

Genesis
1, *26, 27*
1–2, *27*
1–3, *26*
1–11, *25, 26, 29, 30, 31, 32*
1:1, *26*
1:3, *26*
1:4, *26*
1:5, *26*
1:6, *26*
1:7, *26*
1:8, *26*
1:10, *26*
1:12, *26, 27*
1:14-18, *26*
1:18, *26*
1:21, *26, 27*
1:25, *26, 27*
1:26, *26, 28*
1:26-27, *27*
1:28, *26, 28*
1:31, *26, 27*
1:31–2:2, *26*
2, *27*
2:1, *27*
2:10-14, *28*
2:18, *28*
2:22, *28*
2:23, *28*
3, *28*
3–11, *32*
3:8, *56*
3:12-13, *28*
3:14-19, *28*
3:15, *25, 28, 41*
3:16, *28*
3:21, *28*
6, *29*
9:1, *45*
9:9, *41*
10, *29, 30, 31, 33, 45, 57*
10–11, *29, 32, 33, 57*
10:5, *29, 31, 33, 57*
10:18, *29*
10:20, *31, 33, 57*
10:31, *31, 33, 57*
11, *29, 30*
11:1, *29*
11:1-9, *27, 29, 30, 45*
11:10, *32*
11:27, *32*
12, *32, 33, 41*
12:1-3, *32*
12:3, *57*
12:7, *41*
15:6, *51*
17:7, *24*
18:18, *33*

Exodus
6:7, *24*
19, *8*

Leviticus
26:12, *24*

Numbers
11:29, *190*

Deuteronomy
4:6, *34*
6:4, *26*
7:1, *34*
7:6, *24*
15:6, *34*
33:17, *34*

Joshua
2, *37*

1 Kings
17, *37*

2 Kings
5, *37*

Psalms
47:8-9, *34*
50:1, *34*
62, *34*
65:2, *34*
68:18, *55*
72:17, *34*
87:4-6, *34*
148:14, *34*
150:6, *34*

Isaiah
1–39, *36*
2:2-4, *35*
11:10-12, *35*
19:19-25, *35*
25:6-8, *35*
40–55, *36*
40–66, *36*
49:6, *36, 38*
56–66, *36*
56:6-8, *36*
56:7, *38, 42*
65:17, *56*
66:18, *36, 38*
66:18-19, *37*
66:18-23, *36*
66:19, *36*
66:20, *37*
66:23, *37*

Jeremiah
31, *37*
31:33, *24*

Ezekiel
36, *37*
36:27, *190*
36:28, *24*
37:26, *38*

Joel
2, *44, 190*

Amos
9, *35*

Obadiah
1, *35*

Zephaniah
3:1-13, *27*
3:9, *34*

Zechariah
8:8, *24*
8:22, *35*
8:23, *34*
14:16, *35*

Malachi
4, *32*

NEW TESTAMENT

Matthew
1:1, *41*
2:1, *41*
8, *39, 41, 42*
8:1, *41*
8:10, *41*
8:11, *41*
10:5-6, *38*
15, *39, 42*
15:24, *38*
16, *42, 177, 209, 220, 221*
16:13-19, *220*
16:13-20, *176*
16:18, *41, 220*
16:19, *177*
18, *42, 177, 221*
18:15-20, *176, 220, 229*
18:17-18, *220*
18:19-20, *220*
18:20, *4, 42, 67, 168, 177, 190, 219, 220, 221, 222, 230, 250*
24:14, *216*
26:29, *254*
28, *177, 221*
28:18-20, *220*
28:19, *38*
28:20, *221*

Mark
5, *39, 42*
7, *42*
11:17, *36, 42*
12:29, *26*
15:39, *42*

Luke
2:10, *43*

2:31-32, *43*
4:24-27, *43*
17, *39*
17:11-19, *43*
18:8, *94*
24, *37*
24:44-47, *34*
24:47, *43*

John
1:1-14, *26*
1:9, *39*
1:12, *39*
1:29, *39*
3:16, *39*
4, *39*
8:12, *39*
10:16, *36, 39*
12:32, *40*
16:13, *62, 63*
17, *8, 40, 232*
17:2, *40*
17:9, *39*
17:17-19, *8*
17:18, *9, 40*
17:20, *9*
17:21-23, *41*
20:21-23, *40*
20:23, *102*
20:31, *41*

Acts
1, *134*
1–7, *45*
1:8, *43, 45*
1:11, *47*
2, *38, 44, 190*
2:1-3, *27*
2:1-13, *45*
2:17, *44*
2:17-18, *44*
2:19-20, *44*
2:21, *44*
2:38-39, *44*
2:42, *9*
6, *134*
8, *45*
8–12, *45*
8:1, *45*
8:4-25, *46*
8:26-40, *46*
9:31, *197*

10:28, *46*
10:34-35, *46*
11:17-18, *46*
11:20-21, *46*
11:22, *151*
13, *66*
13–28, *45, 46*
15, *46, 66, 134, 150, 163*

Romans
1:8, *47*
1:16, *47*
3:30, *51*
6:17, *62*
9:24-25, *57*
9:26, *24*
10:10, *168*
12, *48*
12:3-8, *9*
12:4-5, *48*
14:1-2, *10*
15, *66*
15:25-26, *179*
15:26, *151*
16:16, *179*

1 Corinthians
1:2, *8, 49, 216*
1:26, *9*
2:12, *190*
2:16, *190*
3:17, *8*
5:4, *221*
5:5, *134*
7:7, *10*
7:40, *134, 190*
8:6, *26*
10, *8*
10:16-17, *48*
10:17, *54*
10:32, *47, 197*
11:22, *134*
11:23, *62*
11:27, *134*
12, *47, 48, 49, 50, 59, 186*
12:1-11, *47*
12:3, *48*
12:4, *9, 48*
12:4-6, *48*
12:4-31, *50*
12:5, *9*

12:7, *47*
12:7-11, *48*
12:11, *47*
12:12, *48, 151*
12:12-27, *48*
12:13, *9*
12:13-14, *48*
12:18-20, *49*
12:22-23, *49*
12:25, *49*
12:27, *48*
12:28, *49, 197*
12:28-31, *47, 48*
12:29, *151*
15:1-5, *9, 213*
15:3, *21, 62*
16:1-3, *180*
16:19, *179*

2 Corinthians
3:17, *250*
5:19, *212*
6:16, *24*
8:1-2, *179*
8:18, *179*
8:19, *151*
8:24, *180*
11:28, *66*
13:13, *179*

Galatians
3, *47, 50, 52, 53, 59, 186*
3:6, *51*
3:7, *50*
3:8, *51*
3:9, *51*
3:9-10, *50*
3:20, *26*
3:26, *51*
3:26-29, *50, 51*
3:27, *51*
3:28, *10, 51*
3:29, *51*
6:16, *47*

Ephesians
1, *8, 53*
1–3, *54*
1:4, *47, 53*
1:5, *53*
1:9-10, *53*
1:10, *56*

1:11, *53*
1:12, *53*
1:14, *53*
1:18, *62*
1:22-23, *53*
1:23, *48*
2, *53, 58*
2–4, *48*
2:14-15, *54*
2:15-16, *53*
2:18, *54*
2:19, *54*
2:20, *9*
3, *54*
3:1-11, *26*
3:2-5, *54*
3:9-11, *54*
3:18, *62*
3:21, *47*
4, *10, 53, 54, 56, 59, 186*
4:1, *54*
4:2-5, *54*
4:3, *54*
4:3-6, *8*
4:4-6, *10, 54*
4:5, *249*
4:6, *26*
4:7, *54*
4:7-16, *10*
4:8-10, *55*

4:11, *55*
4:11-16, *10*
4:12, *55*
4:13, *55*
4:15, *55*
4:16, *10, 55*
5:23, *47, 48*
6:18, *180*

Philippians
2:6, *24*

Colossians
1, *66*
1:6, *47*
1:9, *62*
1:16, *26*
1:18, *47, 48, 189*
1:24, *48*
2:19, *48*
3:11, *10*
3:15, *48*

2 Thessalonians
2:15, *62*
3:6, *62*

1 Timothy
2:5, *26*
3:16, *47*
6:20, *62*

2 Timothy
1:6, *102*
1:14, *62, 102*
4, *66*

Titus
1:5, *102*
2:2-4, *10*

Hebrews
10:19, *134, 190*
12:1, *61*

James
2:1, *9*

1 Peter
1, *8*
2, *8, 58*
2:4-10, *220*
2:9, *134, 190*
2:25, *189*
4:10, *170*
4:10-11, *9*
5:1-5, *176*

2 Peter
1, *66*
1:5, *62*

3 John
5–6, *179*

Jude
3, *62*

Revelation
1:6, *134, 190*
3:3, *62*
4:11, *215*
5:8-9, *215*
5:9, *9, 56, 57*
5:10, *9, 57*
7:9, *56, 57*
10:11, *57*
11:17, *26*
13:7, *57*
14:6, *57*
15:4, *57*
17:15, *57*
20:6, *215*
21–22, *56*
21:3, *24, 56, 58*
21:5-6, *58*
21:7, *58*
21:24, *57*
21:26, *57*
22, *32, 33*
22:2, *57*

THE STUDIES IN CHRISTIAN DOCTRINE AND SCRIPTURE SERIES

Studies in Christian Doctrine and Scripture promotes evangelical contributions to systematic theology, seeking fresh understanding of Christian doctrine through creatively faithful engagement with Scripture in dialogue with catholic tradition(s).

Thus: We aim to publish **contributions to systematic theology** rather than merely descriptive rehearsals of biblical theology, historical retrievals of classic or contemporary theologians, or hermeneutical reflections on theological method—volumes that are plentifully and expertly published elsewhere.

We aim to promote **evangelical** contributions, neither retreating from broader dialogue into a narrow version of this identity on the one hand, nor running away from the biblical preoccupation of our heritage on the other hand.

We seek fresh understanding of Christian doctrine **through creatively faithful engagement with Scripture.** To some fellow evangelicals and interested others today, we commend the classic evangelical commitment of engaging Scripture. To other fellow evangelicals today, we commend a contemporary aim to engage Scripture with creative fidelity. The church is to be always reforming—but always reforming according to the Word of God.

We seek **fresh understanding of Christian doctrine.** We do not promote a singular method; we welcome proposals appealing to biblical theology, the history of interpretation, theological interpretation of Scripture, or still other approaches. We welcome projects that engage in detailed exegesis as well as those that appropriate broader biblical themes and patterns. Ultimately, we hope to promote relating Scripture to doctrinal understanding in material, not just formal, ways.

We promote scriptural engagement **in dialogue with catholic tradition(s).** A periodic evangelical weakness is relative disinterest in the church's shared creedal heritage, in churches' particular confessions and more generally in the history of dogmatic reflection. Beyond existing efforts to enhance understanding of themes and corpora in biblical theology, then, we hope to foster engagement with Scripture that bears upon and learns from loci, themes, or crucial questions in classic dogmatics and contemporary systematic theology.